My Little Monster

3

Robico

CONTENTS

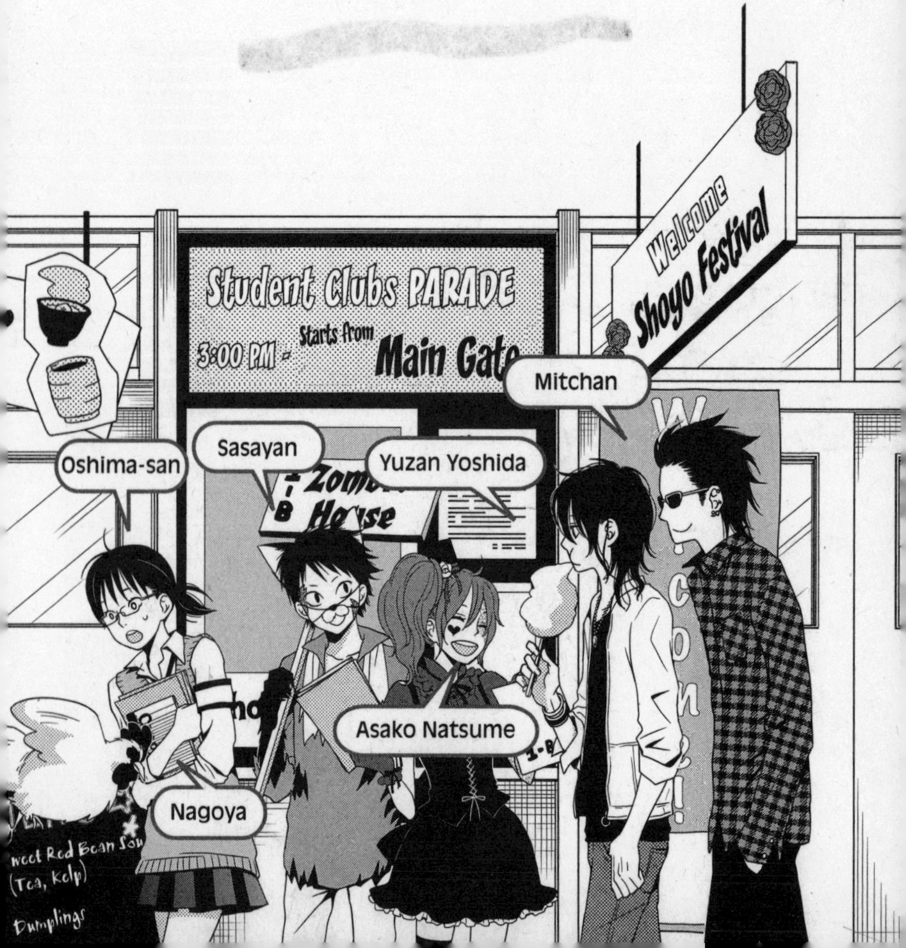
Welcome
Shoyo Festival
Student Clubs PARADE
3:00 PM ~ Starts from Main Gate
Mitchan
Yuzan Yoshida
Sasayan
Oshima-san
Asako Natsume
Nagoya
(Tea, Kelp)
Dumplings

STORY

When Shizuku Mizutani does a little favor for problem child, Haru Yoshida, who sits next to her in school, he develops a huge crush on her. Attracted to his innocence, she eventually falls for him too, but when she asks him out, he inexplicably turns her down. Even so, she determines to win him over and ask him out again.

But then, Haru's brother Yuzan suddenly shows up and tells Shizuku that Haru might have to leave school. At first, this only makes her feelings for Haru stronger. But soon she starts to waver, not knowing how to make him notice her.

Finally, she decides to just give up on love...?

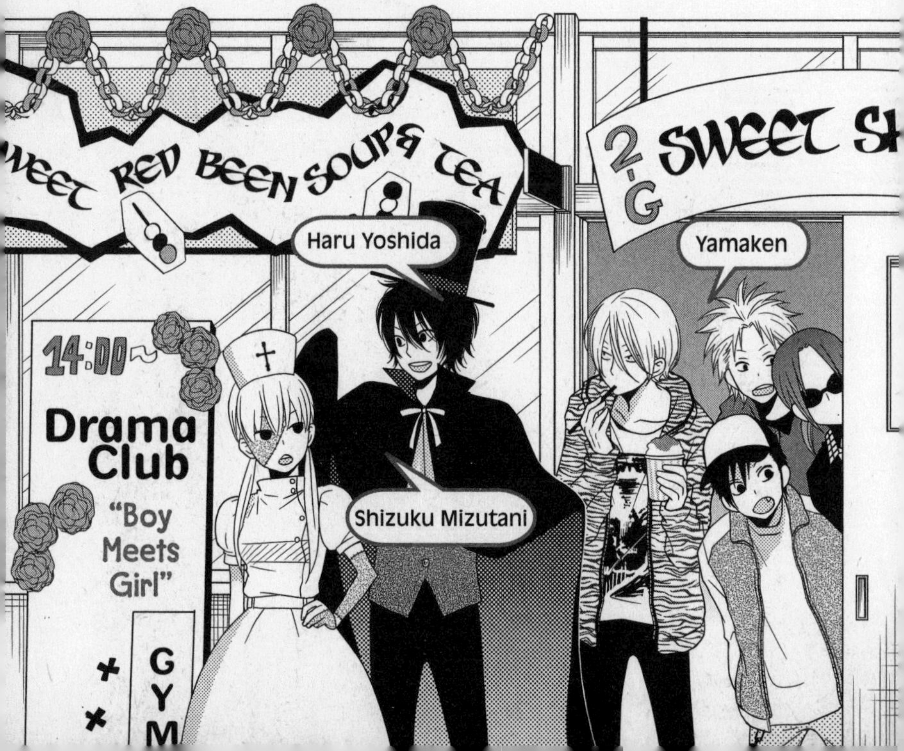
SWEET RED BEEN SOUP & TEA
2-G SWEET SH
Haru Yoshida
Yamaken
14:00~
Drama Club
"Boy Meets Girl"
GYM
Shizuku Mizutani

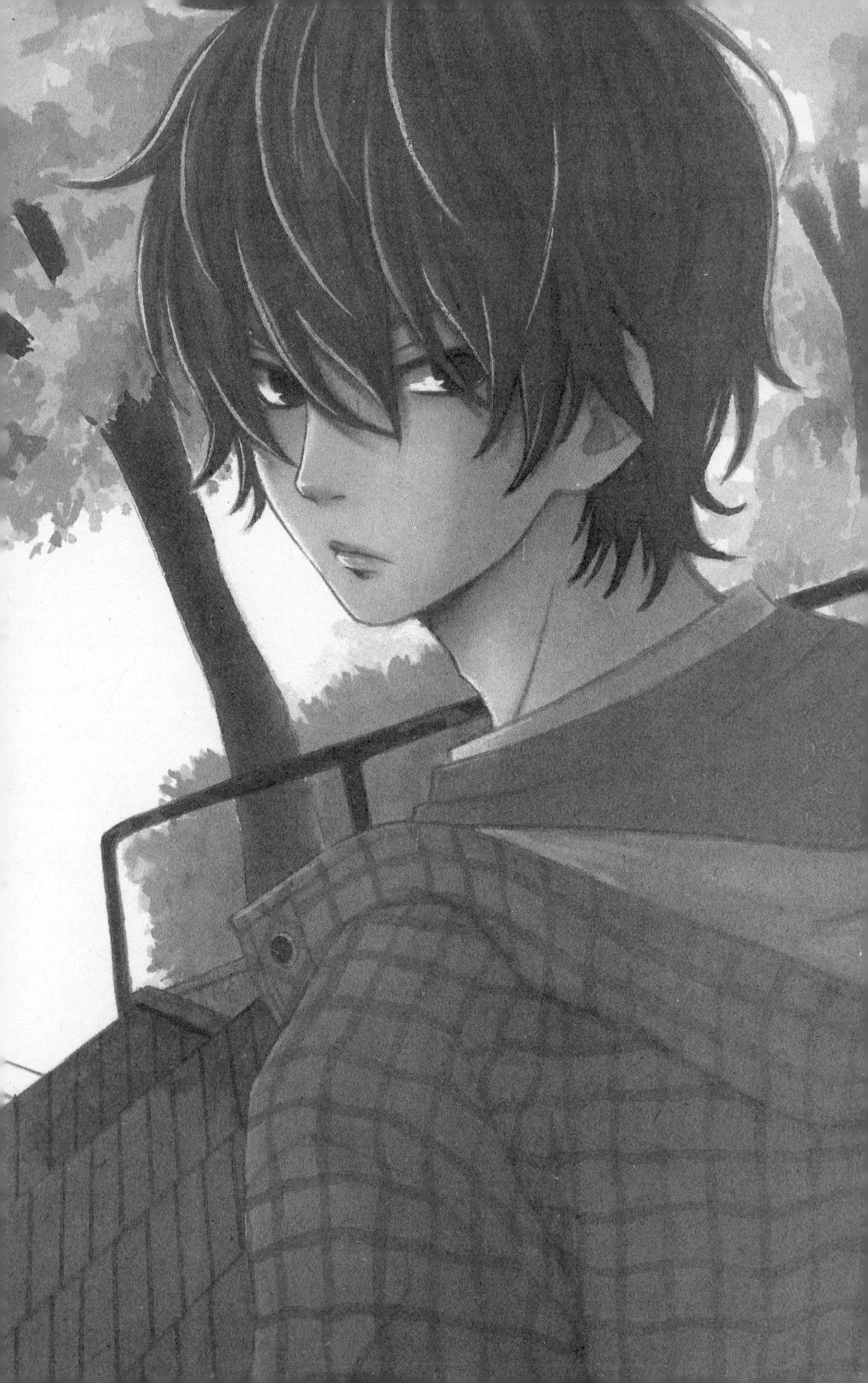

Chapter 9 I Like You

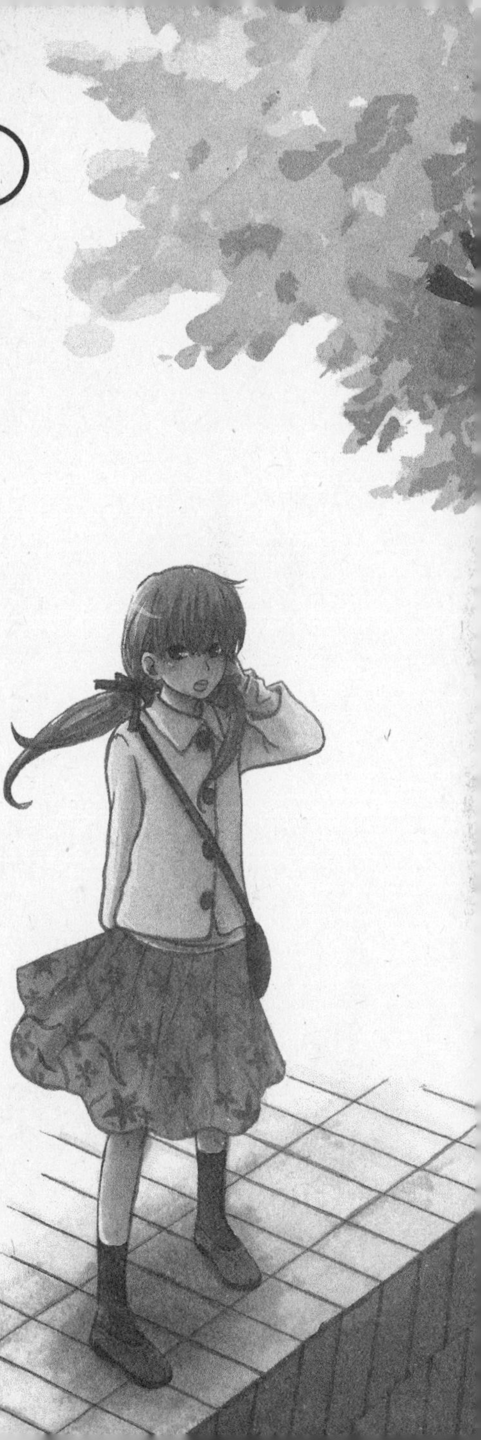

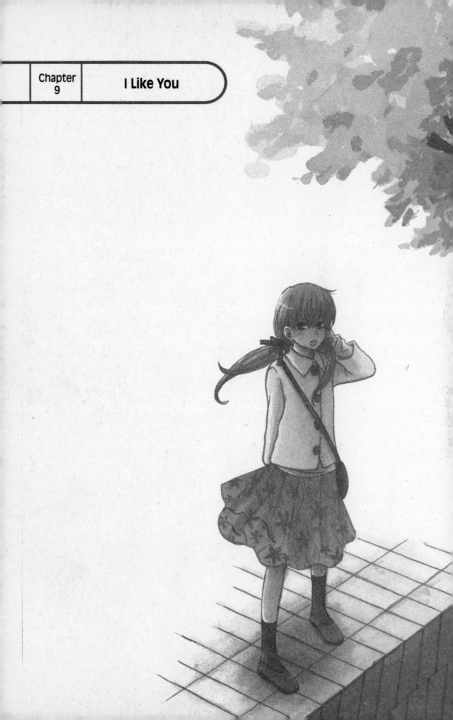

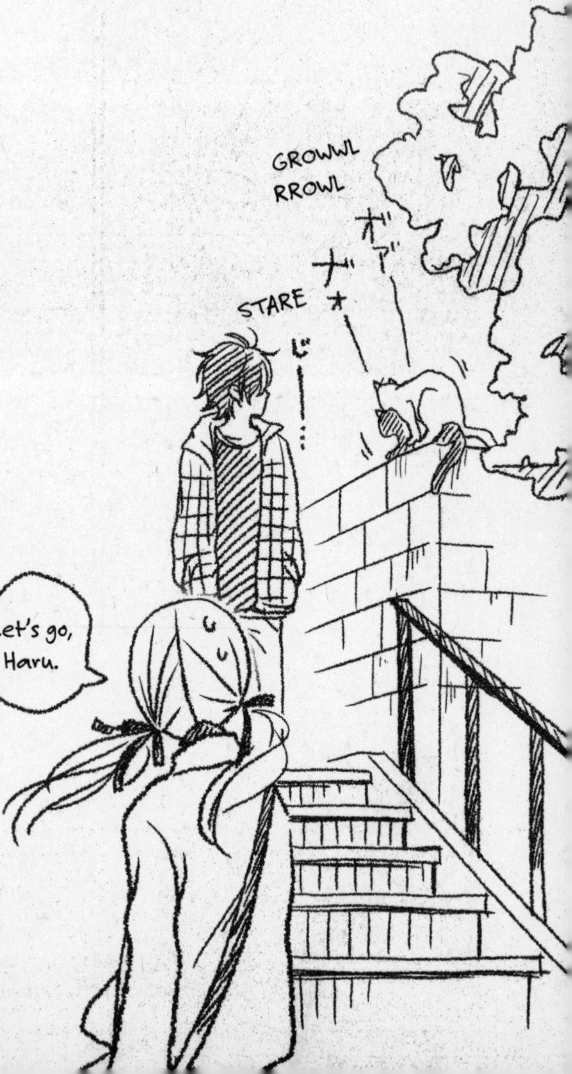
GROWWL
RROWL
STARE
Let's go, Haru.

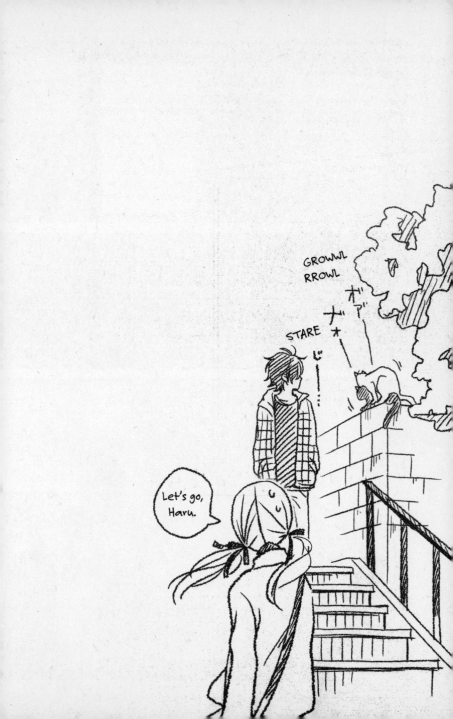

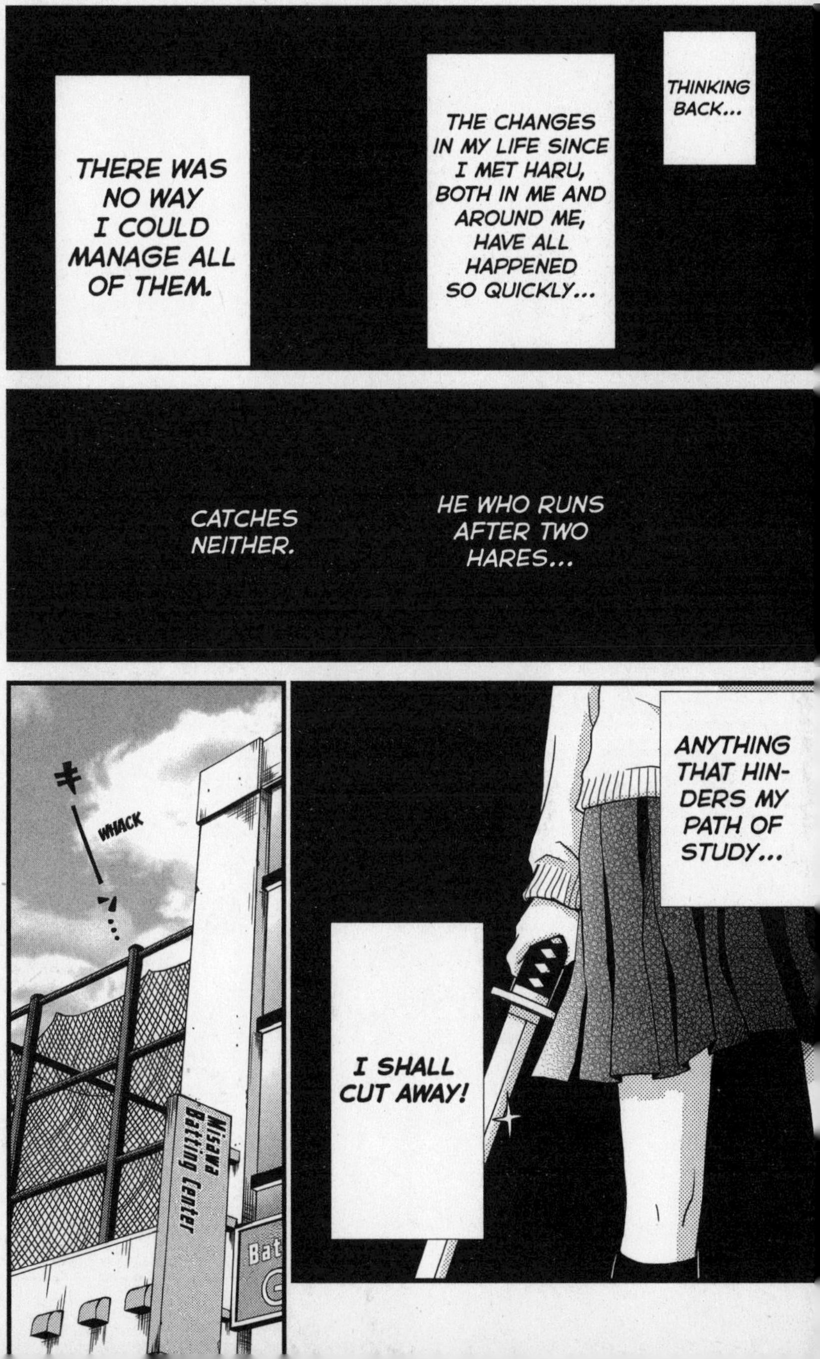
THINKING BACK...
THE CHANGES IN MY LIFE SINCE I MET HARU, BOTH IN ME AND AROUND ME, HAVE ALL HAPPENED SO QUICKLY...
THERE WAS NO WAY I COULD MANAGE ALL OF THEM.
HE WHO RUNS AFTER TWO HARES...
CATCHES NEITHER.
ANYTHING THAT HIN-DERS MY PATH OF STUDY...
I SHALL CUT AWAY!
WHACK
Misawa Batting Center

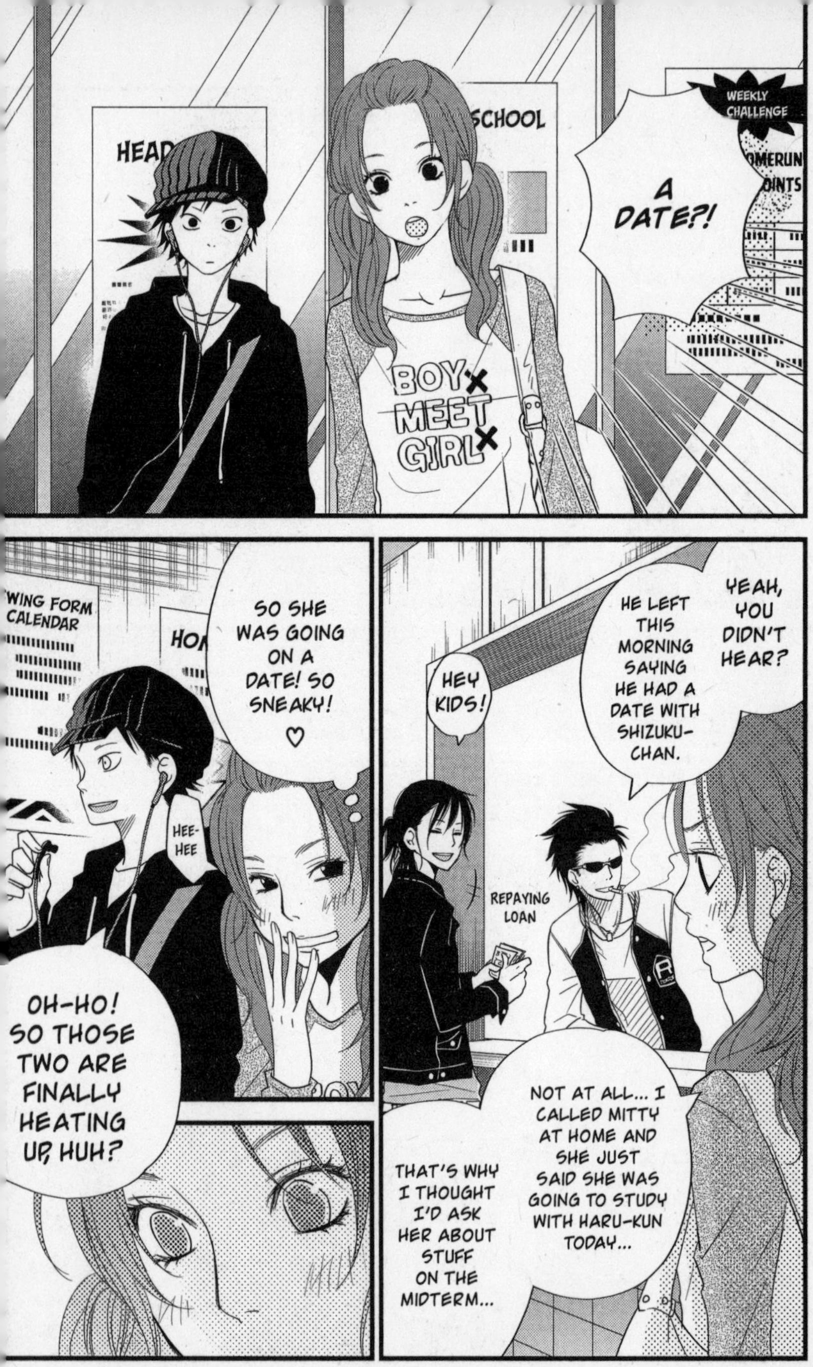
A DATE?!
WEEKLY CHALLENGE
SCHOOL
BOY MEET GIRL
YEAH, YOU DIDN'T HEAR?
HE LEFT THIS MORNING SAYING HE HAD A DATE WITH SHIZUKU-CHAN.
HEY KIDS!
REPAYING LOAN
NOT AT ALL... I CALLED MITTY AT HOME AND SHE JUST SAID SHE WAS GOING TO STUDY WITH HARU-KUN TODAY...
THAT'S WHY I THOUGHT I'D ASK HER ABOUT STUFF ON THE MIDTERM...
SO SHE WAS GOING ON A DATE! SO SNEAKY! ♡
HEE-HEE
OH-HO! SO THOSE TWO ARE FINALLY HEATING UP, HUH?

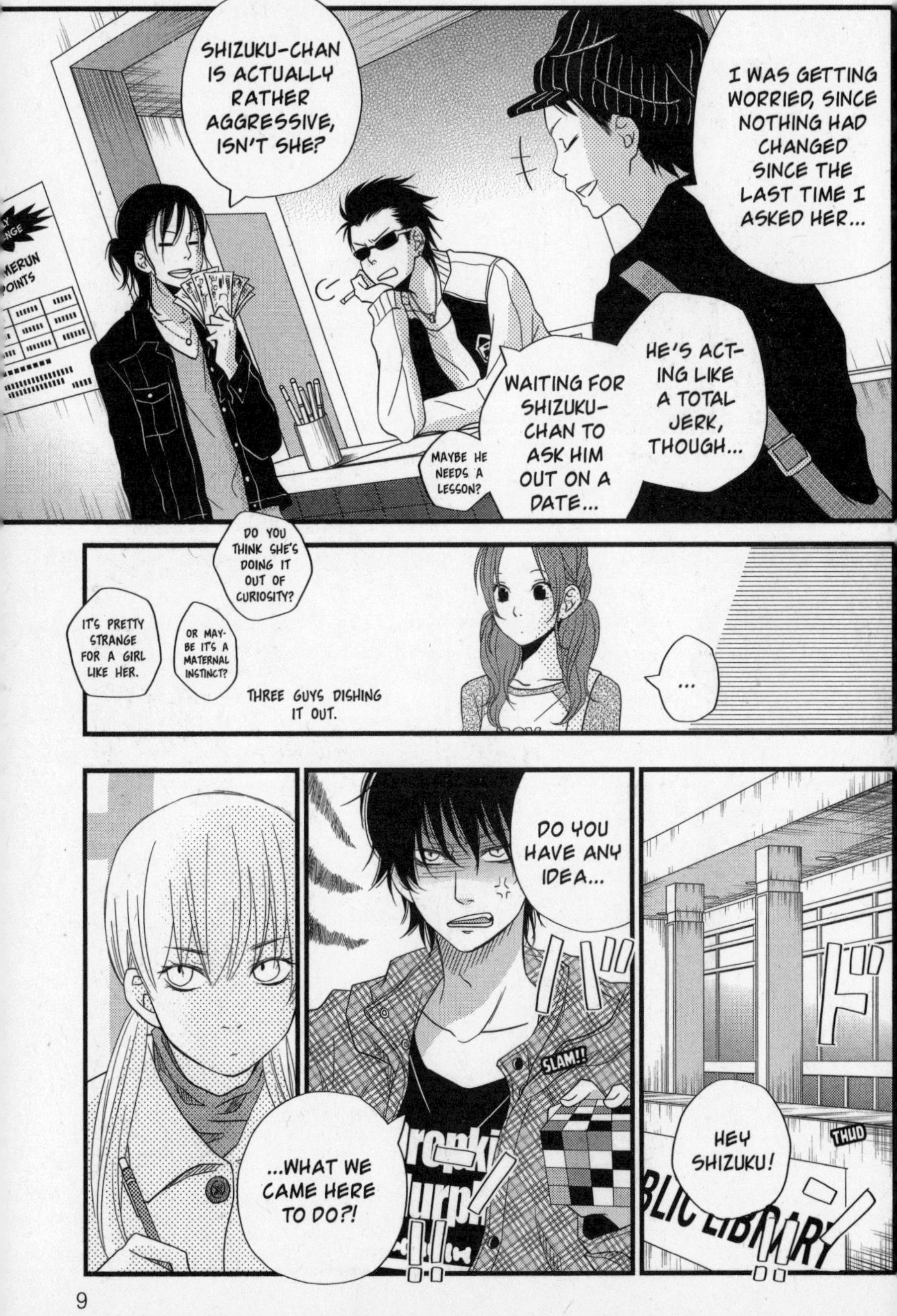
I WAS GETTING WORRIED, SINCE NOTHING HAD CHANGED SINCE THE LAST TIME I ASKED HER...
SHIZUKU-CHAN IS ACTUALLY RATHER AGGRESSIVE, ISN'T SHE?
HE'S ACTING LIKE A TOTAL JERK, THOUGH...
WAITING FOR SHIZUKU-CHAN TO ASK HIM OUT ON A DATE...
MAYBE HE NEEDS A LESSON?
...
DO YOU THINK SHE'S DOING IT OUT OF CURIOSITY?
OR MAYBE IT'S A MATERNAL INSTINCT?
IT'S PRETTY STRANGE FOR A GIRL LIKE HER.
THREE GUYS DISHING IT OUT.
HEY SHIZUKU!
THUD
BLIC LIBRARY
DO YOU HAVE ANY IDEA...
SLAM!!
...WHAT WE CAME HERE TO DO?!

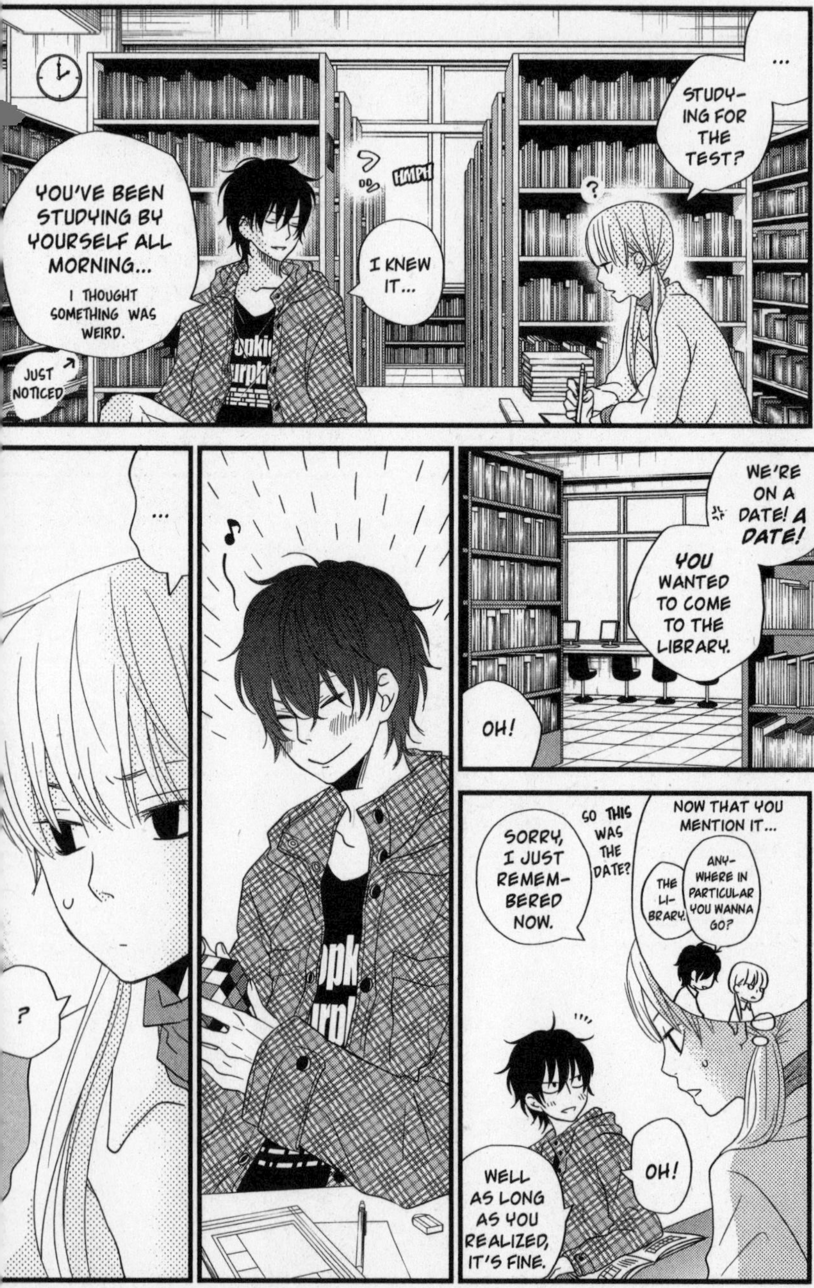
...
STUDYING FOR THE TEST?
?
HMPH
I KNEW IT...
YOU'VE BEEN STUDYING BY YOURSELF ALL MORNING...
I THOUGHT SOMETHING WAS WEIRD.
JUST NOTICED
WE'RE ON A DATE! A DATE!
YOU WANTED TO COME TO THE LIBRARY.
OH!
NOW THAT YOU MENTION IT...
ANYWHERE IN PARTICULAR YOU WANNA GO?
THE LIBRARY.
SO THIS WAS THE DATE?
SORRY, I JUST REMEMBERED NOW.
OH!
WELL AS LONG AS YOU REALIZED, IT'S FINE.
...
?

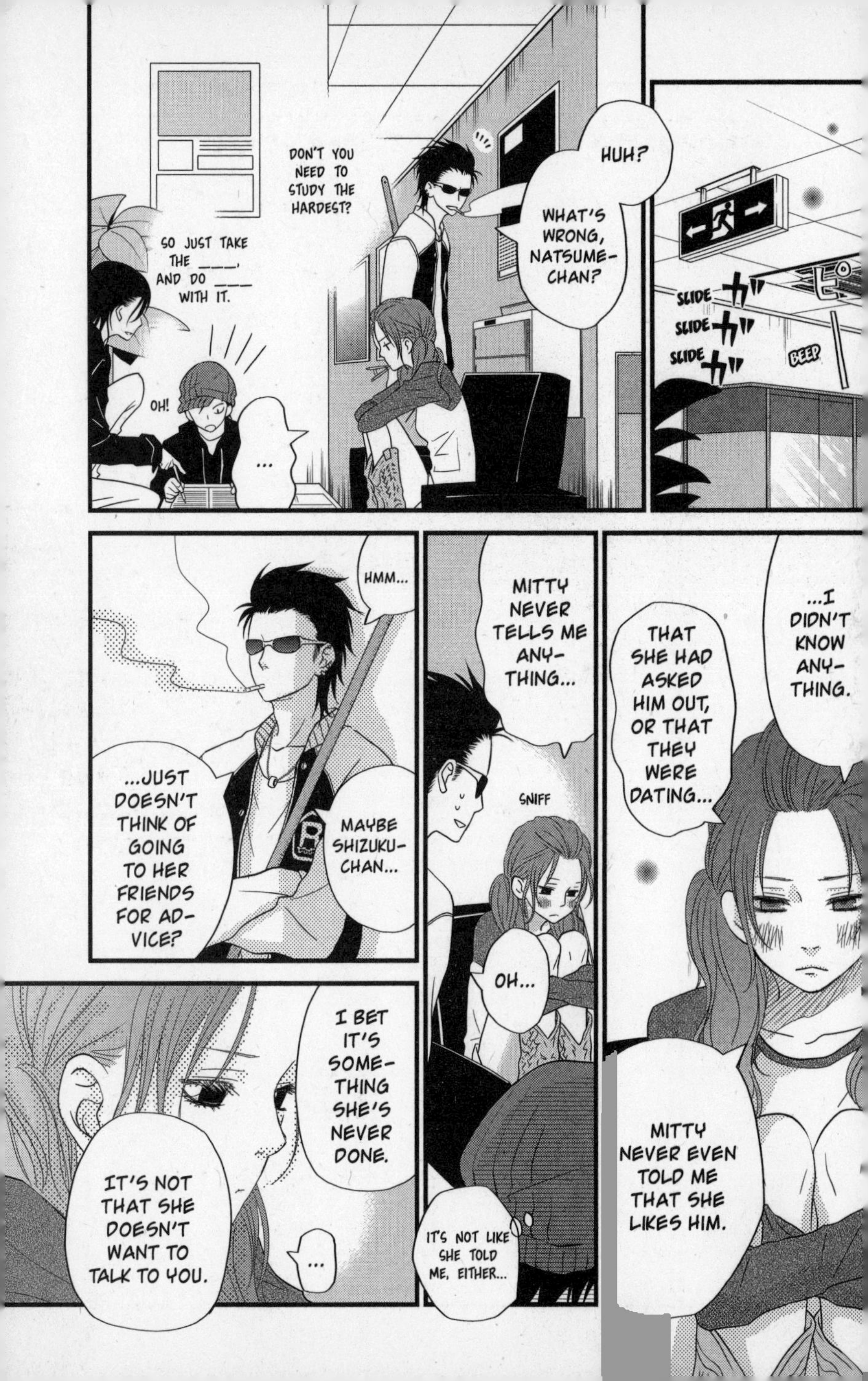
SLIDE
SLIDE
SLIDE
BEEP
HUH?
WHAT'S WRONG, NATSUME-CHAN?
DON'T YOU NEED TO STUDY THE HARDEST?
SO JUST TAKE THE ___, AND DO ___ WITH IT.
OH!
...
...I DIDN'T KNOW ANYTHING.
THAT SHE HAD ASKED HIM OUT, OR THAT THEY WERE DATING...
MITTY NEVER EVEN TOLD ME THAT SHE LIKES HIM.
MITTY NEVER TELLS ME ANYTHING...
SNIFF
OH...
IT'S NOT LIKE SHE TOLD ME, EITHER...
HMM...
MAYBE SHIZUKU-CHAN...
...JUST DOESN'T THINK OF GOING TO HER FRIENDS FOR ADVICE?
I BET IT'S SOMETHING SHE'S NEVER DONE.
IT'S NOT THAT SHE DOESN'T WANT TO TALK TO YOU.
...

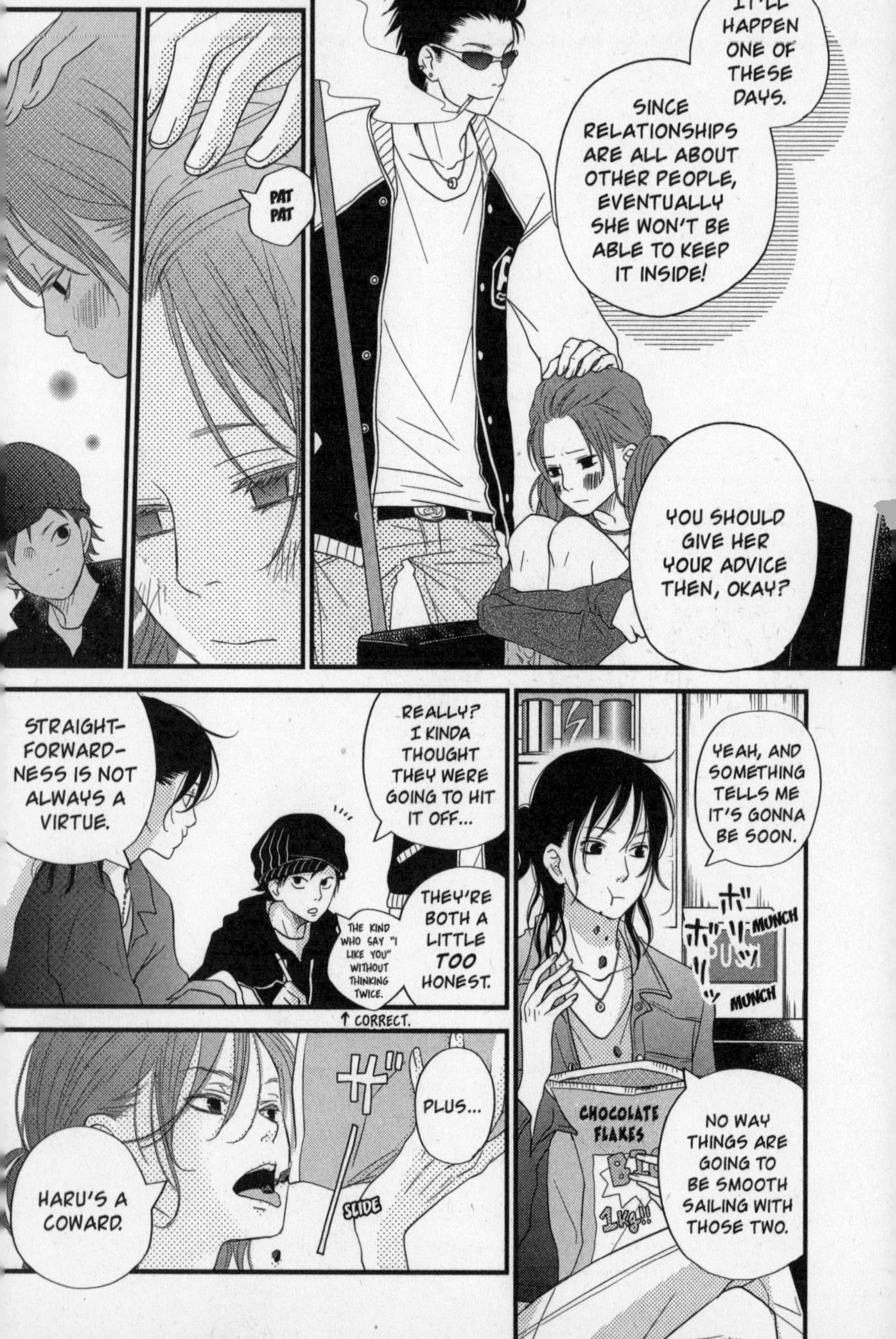
IT'LL HAPPEN ONE OF THESE DAYS.
SINCE RELATIONSHIPS ARE ALL ABOUT OTHER PEOPLE, EVENTUALLY SHE WON'T BE ABLE TO KEEP IT INSIDE!
YOU SHOULD GIVE HER YOUR ADVICE THEN, OKAY?
PAT PAT
YEAH, AND SOMETHING TELLS ME IT'S GONNA BE SOON.
MUNCH
MUNCH
CHOCOLATE FLAKES
1kg!!
NO WAY THINGS ARE GOING TO BE SMOOTH SAILING WITH THOSE TWO.
REALLY? I KINDA THOUGHT THEY WERE GOING TO HIT IT OFF...
THEY'RE BOTH A LITTLE TOO HONEST.
THE KIND WHO SAY "I LIKE YOU" WITHOUT THINKING TWICE.
STRAIGHT-FORWARD-NESS IS NOT ALWAYS A VIRTUE.
↑ CORRECT.
PLUS...
SLIDE
HARU'S A COWARD.

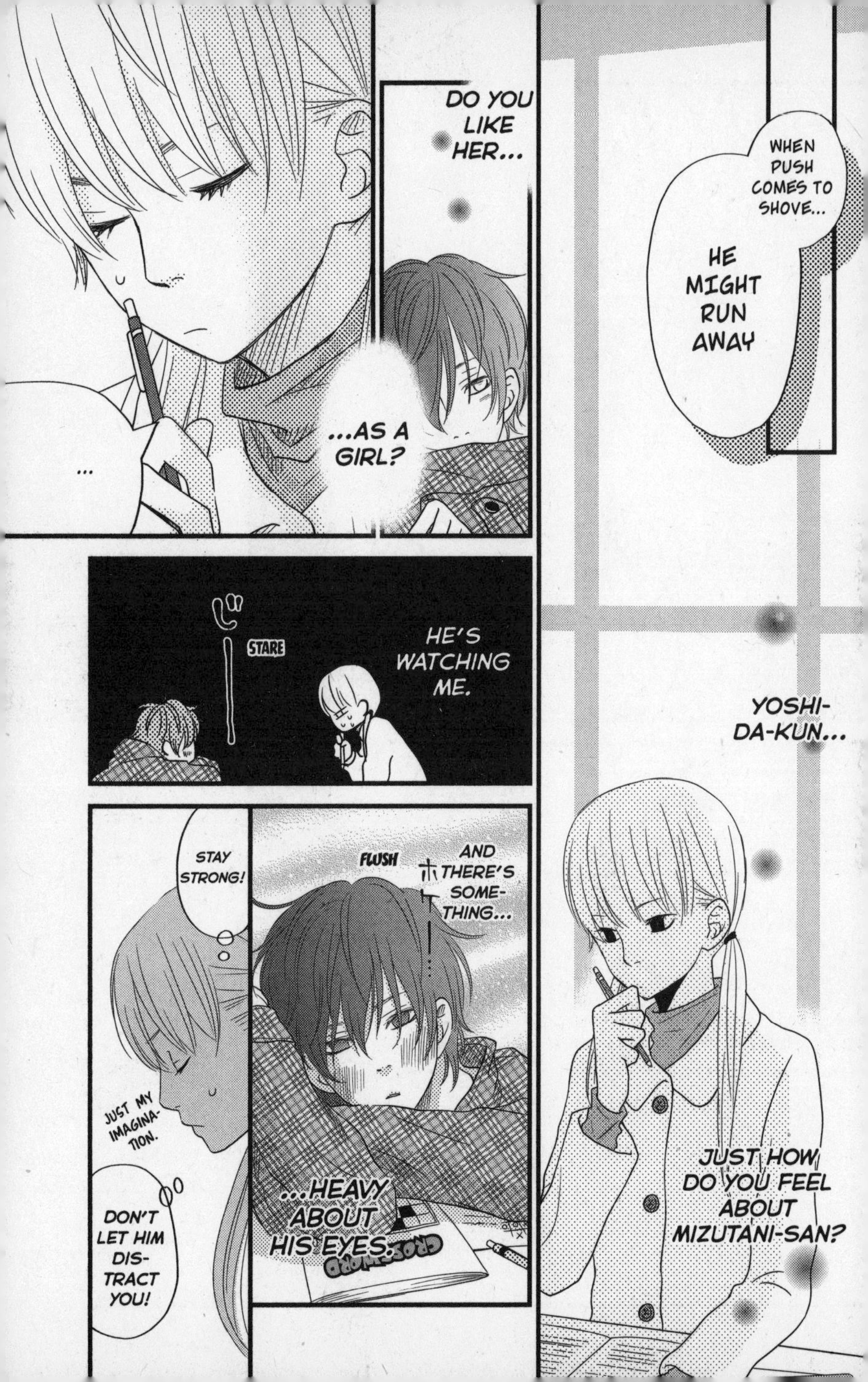
WHEN PUSH COMES TO SHOVE...
HE MIGHT RUN AWAY
YOSHI-DA-KUN...
JUST HOW DO YOU FEEL ABOUT MIZUTANI-SAN?
DO YOU LIKE HER...
...AS A GIRL?
...
HE'S WATCHING ME.
STARE
FLUSH
AND THERE'S SOME-THING...
...HEAVY ABOUT HIS EYES.
STAY STRONG!
JUST MY IMAGINA-TION.
DON'T LET HIM DIS-TRACT YOU!

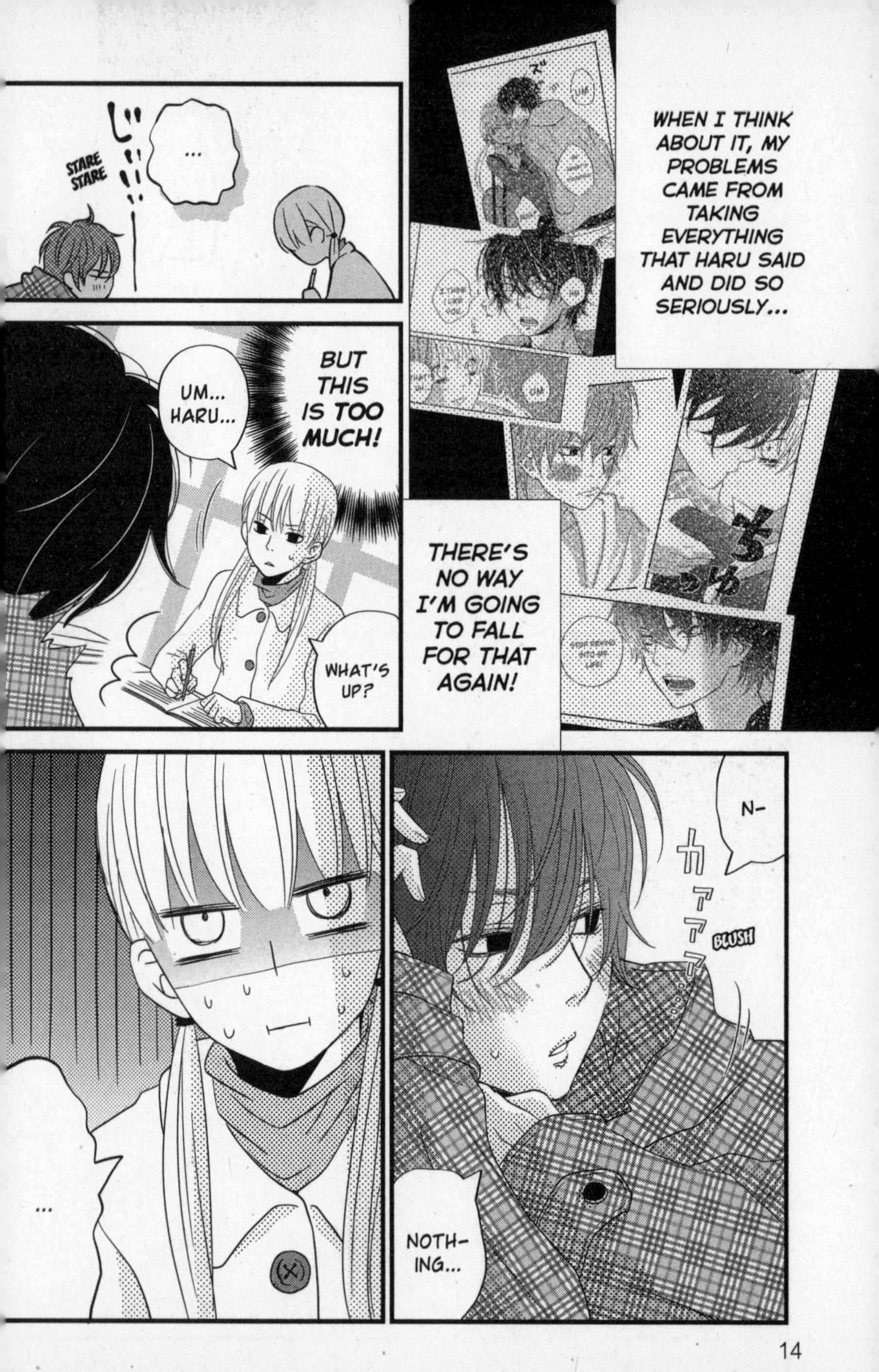
WHEN I THINK ABOUT IT, MY PROBLEMS CAME FROM TAKING EVERYTHING THAT HARU SAID AND DID SO SERIOUSLY...
THERE'S NO WAY I'M GOING TO FALL FOR THAT AGAIN!
STARE STARE
...
UM... HARU...
BUT THIS IS TOO MUCH!
WHAT'S UP?
N-
BLUSH
NOTH-ING...
...

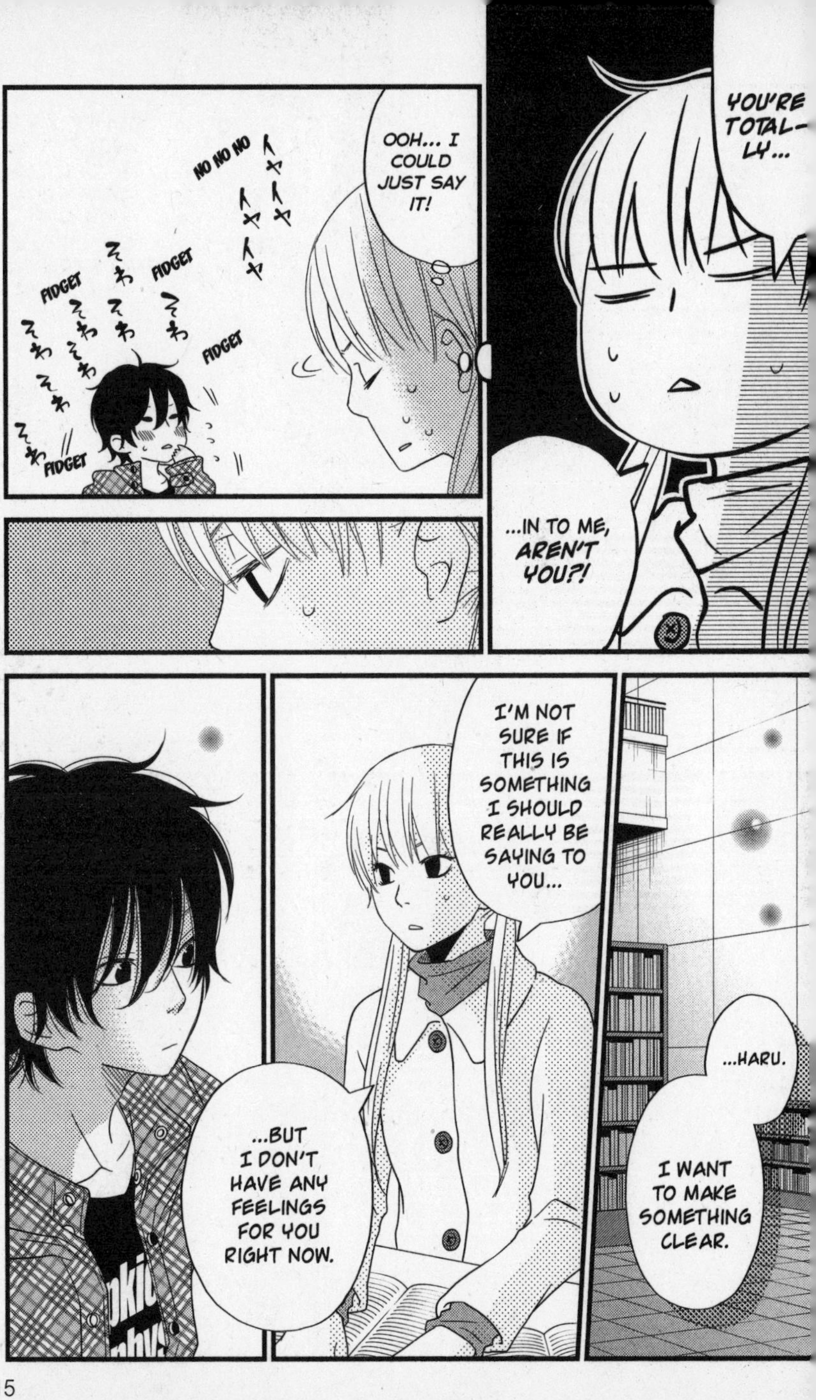
YOU'RE TOTAL-LY...
...IN TO ME, AREN'T YOU?!
OOH... I COULD JUST SAY IT!
NO NO NO
イヤイヤイヤイヤ
FIDGET
FIDGET
FIDGET
FIDGET
...HARU.
I WANT TO MAKE SOMETHING CLEAR.
I'M NOT SURE IF THIS IS SOMETHING I SHOULD REALLY BE SAYING TO YOU...
...BUT I DON'T HAVE ANY FEELINGS FOR YOU RIGHT NOW.

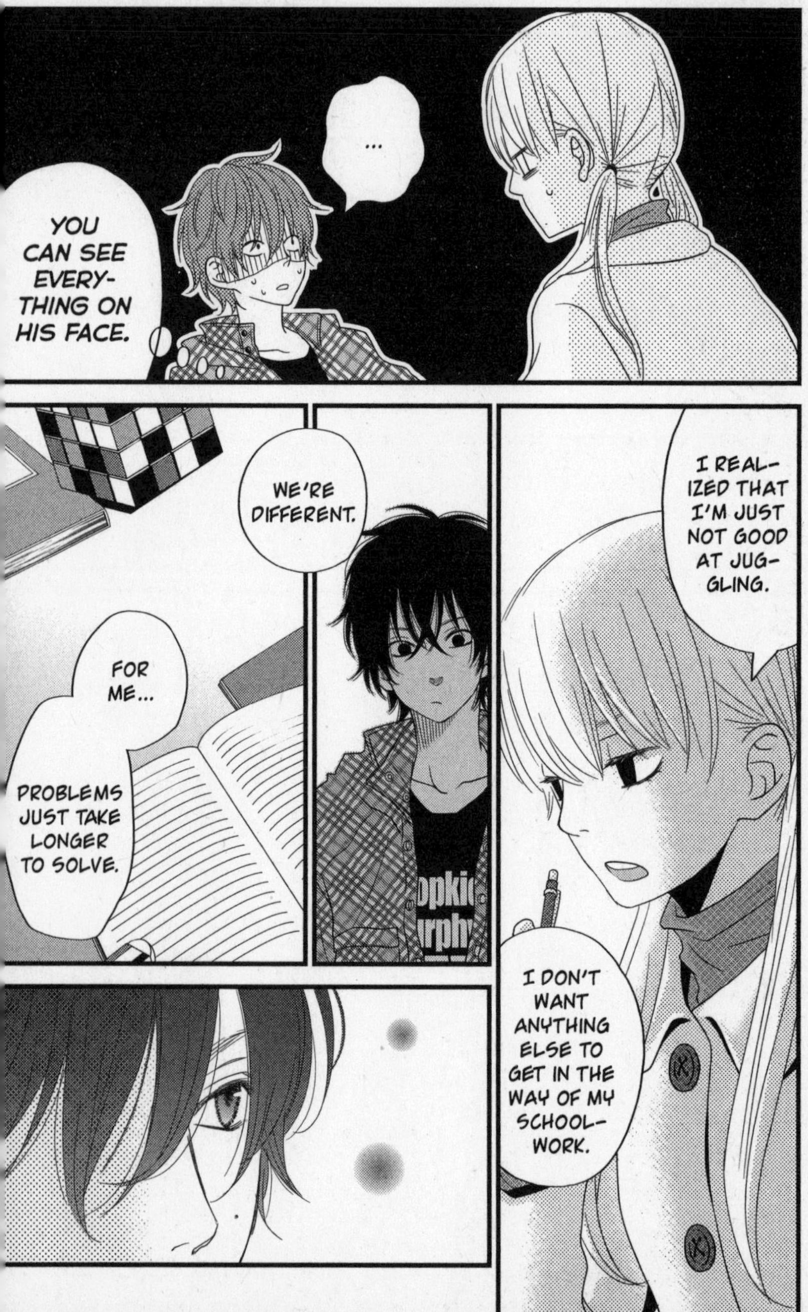
...
YOU CAN SEE EVERY-THING ON HIS FACE.
I REAL-IZED THAT I'M JUST NOT GOOD AT JUG-GLING.
I DON'T WANT ANYTHING ELSE TO GET IN THE WAY OF MY SCHOOL-WORK.
WE'RE DIFFERENT.
FOR ME...
PROBLEMS JUST TAKE LONGER TO SOLVE.

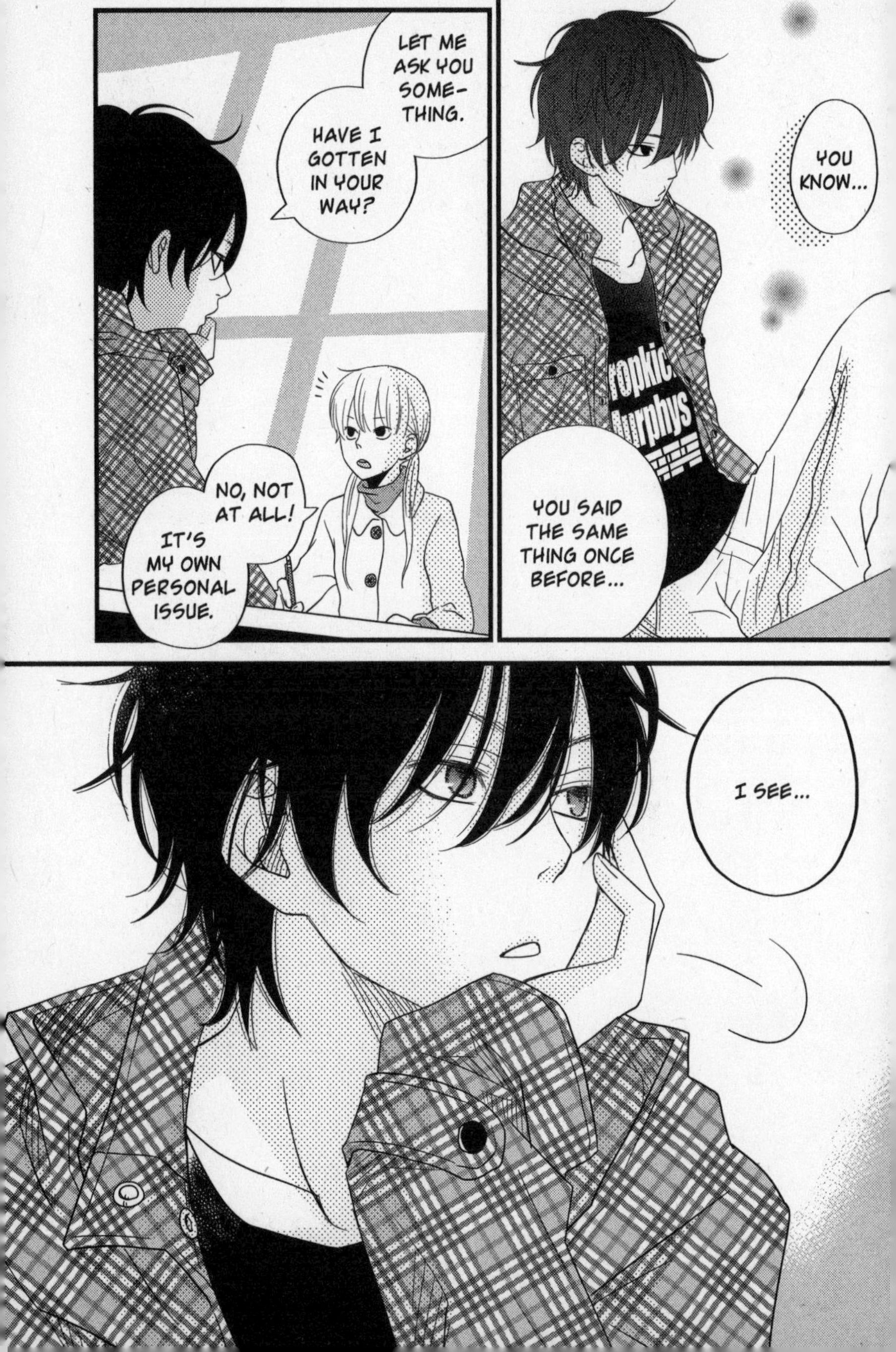
YOU KNOW...
YOU SAID THE SAME THING ONCE BEFORE...
LET ME ASK YOU SOME-THING.
HAVE I GOTTEN IN YOUR WAY?
NO, NOT AT ALL!
IT'S MY OWN PERSONAL ISSUE.
I SEE...

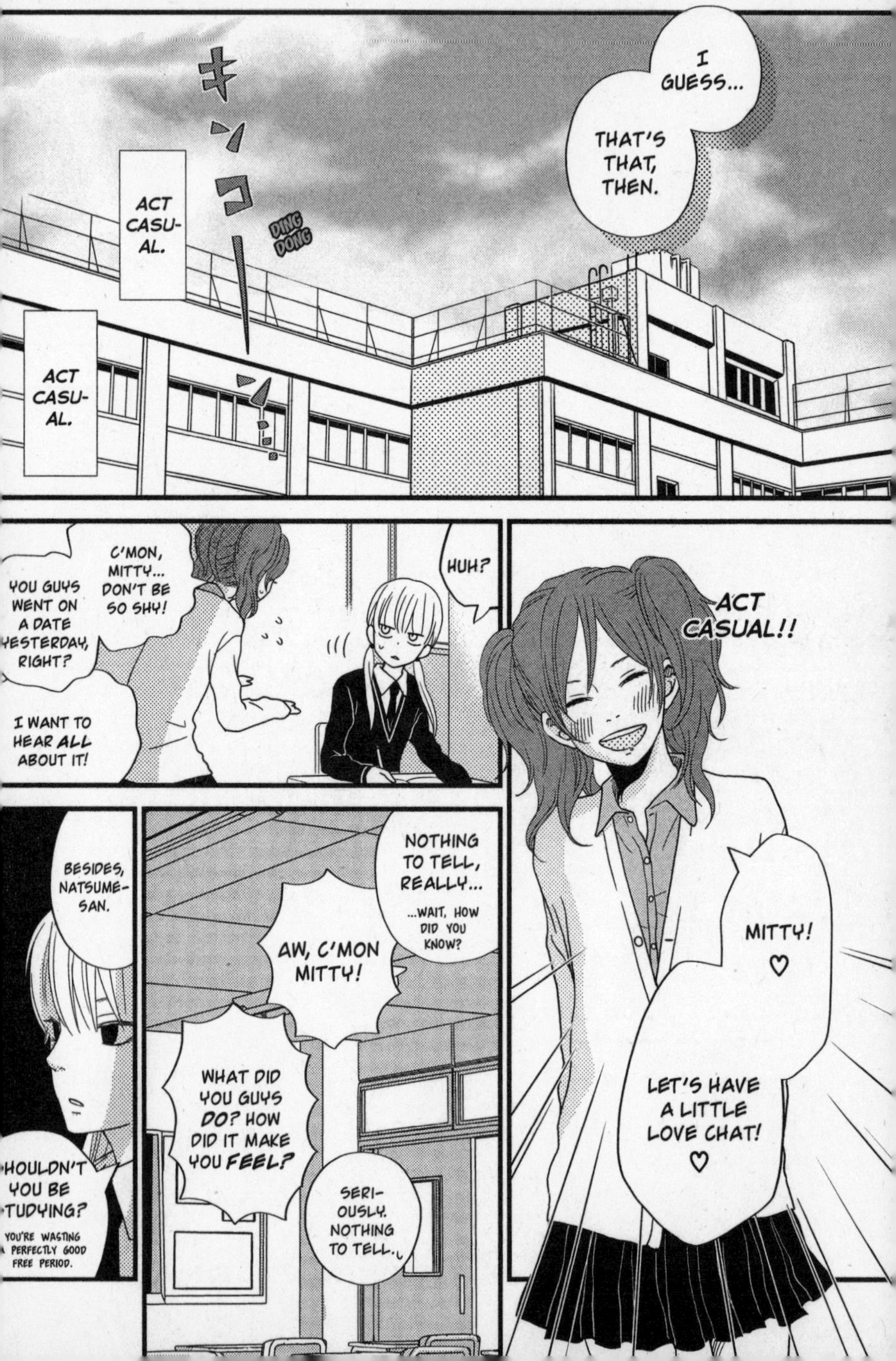
I GUESS...
THAT'S THAT, THEN.
DING DONG
ACT CASUAL.
ACT CASUAL.
ACT CASUAL!!
MITTY! ♡
LET'S HAVE A LITTLE LOVE CHAT! ♡
HUH?
C'MON, MITTY... DON'T BE SO SHY!
YOU GUYS WENT ON A DATE YESTERDAY, RIGHT?
I WANT TO HEAR ALL ABOUT IT!
NOTHING TO TELL, REALLY...
...WAIT, HOW DID YOU KNOW?
AW, C'MON MITTY!
WHAT DID YOU GUYS DO? HOW DID IT MAKE YOU FEEL?
SERIOUSLY. NOTHING TO TELL.
BESIDES, NATSUME-SAN.
HOULDN'T YOU BE TUDYING?
YOU'RE WASTING PERFECTLY GOOD FREE PERIOD.

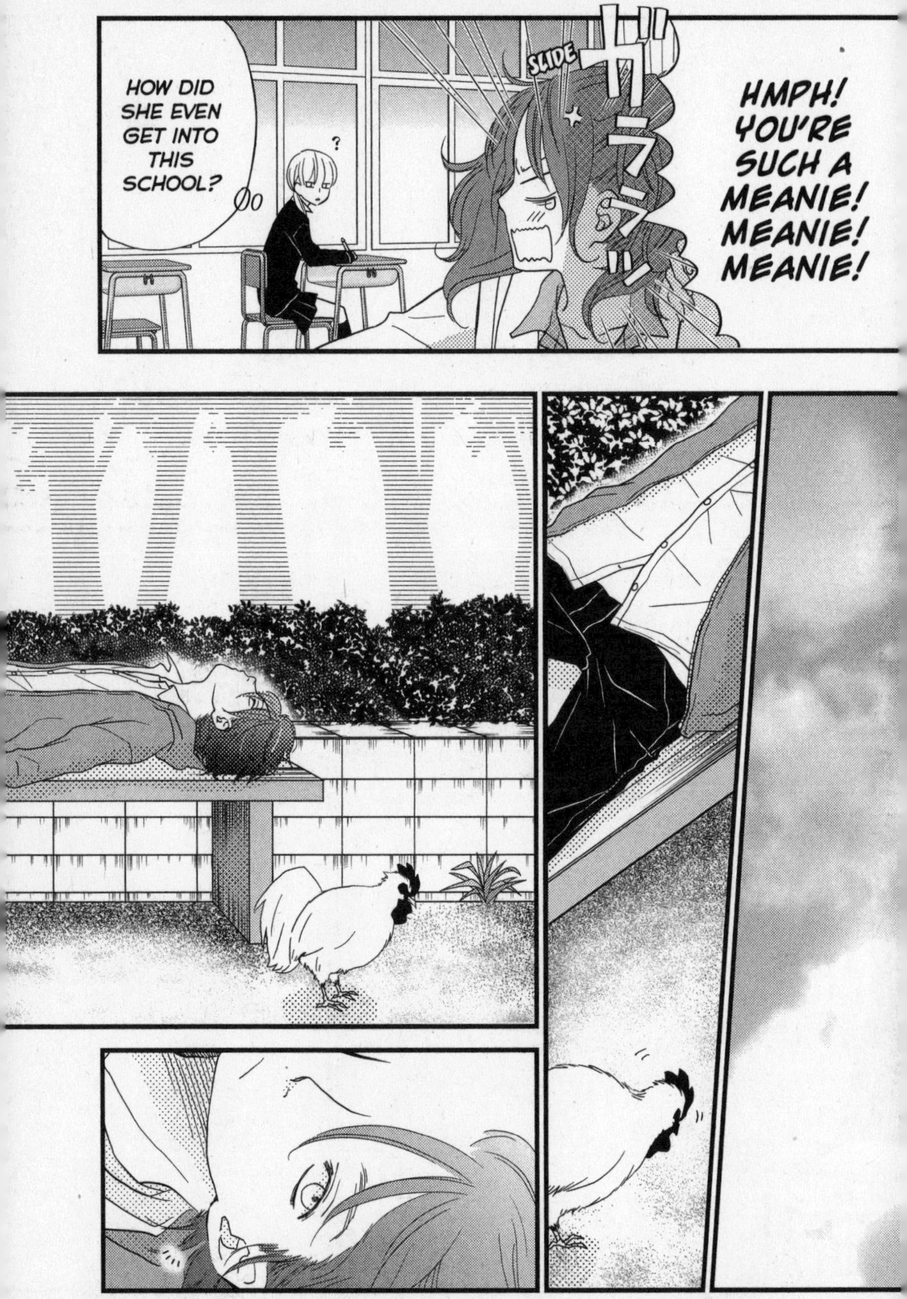
HMPH! YOU'RE SUCH A MEANIE! MEANIE! MEANIE!
SLIDE
?
HOW DID SHE EVEN GET INTO THIS SCHOOL?

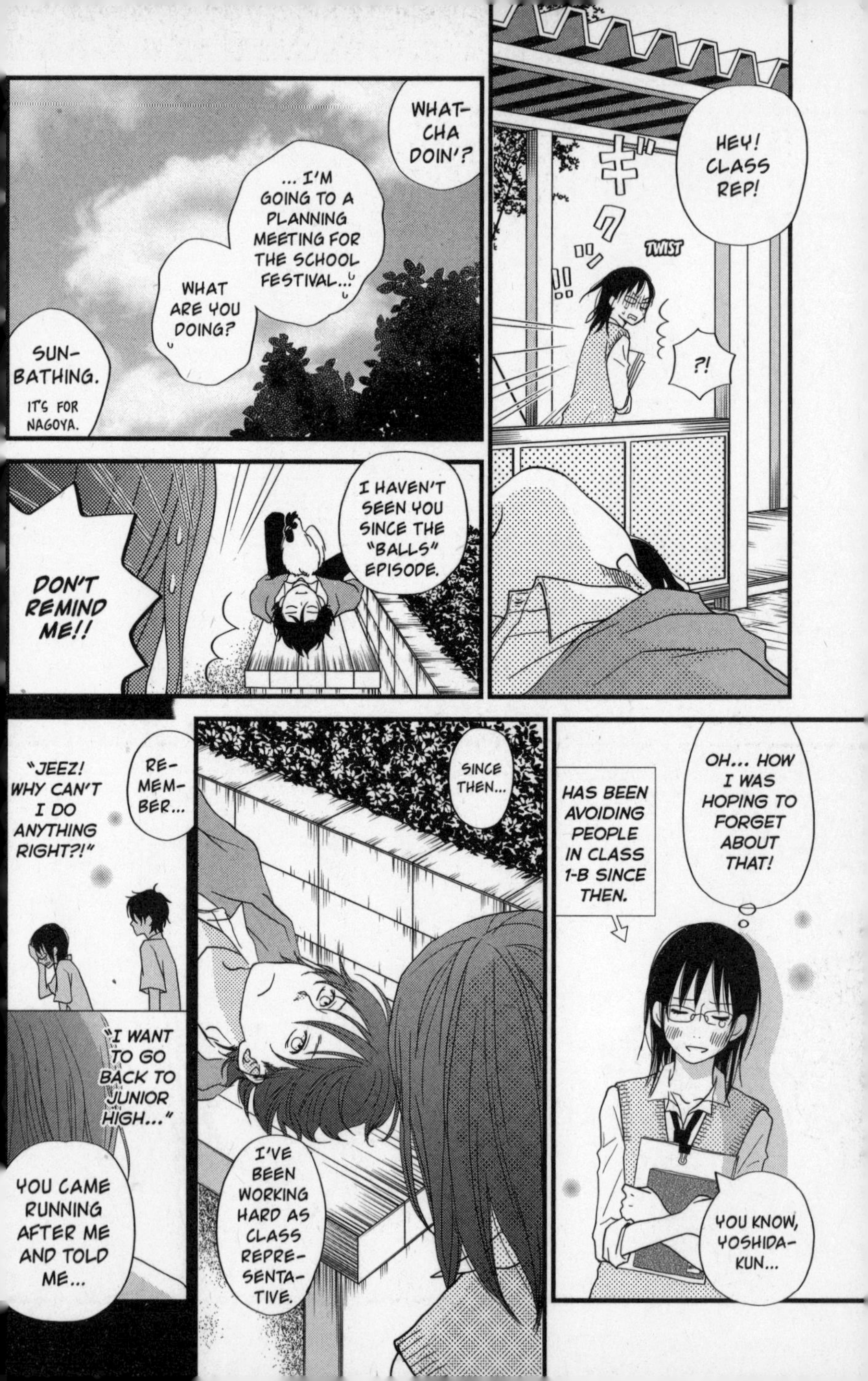
HEY! CLASS REP!
ギク
TWIST
?!
WHAT-CHA DOIN'?
... I'M GOING TO A PLANNING MEETING FOR THE SCHOOL FESTIVAL...
WHAT ARE YOU DOING?
SUN-BATHING.
IT'S FOR NAGOYA.
I HAVEN'T SEEN YOU SINCE THE "BALLS" EPISODE.
DON'T REMIND ME!!
OH... HOW I WAS HOPING TO FORGET ABOUT THAT!
HAS BEEN AVOIDING PEOPLE IN CLASS 1-B SINCE THEN.
YOU KNOW, YOSHIDA-KUN...
SINCE THEN...
I'VE BEEN WORKING HARD AS CLASS REPRE-SENTA-TIVE.
RE-MEM-BER...
"JEEZ! WHY CAN'T I DO ANYTHING RIGHT?!"
"I WANT TO GO BACK TO JUNIOR HIGH..."
YOU CAME RUNNING AFTER ME AND TOLD ME...

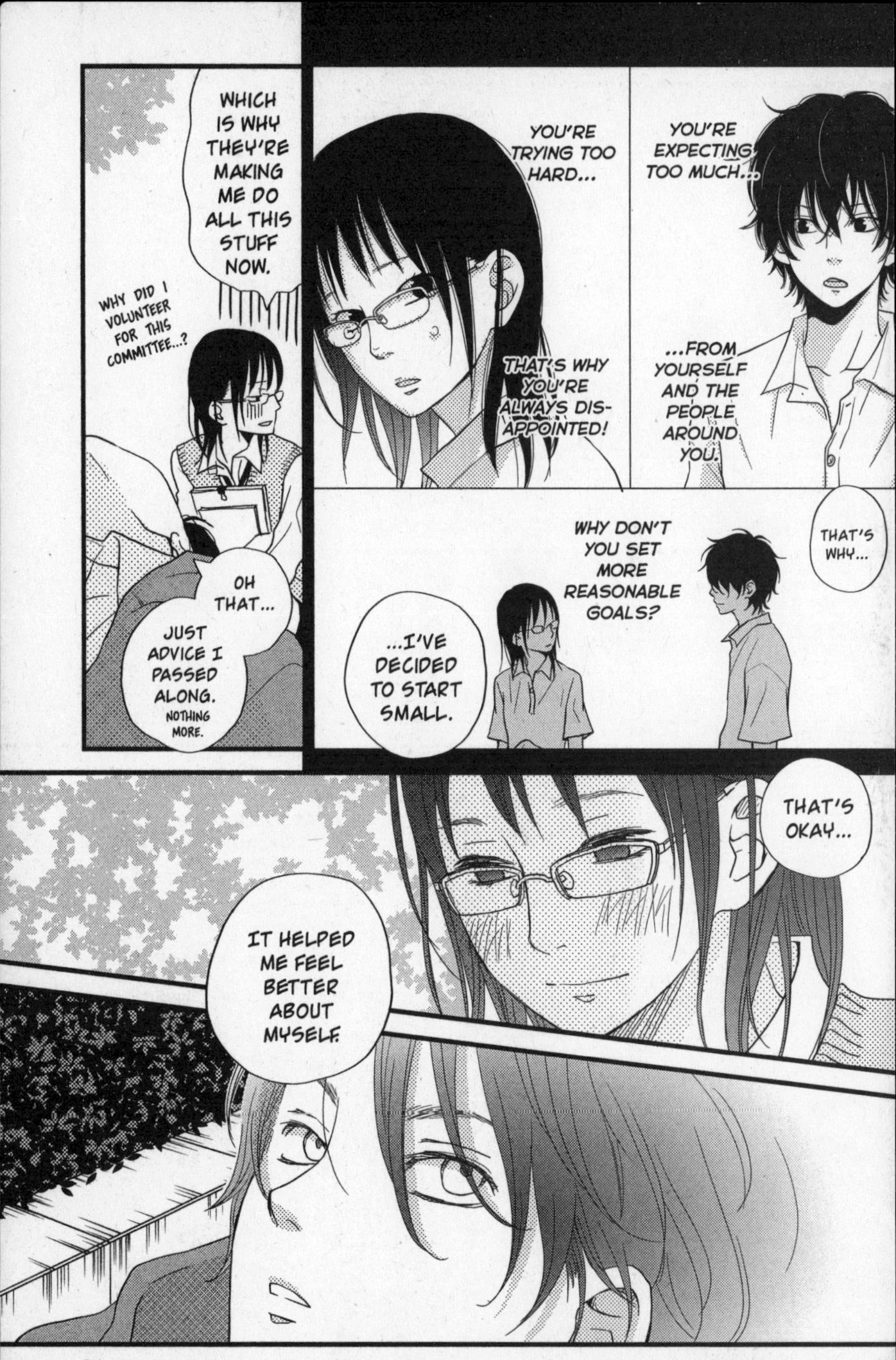
YOU'RE EXPECTING TOO MUCH...
...FROM YOURSELF AND THE PEOPLE AROUND YOU.
YOU'RE TRYING TOO HARD...
THAT'S WHY YOU'RE ALWAYS DIS-APPOINTED!
THAT'S WHY...
WHY DON'T YOU SET MORE REASONABLE GOALS?
...I'VE DECIDED TO START SMALL.
WHICH IS WHY THEY'RE MAKING ME DO ALL THIS STUFF NOW.
WHY DID I VOLUNTEER FOR THIS COMMITTEE...?
OH THAT...
JUST ADVICE I PASSED ALONG. NOTHING MORE.
THAT'S OKAY...
IT HELPED ME FEEL BETTER ABOUT MYSELF.

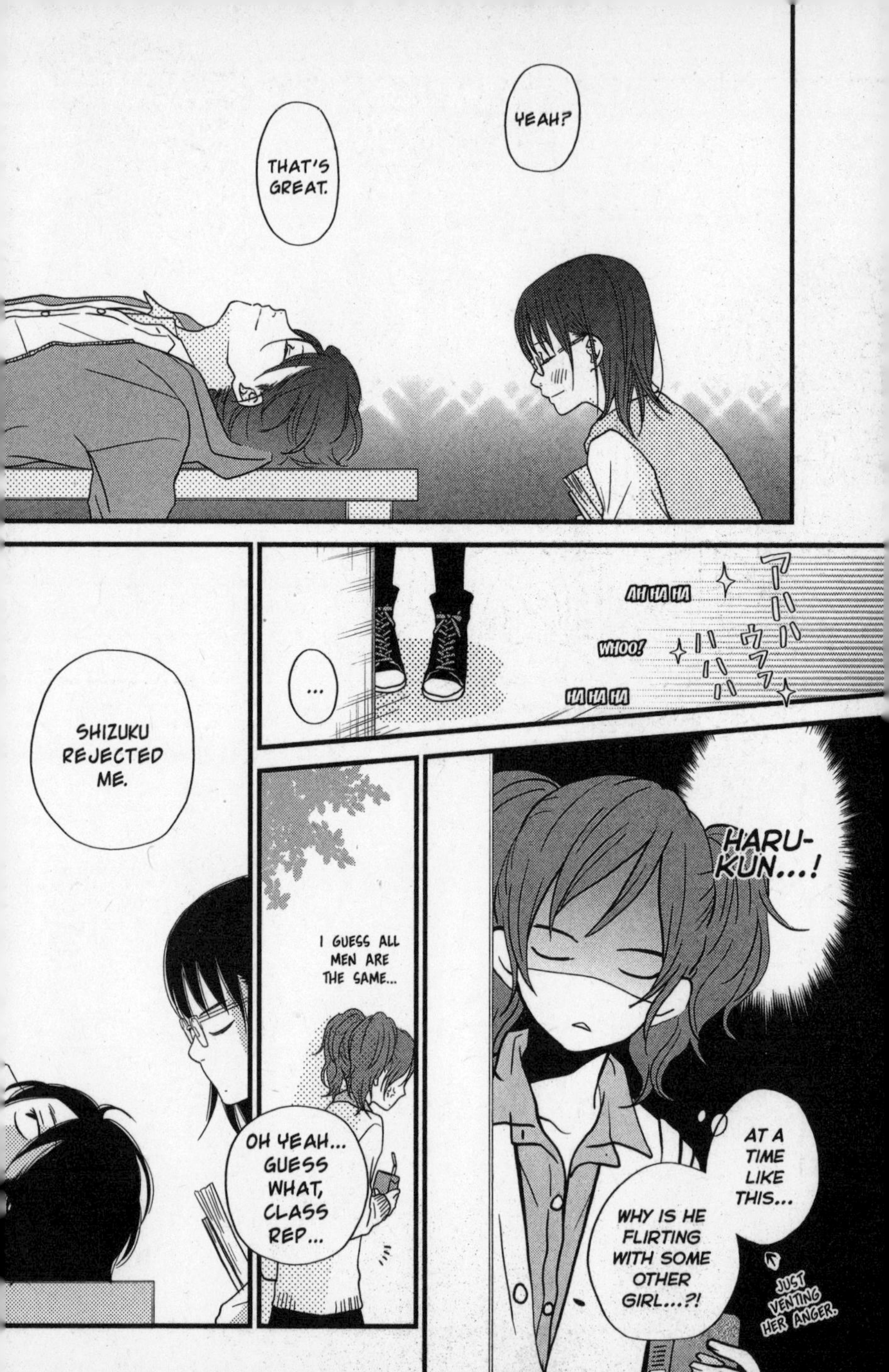
YEAH?
THAT'S GREAT.
AH HA HA
WHOO!
HA HA HA
...
HARU-KUN...!
AT A TIME LIKE THIS...
WHY IS HE FLIRTING WITH SOME OTHER GIRL...?!
JUST VENTING HER ANGER.
I GUESS ALL MEN ARE THE SAME...
OH YEAH... GUESS WHAT, CLASS REP...
SHIZUKU REJECTED ME.

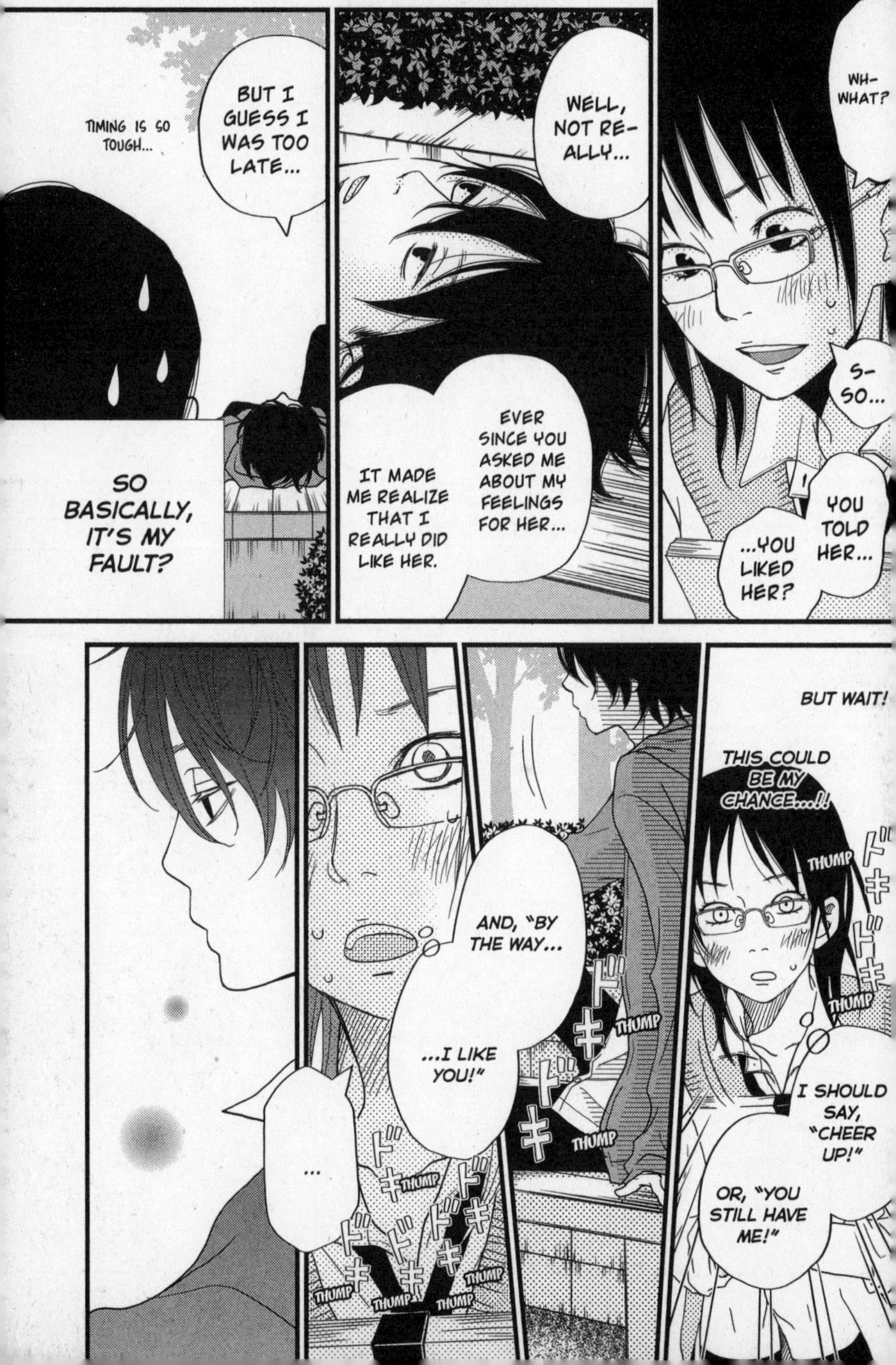
WH-WHAT?
S-SO...
YOU TOLD HER...
...YOU LIKED HER?
WELL, NOT RE-ALLY...
EVER SINCE YOU ASKED ME ABOUT MY FEELINGS FOR HER...
IT MADE ME REALIZE THAT I REALLY DID LIKE HER.
BUT I GUESS I WAS TOO LATE...
TIMING IS SO TOUGH...
SO BASICALLY, IT'S MY FAULT?
BUT WAIT!
THIS COULD BE MY CHANCE...!!
THUMP
THUMP
I SHOULD SAY, "CHEER UP!"
OR, "YOU STILL HAVE ME!"
THUMP
THUMP
AND, "BY THE WAY...
...I LIKE YOU!"
THUMP
THUMP
THUMP
THUMP
THUMP
...

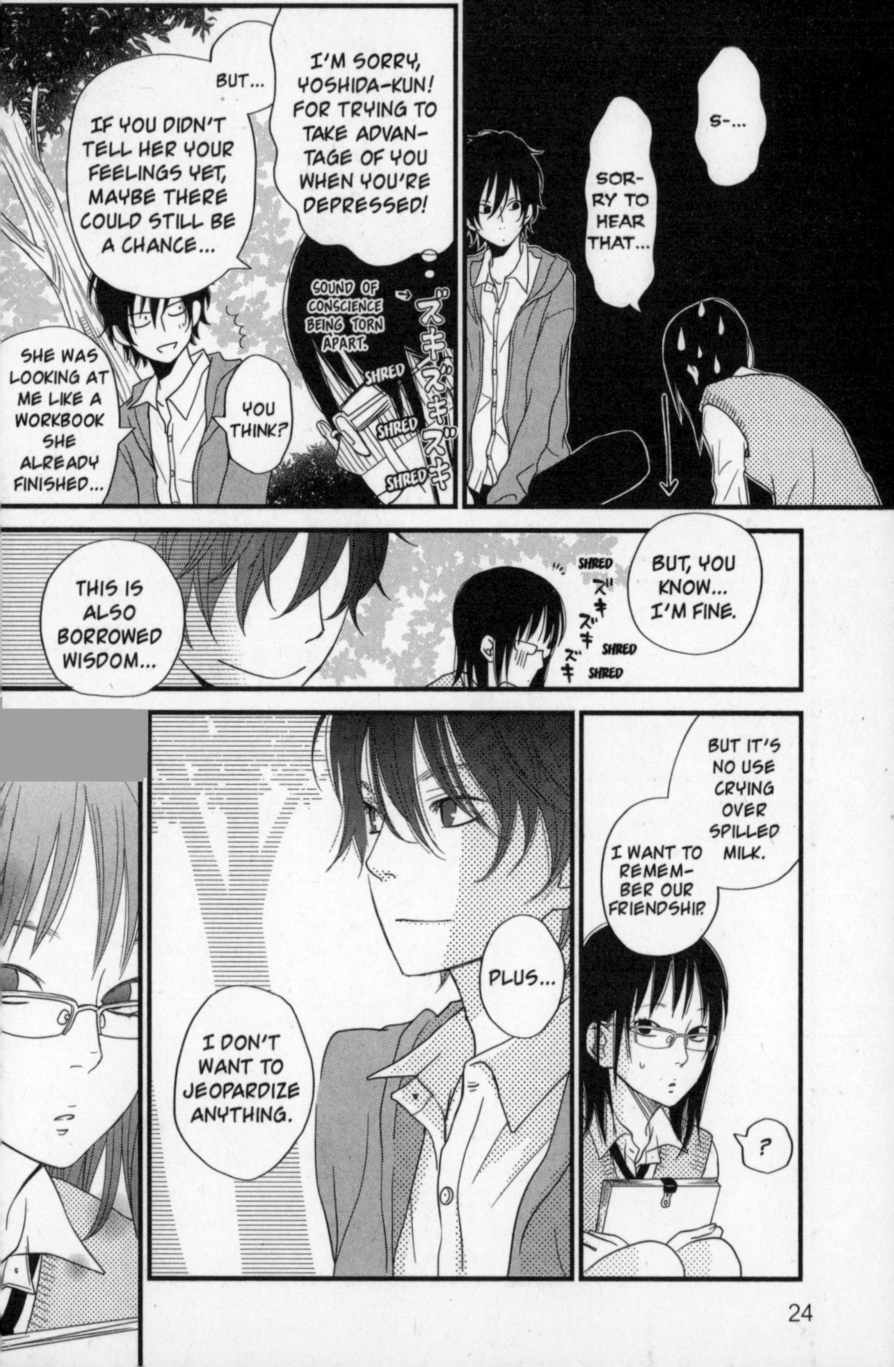
S-...
SOR-RY TO HEAR THAT...
I'M SORRY, YOSHIDA-KUN! FOR TRYING TO TAKE ADVAN-TAGE OF YOU WHEN YOU'RE DEPRESSED!
SOUND OF CONSCIENCE BEING TORN APART.
ズキズキ
SHRED
SHRED
SHRED
BUT...
IF YOU DIDN'T TELL HER YOUR FEELINGS YET, MAYBE THERE COULD STILL BE A CHANCE...
YOU THINK?
SHE WAS LOOKING AT ME LIKE A WORKBOOK SHE ALREADY FINISHED...
BUT, YOU KNOW... I'M FINE.
SHRED
ズキ
ズキ
SHRED
ズキ
SHRED
THIS IS ALSO BORROWED WISDOM...
BUT IT'S NO USE CRYING OVER SPILLED MILK.
I WANT TO REMEM-BER OUR FRIENDSHIP.
?
PLUS...
I DON'T WANT TO JEOPARDIZE ANYTHING.

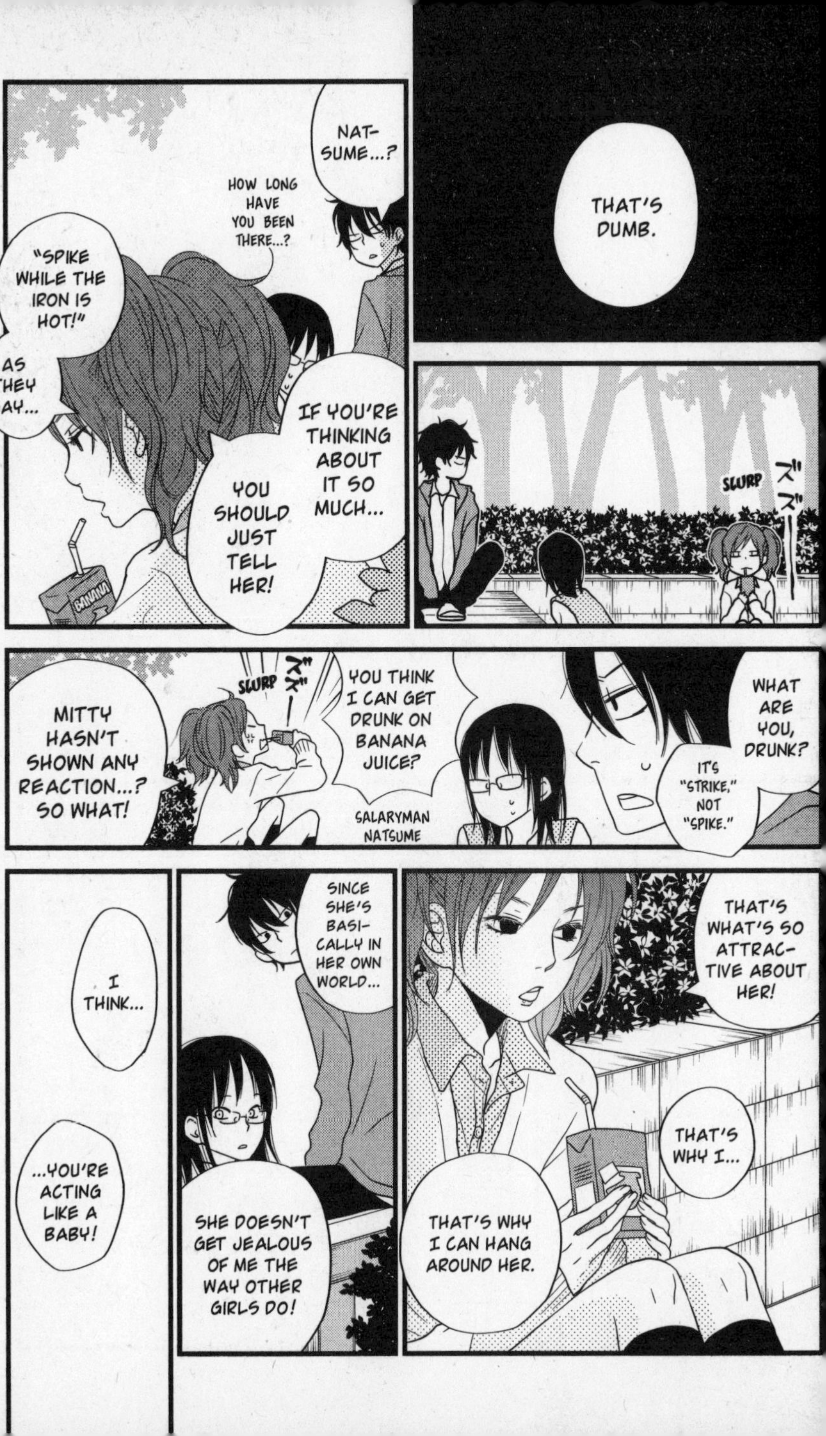
THAT'S DUMB.
ズズー
SLURP
NAT-SUME...?
HOW LONG HAVE YOU BEEN THERE...?
"SPIKE WHILE THE IRON IS HOT!"
AS THEY SAY...
IF YOU'RE THINKING ABOUT IT SO MUCH...
YOU SHOULD JUST TELL HER!
BANANA
WHAT ARE YOU, DRUNK?
IT'S "STRIKE," NOT "SPIKE."
YOU THINK I CAN GET DRUNK ON BANANA JUICE?
SALARYMAN NATSUME
ズズ
SLURP
MITTY HASN'T SHOWN ANY REACTION...? SO WHAT!
THAT'S WHAT'S SO ATTRACTIVE ABOUT HER!
THAT'S WHY I...
THAT'S WHY I CAN HANG AROUND HER.
SINCE SHE'S BASI-CALLY IN HER OWN WORLD...
SHE DOESN'T GET JEALOUS OF ME THE WAY OTHER GIRLS DO!
I THINK...
...YOU'RE ACTING LIKE A BABY!

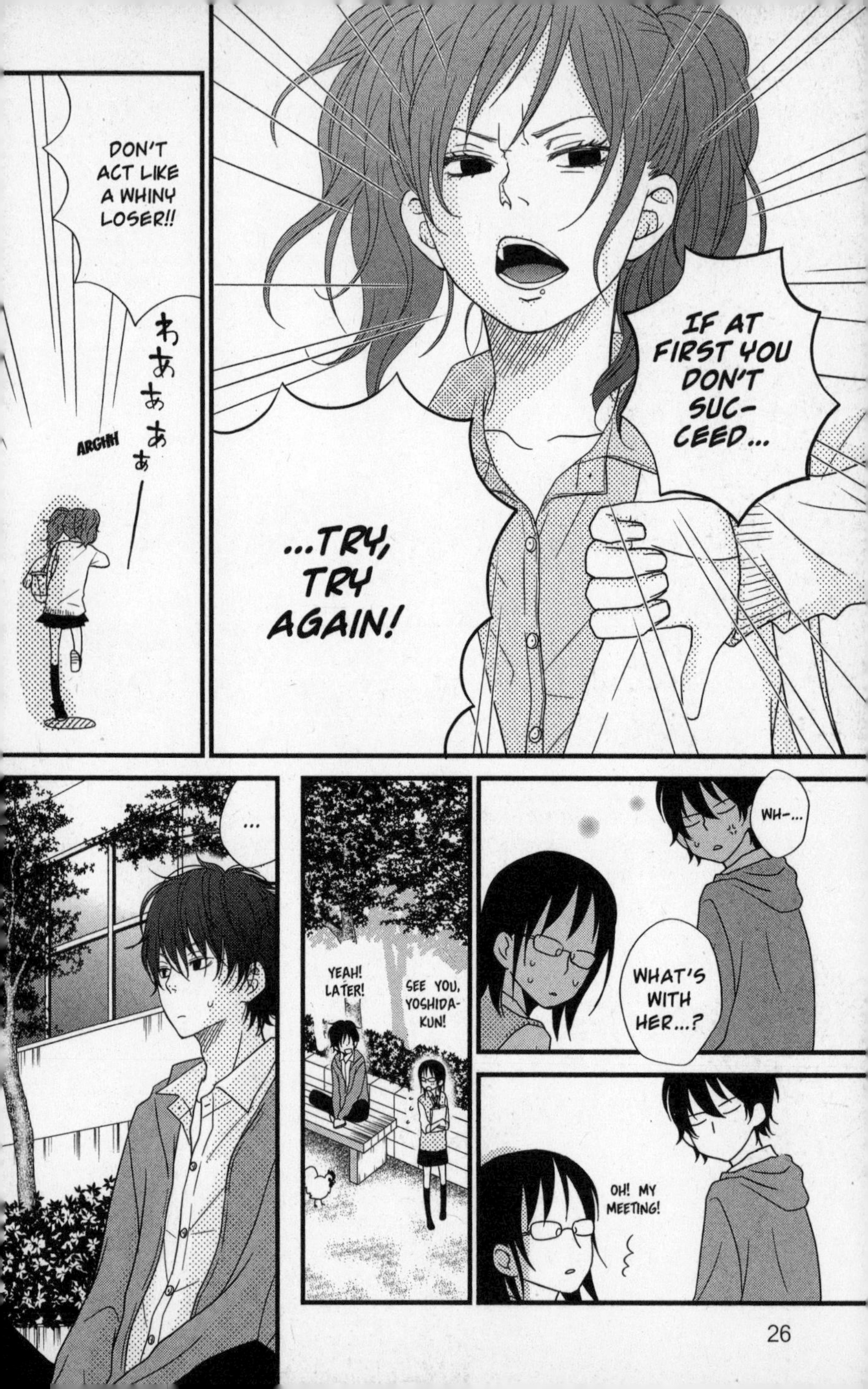

IF AT FIRST YOU DON'T SUC-CEED...
...TRY, TRY AGAIN!
DON'T ACT LIKE A WHINY LOSER!!
わあああぁ
ARGHH
WH-...
WHAT'S WITH HER...?
OH! MY MEETING!
SEE YOU, YOSHIDA-KUN!
YEAH! LATER!
...

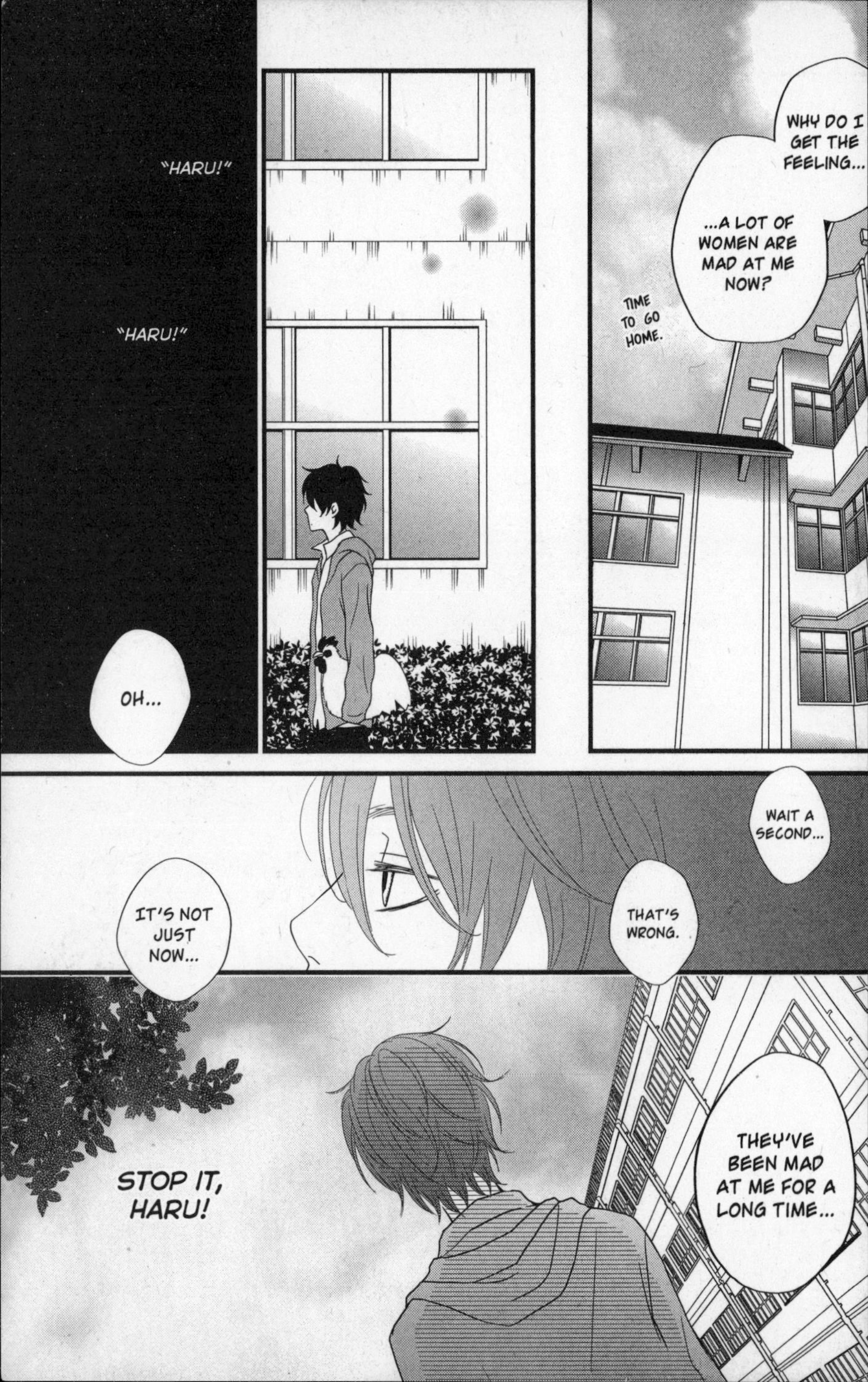
WHY DO I GET THE FEELING...
...A LOT OF WOMEN ARE MAD AT ME NOW?
TIME TO GO HOME.
"HARU!"
"HARU!"
OH...
WAIT A SECOND...
THAT'S WRONG.
IT'S NOT JUST NOW...
THEY'VE BEEN MAD AT ME FOR A LONG TIME...
STOP IT, HARU!

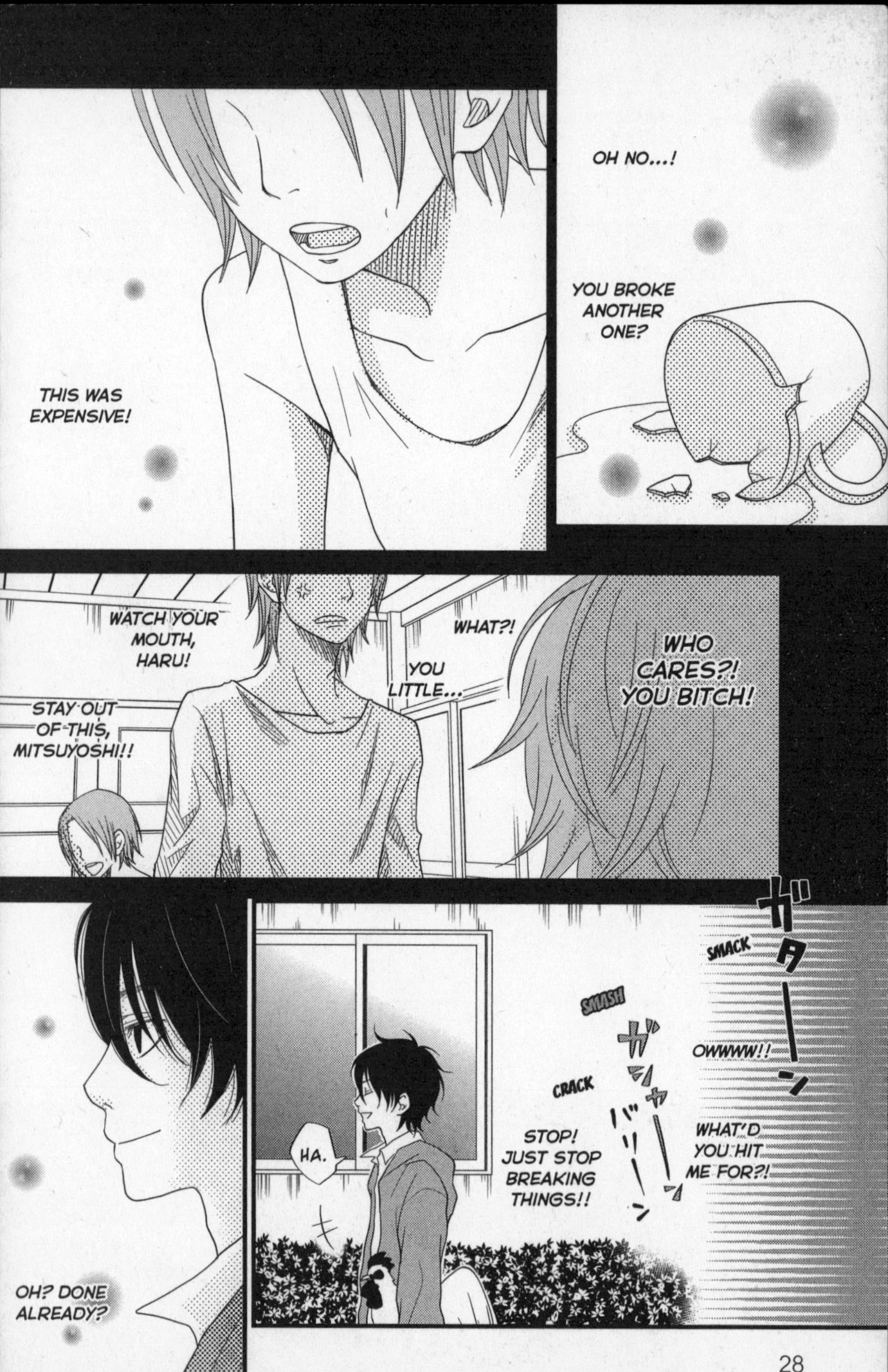
OH NO...!
YOU BROKE ANOTHER ONE?
THIS WAS EXPENSIVE!
WHO CARES?! YOU BITCH!
WHAT?!
YOU LITTLE...
WATCH YOUR MOUTH, HARU!
STAY OUT OF THIS, MITSUYOSHI!!
SMACK
OWWWW!!
WHAT'D YOU HIT ME FOR?!
SMASH
CRACK
STOP! JUST STOP BREAKING THINGS!!
HA.
OH? DONE ALREADY?

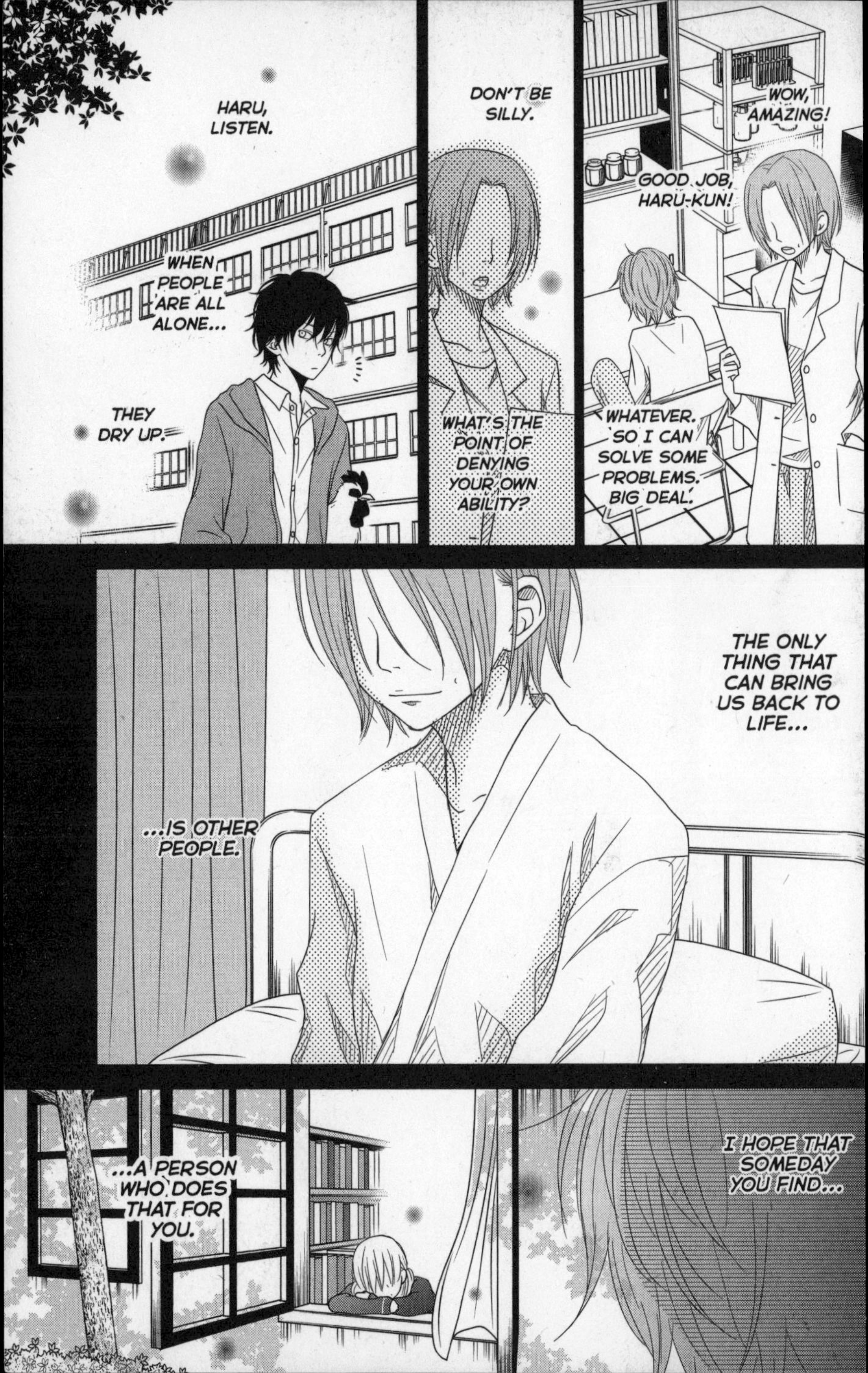

WOW, AMAZING!
GOOD JOB, HARU-KUN!
WHATEVER. SO I CAN SOLVE SOME PROBLEMS. BIG DEAL.
DON'T BE SILLY.
WHAT'S THE POINT OF DENYING YOUR OWN ABILITY?
HARU, LISTEN.
WHEN PEOPLE ARE ALL ALONE...
THEY DRY UP.
THE ONLY THING THAT CAN BRING US BACK TO LIFE...
...IS OTHER PEOPLE.
I HOPE THAT SOMEDAY YOU FIND...
...A PERSON WHO DOES THAT FOR YOU.

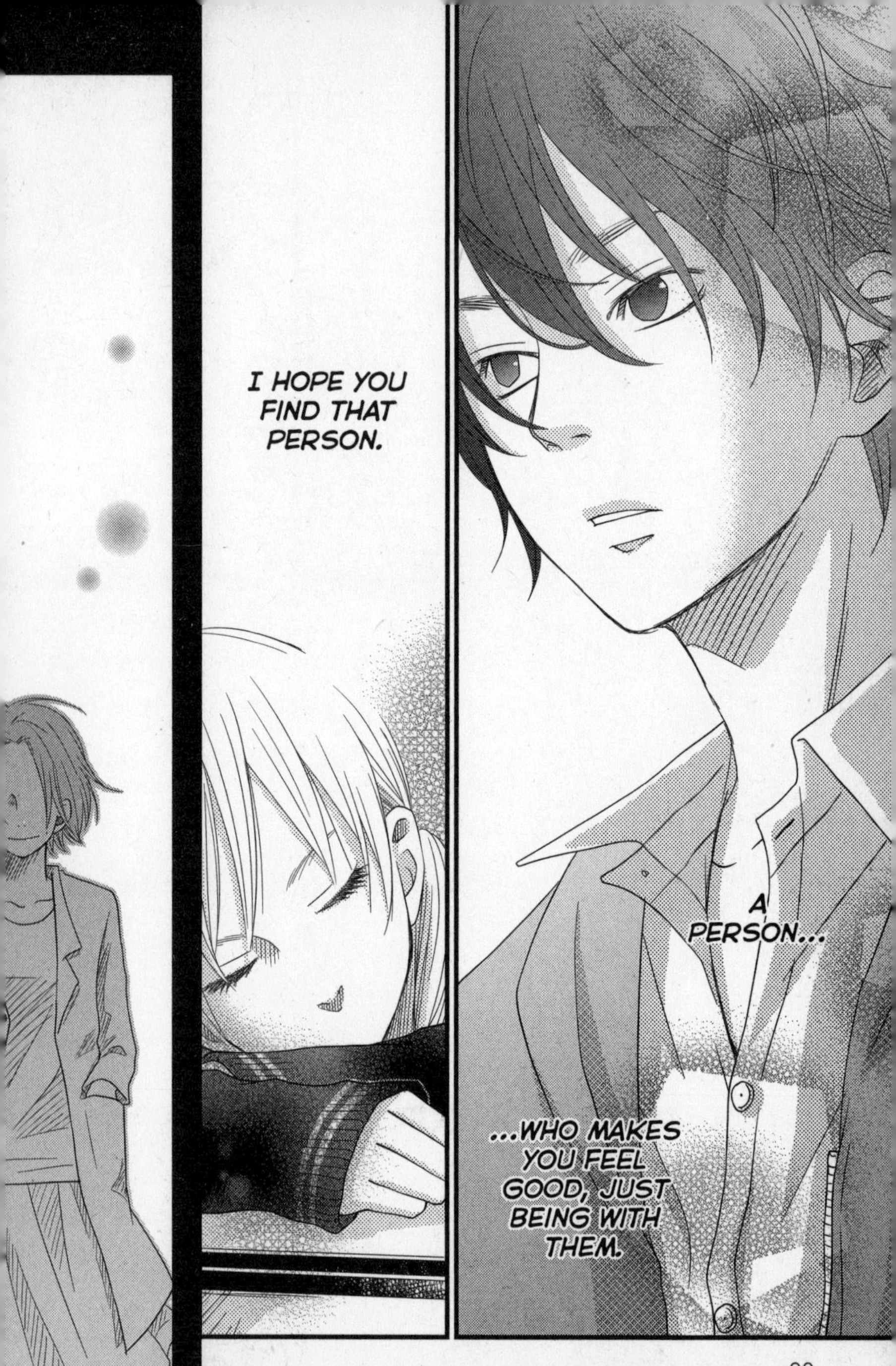
A PERSON...
...WHO MAKES YOU FEEL GOOD, JUST BEING WITH THEM.
I HOPE YOU FIND THAT PERSON.

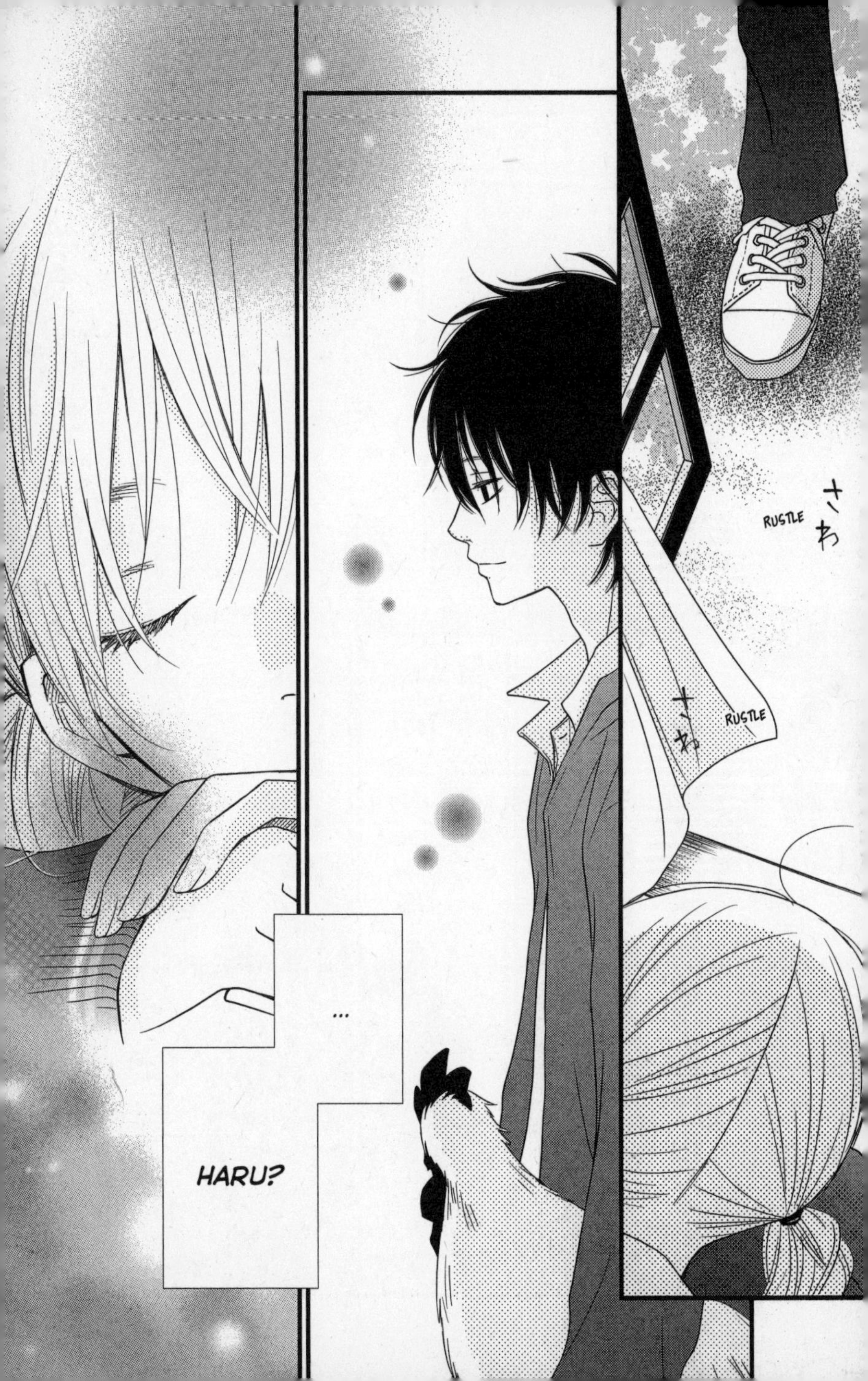
さわ
RUSTLE
さわ
RUSTLE
...
HARU?

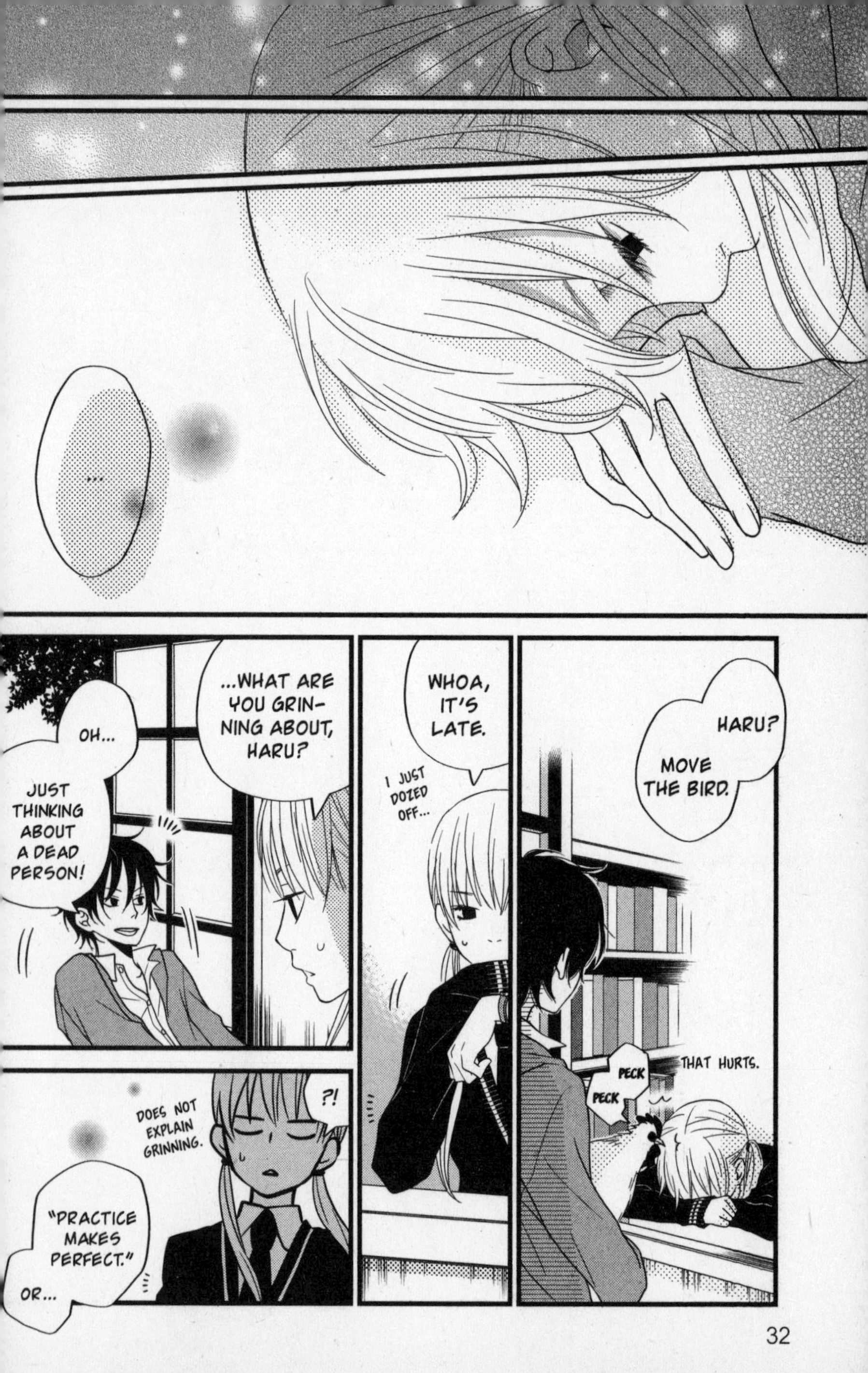
...
HARU? MOVE THE BIRD.
THAT HURTS.
PECK PECK
WHOA, IT'S LATE.
I JUST DOZED OFF...
...WHAT ARE YOU GRINNING ABOUT, HARU?
OH... JUST THINKING ABOUT A DEAD PERSON!
?!
DOES NOT EXPLAIN GRINNING.
"PRACTICE MAKES PERFECT." OR...

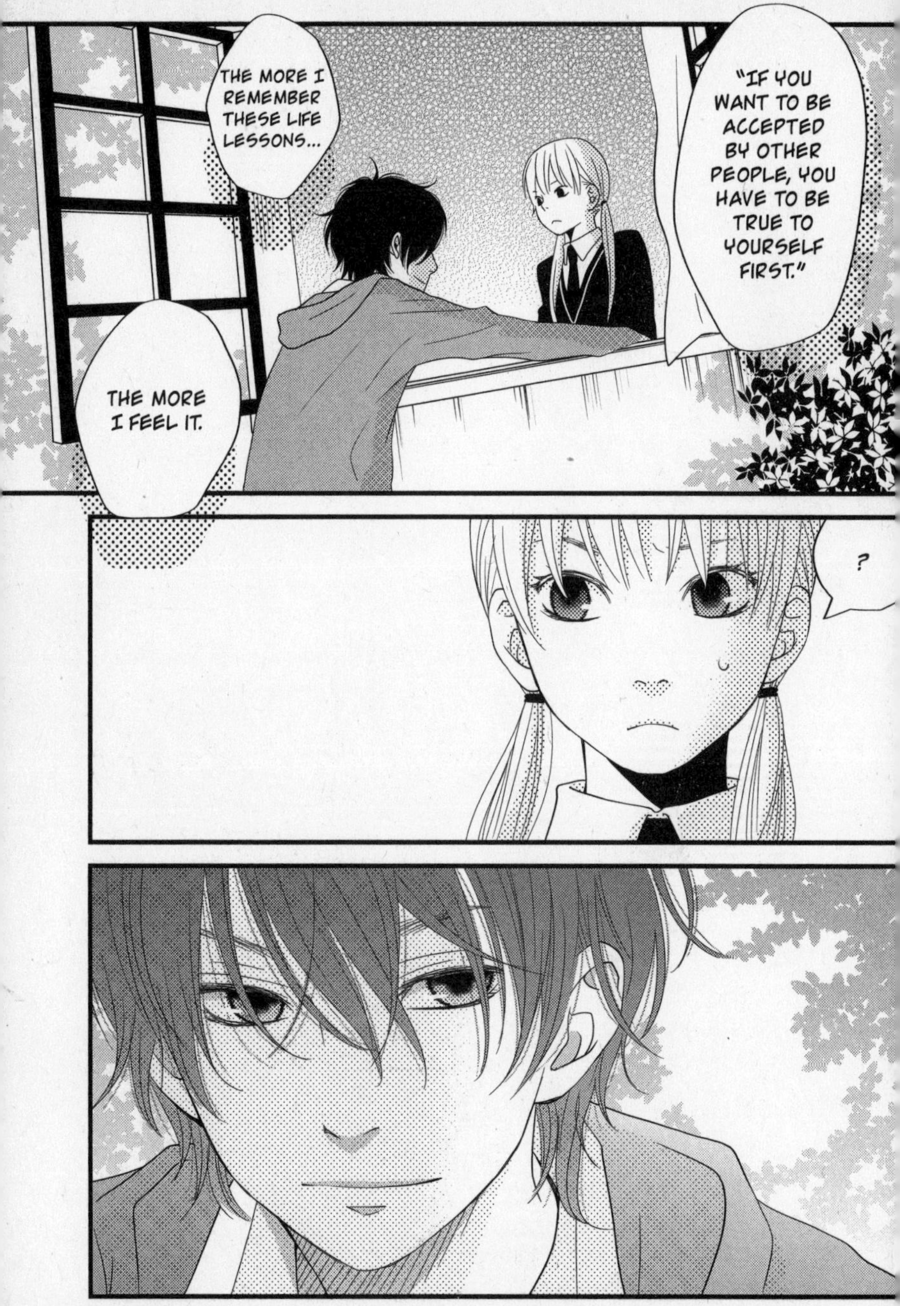
"IF YOU WANT TO BE ACCEPTED BY OTHER PEOPLE, YOU HAVE TO BE TRUE TO YOURSELF FIRST."
THE MORE I REMEMBER THESE LIFE LESSONS...
THE MORE I FEEL IT.
?

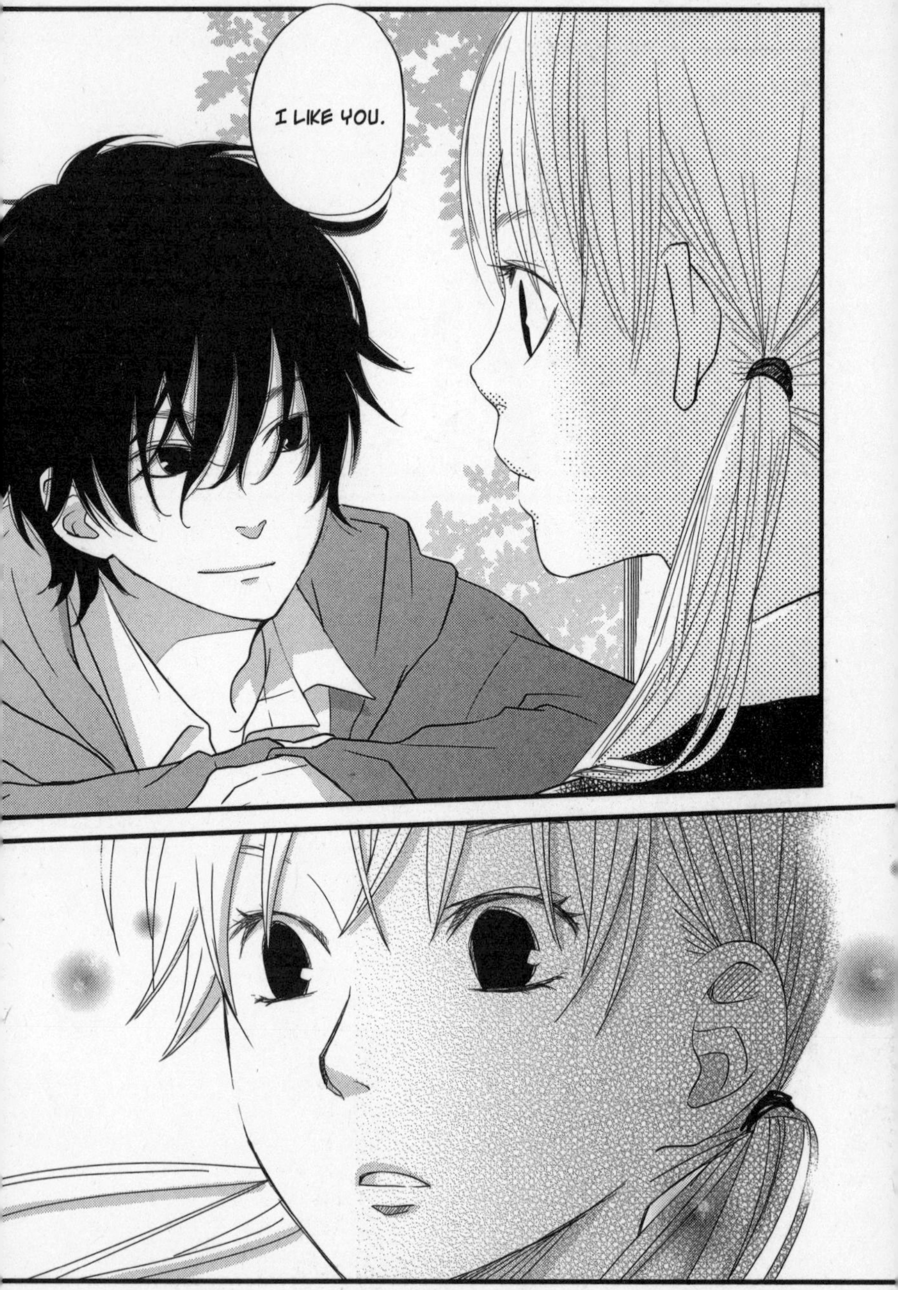
I LIKE YOU.

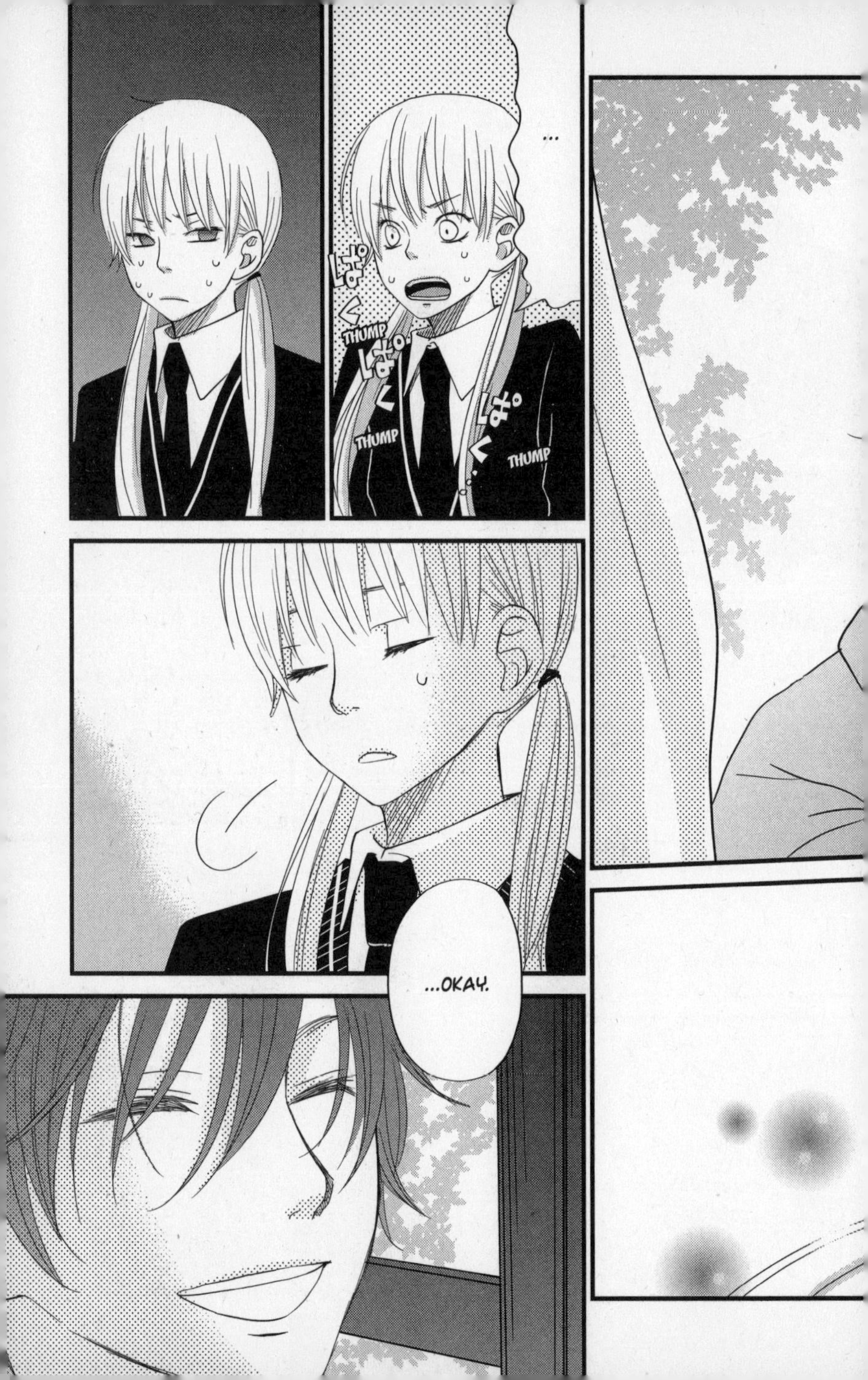
...
THUMP
THUMP
THUMP
...OKAY.

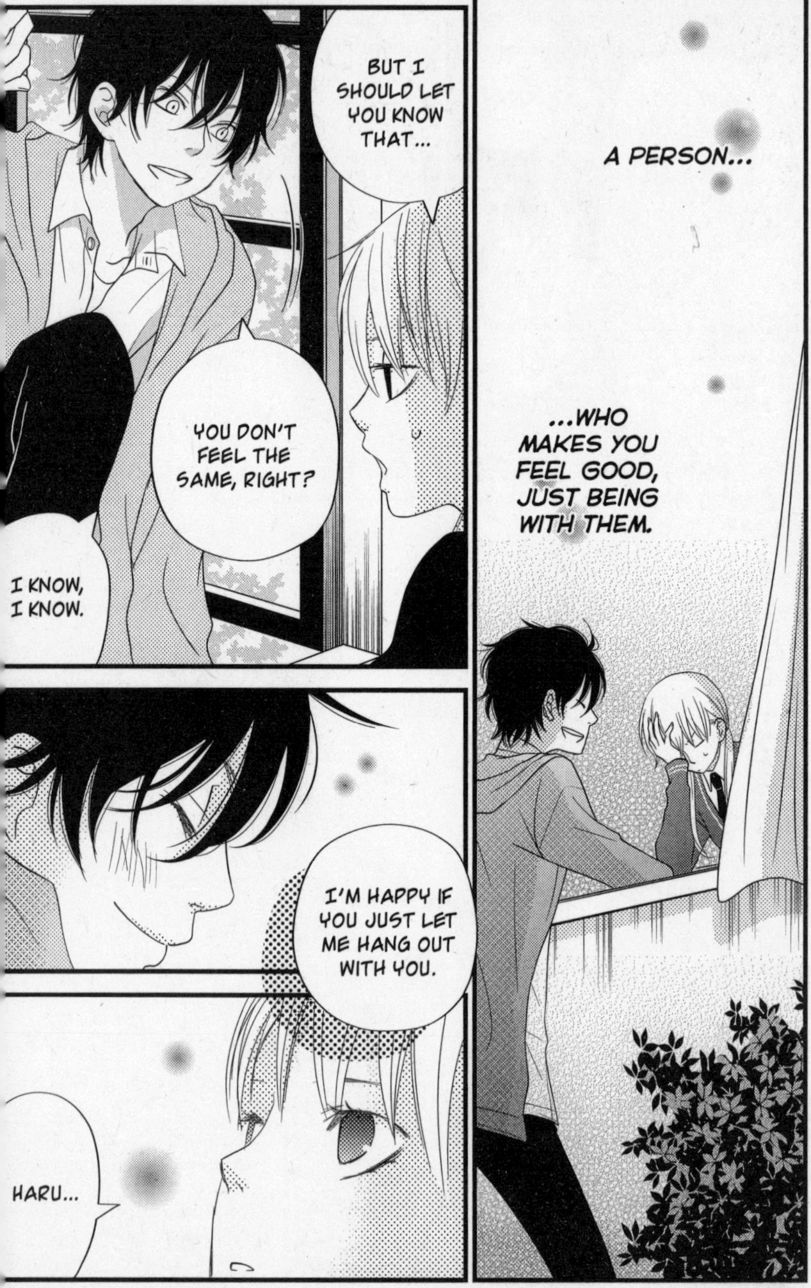
A PERSON...
...WHO MAKES YOU FEEL GOOD, JUST BEING WITH THEM.
BUT I SHOULD LET YOU KNOW THAT...
YOU DON'T FEEL THE SAME, RIGHT?
I KNOW, I KNOW.
I'M HAPPY IF YOU JUST LET ME HANG OUT WITH YOU.
HARU...

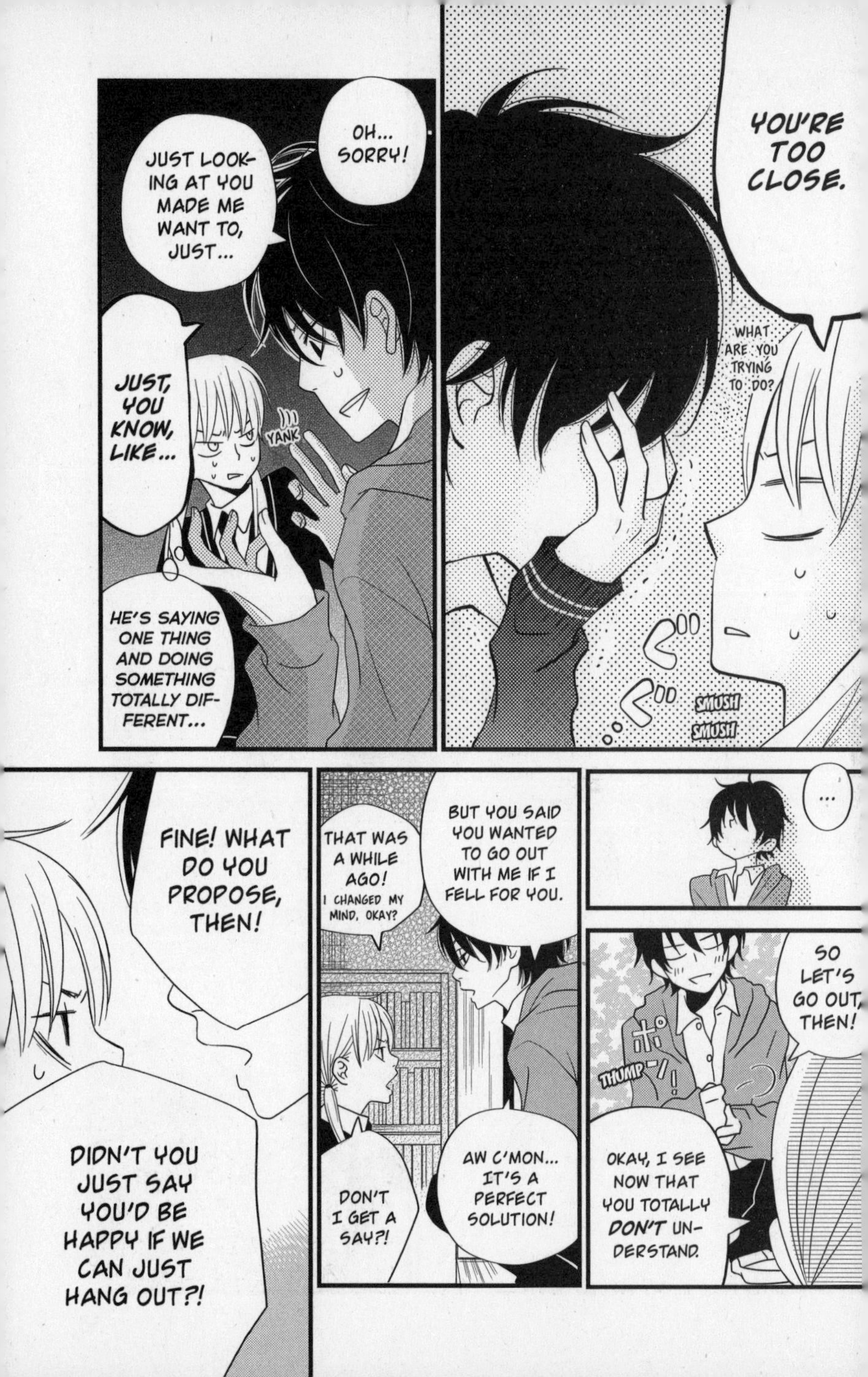
YOU'RE TOO CLOSE.
WHAT ARE YOU TRYING TO DO?
SMUSH
SMUSH
OH... SORRY!
JUST LOOKING AT YOU MADE ME WANT TO, JUST...
YANK
JUST, YOU KNOW, LIKE...
HE'S SAYING ONE THING AND DOING SOMETHING TOTALLY DIFFERENT...
...
SO LET'S GO OUT, THEN!
THUMP
OKAY, I SEE NOW THAT YOU TOTALLY *DON'T* UNDERSTAND.
BUT YOU SAID YOU WANTED TO GO OUT WITH ME IF I FELL FOR YOU.
THAT WAS A WHILE AGO! I CHANGED MY MIND, OKAY?
AW C'MON... IT'S A PERFECT SOLUTION!
DON'T I GET A SAY?!
FINE! WHAT DO YOU PROPOSE, THEN!
DIDN'T YOU JUST SAY YOU'D BE HAPPY IF WE CAN JUST HANG OUT?!

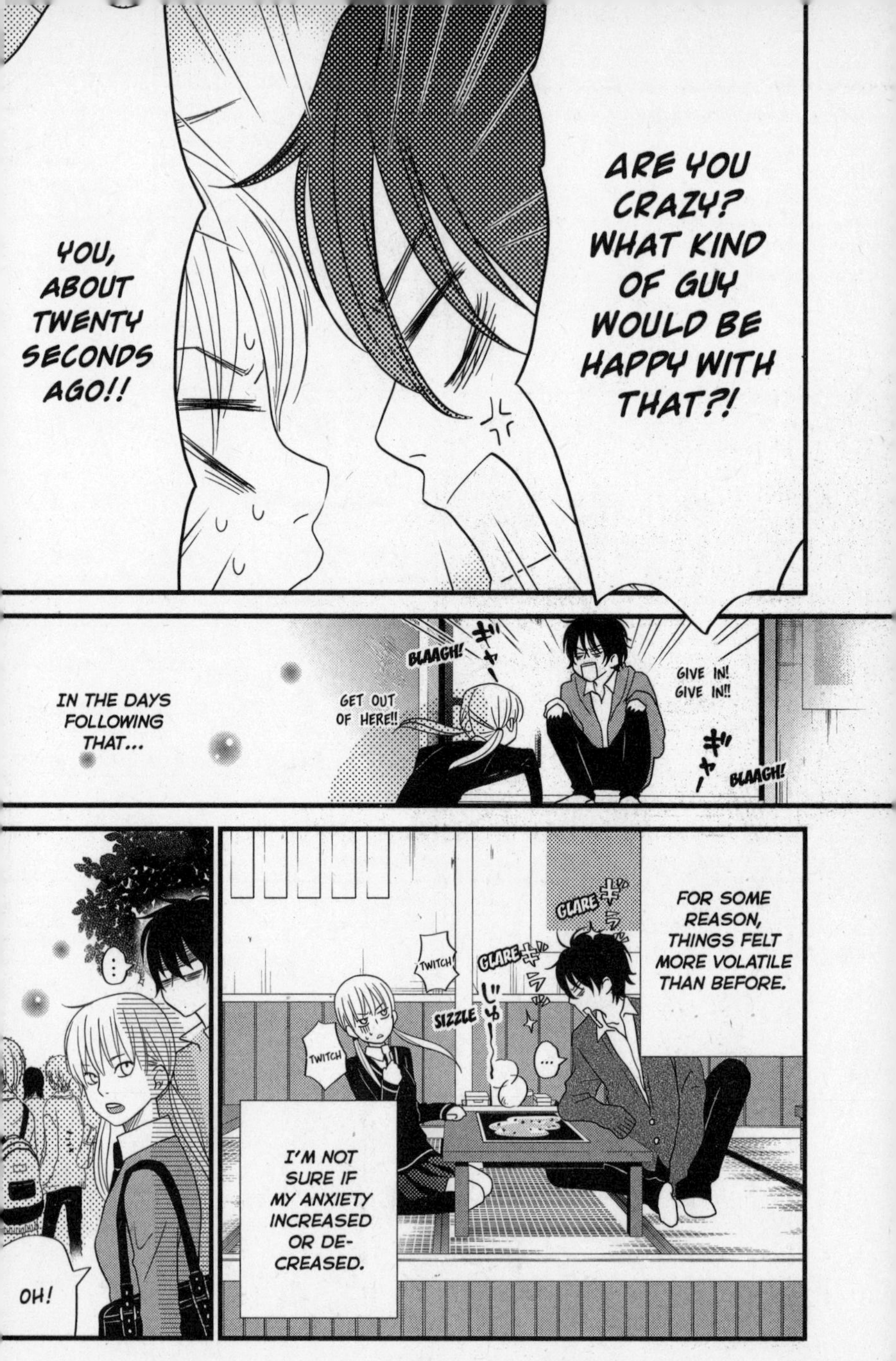
ARE YOU CRAZY? WHAT KIND OF GUY WOULD BE HAPPY WITH THAT?!
YOU, ABOUT TWENTY SECONDS AGO!!
GIVE IN! GIVE IN!!
ギャー
BLAAGH!
ギャー
BLAAGH!
GET OUT OF HERE!!
IN THE DAYS FOLLOWING THAT...
FOR SOME REASON, THINGS FELT MORE VOLATILE THAN BEFORE.
ギラ
GLARE
ギラ
GLARE
TWITCH
じゅー
SIZZLE
...
TWITCH
I'M NOT SURE IF MY ANXIETY INCREASED OR DE-CREASED.
...
OH!

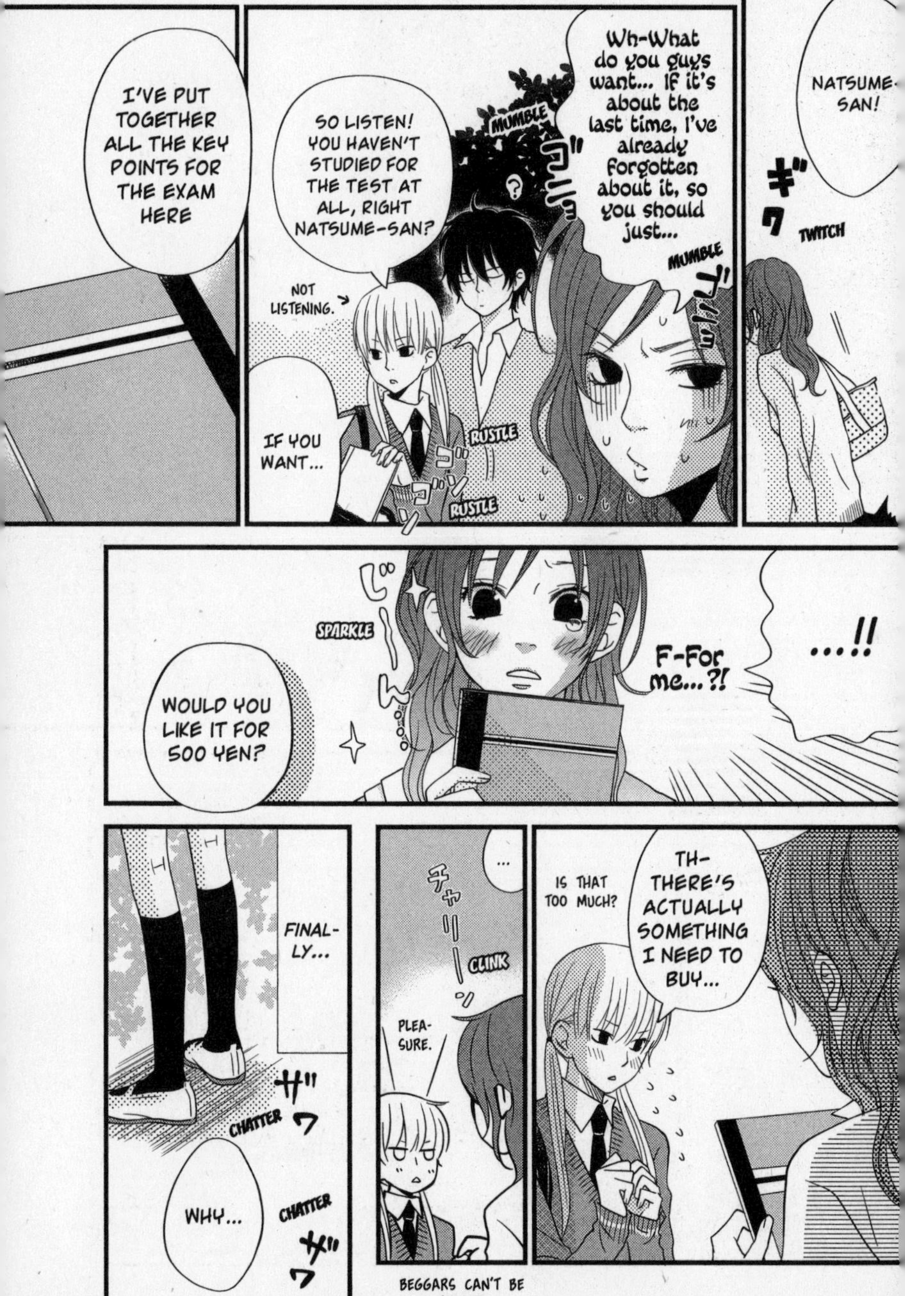
NATSUME-SAN!
TWITCH
Wh-What do you guys want... If it's about the last time, I've already forgotten about it, so you should just...
MUMBLE
MUMBLE
SO LISTEN! YOU HAVEN'T STUDIED FOR THE TEST AT ALL, RIGHT NATSUME-SAN?
NOT LISTENING.
IF YOU WANT...
RUSTLE
RUSTLE
I'VE PUT TOGETHER ALL THE KEY POINTS FOR THE EXAM HERE
...!!
F-For me...?!
SPARKLE
WOULD YOU LIKE IT FOR 500 YEN?
TH-THERE'S ACTUALLY SOMETHING I NEED TO BUY...
IS THAT TOO MUCH?
...
CLINK
PLEASURE.
BEGGARS CAN'T BE CHOOSERS.
FINAL-LY...
CHATTER
CHATTER
WHY...

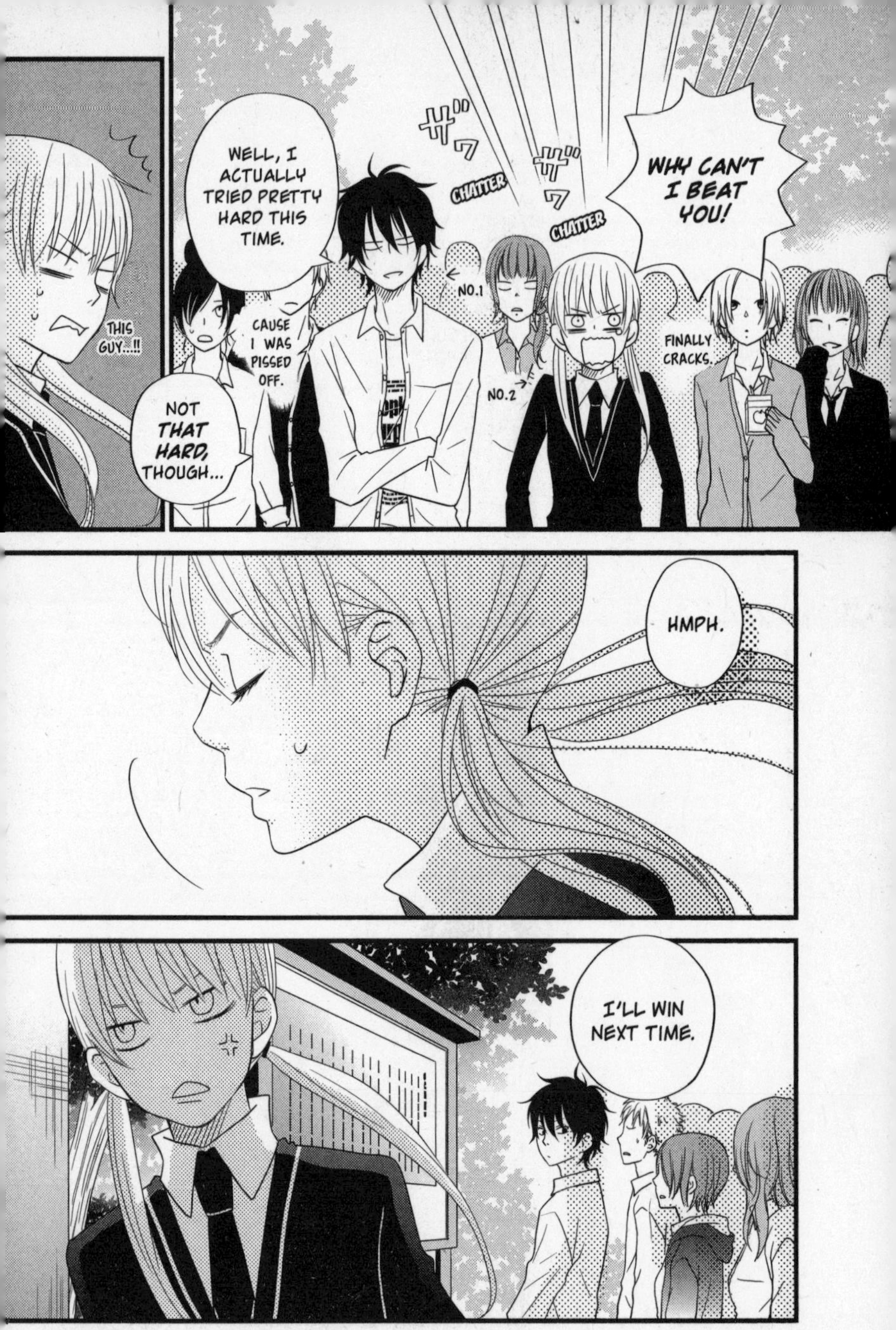
WHY CAN'T I BEAT YOU!
FINALLY CRACKS.
ザワ CHATTER
ザワ CHATTER
NO.1
NO.2
WELL, I ACTUALLY TRIED PRETTY HARD THIS TIME.
CAUSE I WAS PISSED OFF.
NOT THAT HARD, THOUGH...
THIS GUY...!!
HMPH.
I'LL WIN NEXT TIME.

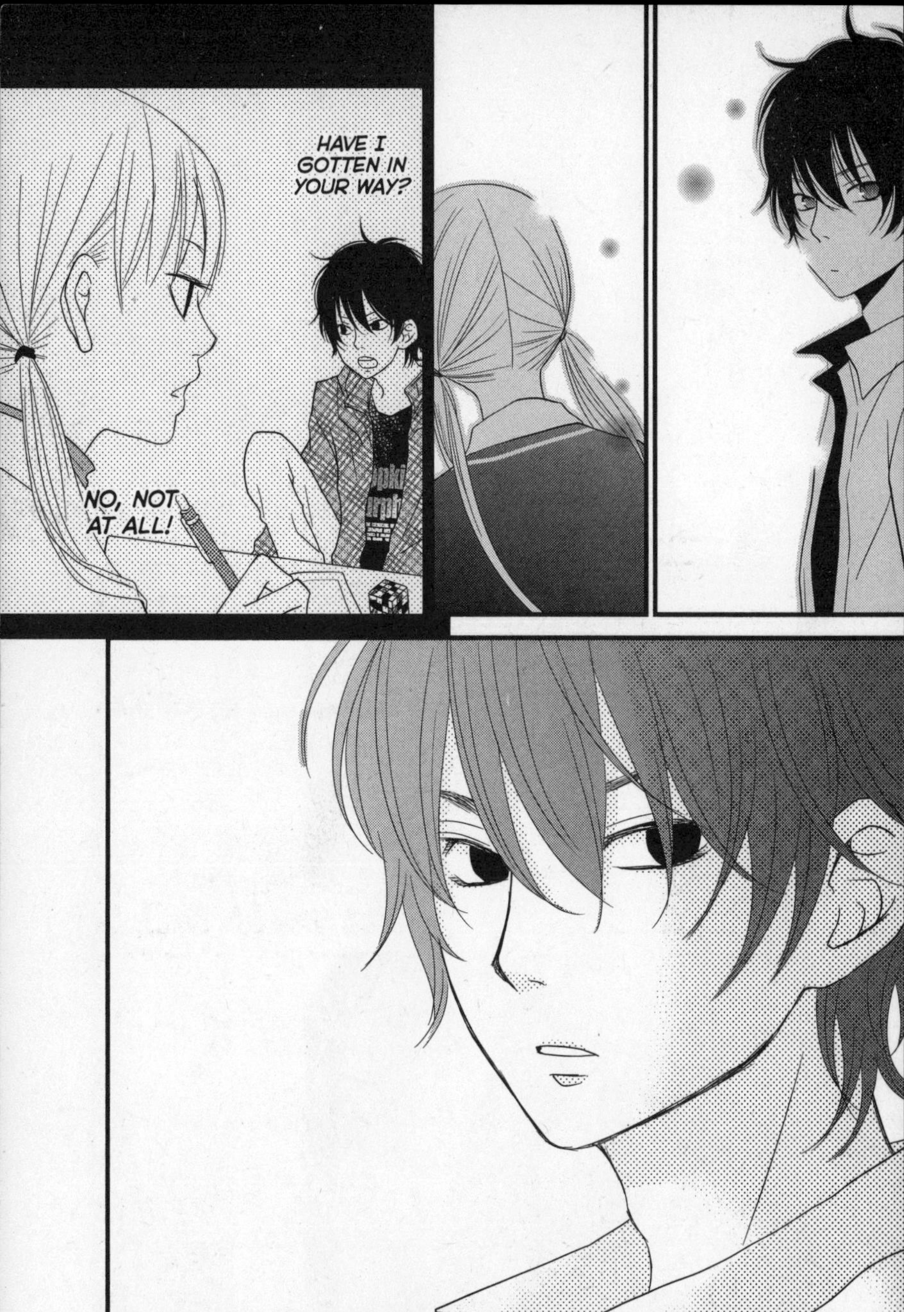
HAVE I GOTTEN IN YOUR WAY?
NO, NOT AT ALL!

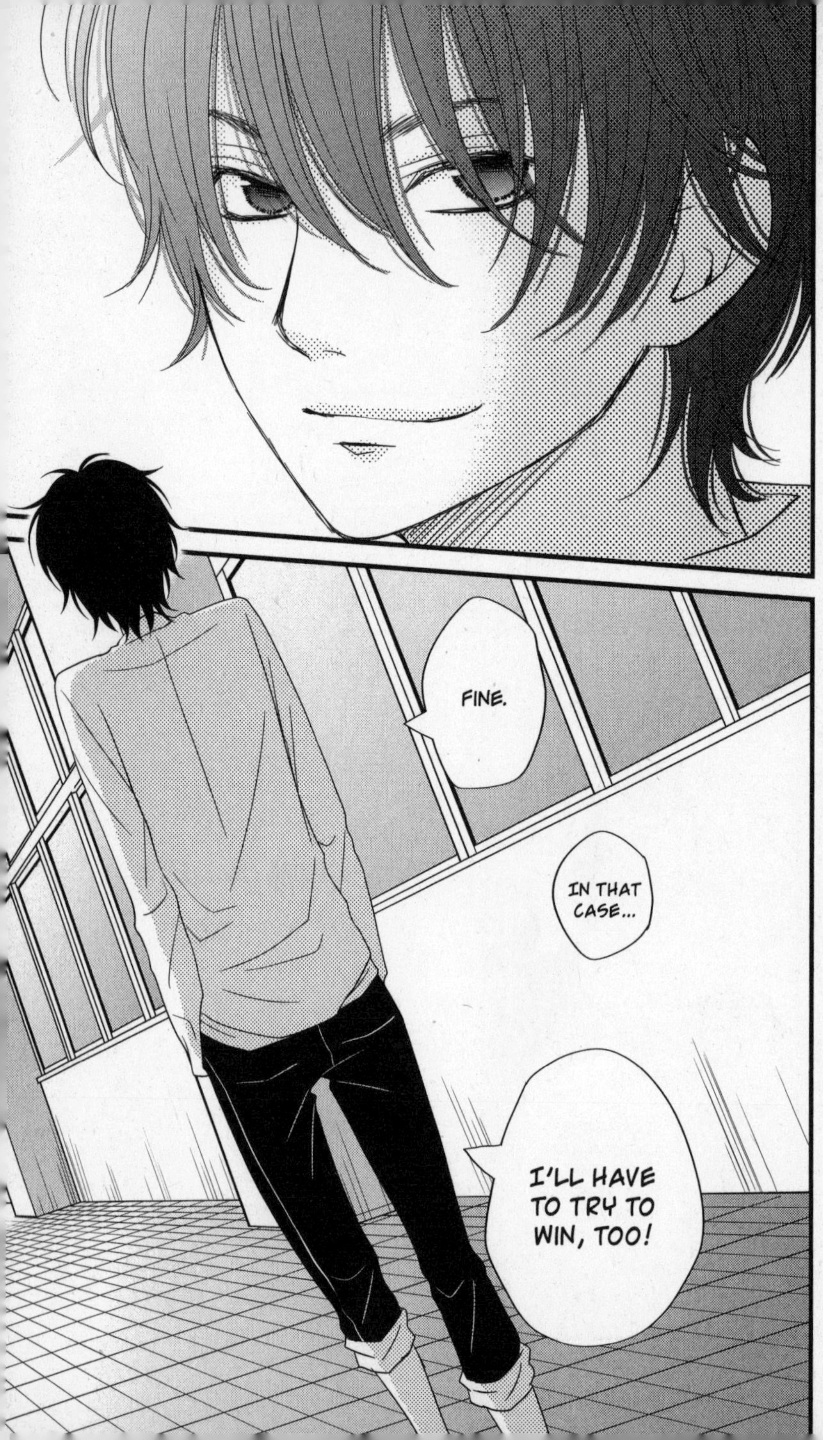
FINE.
IN THAT CASE...
I'LL HAVE TO TRY TO WIN, TOO!

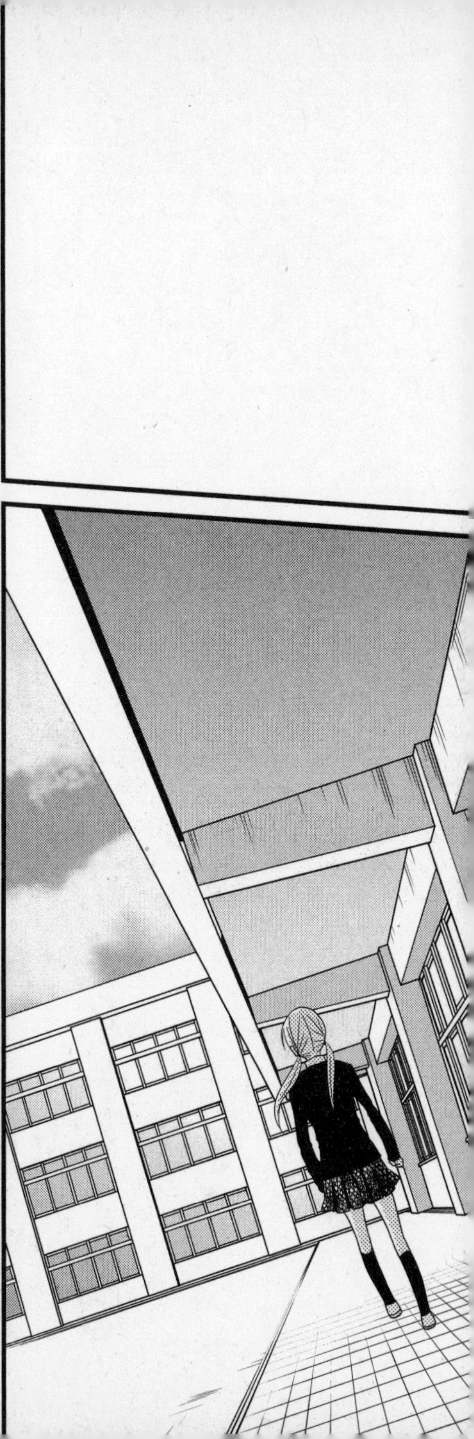
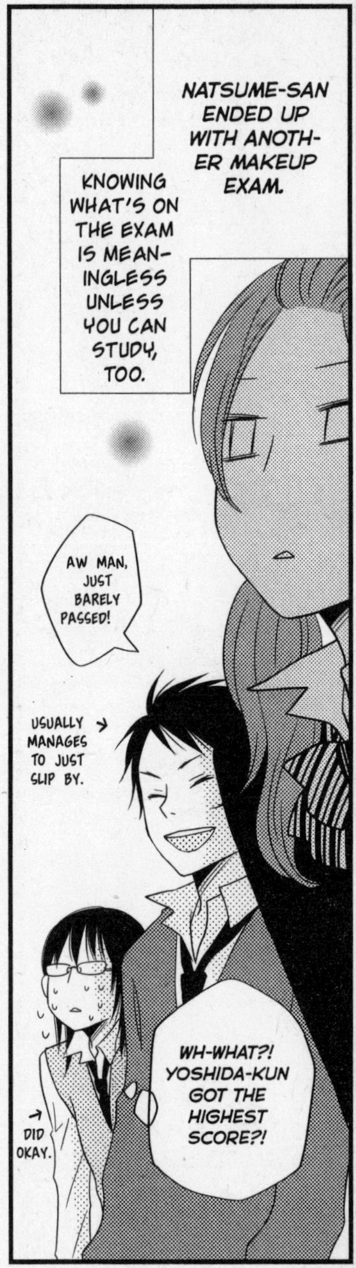
NATSUME-SAN ENDED UP WITH ANOTHER MAKEUP EXAM.
KNOWING WHAT'S ON THE EXAM IS MEANINGLESS UNLESS YOU CAN STUDY, TOO.
AW MAN, JUST BARELY PASSED!
USUALLY MANAGES TO JUST SLIP BY.
WH-WHAT?! YOSHIDA-KUN GOT THE HIGHEST SCORE?!
DID OKAY.

Explanation

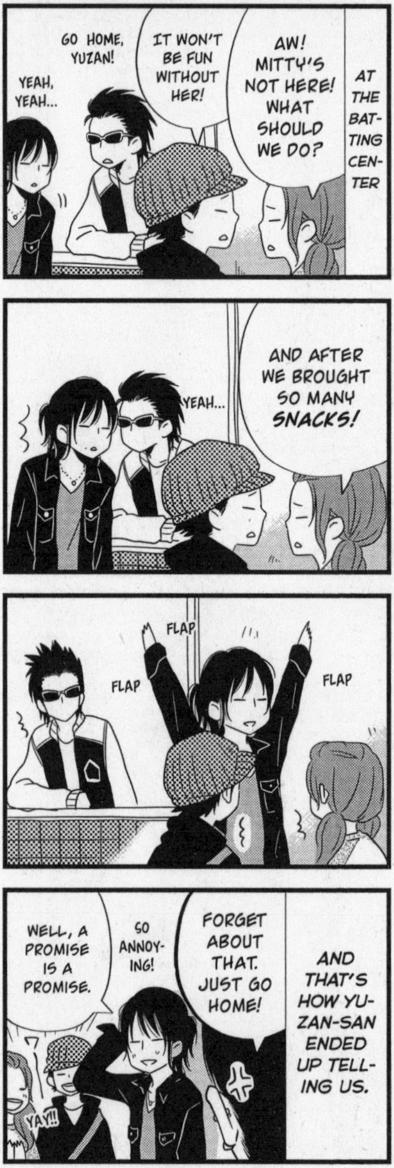
AT THE BATTING CENTER
AW! MITTY'S NOT HERE! WHAT SHOULD WE DO?
IT WON'T BE FUN WITHOUT HER!
GO HOME, YUZAN!
YEAH, YEAH...
AND AFTER WE BROUGHT SO MANY SNACKS!
YEAH...
FLAP
FLAP
FLAP
AND THAT'S HOW YUZAN-SAN ENDED UP TELLING US.
FORGET ABOUT THAT. JUST GO HOME!
SO ANNOYING!
WELL, A PROMISE IS A PROMISE.
YAY!!

Thought Process

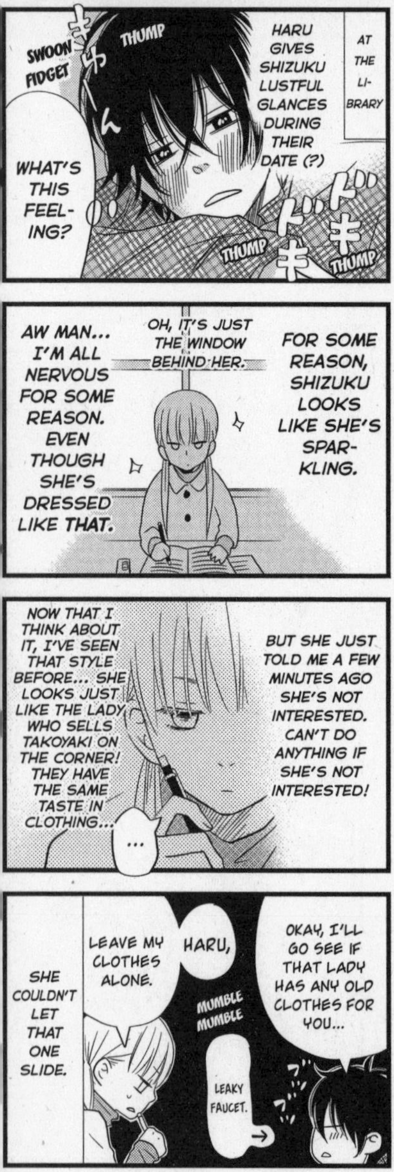
AT THE LIBRARY
HARU GIVES SHIZUKU LUSTFUL GLANCES DURING THEIR DATE (?)
THUMP
SWOON
FIDGET
WHAT'S THIS FEELING?
THUMP
THUMP
FOR SOME REASON, SHIZUKU LOOKS LIKE SHE'S SPARKLING.
OH, IT'S JUST THE WINDOW BEHIND HER.
AW MAN... I'M ALL NERVOUS FOR SOME REASON. EVEN THOUGH SHE'S DRESSED LIKE THAT.
BUT SHE JUST TOLD ME A FEW MINUTES AGO SHE'S NOT INTERESTED. CAN'T DO ANYTHING IF SHE'S NOT INTERESTED!
NOW THAT I THINK ABOUT IT, I'VE SEEN THAT STYLE BEFORE... SHE LOOKS JUST LIKE THE LADY WHO SELLS TAKOYAKI ON THE CORNER! THEY HAVE THE SAME TASTE IN CLOTHING...
...
OKAY, I'LL GO SEE IF THAT LADY HAS ANY OLD CLOTHES FOR YOU...
HARU,
LEAVE MY CLOTHES ALONE.
MUMBLE MUMBLE
LEAKY FAUCET.
SHE COULDN'T LET THAT ONE SLIDE.

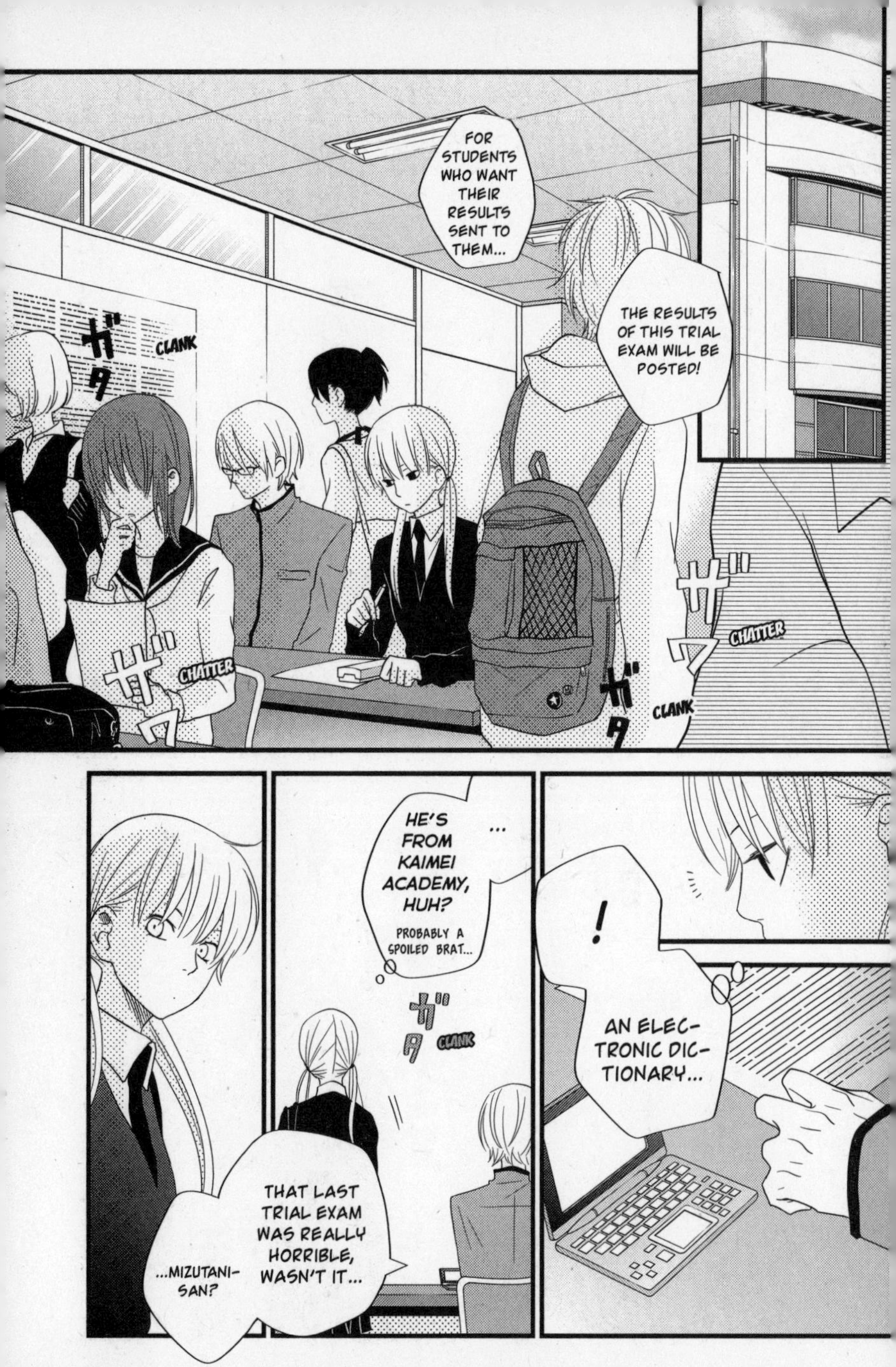
THE RESULTS OF THIS TRIAL EXAM WILL BE POSTED!
FOR STUDENTS WHO WANT THEIR RESULTS SENT TO THEM...
ザワ CHATTER
ガタ CLANK
ガタ CLANK
ザワ CHATTER
!
AN ELEC-TRONIC DIC-TIONARY...
...
HE'S FROM KAIMEI ACADEMY, HUH?
PROBABLY A SPOILED BRAT...
ガタ CLANK
THAT LAST TRIAL EXAM WAS REALLY HORRIBLE, WASN'T IT...
...MIZUTANI-SAN?

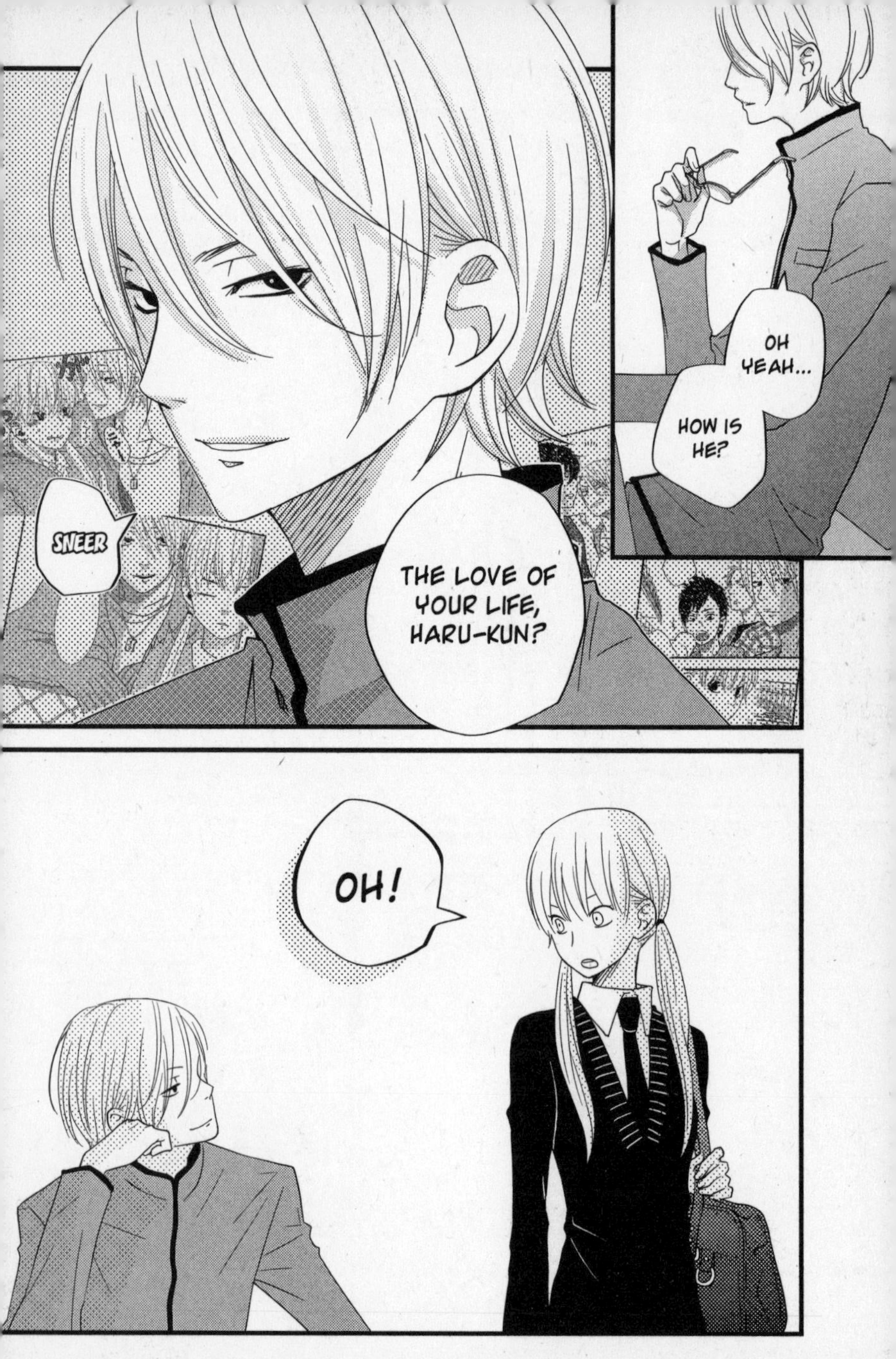
OH YEAH...
HOW IS HE?
THE LOVE OF YOUR LIFE, HARU-KUN?
SNEER
OH!

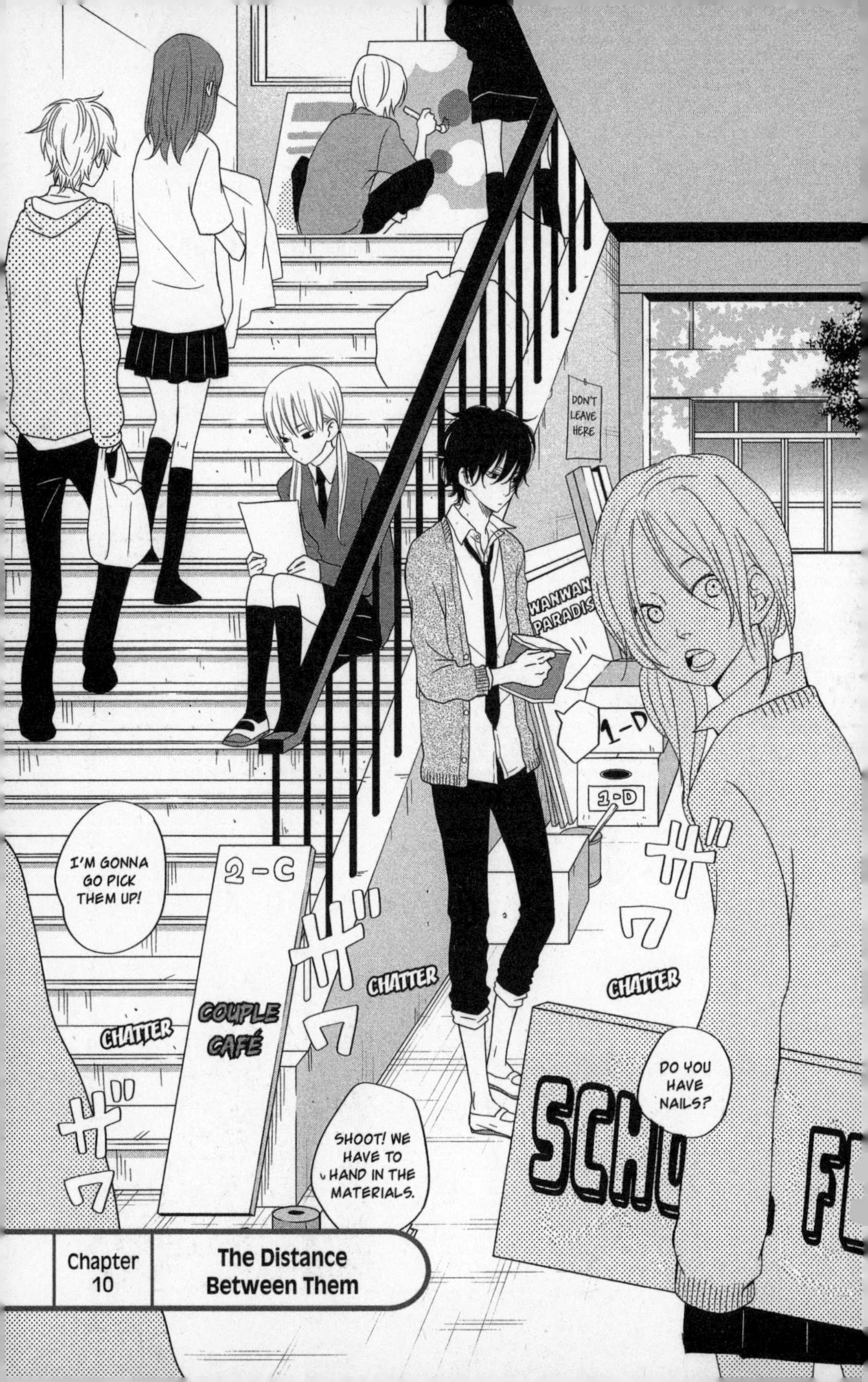
DON'T LEAVE HERE
1-D
1-D
DO YOU HAVE NAILS?
ザワ
CHATTER
SHOOT! WE HAVE TO HAND IN THE MATERIALS.
CHATTER
ザワ
2-C
COUPLE CAFÉ
I'M GONNA GO PICK THEM UP!
CHATTER
ザワ

Chapter 10
The Distance Between Them

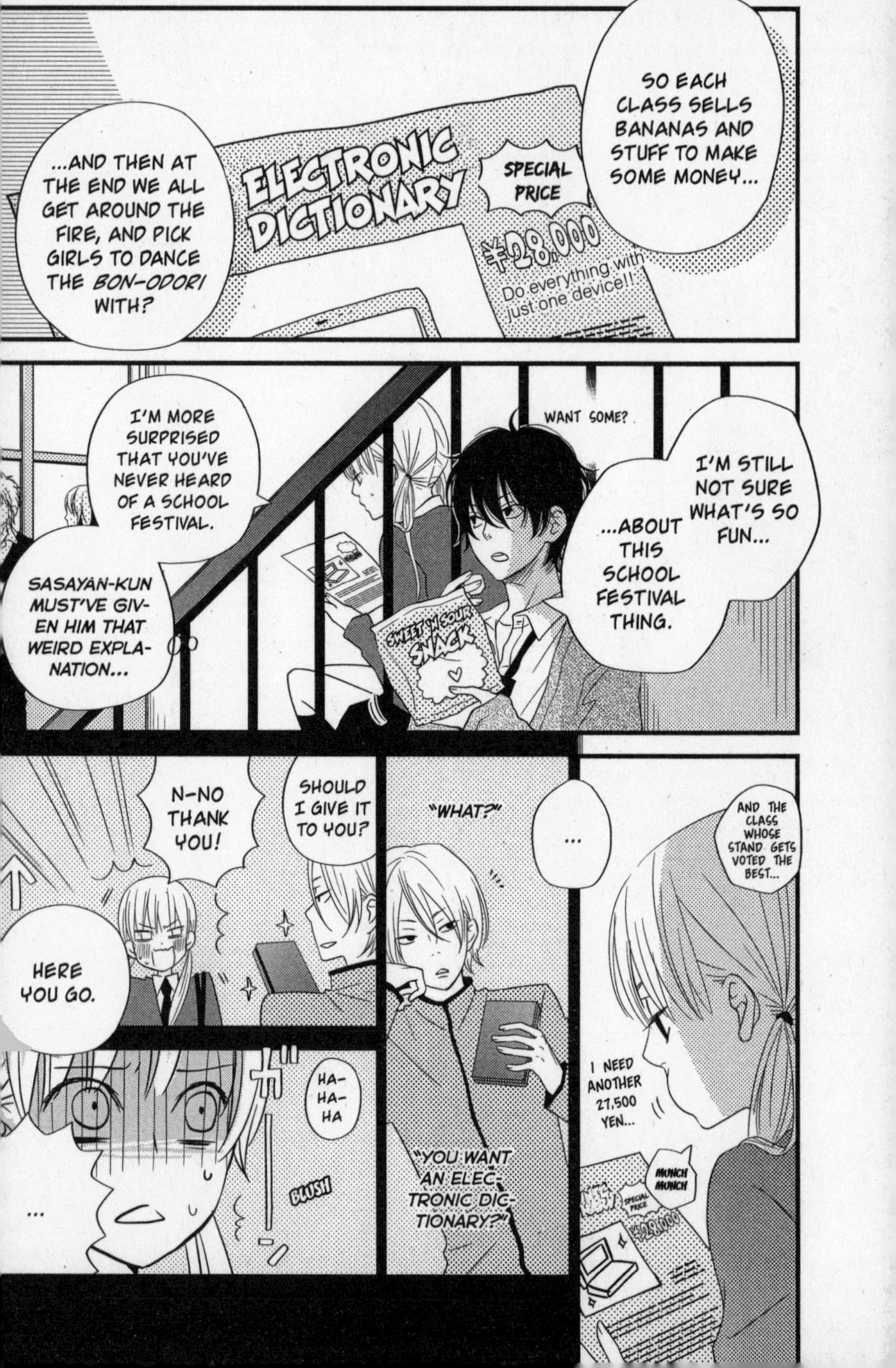
SO EACH CLASS SELLS BANANAS AND STUFF TO MAKE SOME MONEY...
ELECTRONIC DICTIONARY
SPECIAL PRICE
¥28,000
Do everything with just one device!!
...AND THEN AT THE END WE ALL GET AROUND THE FIRE, AND PICK GIRLS TO DANCE THE *BON-ODORI* WITH?
I'M STILL NOT SURE WHAT'S SO FUN...
...ABOUT THIS SCHOOL FESTIVAL THING.
WANT SOME?
SWEET 'N SOUR SNACK
I'M MORE SURPRISED THAT YOU'VE NEVER HEARD OF A SCHOOL FESTIVAL.
SASAYAN-KUN MUST'VE GIV-EN HIM THAT WEIRD EXPLA-NATION...
AND THE CLASS WHOSE STAND GETS VOTED THE BEST...
...
I NEED ANOTHER 27,500 YEN...
MUNCH MUNCH
SPECIAL PRICE
¥28,000
"WHAT?"
"YOU WANT AN ELEC-TRONIC DIC-TIONARY?"
SHOULD I GIVE IT TO YOU?
N-NO THANK YOU!
HERE YOU GO.
HA-HA-HA
BLUSH
...

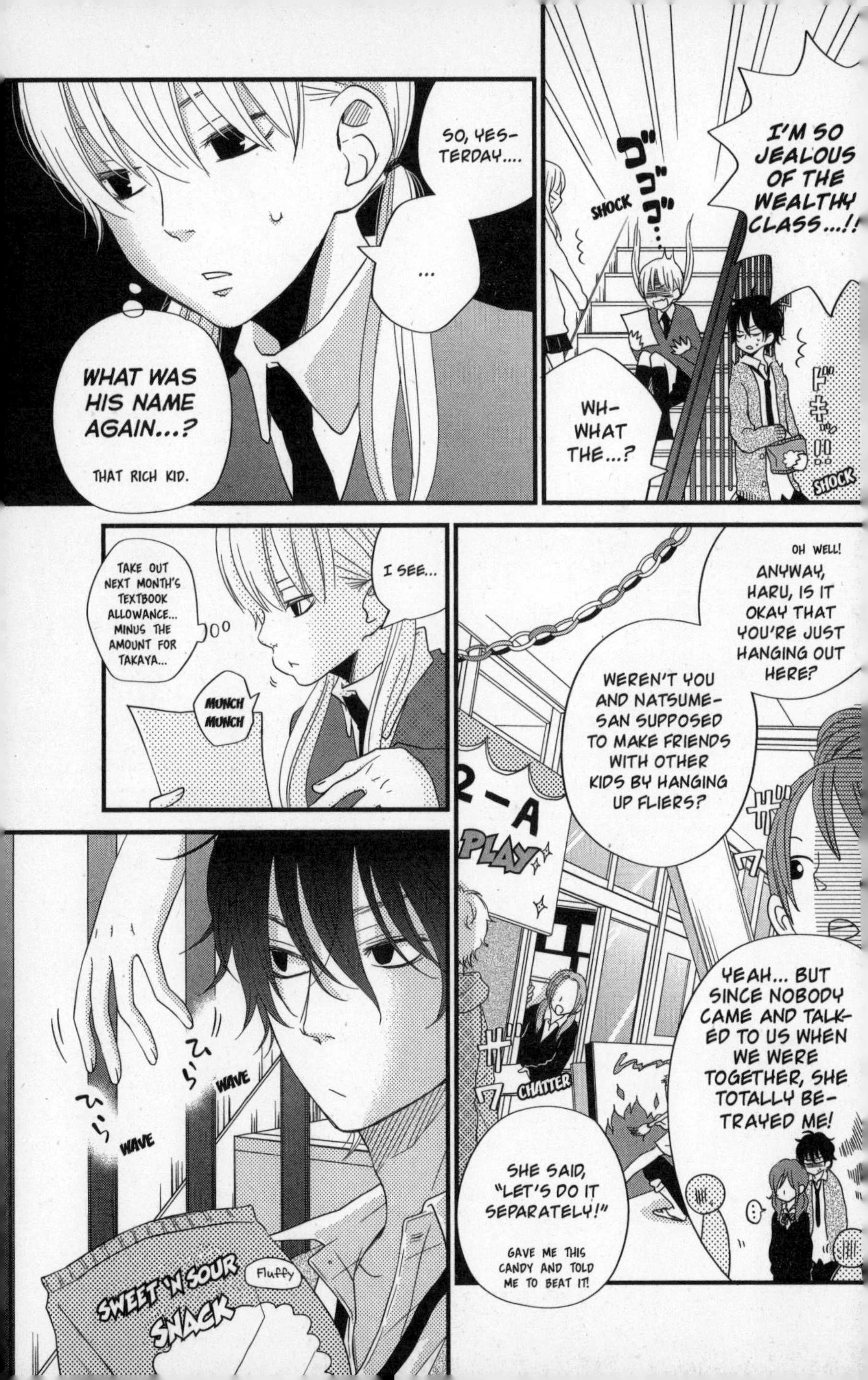
I'M SO JEALOUS OF THE WEALTHY CLASS...!!
SHOCK
WH- WHAT THE...?
SHOCK
SO, YES-TERDAY....
...
WHAT WAS HIS NAME AGAIN...?
THAT RICH KID.
OH WELL!
ANYWAY, HARU, IS IT OKAY THAT YOU'RE JUST HANGING OUT HERE?
WEREN'T YOU AND NATSUME-SAN SUPPOSED TO MAKE FRIENDS WITH OTHER KIDS BY HANGING UP FLIERS?
2-A
PLAY
CHATTER
YEAH... BUT SINCE NOBODY CAME AND TALK-ED TO US WHEN WE WERE TOGETHER, SHE TOTALLY BE-TRAYED ME!
SHE SAID, "LET'S DO IT SEPARATELY!"
GAVE ME THIS CANDY AND TOLD ME TO BEAT IT!
...
I SEE...
TAKE OUT NEXT MONTH'S TEXTBOOK ALLOWANCE... MINUS THE AMOUNT FOR TAKAYA...
MUNCH MUNCH
WAVE
WAVE
SWEET 'N SOUR SNACK
Fluffy

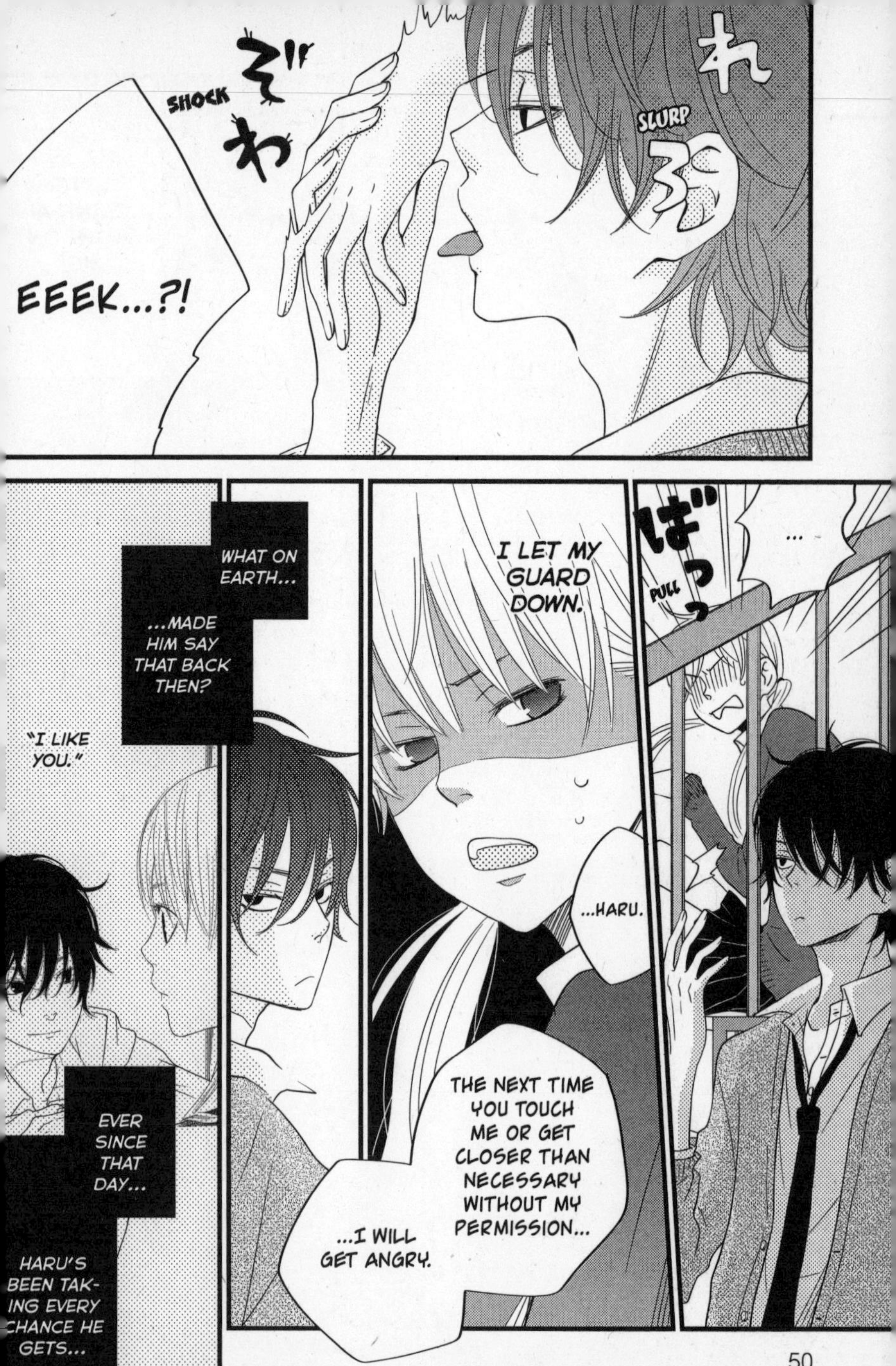
れ
SLURP
ろ
SHOCK
ぞ
わ
EEEK...?!
...
ばっ
PULL
...HARU.
I LET MY GUARD DOWN.
THE NEXT TIME YOU TOUCH ME OR GET CLOSER THAN NECESSARY WITHOUT MY PERMISSION...
...I WILL GET ANGRY.
WHAT ON EARTH...
...MADE HIM SAY THAT BACK THEN?
"I LIKE YOU."
EVER SINCE THAT DAY...
HARU'S BEEN TAKING EVERY CHANCE HE GETS...

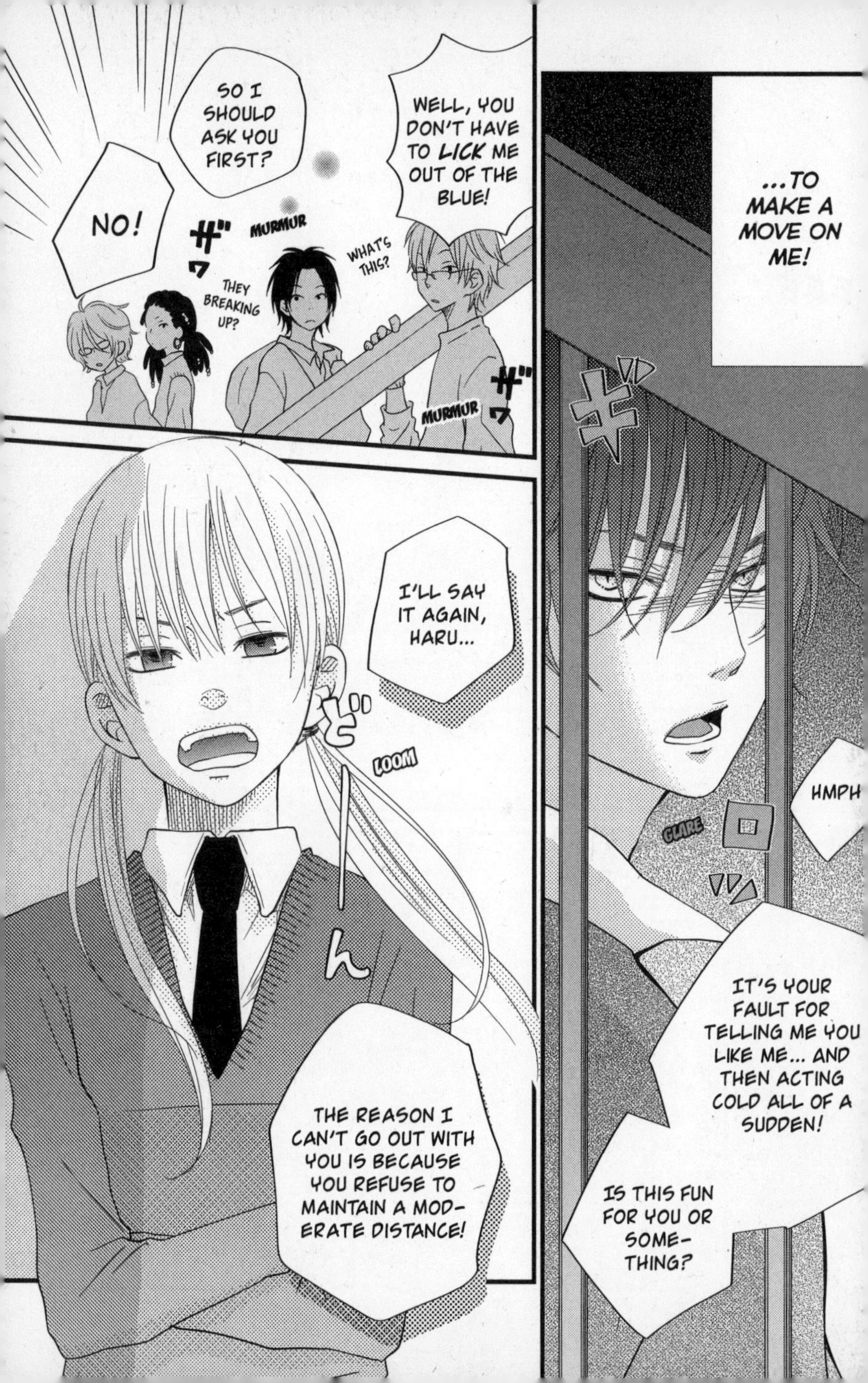
...TO MAKE A MOVE ON ME!
HMPH
GLARE
IT'S YOUR FAULT FOR TELLING ME YOU LIKE ME... AND THEN ACTING COLD ALL OF A SUDDEN!
IS THIS FUN FOR YOU OR SOME-THING?
WELL, YOU DON'T HAVE TO LICK ME OUT OF THE BLUE!
SO I SHOULD ASK YOU FIRST?
NO!
MURMUR
WHAT'S THIS?
THEY BREAKING UP?
MURMUR
I'LL SAY IT AGAIN, HARU...
LOOM
THE REASON I CAN'T GO OUT WITH YOU IS BECAUSE YOU REFUSE TO MAINTAIN A MOD-ERATE DISTANCE!

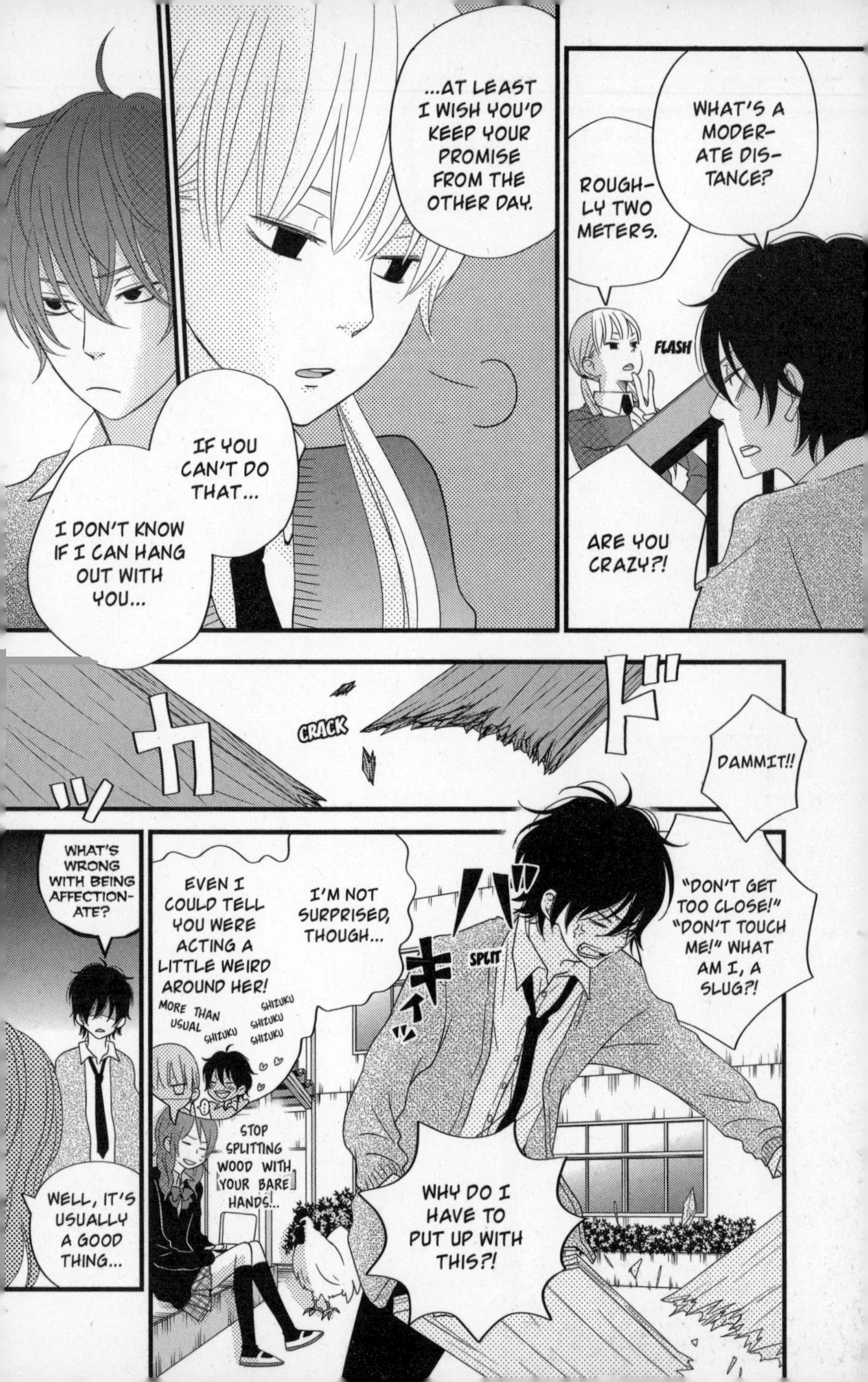
WHAT'S A MODERATE DISTANCE?
ROUGHLY TWO METERS.
FLASH
ARE YOU CRAZY?!
...AT LEAST I WISH YOU'D KEEP YOUR PROMISE FROM THE OTHER DAY.
IF YOU CAN'T DO THAT...
I DON'T KNOW IF I CAN HANG OUT WITH YOU...
ド
DAMMIT!!
CRACK
カッ
"DON'T GET TOO CLOSE!" "DON'T TOUCH ME!" WHAT AM I, A SLUG?!
バキィッ
SPLIT
WHY DO I HAVE TO PUT UP WITH THIS?!
I'M NOT SURPRISED, THOUGH...
EVEN I COULD TELL YOU WERE ACTING A LITTLE WEIRD AROUND HER!
MORE THAN USUAL
SHIZUKU SHIZUKU SHIZUKU SHIZUKU
STOP SPLITTING WOOD WITH YOUR BARE HANDS...
WHAT'S WRONG WITH BEING AFFECTIONATE?
WELL, IT'S USUALLY A GOOD THING...

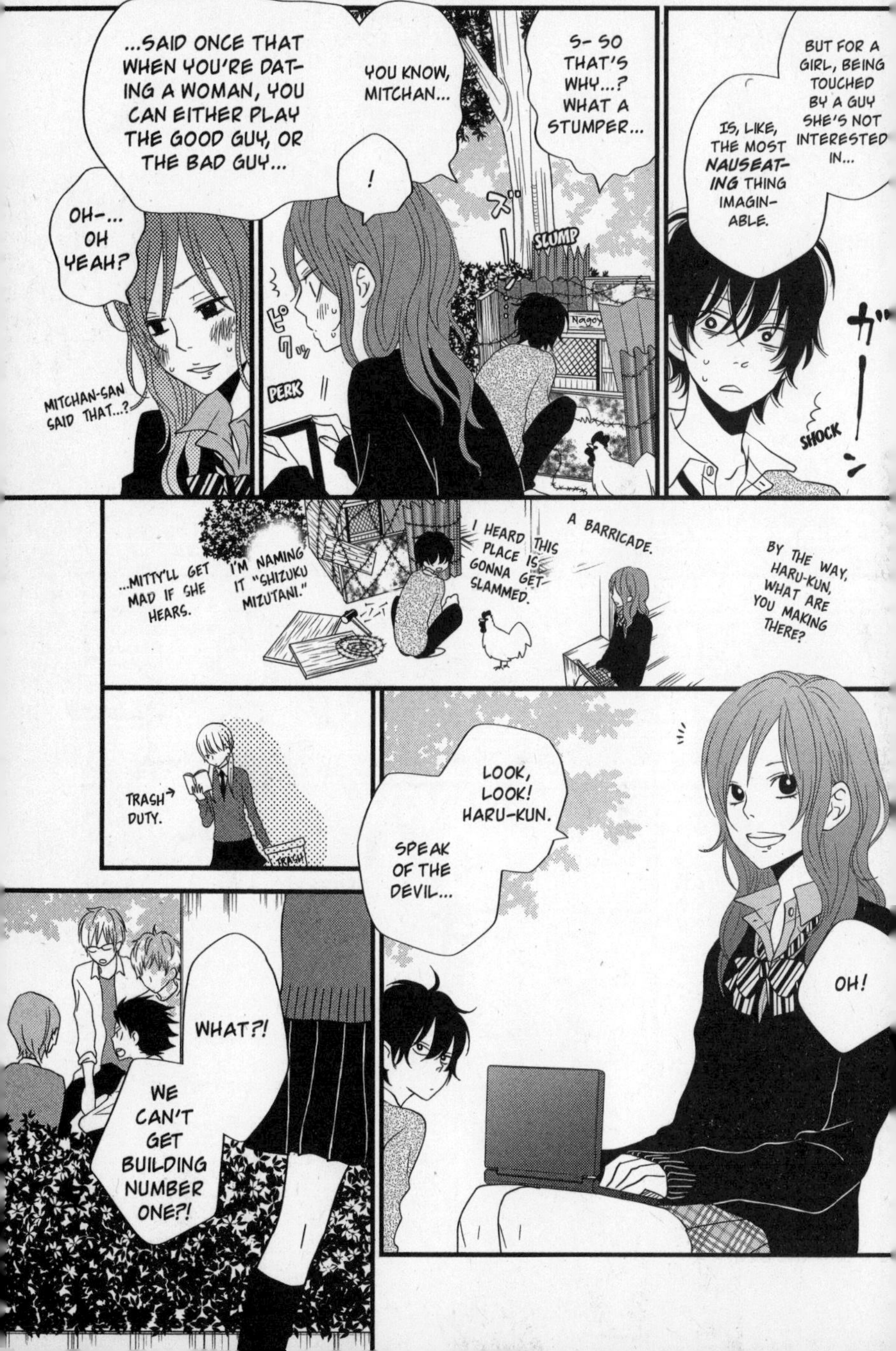

BUT FOR A GIRL, BEING TOUCHED BY A GUY SHE'S NOT INTERESTED IN...
IS, LIKE, THE MOST NAUSEATING THING IMAGINABLE.
SHOCK
S- SO THAT'S WHY...? WHAT A STUMPER...
SLUMP
YOU KNOW, MITCHAN...
...SAID ONCE THAT WHEN YOU'RE DATING A WOMAN, YOU CAN EITHER PLAY THE GOOD GUY, OR THE BAD GUY...
!
PERK
OH-... OH YEAH?
MITCHAN-SAN SAID THAT...?
BY THE WAY, HARU-KUN, WHAT ARE YOU MAKING THERE?
A BARRICADE.
I HEARD THIS PLACE IS GONNA GET SLAMMED.
I'M NAMING IT "SHIZUKU MIZUTANI."
...MITTY'LL GET MAD IF SHE HEARS.
OH!
LOOK, LOOK! HARU-KUN.
SPEAK OF THE DEVIL...
TRASH DUTY.
TRASH
WHAT?!
WE CAN'T GET BUILDING NUMBER ONE?!

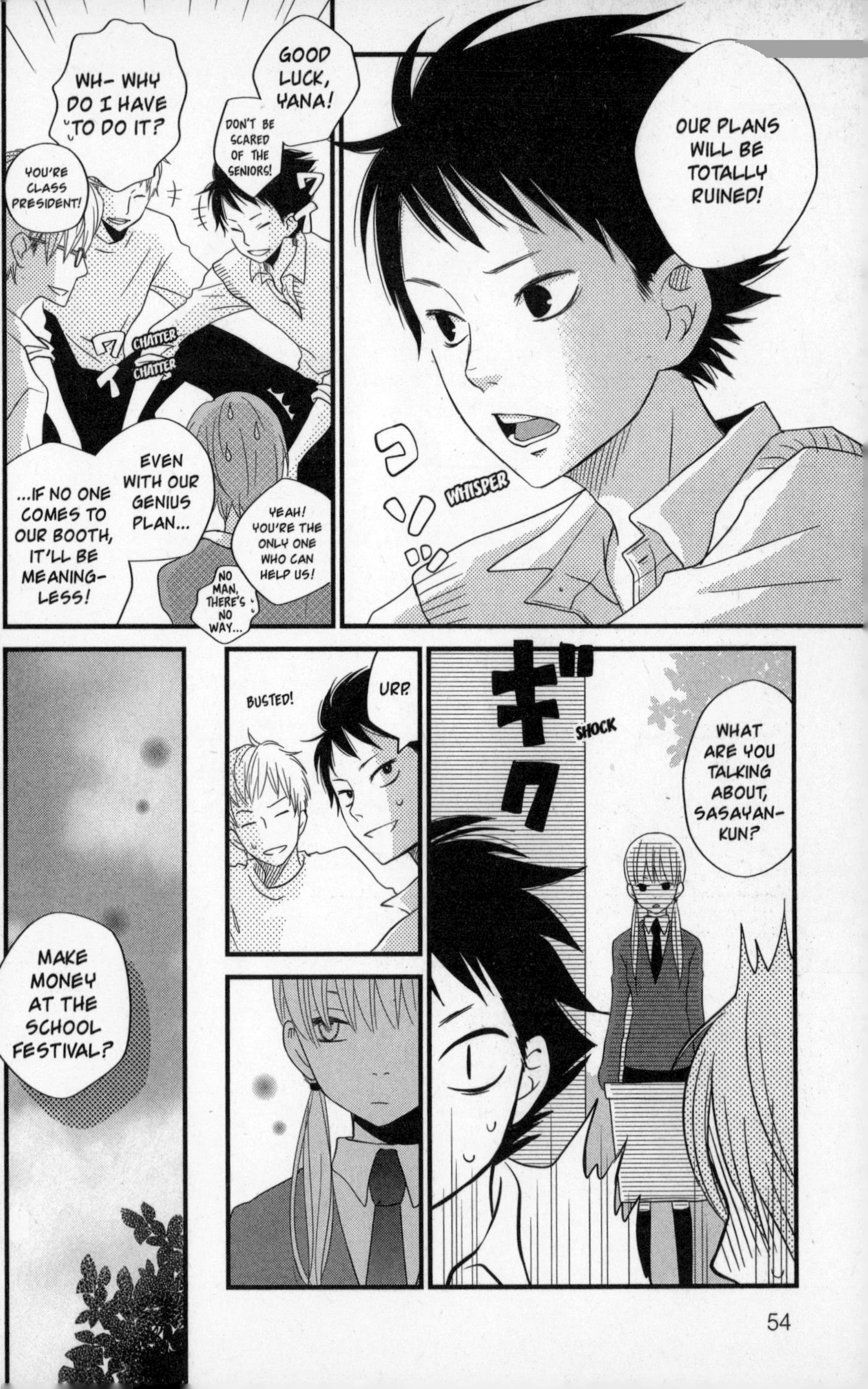
OUR PLANS WILL BE TOTALLY RUINED!
WHISPER
GOOD LUCK, YANA!
DON'T BE SCARED OF THE SENIORS!
WH- WHY DO I HAVE TO DO IT?
YOU'RE CLASS PRESIDENT!
CHATTER
CHATTER
EVEN WITH OUR GENIUS PLAN...
...IF NO ONE COMES TO OUR BOOTH, IT'LL BE MEANING-LESS!
YEAH! YOU'RE THE ONLY ONE WHO CAN HELP US!
NO MAN, THERE'S NO WAY...
SHOCK
WHAT ARE YOU TALKING ABOUT, SASAYAN-KUN?
URP.
BUSTED!
MAKE MONEY AT THE SCHOOL FESTIVAL?

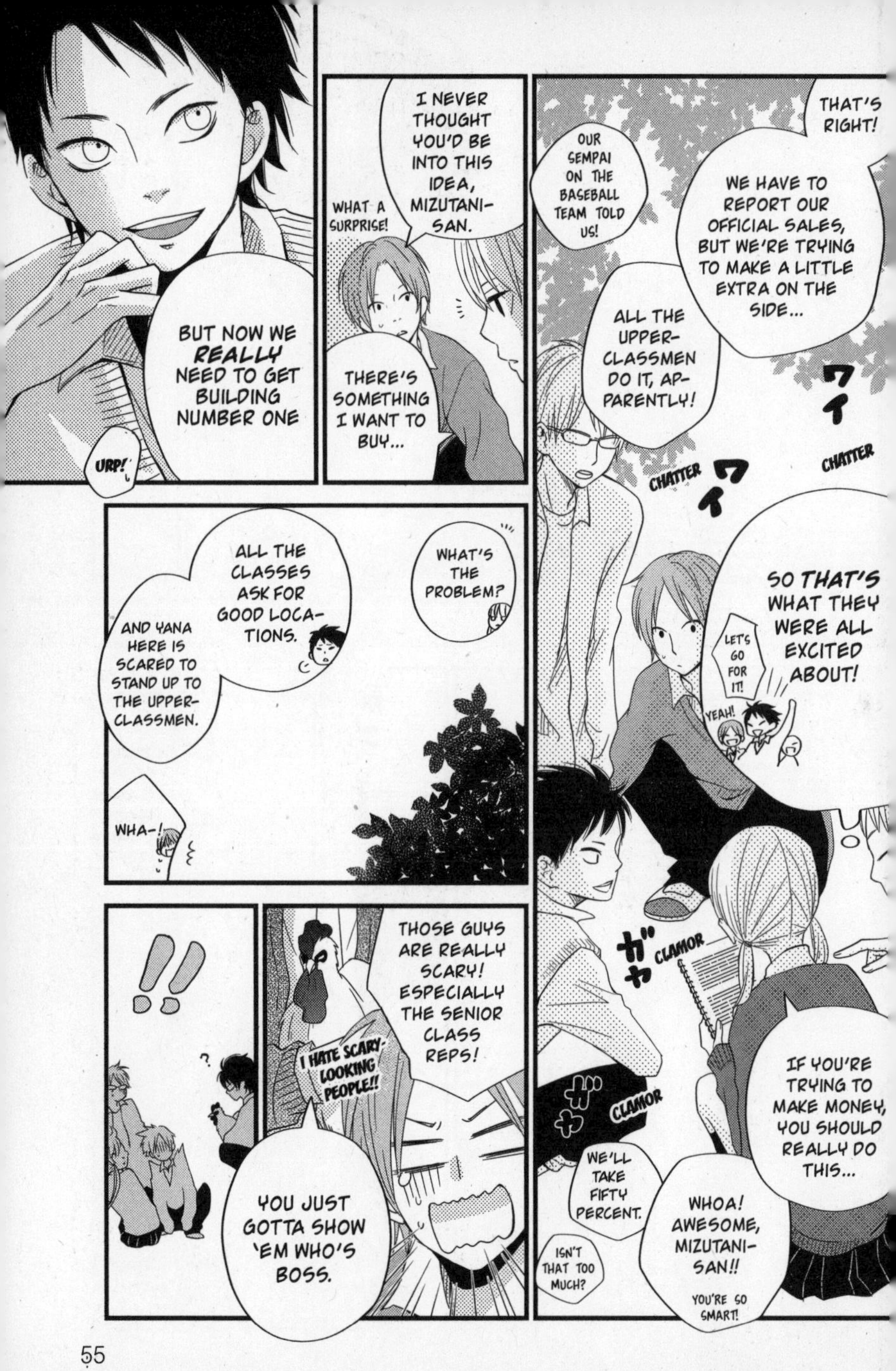
THAT'S RIGHT!
OUR SEMPAI ON THE BASEBALL TEAM TOLD US!
WE HAVE TO REPORT OUR OFFICIAL SALES, BUT WE'RE TRYING TO MAKE A LITTLE EXTRA ON THE SIDE...
ALL THE UPPERCLASSMEN DO IT, APPARENTLY!
ワイ
CHATTER
ワイ
CHATTER
SO THAT'S WHAT THEY WERE ALL EXCITED ABOUT!
LET'S GO FOR IT!
YEAH!
ガヤ
CLAMOR
IF YOU'RE TRYING TO MAKE MONEY, YOU SHOULD REALLY DO THIS...
ガヤ
CLAMOR
WE'LL TAKE FIFTY PERCENT.
WHOA! AWESOME, MIZUTANI-SAN!!
YOU'RE SO SMART!
ISN'T THAT TOO MUCH?
I NEVER THOUGHT YOU'D BE INTO THIS IDEA, MIZUTANI-SAN.
WHAT A SURPRISE!
THERE'S SOMETHING I WANT TO BUY...
BUT NOW WE REALLY NEED TO GET BUILDING NUMBER ONE
URP!
WHAT'S THE PROBLEM?
ALL THE CLASSES ASK FOR GOOD LOCATIONS.
AND YANA HERE IS SCARED TO STAND UP TO THE UPPERCLASSMEN.
WHA-!
THOSE GUYS ARE REALLY SCARY! ESPECIALLY THE SENIOR CLASS REPS!
I HATE SCARY-LOOKING PEOPLE!!
YOU JUST GOTTA SHOW 'EM WHO'S BOSS.
!!
?

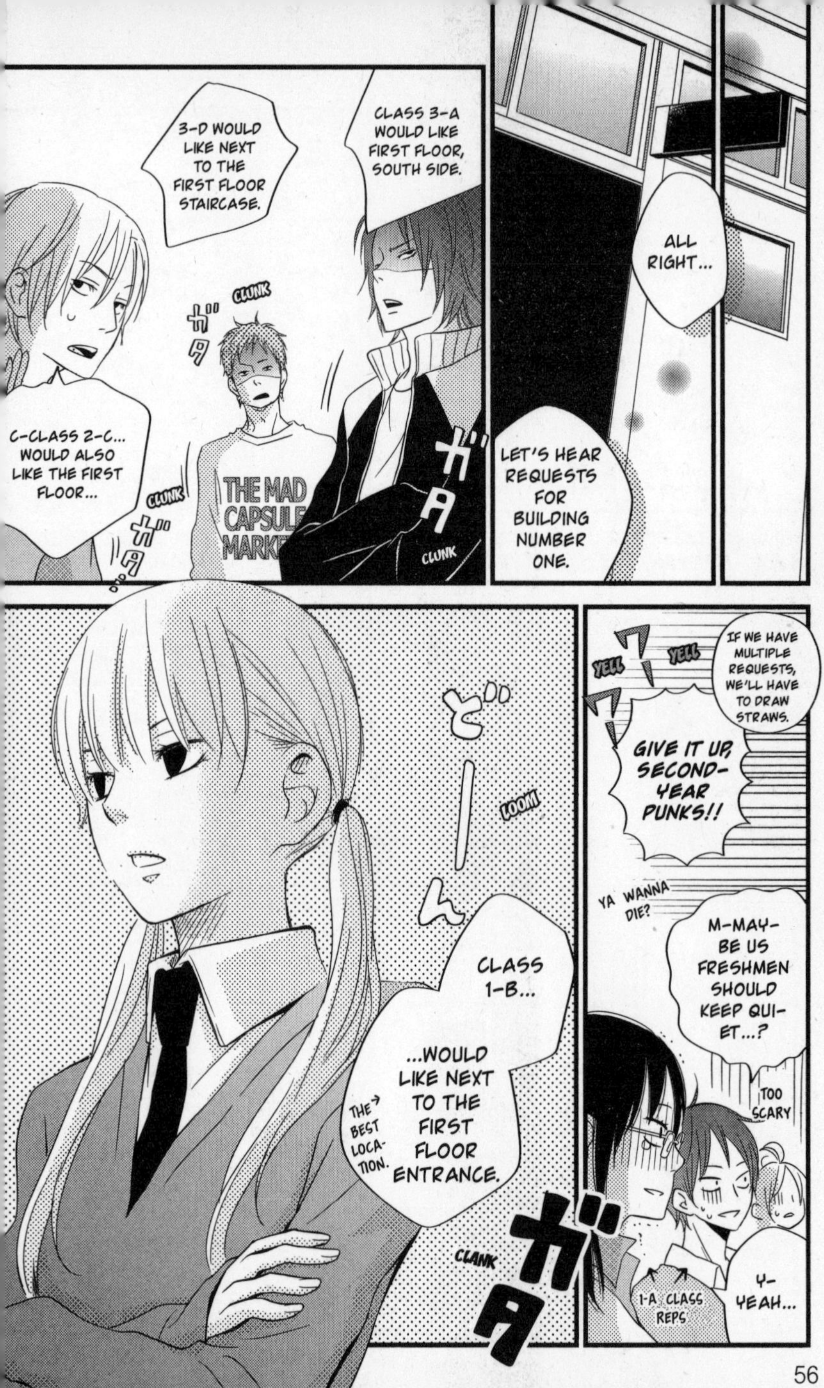
ALL RIGHT...
LET'S HEAR REQUESTS FOR BUILDING NUMBER ONE.
CLASS 3-A WOULD LIKE FIRST FLOOR, SOUTH SIDE.
3-D WOULD LIKE NEXT TO THE FIRST FLOOR STAIRCASE.
CLUNK
CLUNK
CLUNK
C-CLASS 2-C... WOULD ALSO LIKE THE FIRST FLOOR...
IF WE HAVE MULTIPLE REQUESTS, WE'LL HAVE TO DRAW STRAWS.
YELL
YELL
GIVE IT UP, SECOND-YEAR PUNKS!!
YA WANNA DIE?
M-MAY-BE US FRESHMEN SHOULD KEEP QUI-ET...?
TOO SCARY
Y-YEAH...
1-A CLASS REPS
LOOM
CLASS 1-B...
...WOULD LIKE NEXT TO THE FIRST FLOOR ENTRANCE.
THE BEST LOCA-TION.
CLANK

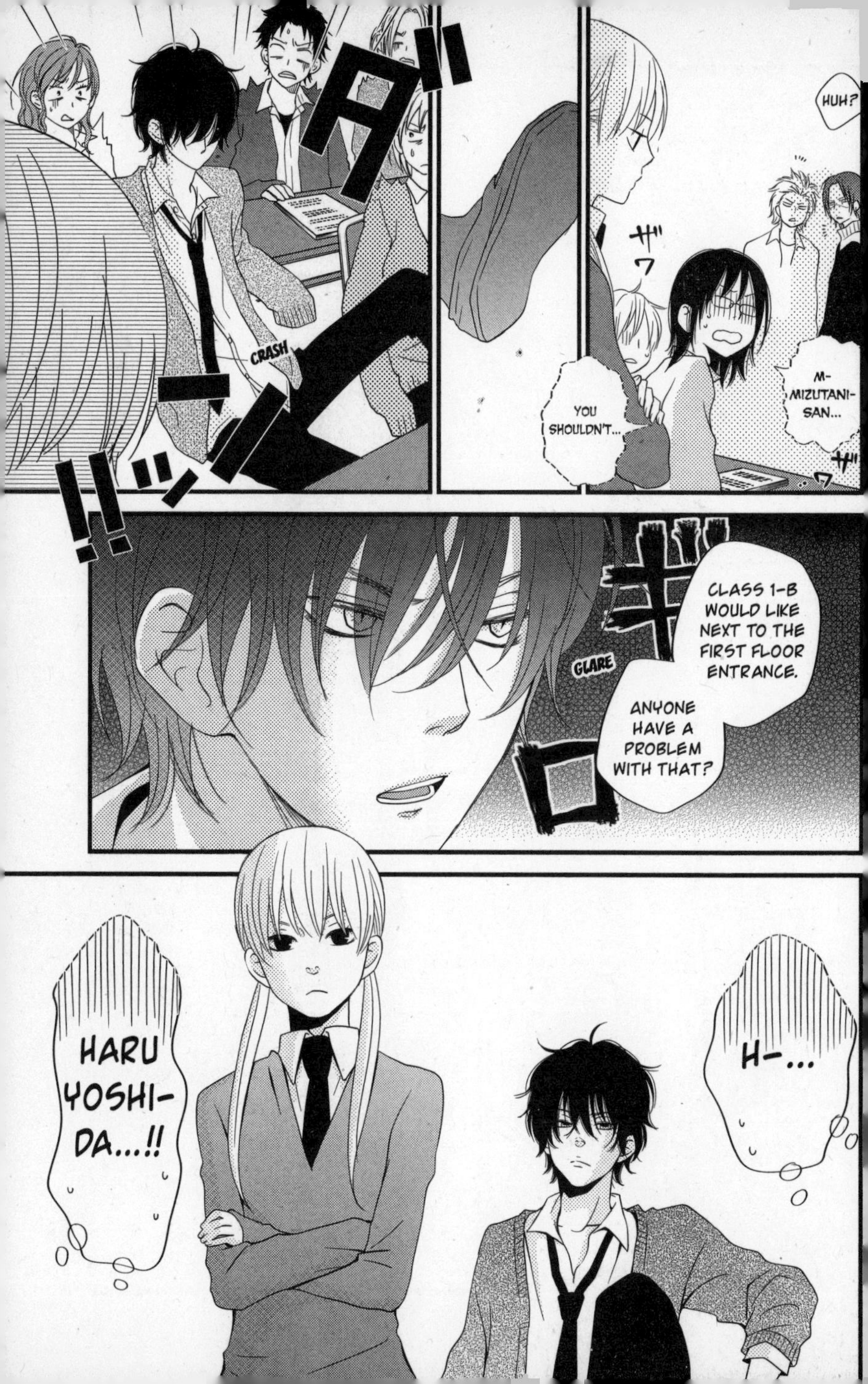
HUH?
M-MIZUTANI-SAN...
YOU SHOULDN'T...
CRASH
CLASS 1-B WOULD LIKE NEXT TO THE FIRST FLOOR ENTRANCE.
GLARE
ANYONE HAVE A PROBLEM WITH THAT?
H-...
HARU YOSHIDA...!!

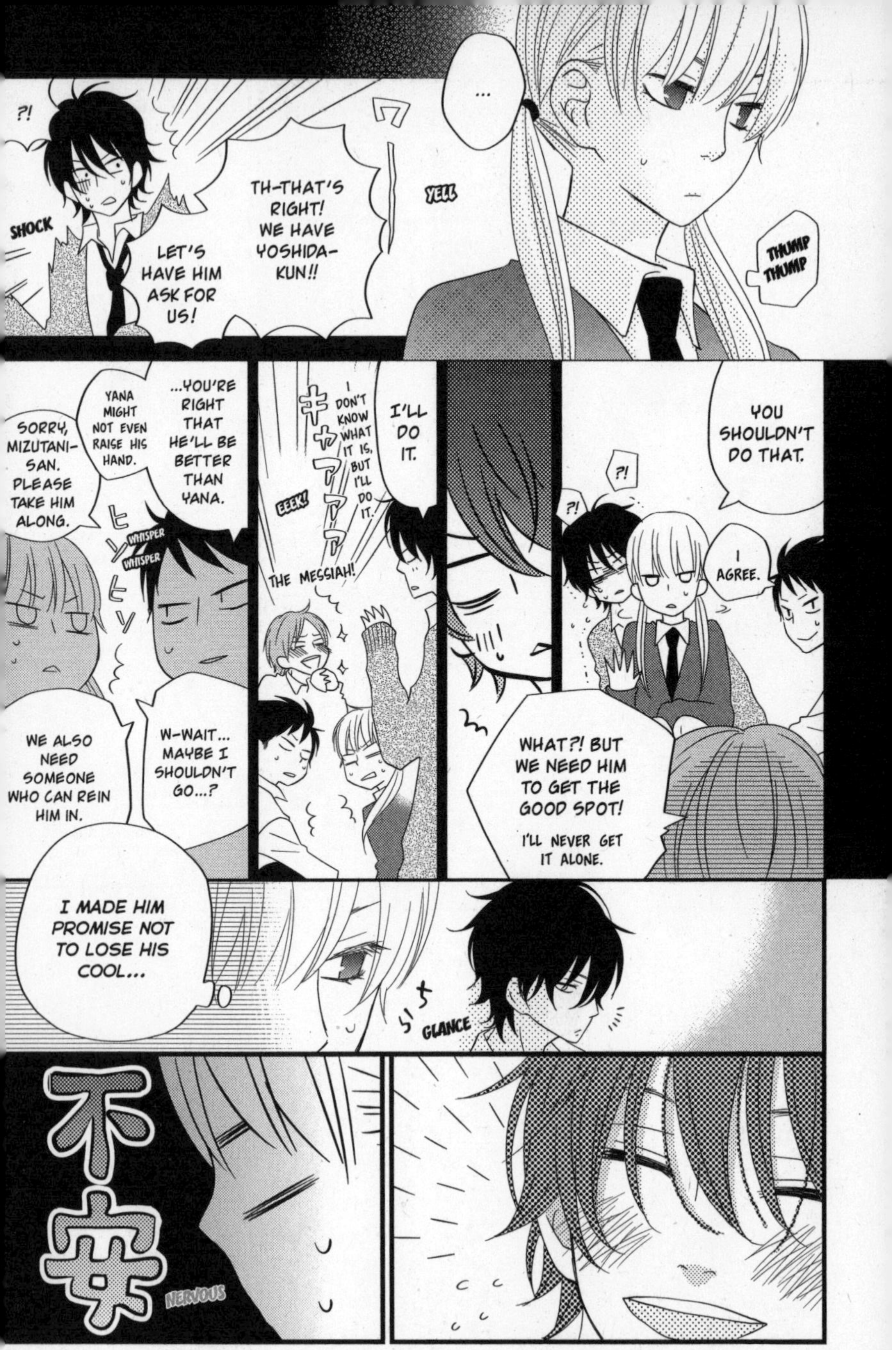
...
THUMP THUMP
TH-THAT'S RIGHT! WE HAVE YOSHIDA-KUN!!
YELL
?!
SHOCK
LET'S HAVE HIM ASK FOR US!
YOU SHOULDN'T DO THAT.
?!
?!
I AGREE.
WHAT?! BUT WE NEED HIM TO GET THE GOOD SPOT!
I'LL NEVER GET IT ALONE.
I'LL DO IT.
I DON'T KNOW WHAT IT IS, BUT I'LL DO IT.
EEEK!
THE MESSIAH!
...YOU'RE RIGHT THAT HE'LL BE BETTER THAN YANA.
YANA MIGHT NOT EVEN RAISE HIS HAND.
SORRY, MIZUTANI-SAN. PLEASE TAKE HIM ALONG.
WHISPER WHISPER
W-WAIT... MAYBE I SHOULDN'T GO...?
WE ALSO NEED SOMEONE WHO CAN REIN HIM IN.
GLANCE
I MADE HIM PROMISE NOT TO LOSE HIS COOL...
NERVOUS

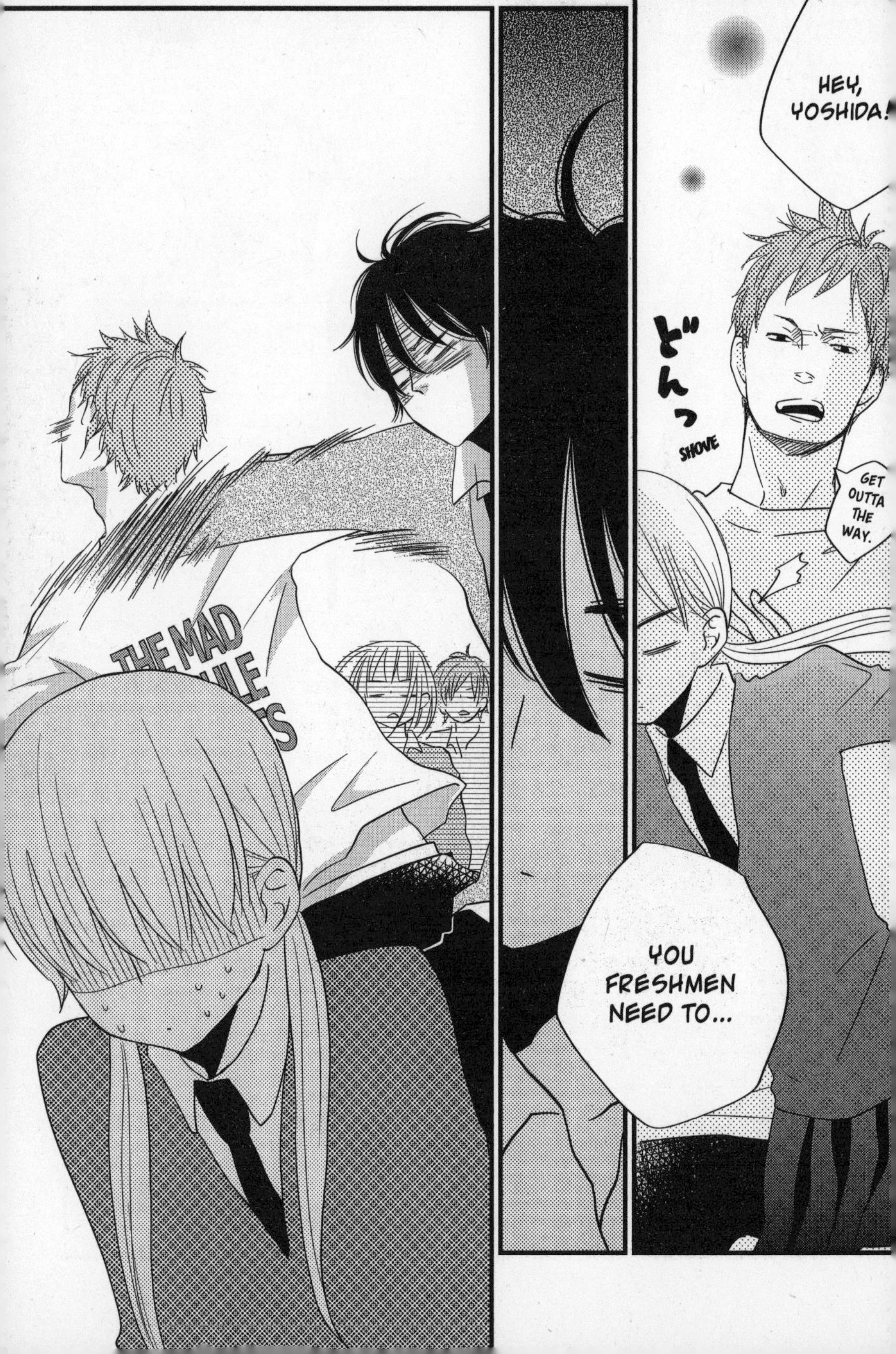
HEY, YOSHIDA!
どんっ
SHOVE
GET OUTTA THE WAY.
YOU FRESHMEN NEED TO...
THE MAD

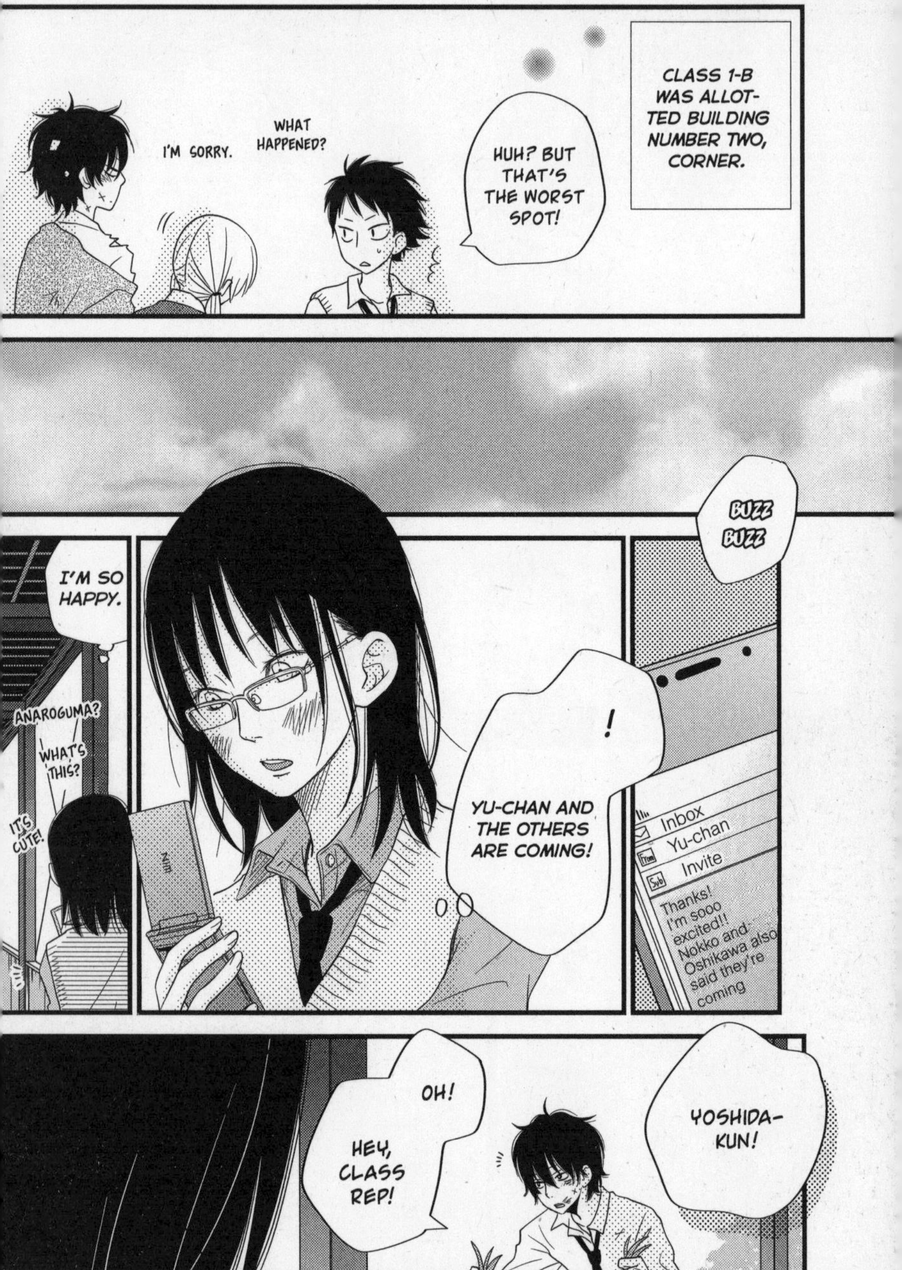
CLASS 1-B WAS ALLOTTED BUILDING NUMBER TWO, CORNER.
HUH? BUT THAT'S THE WORST SPOT!
WHAT HAPPENED?
I'M SORRY.
BUZZ BUZZ
Inbox
From Yu-chan
Sub Invite
Thanks! I'm sooo excited!! Nokko and Oshikawa also said they're coming
!
YU-CHAN AND THE OTHERS ARE COMING!
I'M SO HAPPY.
ANAROGUMA?
WHAT'S THIS?
IT'S CUTE!
YOSHIDA-KUN!
OH!
HEY, CLASS REP!

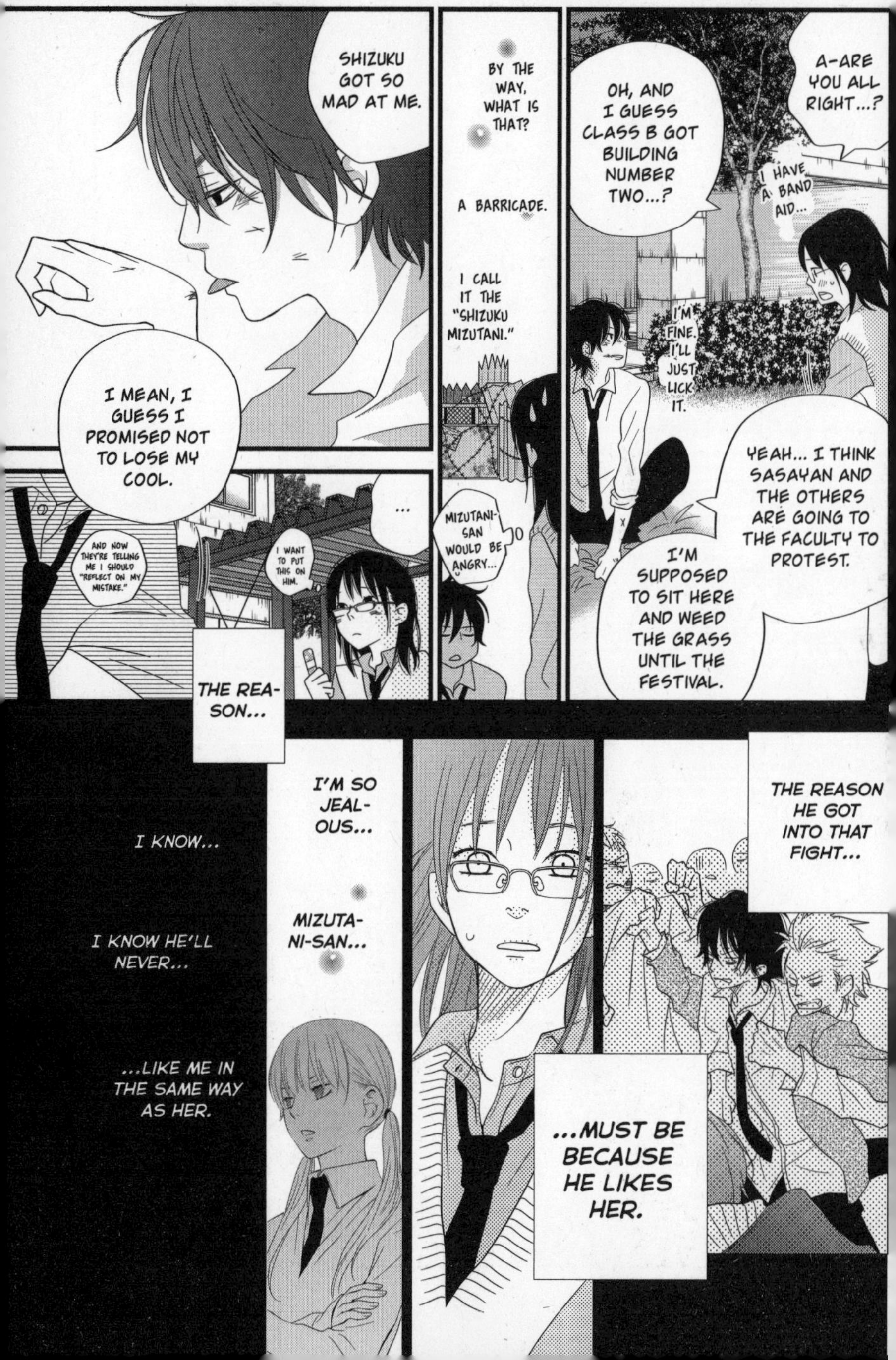
A-ARE YOU ALL RIGHT...?
I HAVE A BAND AID...
OH, AND I GUESS CLASS B GOT BUILDING NUMBER TWO...?
I'M FINE. I'LL JUST LICK IT.
YEAH... I THINK SASAYAN AND THE OTHERS ARE GOING TO THE FACULTY TO PROTEST.
I'M SUPPOSED TO SIT HERE AND WEED THE GRASS UNTIL THE FESTIVAL.
BY THE WAY, WHAT IS THAT?
A BARRICADE.
I CALL IT THE "SHIZUKU MIZUTANI."
MIZUTANI-SAN WOULD BE ANGRY...
SHIZUKU GOT SO MAD AT ME.
I MEAN, I GUESS I PROMISED NOT TO LOSE MY COOL.
...
I WANT TO PUT THIS ON HIM.
AND NOW THEY'RE TELLING ME I SHOULD "REFLECT ON MY MISTAKE."
THE REA-SON...
THE REASON HE GOT INTO THAT FIGHT...
...MUST BE BECAUSE HE LIKES HER.
I'M SO JEAL-OUS...
MIZUTA-NI-SAN...
I KNOW...
I KNOW HE'LL NEVER...
...LIKE ME IN THE SAME WAY AS HER.

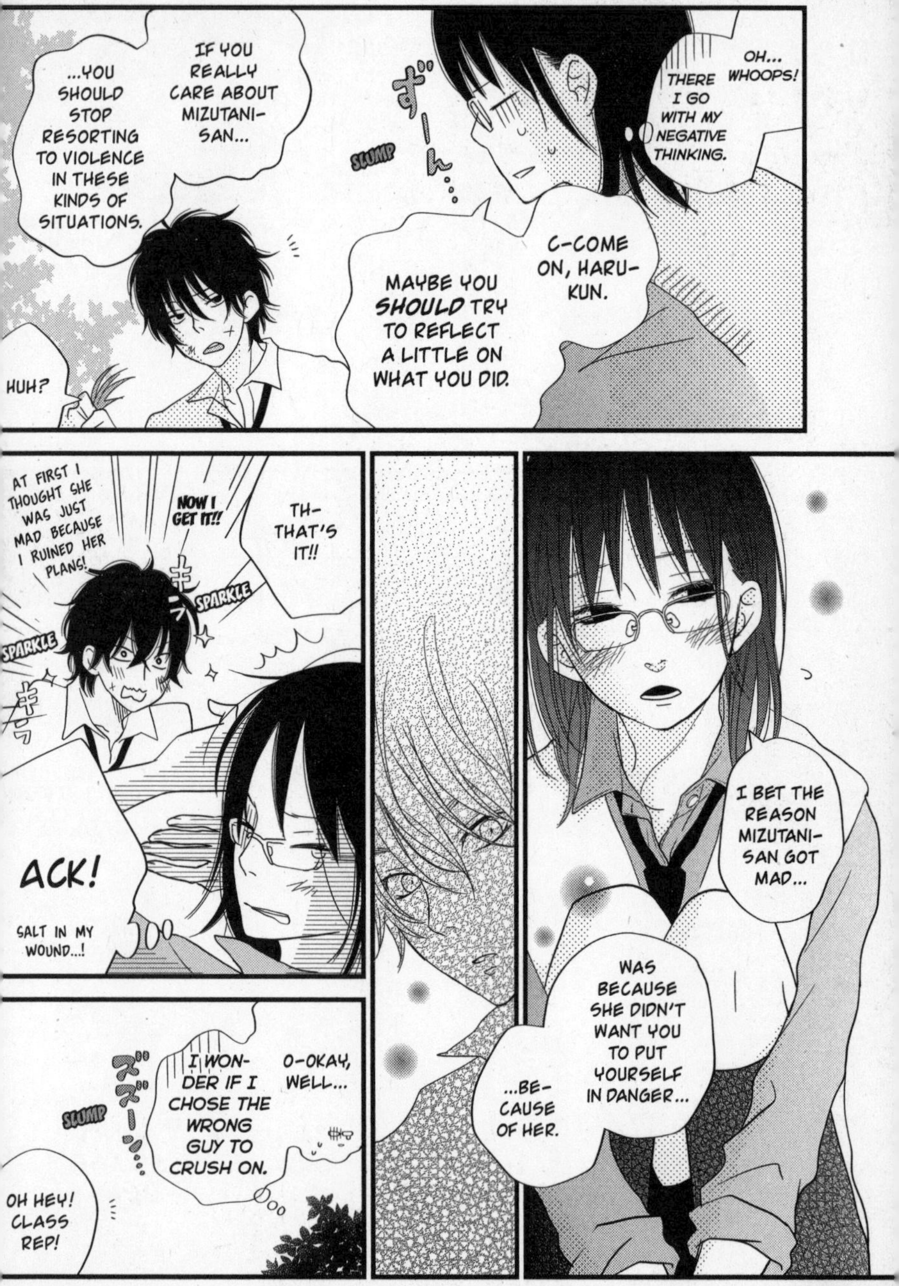
OH... WHOOPS!
THERE I GO WITH MY NEGATIVE THINKING.
SLUMP
C-COME ON, HARU-KUN.
MAYBE YOU SHOULD TRY TO REFLECT A LITTLE ON WHAT YOU DID.
IF YOU REALLY CARE ABOUT MIZUTANI-SAN...
...YOU SHOULD STOP RESORTING TO VIOLENCE IN THESE KINDS OF SITUATIONS.
HUH?
I BET THE REASON MIZUTANI-SAN GOT MAD...
WAS BECAUSE SHE DIDN'T WANT YOU TO PUT YOURSELF IN DANGER...
...BE-CAUSE OF HER.
TH-THAT'S IT!!
NOW I GET IT!!
AT FIRST I THOUGHT SHE WAS JUST MAD BECAUSE I RUINED HER PLANS!
SPARKLE
SPARKLE
ACK!
SALT IN MY WOUND...!
O-OKAY, WELL...
I WONDER IF I CHOSE THE WRONG GUY TO CRUSH ON.
SLUMP
OH HEY! CLASS REP!

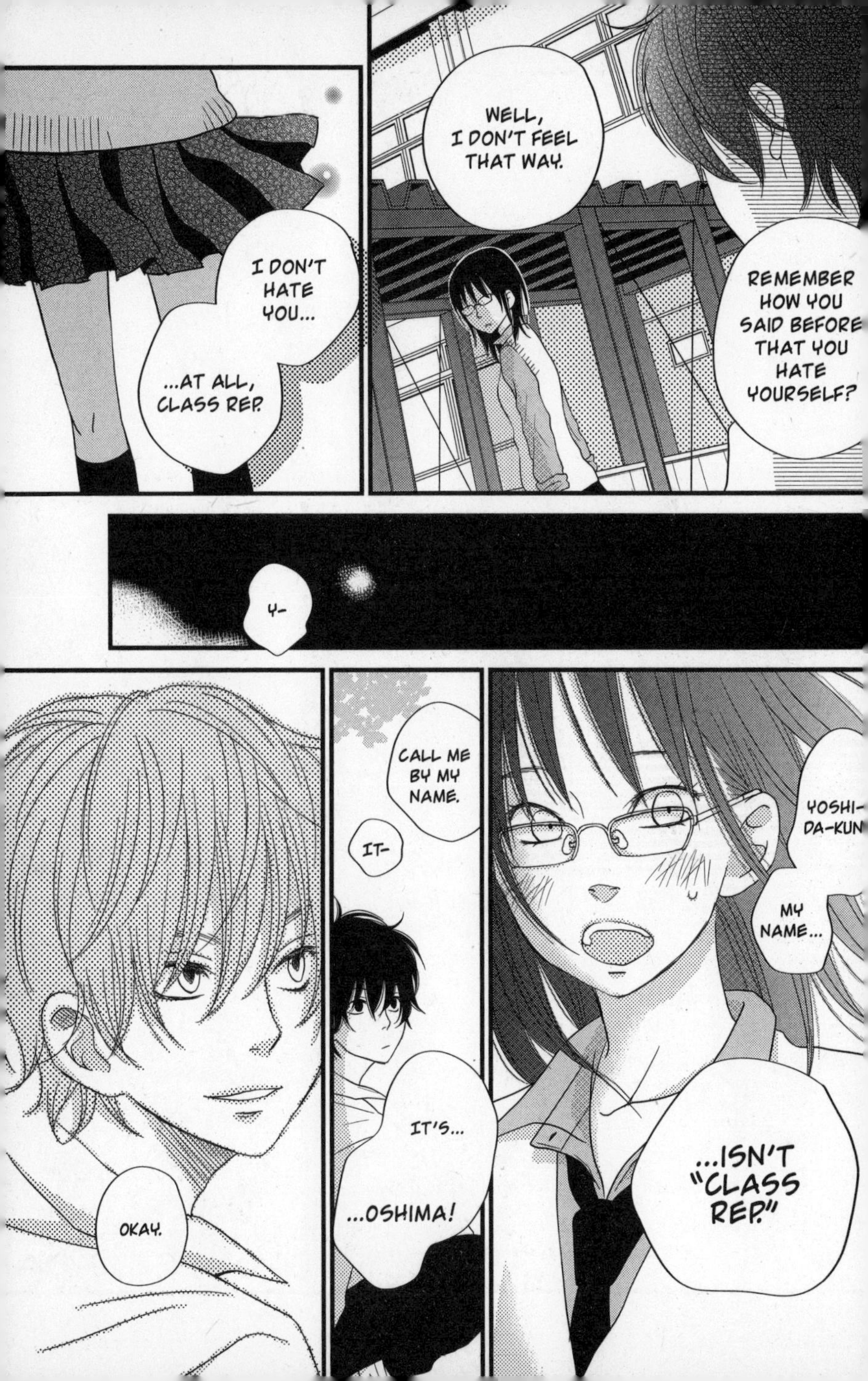
REMEMBER HOW YOU SAID BEFORE THAT YOU HATE YOURSELF?
WELL, I DON'T FEEL THAT WAY.
I DON'T HATE YOU...
...AT ALL, CLASS REP.
Y-
YOSHIDA-KUN
MY NAME...
...ISN'T "CLASS REP."
CALL ME BY MY NAME.
IT-
IT'S...
...OSHIMA!
OKAY.

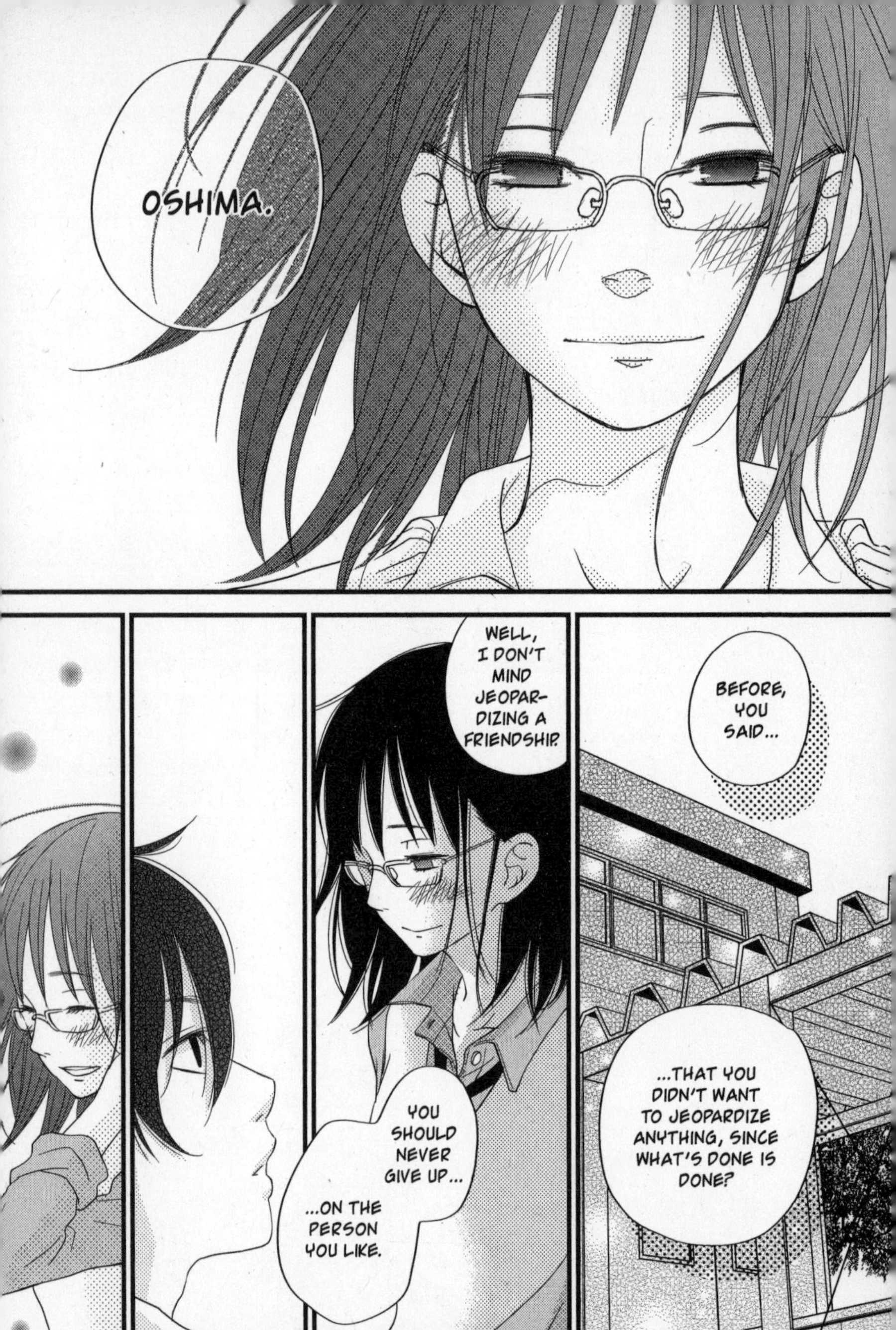
OSHIMA.
BEFORE, YOU SAID...
...THAT YOU DIDN'T WANT TO JEOPARDIZE ANYTHING, SINCE WHAT'S DONE IS DONE?
WELL, I DON'T MIND JEOPARDIZING A FRIENDSHIP.
YOU SHOULD NEVER GIVE UP...
...ON THE PERSON YOU LIKE.

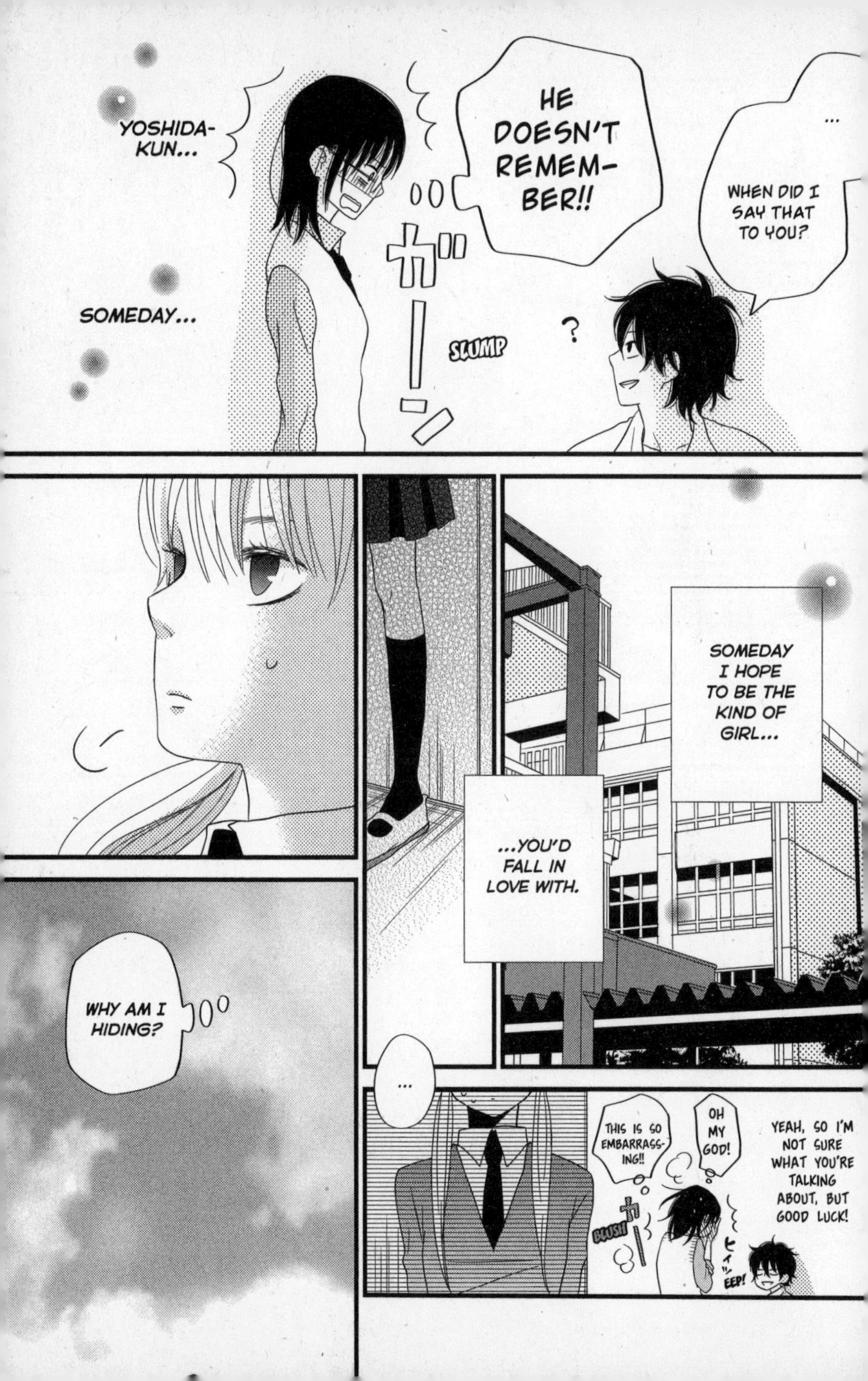
...
WHEN DID I SAY THAT TO YOU?
?
HE DOESN'T REMEMBER!!
ガーン
SLUMP
YOSHIDA-KUN...
SOMEDAY...
SOMEDAY I HOPE TO BE THE KIND OF GIRL...
...YOU'D FALL IN LOVE WITH.
YEAH, SO I'M NOT SURE WHAT YOU'RE TALKING ABOUT, BUT GOOD LUCK!
ヒィッ
EEP!
OH MY GOD!
THIS IS SO EMBARRASSING!!
BLUSH
...
WHY AM I HIDING?

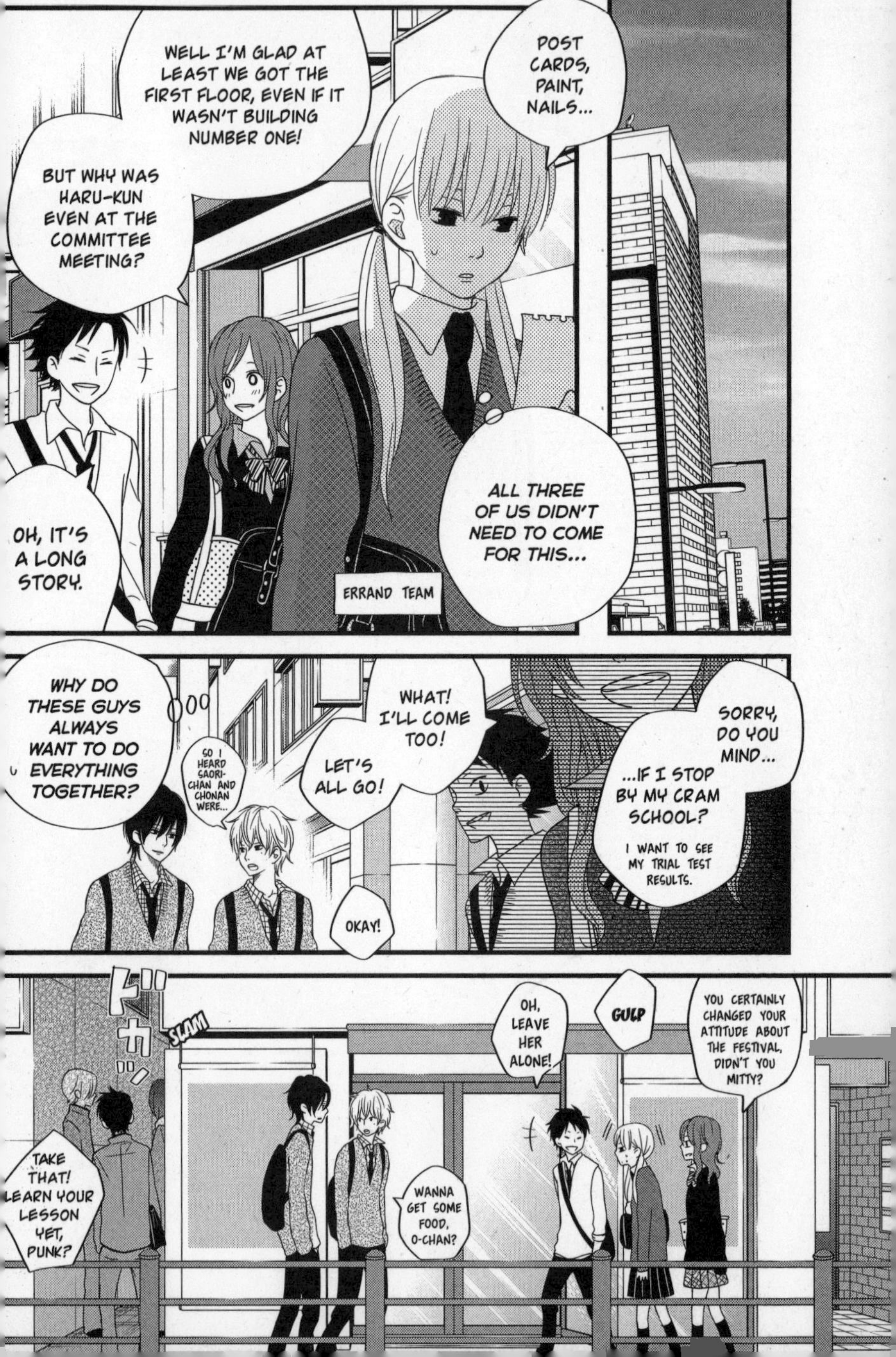
POST CARDS, PAINT, NAILS...
WELL I'M GLAD AT LEAST WE GOT THE FIRST FLOOR, EVEN IF IT WASN'T BUILDING NUMBER ONE!
BUT WHY WAS HARU-KUN EVEN AT THE COMMITTEE MEETING?
ALL THREE OF US DIDN'T NEED TO COME FOR THIS...
OH, IT'S A LONG STORY.
ERRAND TEAM
SORRY, DO YOU MIND...
...IF I STOP BY MY CRAM SCHOOL?
I WANT TO SEE MY TRIAL TEST RESULTS.
WHAT! I'LL COME TOO!
LET'S ALL GO!
OKAY!
SO I HEARD SAORI-CHAN AND CHONAN WERE...
WHY DO THESE GUYS ALWAYS WANT TO DO EVERYTHING TOGETHER?
YOU CERTAINLY CHANGED YOUR ATTITUDE ABOUT THE FESTIVAL, DIDN'T YOU MITTY?
GULP
OH, LEAVE HER ALONE!
WANNA GET SOME FOOD, O-CHAN?
SLAM
TAKE THAT! LEARN YOUR LESSON YET, PUNK?

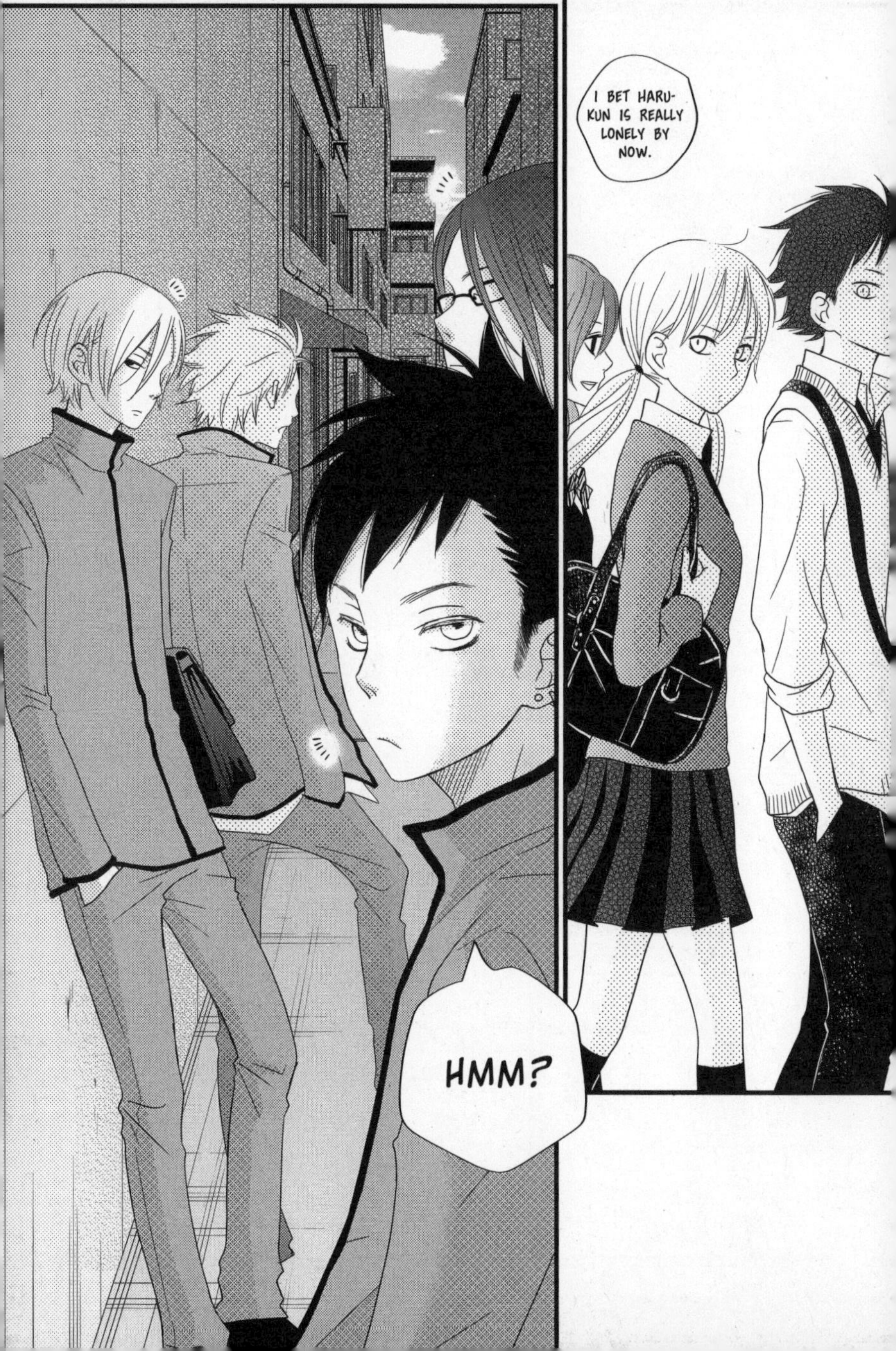
I BET HARU-KUN IS REALLY LONELY BY NOW.
HMM?

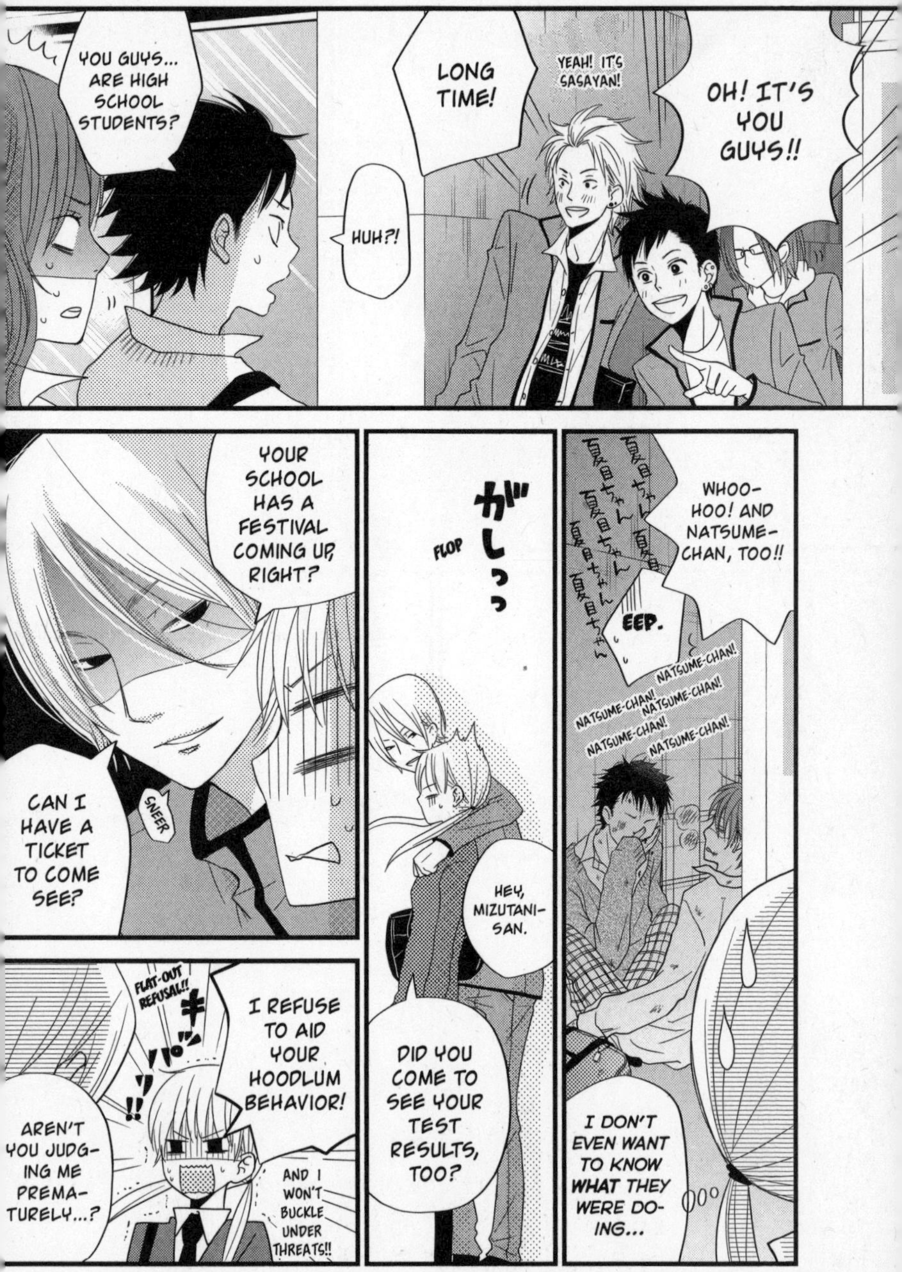
OH! IT'S YOU GUYS!!
YEAH! IT'S SASAYAN!
LONG TIME!
HUH?!
YOU GUYS... ARE HIGH SCHOOL STUDENTS?
WHOO-HOO! AND NATSUME-CHAN, TOO!!
夏目ちゃん夏目ちゃん夏目ちゃん夏目ちゃん夏目ちゃん
EEP.
NATSUME-CHAN! NATSUME-CHAN! NATSUME-CHAN! NATSUME-CHAN! NATSUME-CHAN! NATSUME-CHAN!
I DON'T EVEN WANT TO KNOW WHAT THEY WERE DOING...
がしっ
FLOP
HEY, MIZUTANI-SAN.
DID YOU COME TO SEE YOUR TEST RESULTS, TOO?
YOUR SCHOOL HAS A FESTIVAL COMING UP, RIGHT?
SNEER
CAN I HAVE A TICKET TO COME SEE?
FLAT-OUT REFUSAL!!
キッパリ!!
I REFUSE TO AID YOUR HOODLUM BEHAVIOR!
AND I WON'T BUCKLE UNDER THREATS!!
AREN'T YOU JUDGING ME PREMATURELY...?

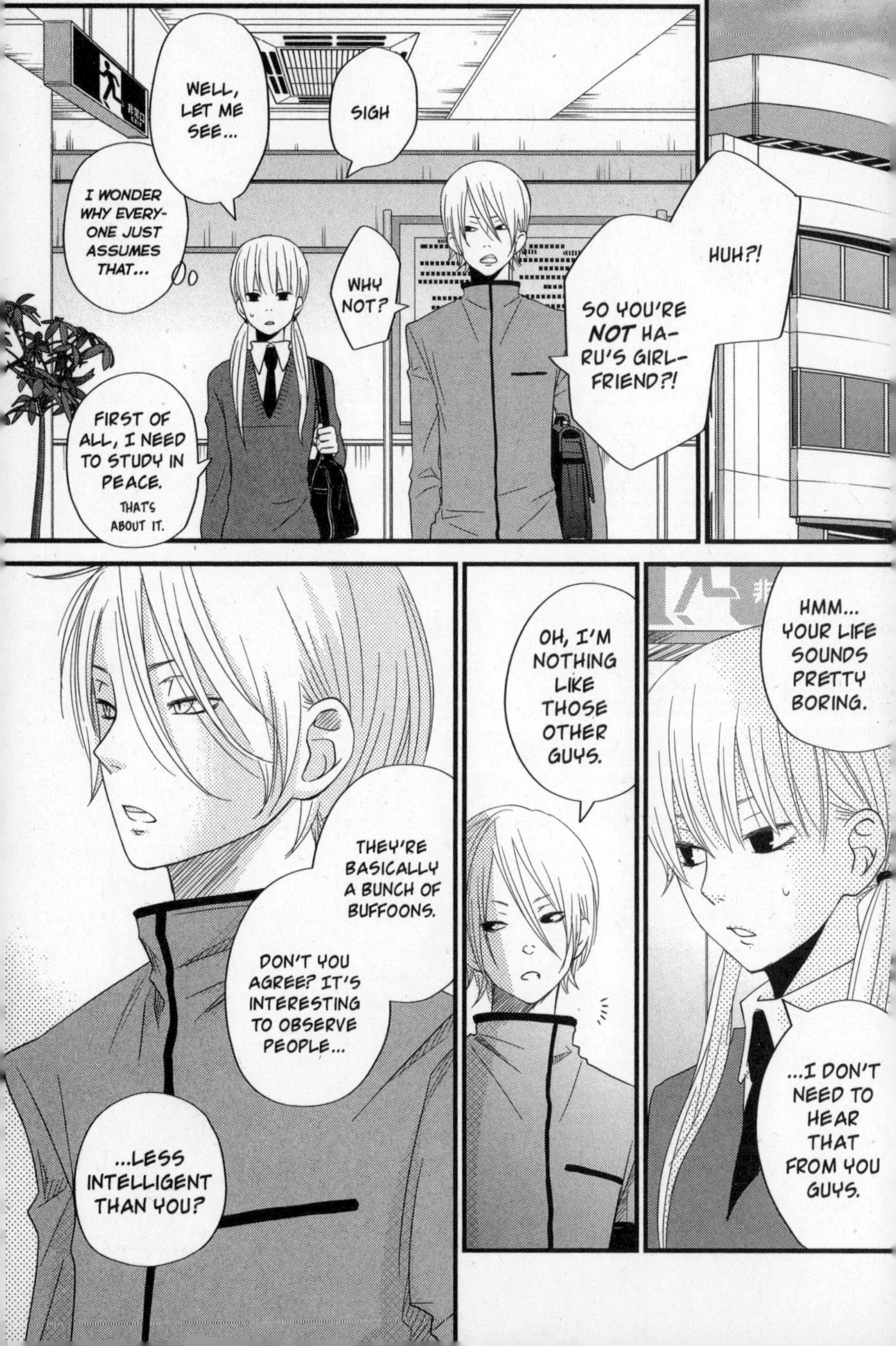
HUH?!
SO YOU'RE NOT HARU'S GIRLFRIEND?!
SIGH
WELL, LET ME SEE...
WHY NOT?
I WONDER WHY EVERYONE JUST ASSUMES THAT...
FIRST OF ALL, I NEED TO STUDY IN PEACE.
THAT'S ABOUT IT.
HMM... YOUR LIFE SOUNDS PRETTY BORING.
...I DON'T NEED TO HEAR THAT FROM YOU GUYS.
OH, I'M NOTHING LIKE THOSE OTHER GUYS.
THEY'RE BASICALLY A BUNCH OF BUFFOONS.
DON'T YOU AGREE? IT'S INTERESTING TO OBSERVE PEOPLE...
...LESS INTELLIGENT THAN YOU?

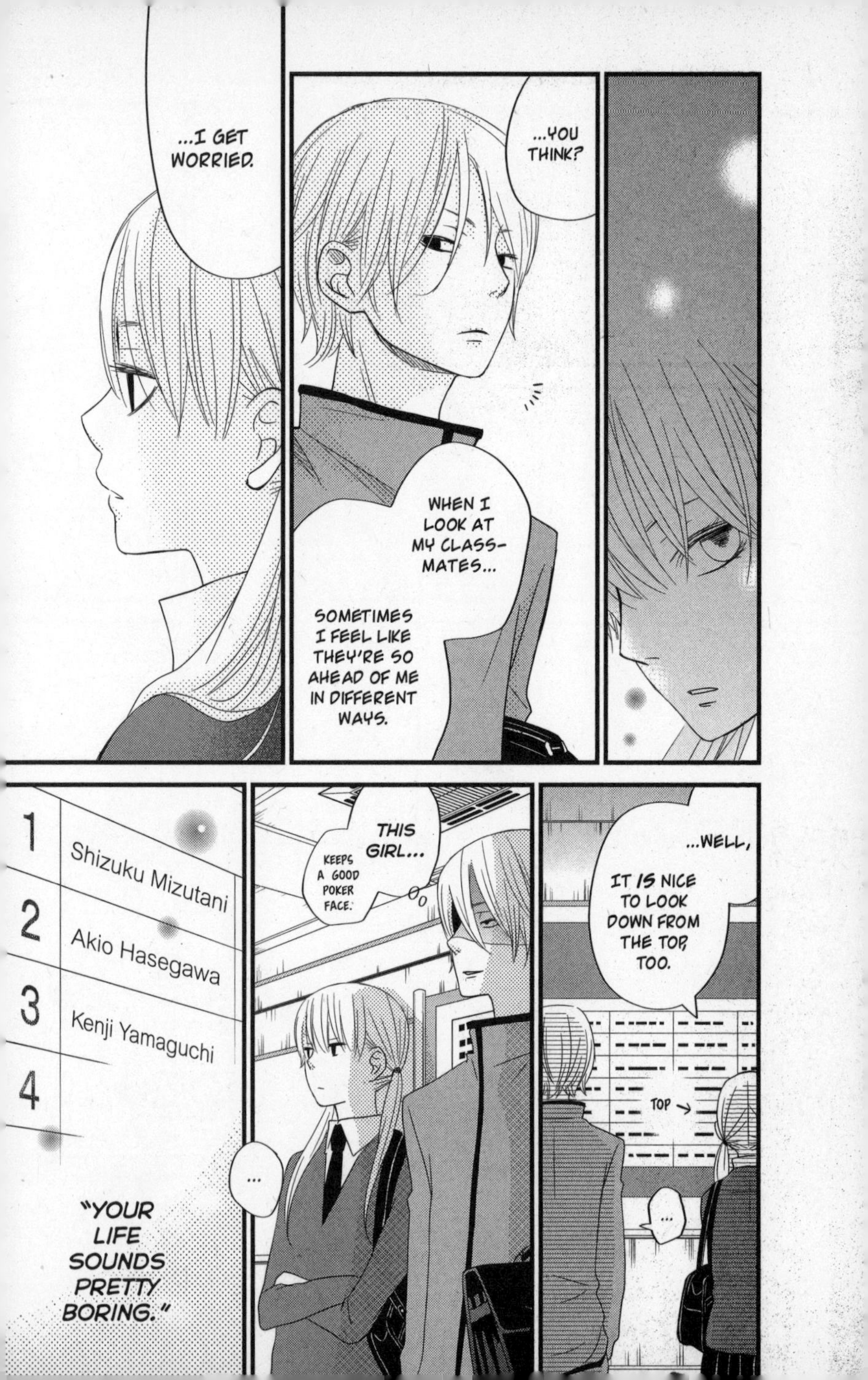

...YOU THINK?
WHEN I LOOK AT MY CLASSMATES...
SOMETIMES I FEEL LIKE THEY'RE SO AHEAD OF ME IN DIFFERENT WAYS.
...I GET WORRIED.
...WELL,
IT IS NICE TO LOOK DOWN FROM THE TOP, TOO.
TOP →
...
THIS GIRL...
KEEPS A GOOD POKER FACE.
...
1 Shizuku Mizutani
2 Akio Hasegawa
3 Kenji Yamaguchi
4
"YOUR LIFE SOUNDS PRETTY BORING."

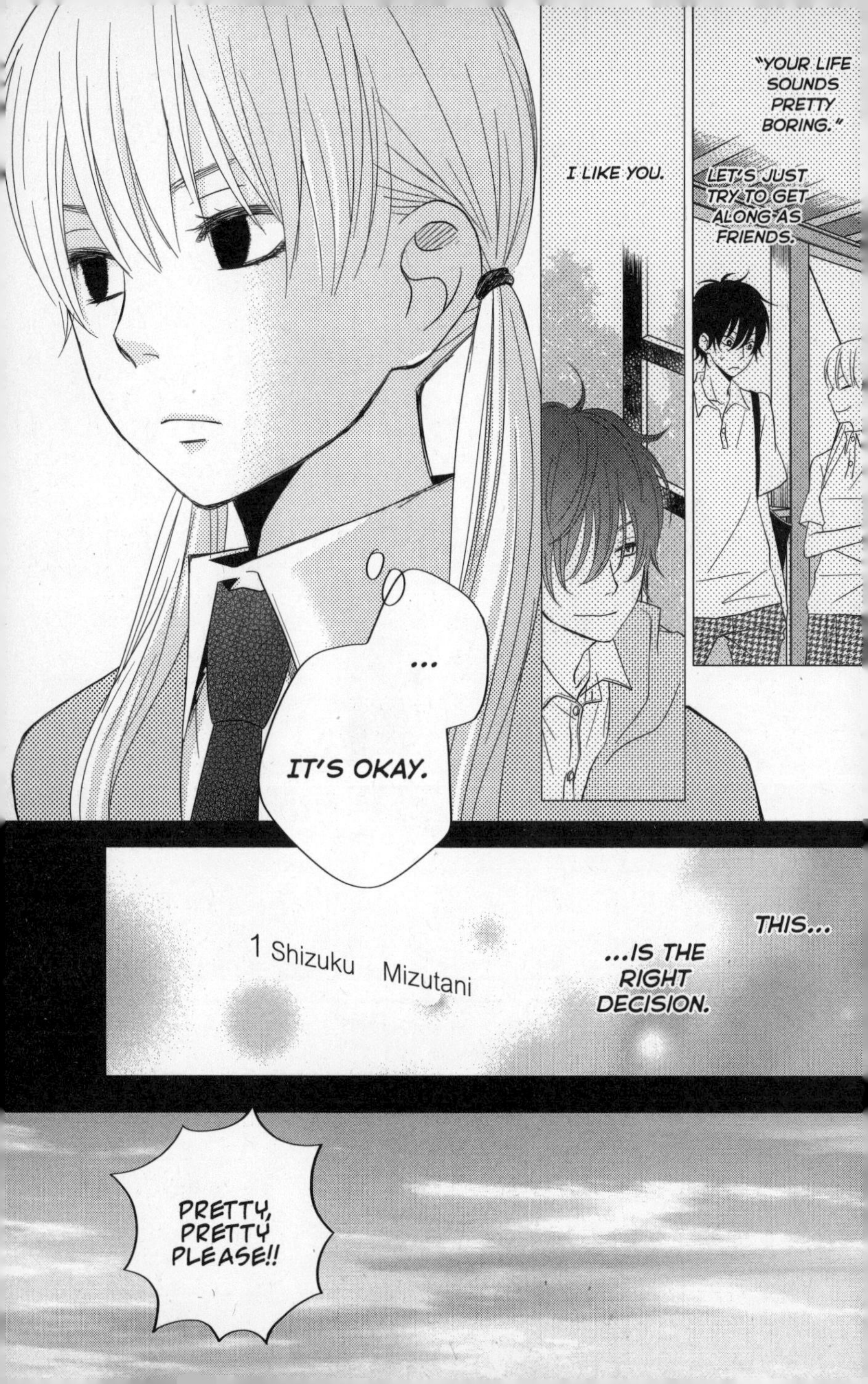
"YOUR LIFE SOUNDS PRETTY BORING."
LET'S JUST TRY TO GET ALONG AS FRIENDS.
I LIKE YOU.
...
IT'S OKAY.
THIS...
...IS THE RIGHT DECISION.
1 Shizuku Mizutani
PRETTY, PRETTY PLEASE!!

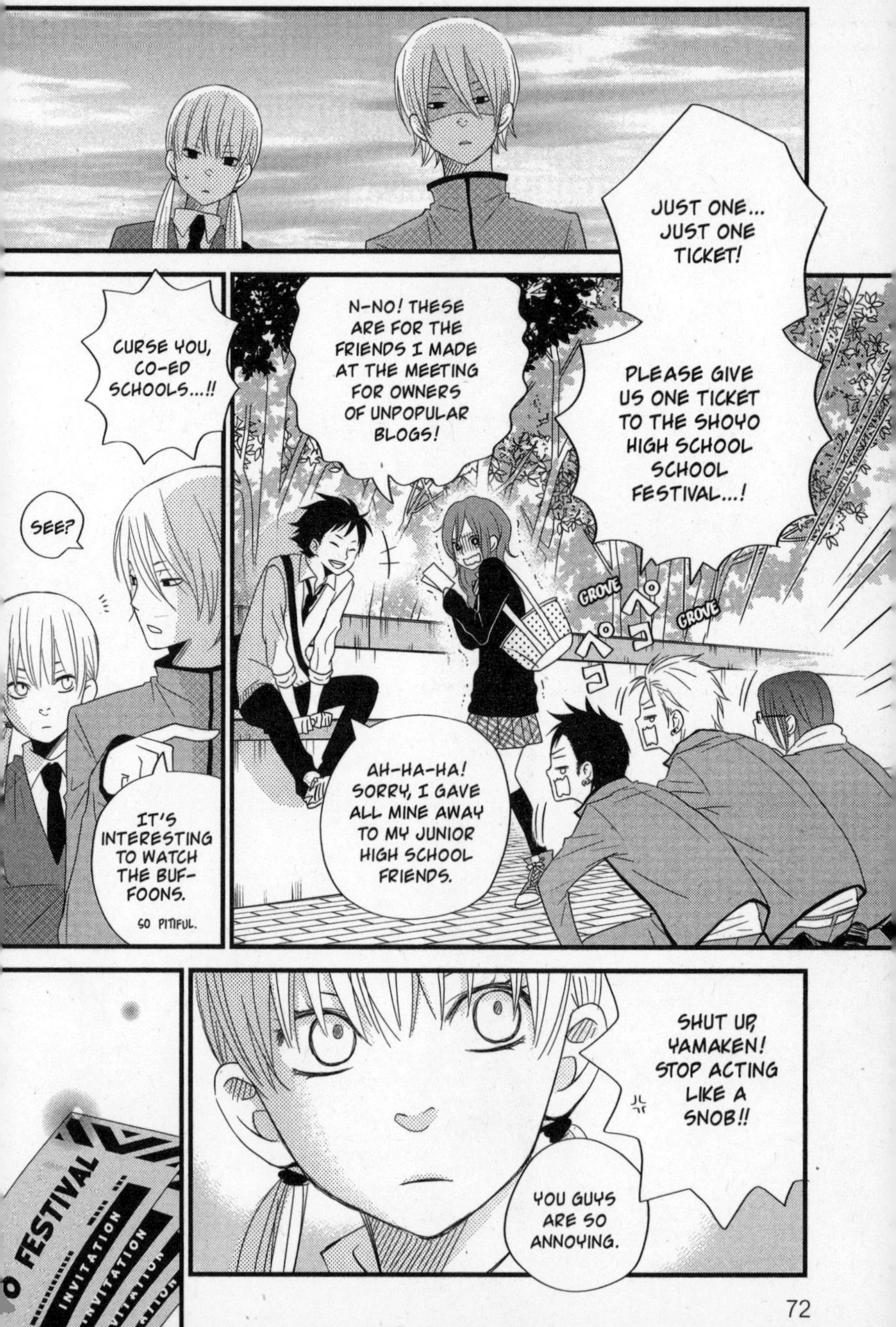
JUST ONE... JUST ONE TICKET!
PLEASE GIVE US ONE TICKET TO THE SHOYO HIGH SCHOOL SCHOOL FESTIVAL...!
N-NO! THESE ARE FOR THE FRIENDS I MADE AT THE MEETING FOR OWNERS OF UNPOPULAR BLOGS!
GROVE
GROVE
AH-HA-HA! SORRY, I GAVE ALL MINE AWAY TO MY JUNIOR HIGH SCHOOL FRIENDS.
CURSE YOU, CO-ED SCHOOLS...!!
SEE?
IT'S INTERESTING TO WATCH THE BUF-FOONS.
SO PITIFUL.
SHUT UP, YAMAKEN! STOP ACTING LIKE A SNOB!!
YOU GUYS ARE SO ANNOYING.
FESTIVAL
INVITATION
INVITATION

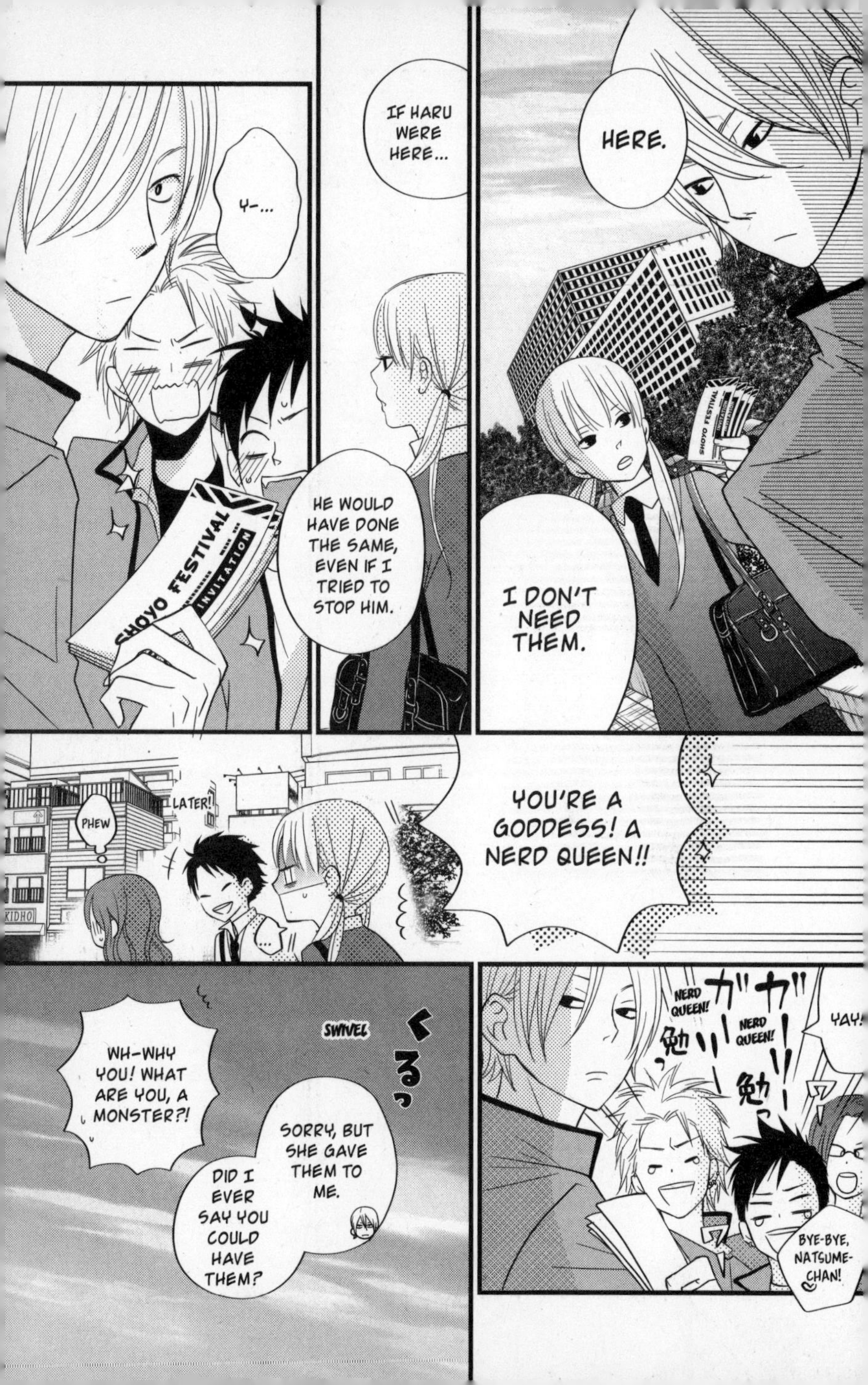
HERE.
SHOYO FESTIVAL
I DON'T NEED THEM.
IF HARU WERE HERE...
HE WOULD HAVE DONE THE SAME, EVEN IF I TRIED TO STOP HIM.
Y-...
SHOYO FESTIVAL
INVITATION
YOU'RE A GODDESS! A NERD QUEEN!!
LATER!
PHEW
...
YAY!
NERD QUEEN!
NERD QUEEN!
BYE-BYE, NATSUME-CHAN!
SWIVEL
くるっ
WH-WHY YOU! WHAT ARE YOU, A MONSTER?!
SORRY, BUT SHE GAVE THEM TO ME.
DID I EVER SAY YOU COULD HAVE THEM?

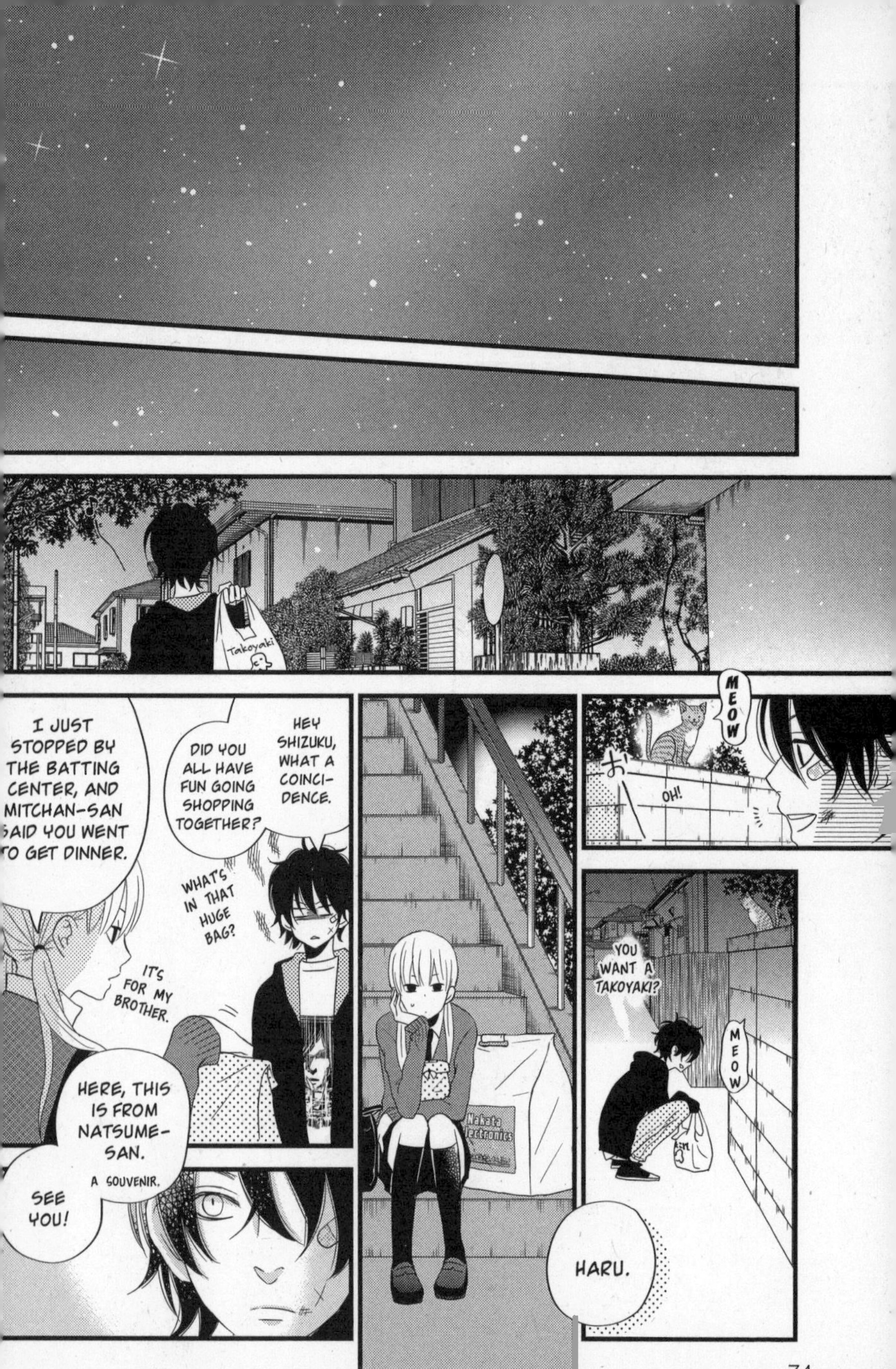
Takoyaki
MEOW
お
OH!
YOU WANT A TAKOYAKI?
MEOW
HARU.
Nakata Electronics
HEY SHIZUKU, WHAT A COINCIDENCE.
DID YOU ALL HAVE FUN GOING SHOPPING TOGETHER?
I JUST STOPPED BY THE BATTING CENTER, AND MITCHAN-SAN SAID YOU WENT TO GET DINNER.
WHAT'S IN THAT HUGE BAG?
IT'S FOR MY BROTHER.
HERE, THIS IS FROM NATSUME-SAN.
A SOUVENIR.
SEE YOU!

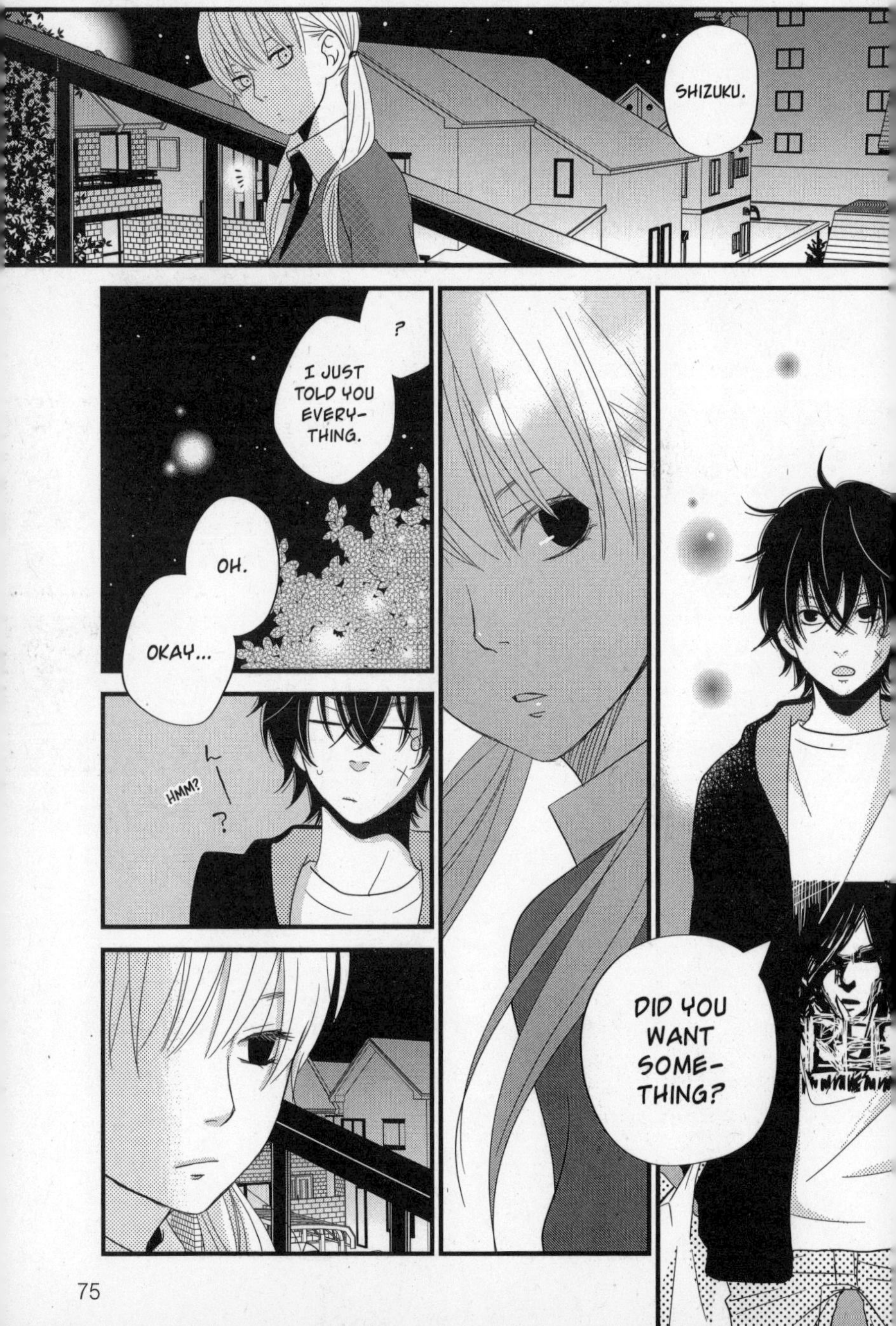
SHIZUKU.
DID YOU WANT SOMETHING?
?
I JUST TOLD YOU EVERYTHING.
OH.
OKAY...
HMM?

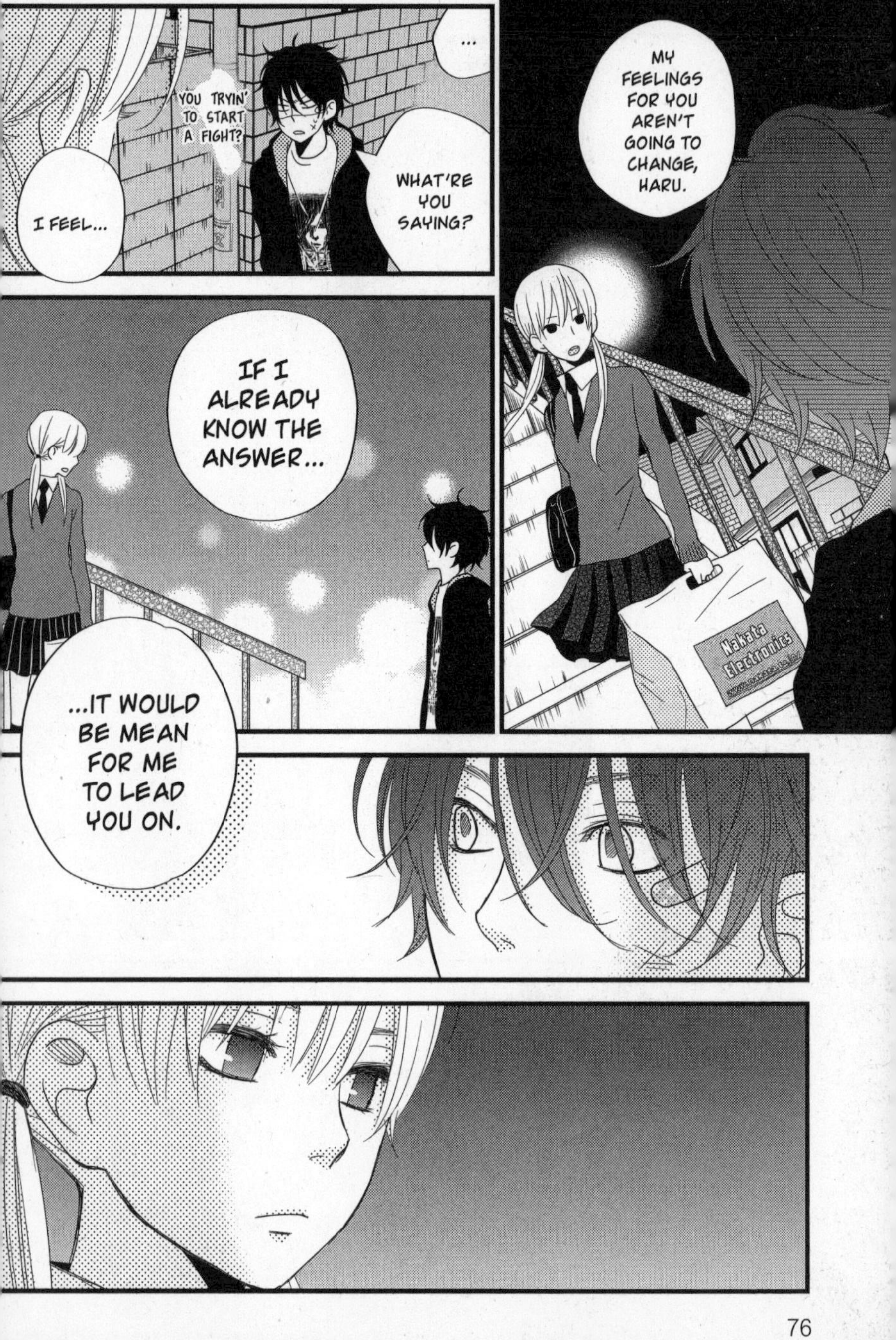
MY FEELINGS FOR YOU AREN'T GOING TO CHANGE, HARU.
Nakata Electronics
...
WHAT'RE YOU SAYING?
YOU TRYIN' TO START A FIGHT?
I FEEL...
IF I ALREADY KNOW THE ANSWER...
...IT WOULD BE MEAN FOR ME TO LEAD YOU ON.

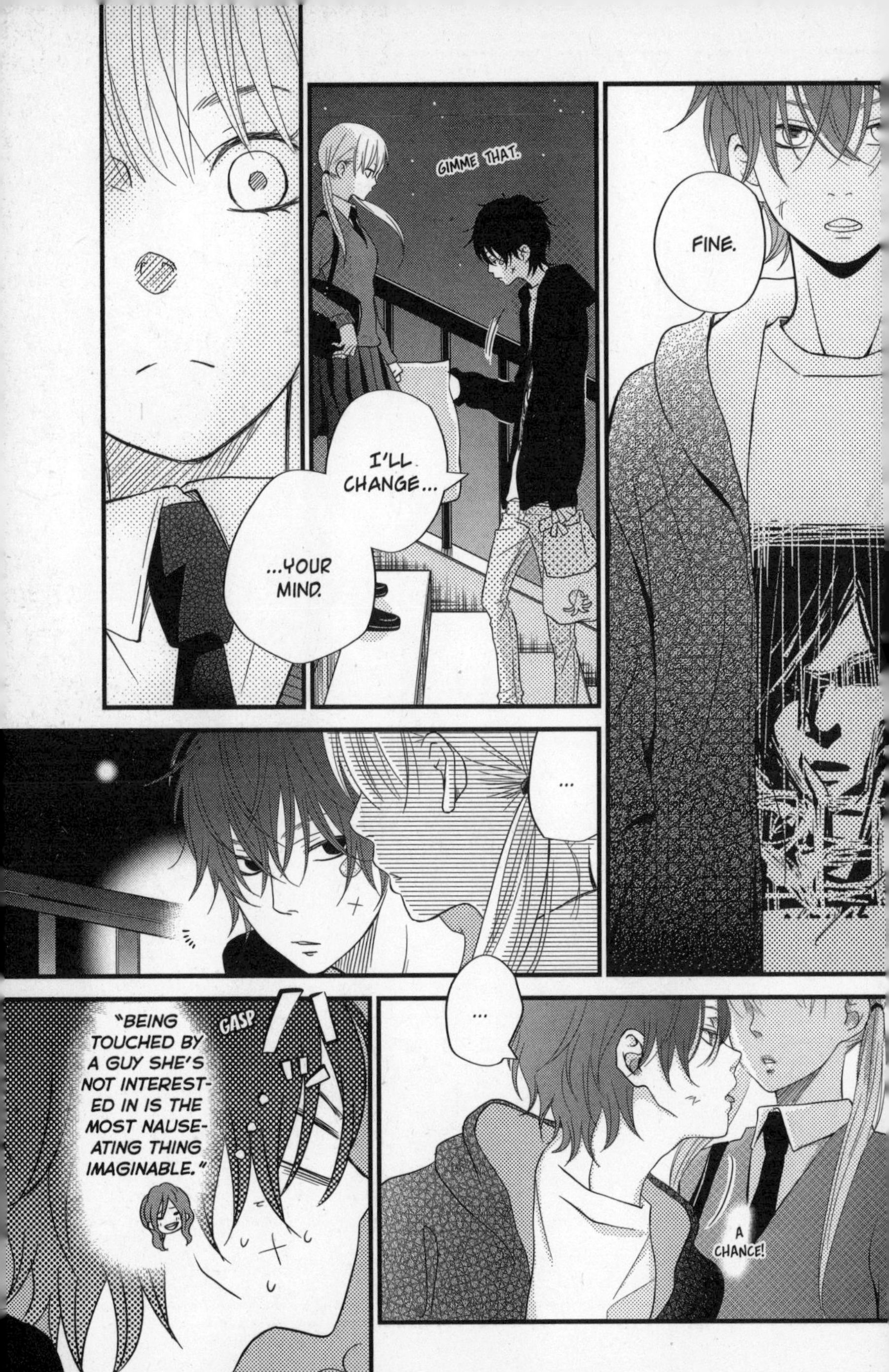
FINE.
GIMME THAT.
I'LL CHANGE...
...YOUR MIND.
...
...
A CHANCE!
GASP
"BEING TOUCHED BY A GUY SHE'S NOT INTERESTED IN IS THE MOST NAUSEATING THING IMAGINABLE."

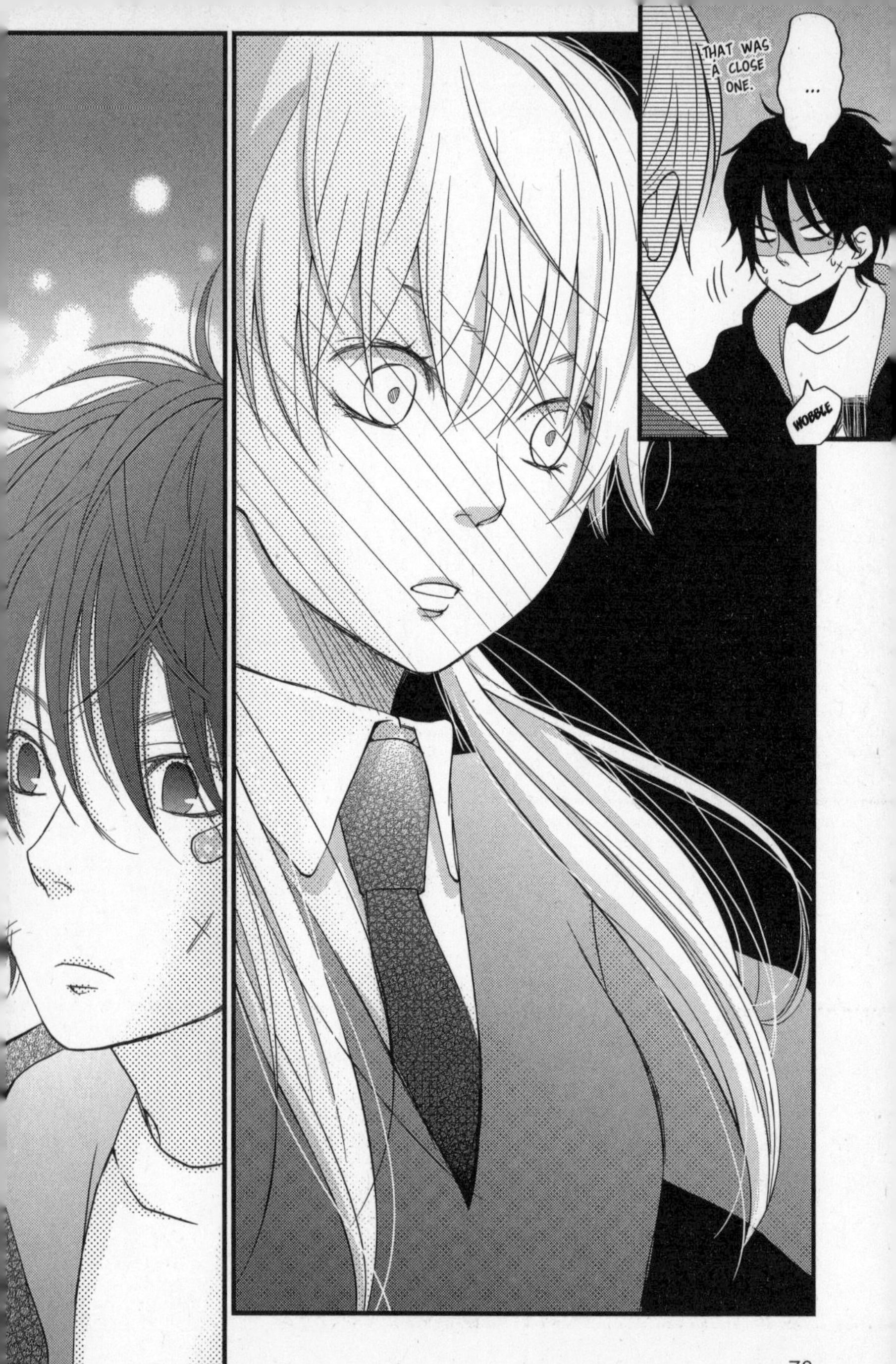
THAT WAS A CLOSE ONE.
...
WOBBLE

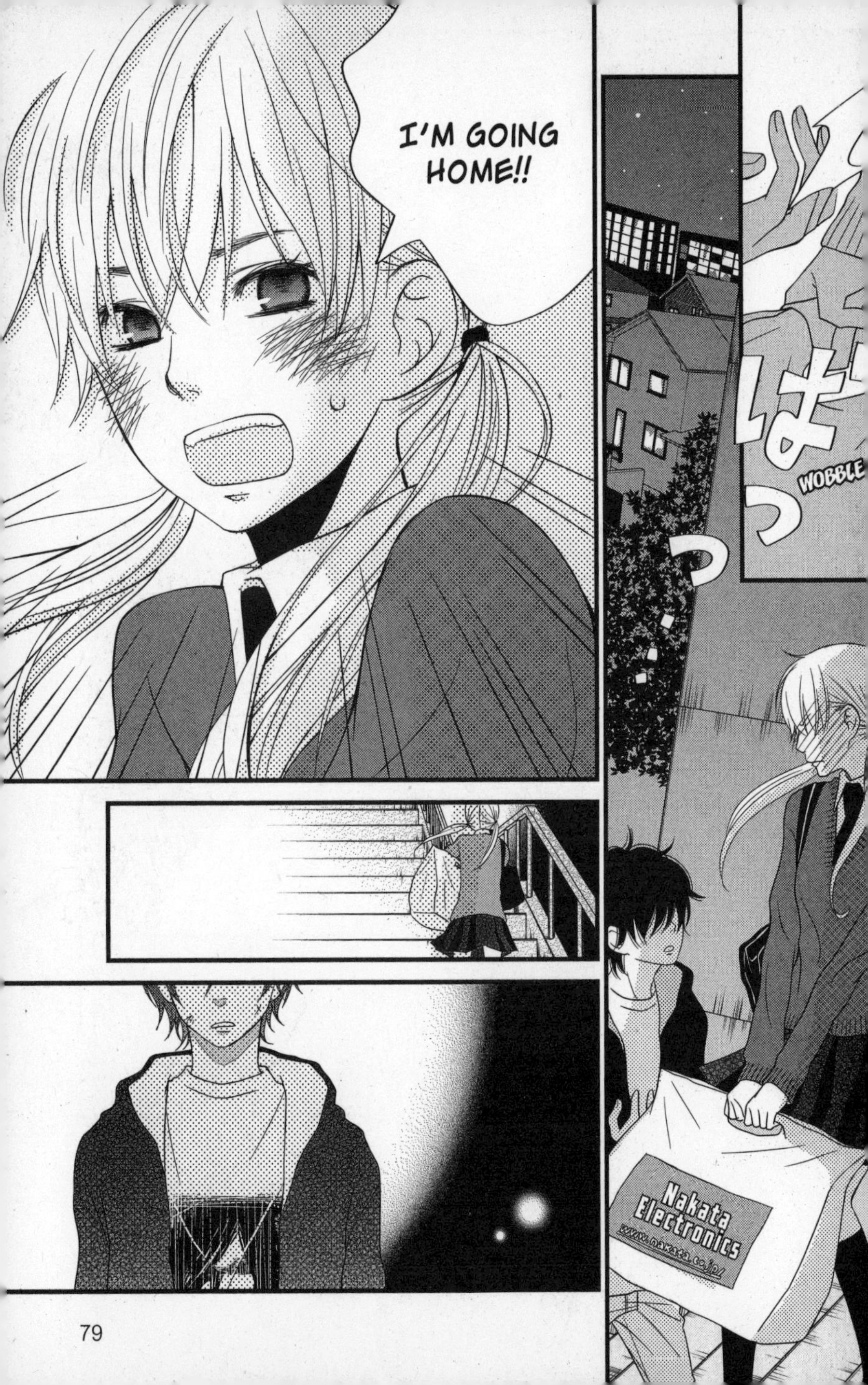
はっ
WOBBLE
つ
Nakata Electronics
www.nakata.co.jp/
I'M GOING HOME!!

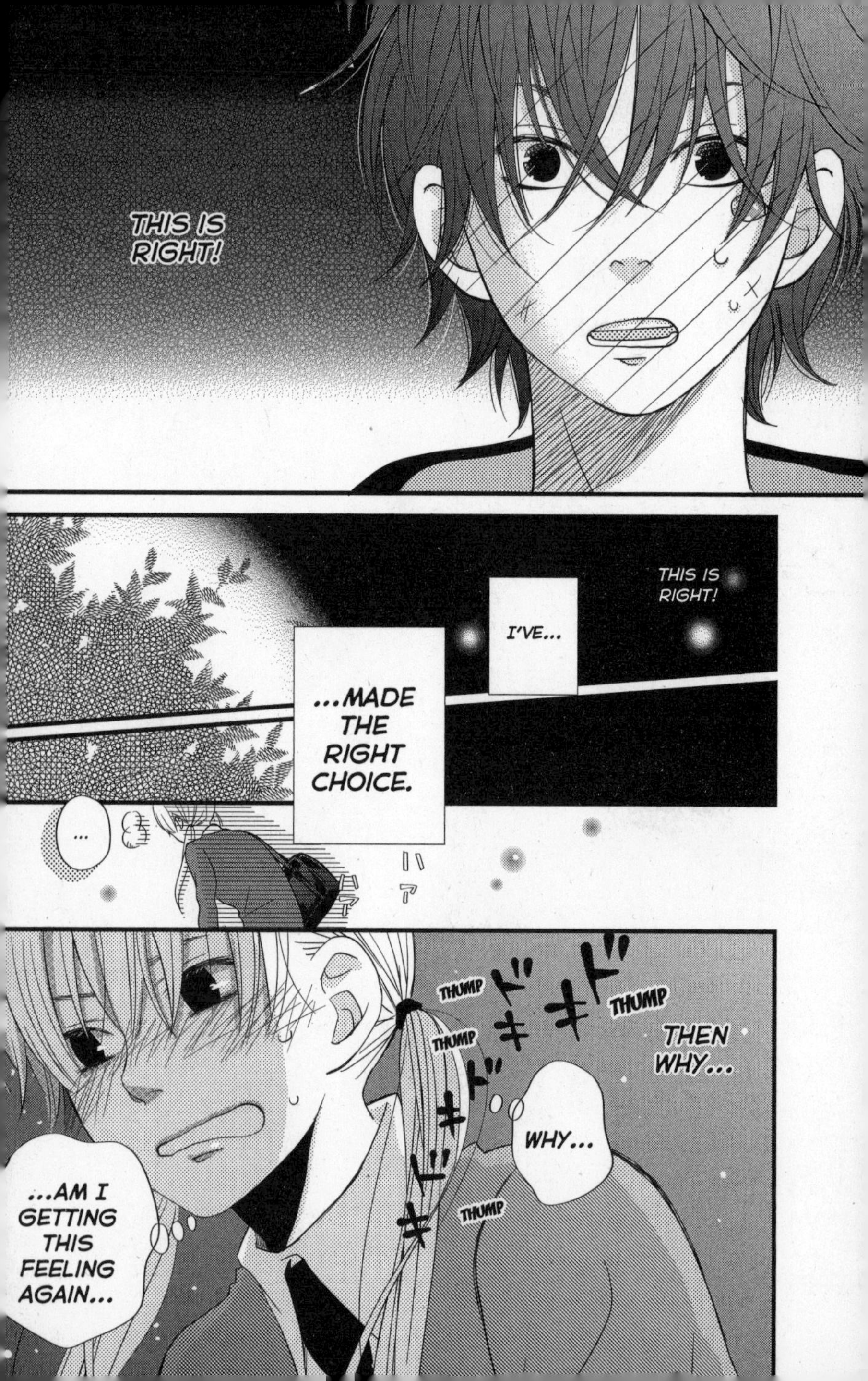
THIS IS RIGHT!
THIS IS RIGHT!
I'VE...
...MADE THE RIGHT CHOICE.
...
ハァ
THUMP
THUMP
THUMP
THEN WHY...
WHY...
THUMP
...AM I GETTING THIS FEELING AGAIN...

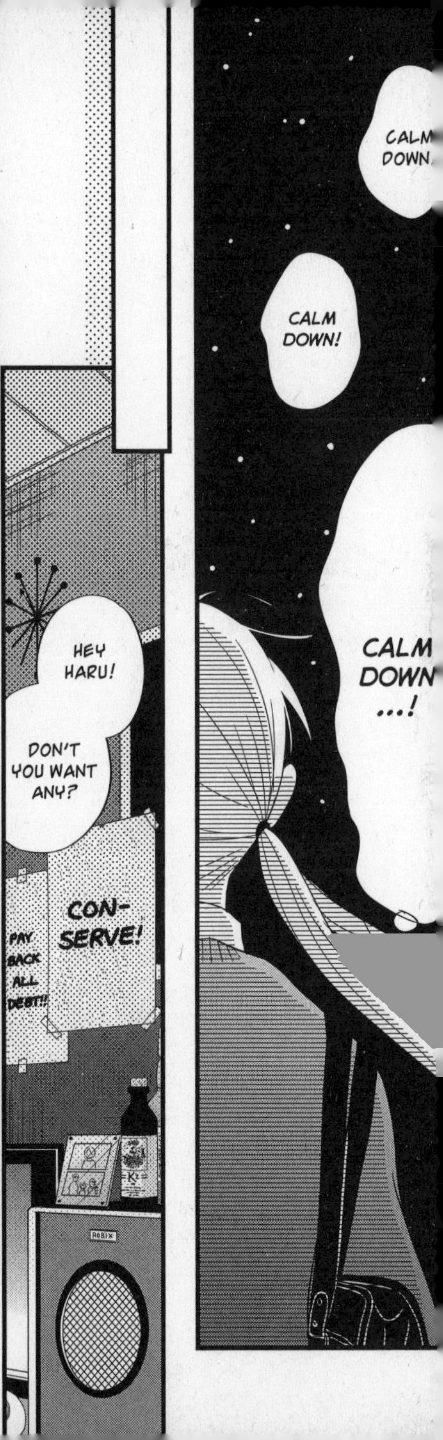
CALM DOWN
CALM DOWN!
CALM DOWN...!
HEY HARU!
DON'T YOU WANT ANY?
CON-SERVE!
PAY BACK ALL DEBT!!

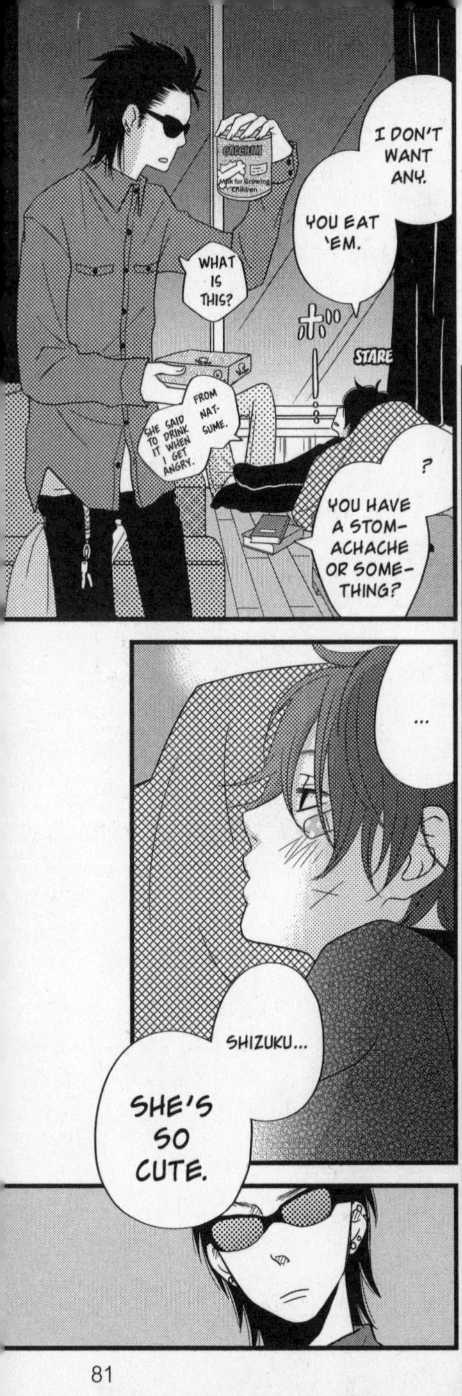
I DON'T WANT ANY.
YOU EAT 'EM.
CALCIUM
Milk for Growing Children
WHAT IS THIS?
STARE
?
YOU HAVE A STOMACHACHE OR SOMETHING?
FROM NATSUME.
SHE SAID TO DRINK IT WHEN I GET ANGRY.
...
SHIZUKU...
SHE'S SO CUTE.

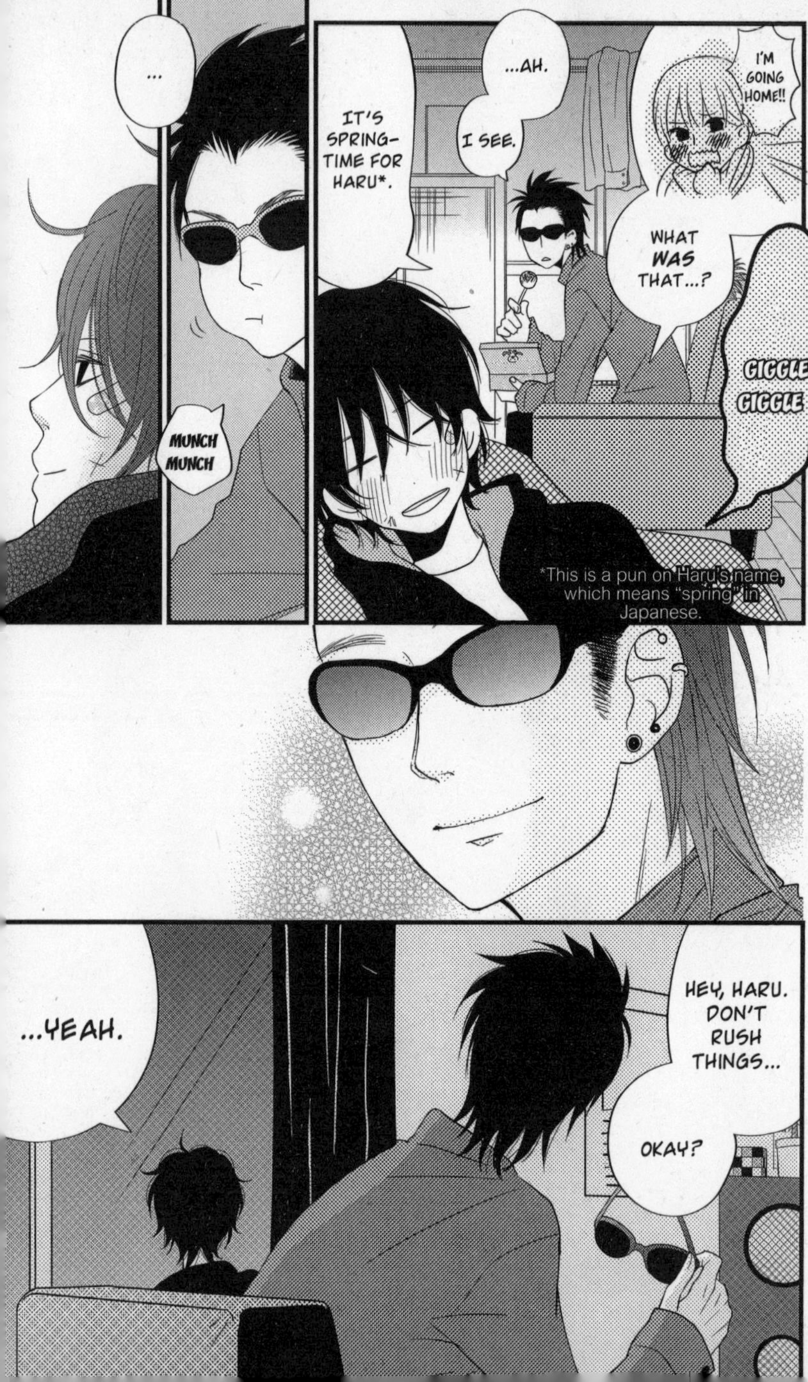
I'M GOING HOME!!
...AH.
I SEE.
WHAT WAS THAT...?
GIGGLE GIGGLE
IT'S SPRING-TIME FOR HARU*.
...
MUNCH MUNCH
HEY, HARU. DON'T RUSH THINGS...
OKAY?
...YEAH.
*This is a pun on Haru's name, which means "spring" in Japanese.

Rational

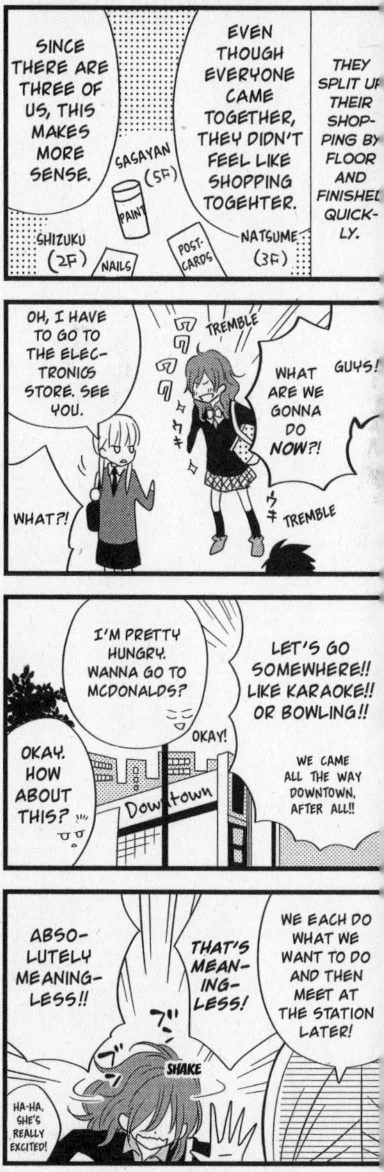

THEY SPLIT UP THEIR SHOPPING BY FLOOR AND FINISHED QUICKLY.
EVEN THOUGH EVERYONE CAME TOGETHER, THEY DIDN'T FEEL LIKE SHOPPING TOGEHTER.
SINCE THERE ARE THREE OF US, THIS MAKES MORE SENSE.
SASAYAN (5F)
PAINT
NATSUME (3F)
POST-CARDS
NAILS
SHIZUKU (2F)
GUYS!
WHAT ARE WE GONNA DO NOW?!
TREMBLE
TREMBLE
OH, I HAVE TO GO TO THE ELECTRONICS STORE. SEE YOU.
WHAT?!
LET'S GO SOMEWHERE!! LIKE KARAOKE!! OR BOWLING!!
WE CAME ALL THE WAY DOWNTOWN, AFTER ALL!!
I'M PRETTY HUNGRY. WANNA GO TO MCDONALDS?
OKAY!
OKAY. HOW ABOUT THIS?
Downtown
WE EACH DO WHAT WE WANT TO DO AND THEN MEET AT THE STATION LATER!
THAT'S MEANINGLESS!
SHAKE
ABSOLUTELY MEANINGLESS!!
HA-HA, SHE'S REALLY EXCITED!

After School

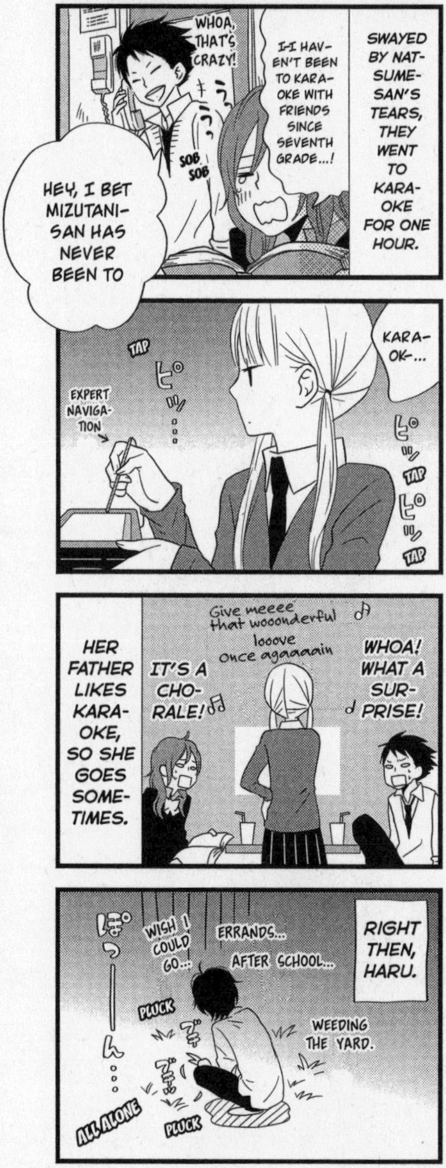

SWAYED BY NATSUME-SAN'S TEARS, THEY WENT TO KARAOKE FOR ONE HOUR.
I-I HAVEN'T BEEN TO KARAOKE WITH FRIENDS SINCE SEVENTH GRADE...!
WHOA, THAT'S CRAZY!
SOB SOB
HEY, I BET MIZUTANI-SAN HAS NEVER BEEN TO
KARA-OK-...
TAP
EXPERT NAVIGATION
TAP
TAP
WHOA! WHAT A SURPRISE!
Give meeee that wooonderful looove once agaaaain
IT'S A CHORALE!
HER FATHER LIKES KARAOKE, SO SHE GOES SOMETIMES.
RIGHT THEN, HARU.
ERRANDS... AFTER SCHOOL...
WISH I COULD GO...
WEEDING THE YARD.
PLUCK
PLUCK
ALL ALONE

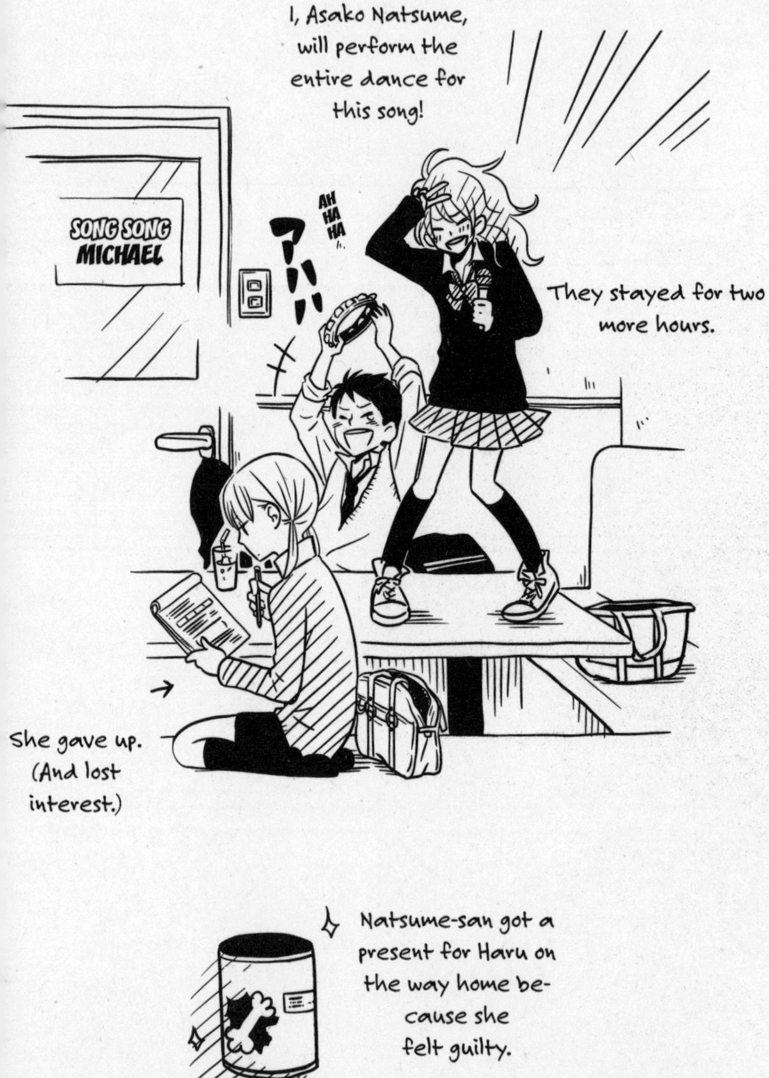

I, Asako Natsume, will perform the entire dance for this song!
AH HA HA
SONG SONG MICHAEL
They stayed for two more hours.
She gave up. (And lost interest.)
Natsume-san got a present for Haru on the way home be-cause she felt guilty.

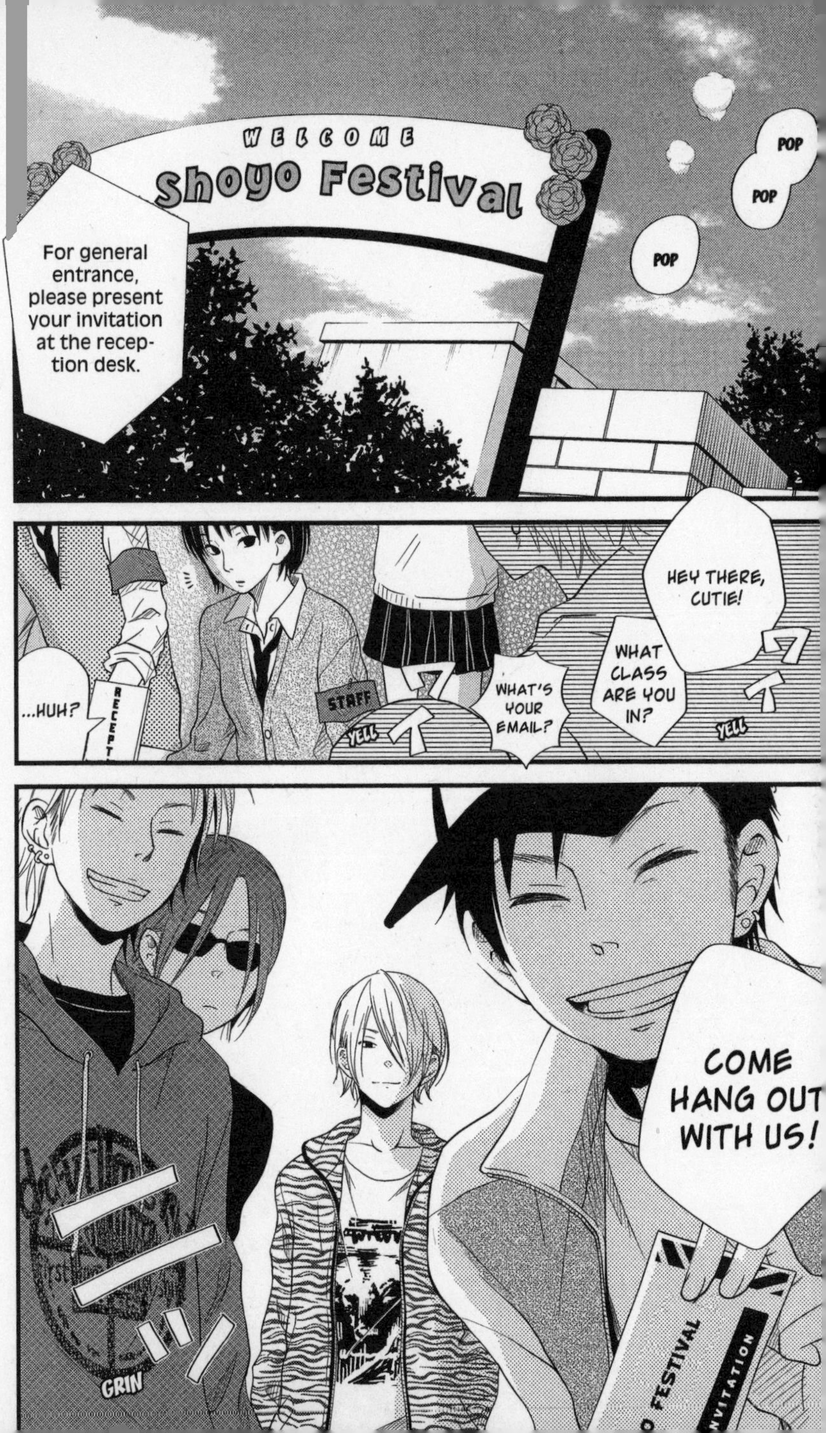
POP
POP
POP
WELCOME
Shoyo Festival
For general entrance, please present your invitation at the reception desk.
HEY THERE, CUTIE!
WHAT CLASS ARE YOU IN?
YELL
WHAT'S YOUR EMAIL?
YELL
STAFF
...HUH?
COME HANG OUT WITH US!
GRIN

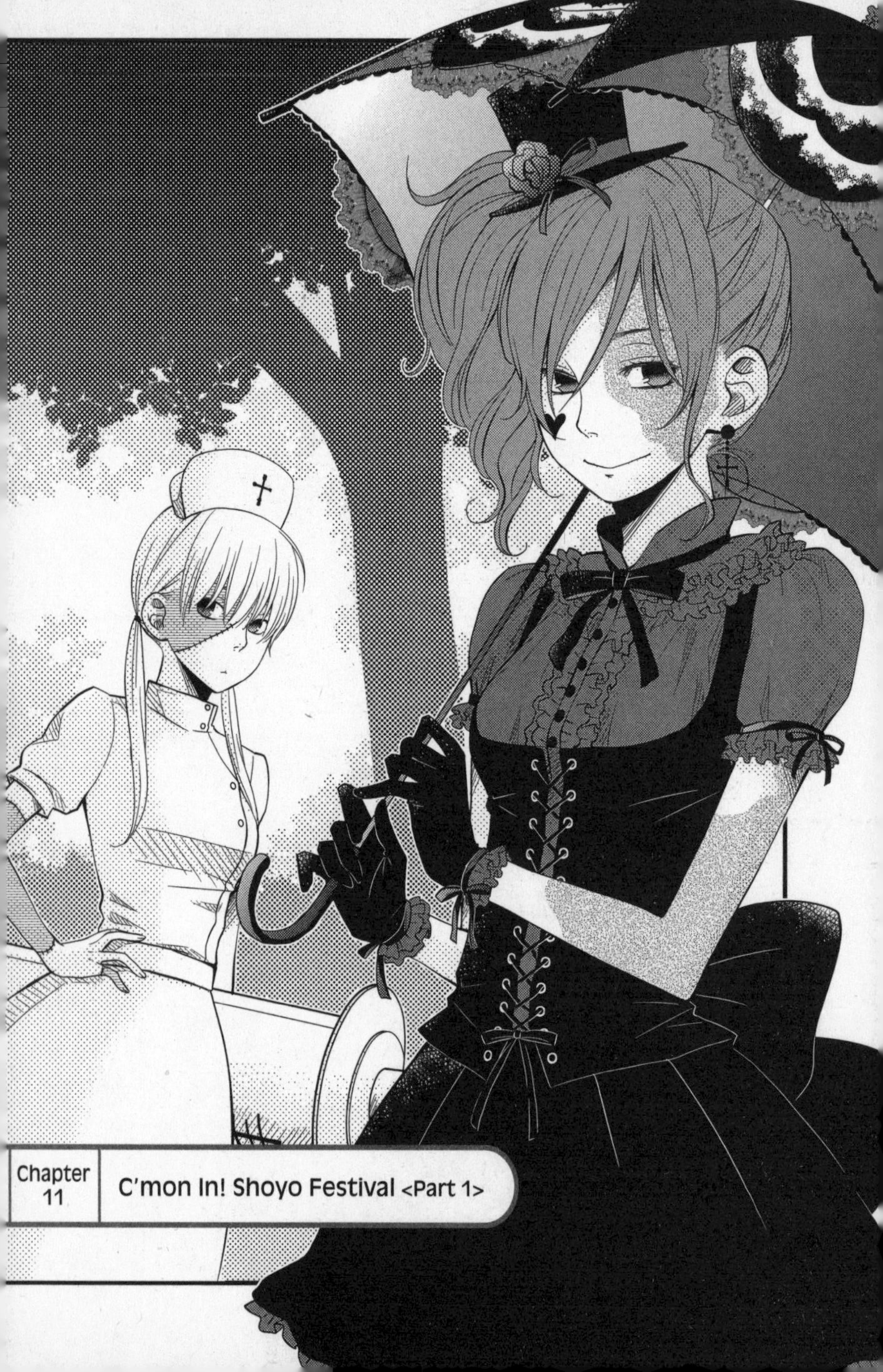
Chapter 11
C'mon In! Shoyo Festival <Part 1>

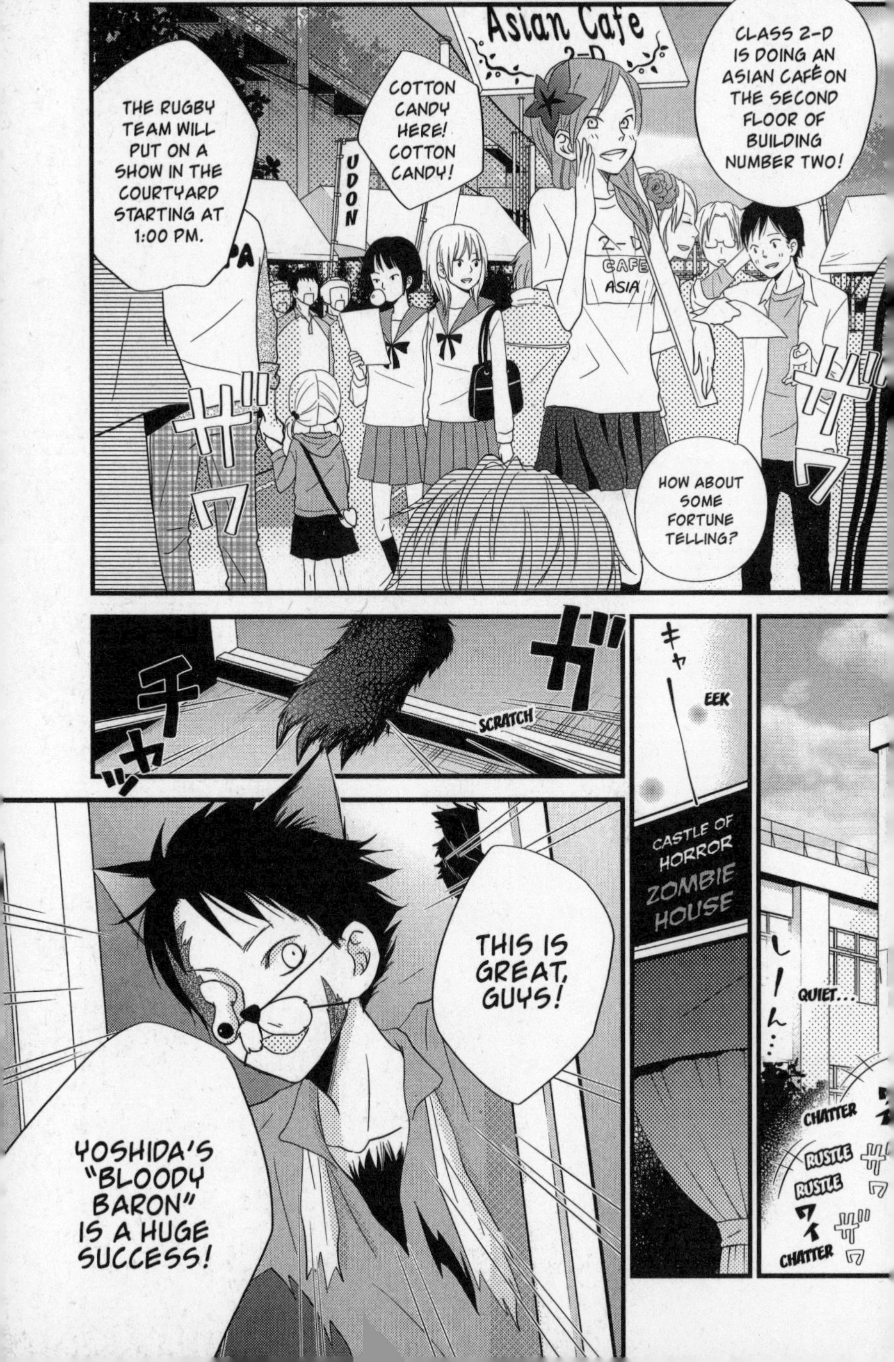
Asian Cafe
2-D
CLASS 2-D IS DOING AN ASIAN CAFÉ ON THE SECOND FLOOR OF BUILDING NUMBER TWO!
2-D CAFE ASIA
HOW ABOUT SOME FORTUNE TELLING?
ザワ
COTTON CANDY HERE! COTTON CANDY!
UDON
THE RUGBY TEAM WILL PUT ON A SHOW IN THE COURTYARD STARTING AT 1:00 PM.
ザワ
しーん…
QUIET…
CHATTER
RUSTLE
RUSTLE
ザワ
CHATTER
キャー
EEK
CASTLE OF HORROR
ZOMBIE HOUSE
ガ
SCRATCH
チャッ
THIS IS GREAT, GUYS!
YOSHIDA'S "BLOODY BARON" IS A HUGE SUCCESS!

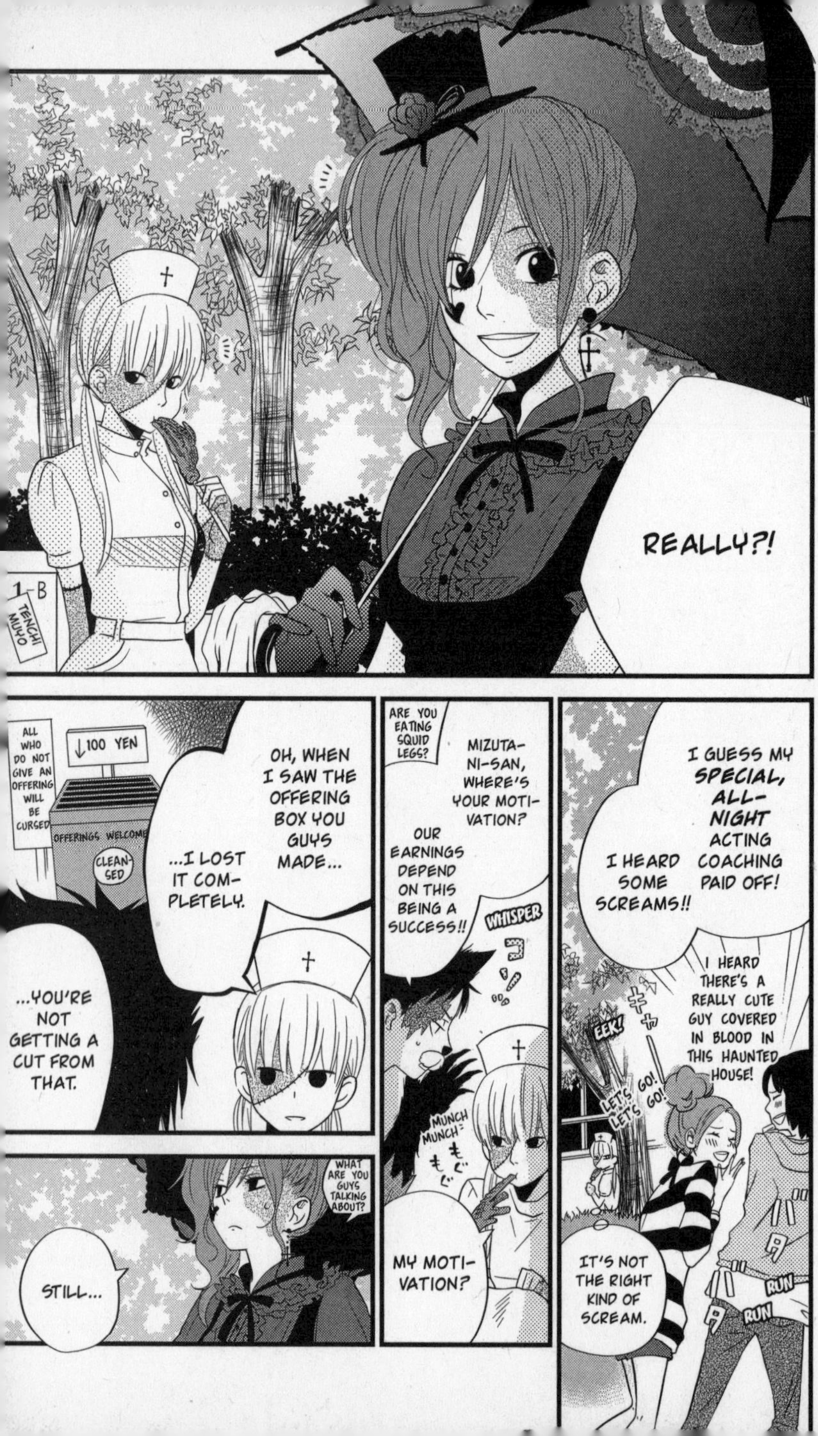
REALLY?!
1-B
TENCHI MUYO
I GUESS MY SPECIAL, ALL-NIGHT ACTING COACHING PAID OFF!
I HEARD SOME SCREAMS!!
I HEARD THERE'S A REALLY CUTE GUY COVERED IN BLOOD IN THIS HAUNTED HOUSE!
EEK!
LET'S GO! LET'S GO!
IT'S NOT THE RIGHT KIND OF SCREAM.
RUN
RUN
MIZUTANI-SAN, WHERE'S YOUR MOTIVATION?
ARE YOU EATING SQUID LEGS?
OUR EARNINGS DEPEND ON THIS BEING A SUCCESS!!
WHISPER
OH, WHEN I SAW THE OFFERING BOX YOU GUYS MADE...
...I LOST IT COMPLETELY.
↓100 YEN
ALL WHO DO NOT GIVE AN OFFERING WILL BE CURSED
OFFERINGS WELCOME
CLEANSED
...YOU'RE NOT GETTING A CUT FROM THAT.
MUNCH MUNCH
MY MOTIVATION?
WHAT ARE YOU GUYS TALKING ABOUT?
STILL...

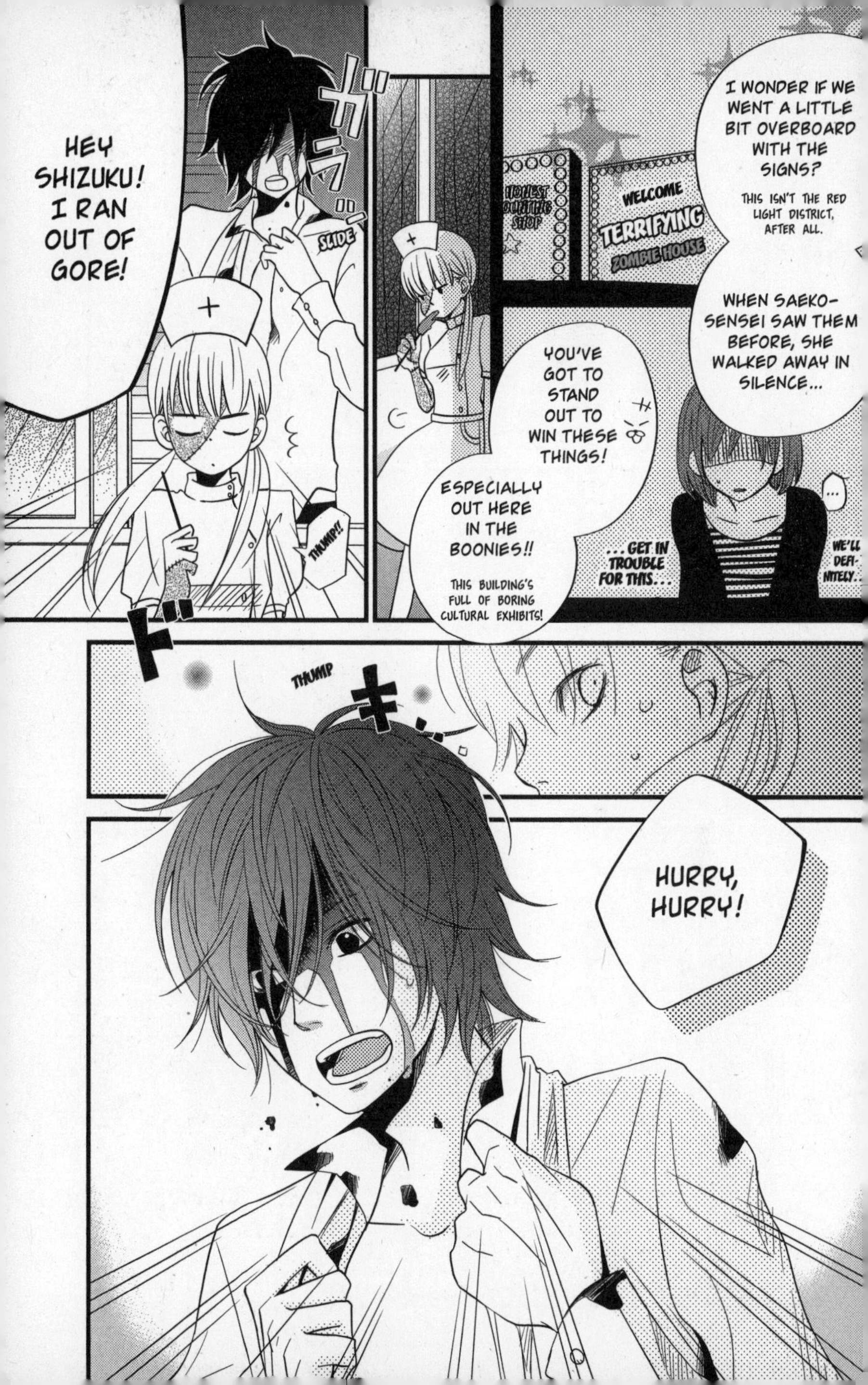
I WONDER IF WE WENT A LITTLE BIT OVERBOARD WITH THE SIGNS?
THIS ISN'T THE RED LIGHT DISTRICT, AFTER ALL.
WELCOME
TERRIFYING
ZOMBIE HOUSE
WHEN SAEKO-SENSEI SAW THEM BEFORE, SHE WALKED AWAY IN SILENCE...
...
WE'LL DEFI-NITELY...
...GET IN TROUBLE FOR THIS...
YOU'VE GOT TO STAND OUT TO WIN THESE THINGS!
ESPECIALLY OUT HERE IN THE BOONIES!!
THIS BUILDING'S FULL OF BORING CULTURAL EXHIBITS!
SLIDE
HEY SHIZUKU! I RAN OUT OF GORE!
THUMP!!
THUMP
HURRY, HURRY!

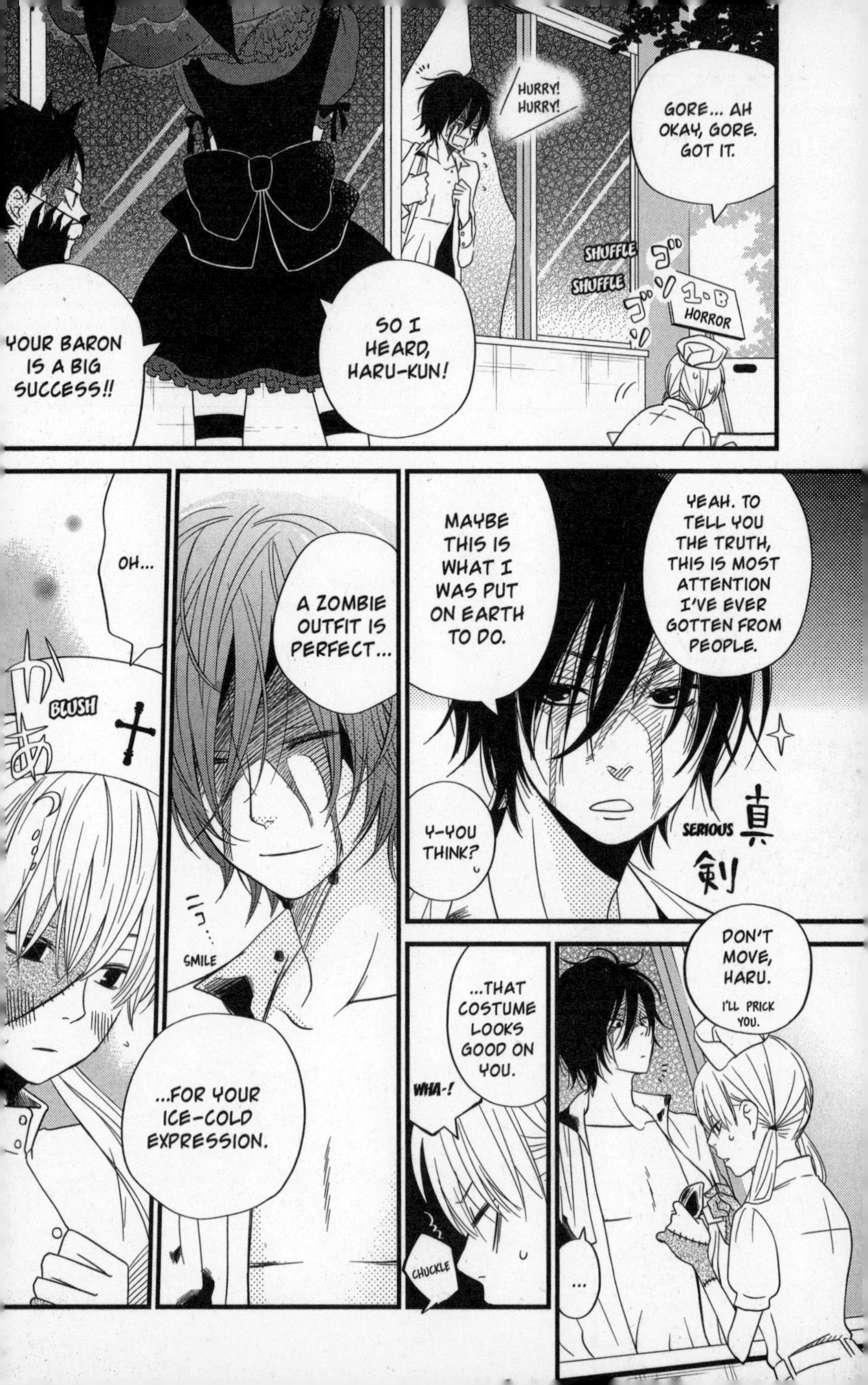
GORE... AH OKAY, GORE. GOT IT.
HURRY! HURRY!
SHUFFLE
SHUFFLE
1-B
HORROR
SO I HEARD, HARU-KUN!
YOUR BARON IS A BIG SUCCESS!!
YEAH. TO TELL YOU THE TRUTH, THIS IS MOST ATTENTION I'VE EVER GOTTEN FROM PEOPLE.
MAYBE THIS IS WHAT I WAS PUT ON EARTH TO DO.
SERIOUS
Y-YOU THINK?
DON'T MOVE, HARU.
I'LL PRICK YOU.
...THAT COSTUME LOOKS GOOD ON YOU.
WHA-!
CHUCKLE
...
A ZOMBIE OUTFIT IS PERFECT...
SMILE
...FOR YOUR ICE-COLD EXPRESSION.
OH...
BLUSH

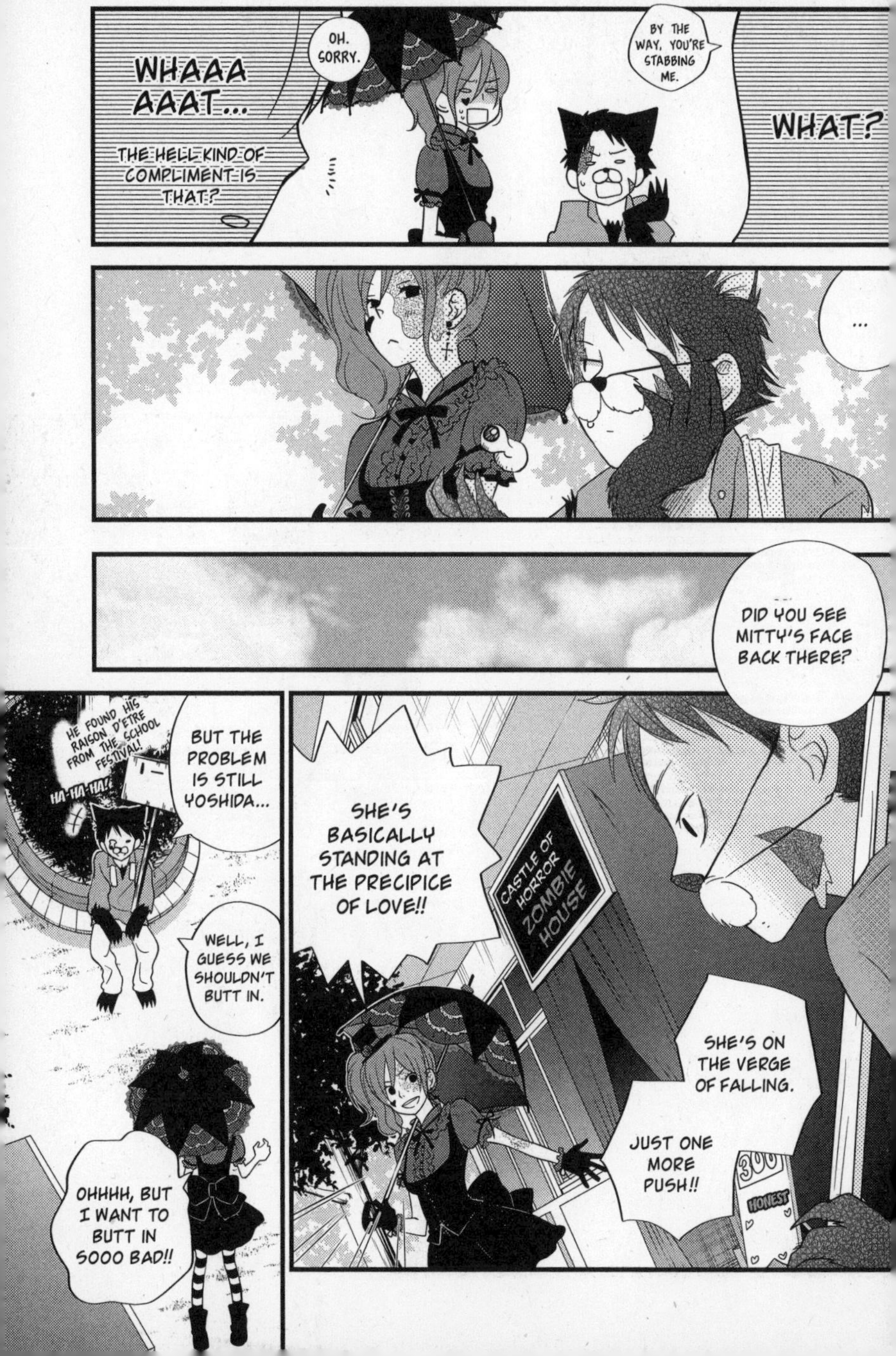
BY THE WAY, YOU'RE STABBING ME.
OH. SORRY.
WHAT?
WHAAAAAAT...
THE HELL KIND OF COMPLIMENT IS THAT?
...
DID YOU SEE MITTY'S FACE BACK THERE?
SHE'S BASICALLY STANDING AT THE PRECIPICE OF LOVE!!
CASTLE OF HORROR ZOMBIE HOUSE
SHE'S ON THE VERGE OF FALLING.
JUST ONE MORE PUSH!!
300
HONEST
BUT THE PROBLEM IS STILL YOSHIDA...
HE FOUND HIS RAISON D'ETRE FROM THE SCHOOL FESTIVAL!
HA-HA-HA!
WELL, I GUESS WE SHOULDN'T BUTT IN.
OHHHH, BUT I WANT TO BUTT IN SOOO BAD!!

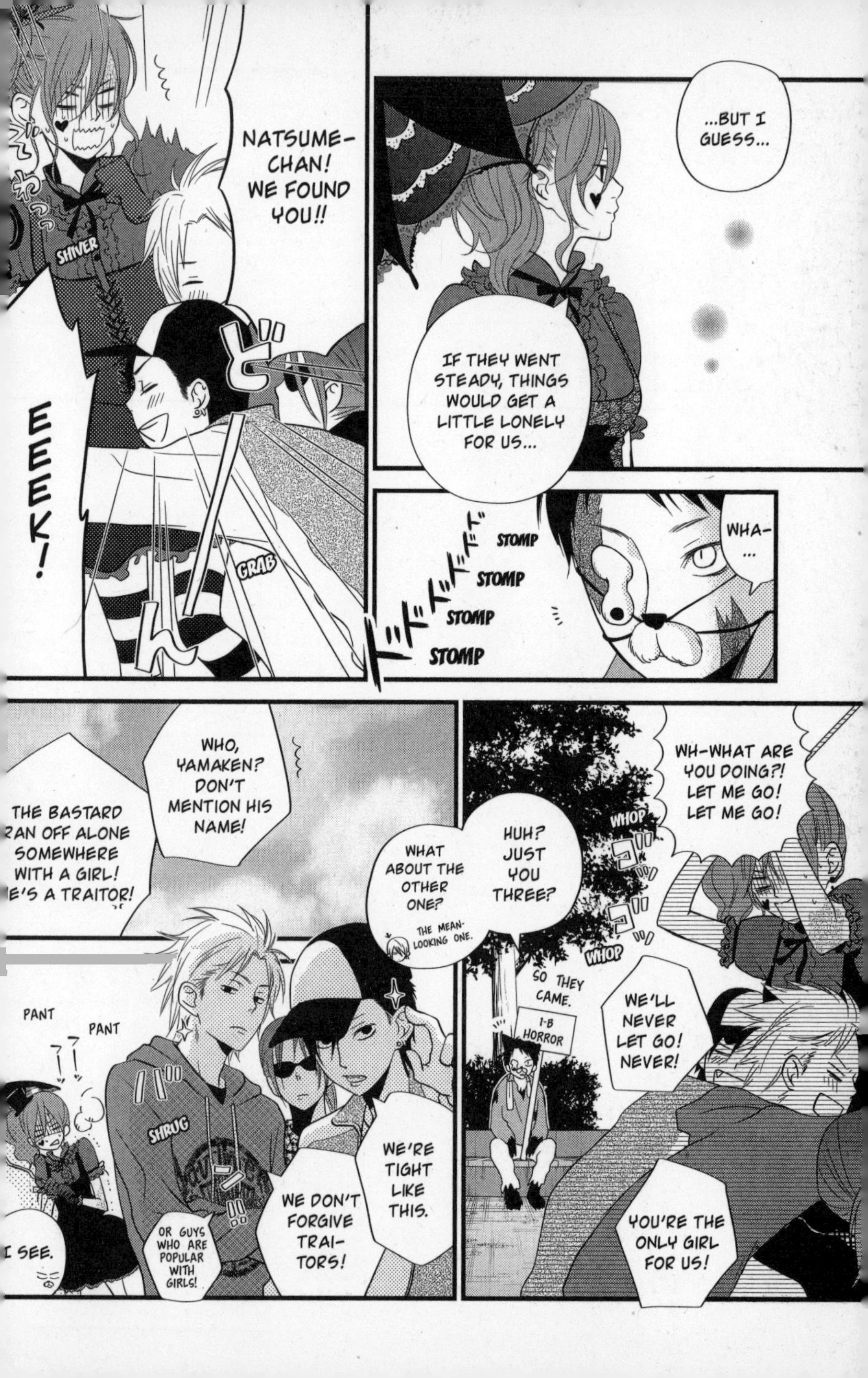
...BUT I GUESS...
IF THEY WENT STEADY, THINGS WOULD GET A LITTLE LONELY FOR US...
WHA-...
STOMP
STOMP
STOMP
STOMP
NATSUME-CHAN! WE FOUND YOU!!
SHIVER
EEEEK!
GRAB
WH-WHAT ARE YOU DOING?! LET ME GO! LET ME GO!
WHOP
WHOP
SO THEY CAME.
1-B HORROR
WE'LL NEVER LET GO! NEVER!
YOU'RE THE ONLY GIRL FOR US!
HUH? JUST YOU THREE?
WHAT ABOUT THE OTHER ONE?
THE MEAN-LOOKING ONE.
WHO, YAMAKEN? DON'T MENTION HIS NAME!
THE BASTARD RAN OFF ALONE SOMEWHERE WITH A GIRL! E'S A TRAITOR!
WE'RE TIGHT LIKE THIS.
WE DON'T FORGIVE TRAI-TORS!
OR GUYS WHO ARE POPULAR WITH GIRLS!
SHRUG
PANT
PANT
I SEE.

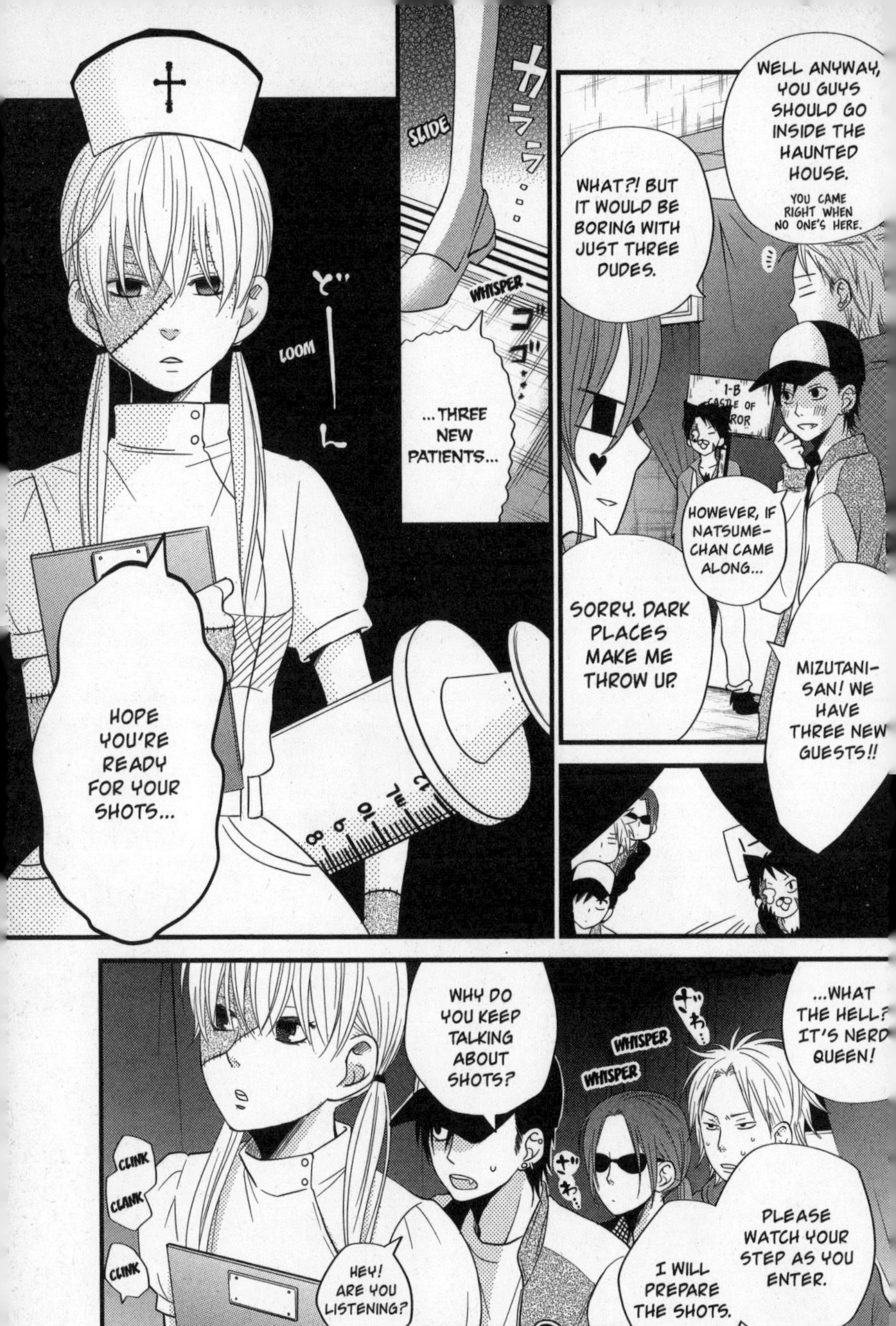
WELL ANYWAY, YOU GUYS SHOULD GO INSIDE THE HAUNTED HOUSE.
YOU CAME RIGHT WHEN NO ONE'S HERE.
WHAT?! BUT IT WOULD BE BORING WITH JUST THREE DUDES.
!
1-B
HOWEVER, IF NATSUME-CHAN CAME ALONG...
SORRY. DARK PLACES MAKE ME THROW UP.
MIZUTANI-SAN! WE HAVE THREE NEW GUESTS!!
カララ...
SLIDE
ゴゴ...
WHISPER
...THREE NEW PATIENTS...
どーん
LOOM
HOPE YOU'RE READY FOR YOUR SHOTS...
...WHAT THE HELL? IT'S NERD QUEEN!
ざわ...
WHISPER
WHISPER
ざわ...
WHY DO YOU KEEP TALKING ABOUT SHOTS?
PLEASE WATCH YOUR STEP AS YOU ENTER.
I WILL PREPARE THE SHOTS.
HEY! ARE YOU LISTENING?
CLINK
CLANK
CLINK

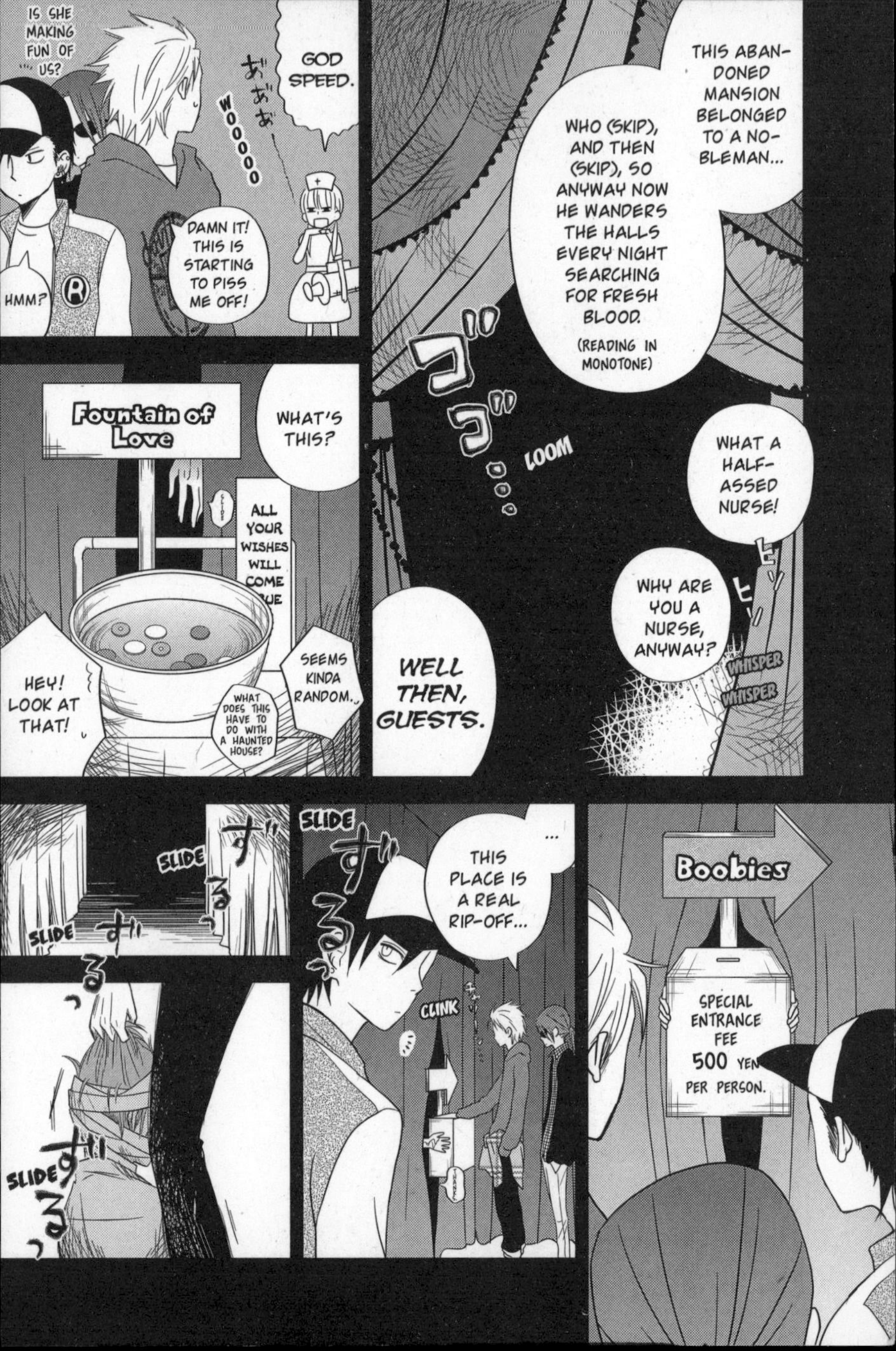
THIS ABANDONED MANSION BELONGED TO A NOBLEMAN...
WHO (SKIP), AND THEN (SKIP), SO ANYWAY NOW HE WANDERS THE HALLS EVERY NIGHT SEARCHING FOR FRESH BLOOD.
(READING IN MONOTONE)
LOOM
WHAT A HALF-ASSED NURSE!
WHY ARE YOU A NURSE, ANYWAY?
WHISPER
WHISPER
WELL THEN, GUESTS.
GOD SPEED.
WOOOOOO
IS SHE MAKING FUN OF US?
DAMN IT! THIS IS STARTING TO PISS ME OFF!
HMM?
WHAT'S THIS?
Fountain of Love
ALL YOUR WISHES WILL COME
SEEMS KINDA RANDOM...
WHAT DOES THIS HAVE TO DO WITH A HAUNTED HOUSE?
HEY! LOOK AT THAT!
Boobies
SPECIAL ENTRANCE FEE 500 YEN PER PERSON.
...
THIS PLACE IS A REAL RIP-OFF...
SLIDE
CLINK
...
SLIDE
SLIDE
SLIDE

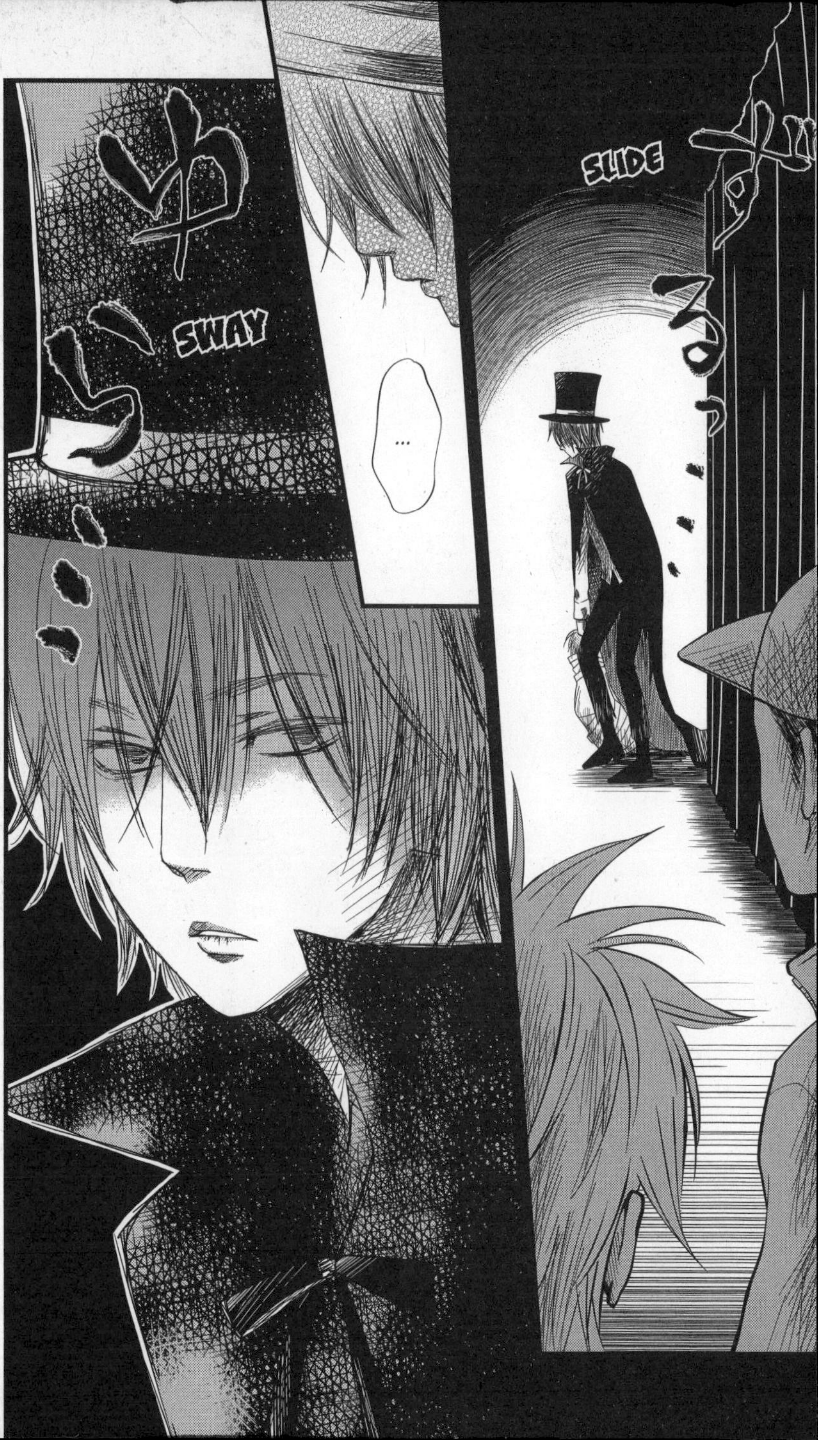
SLIDE
...
SWAY

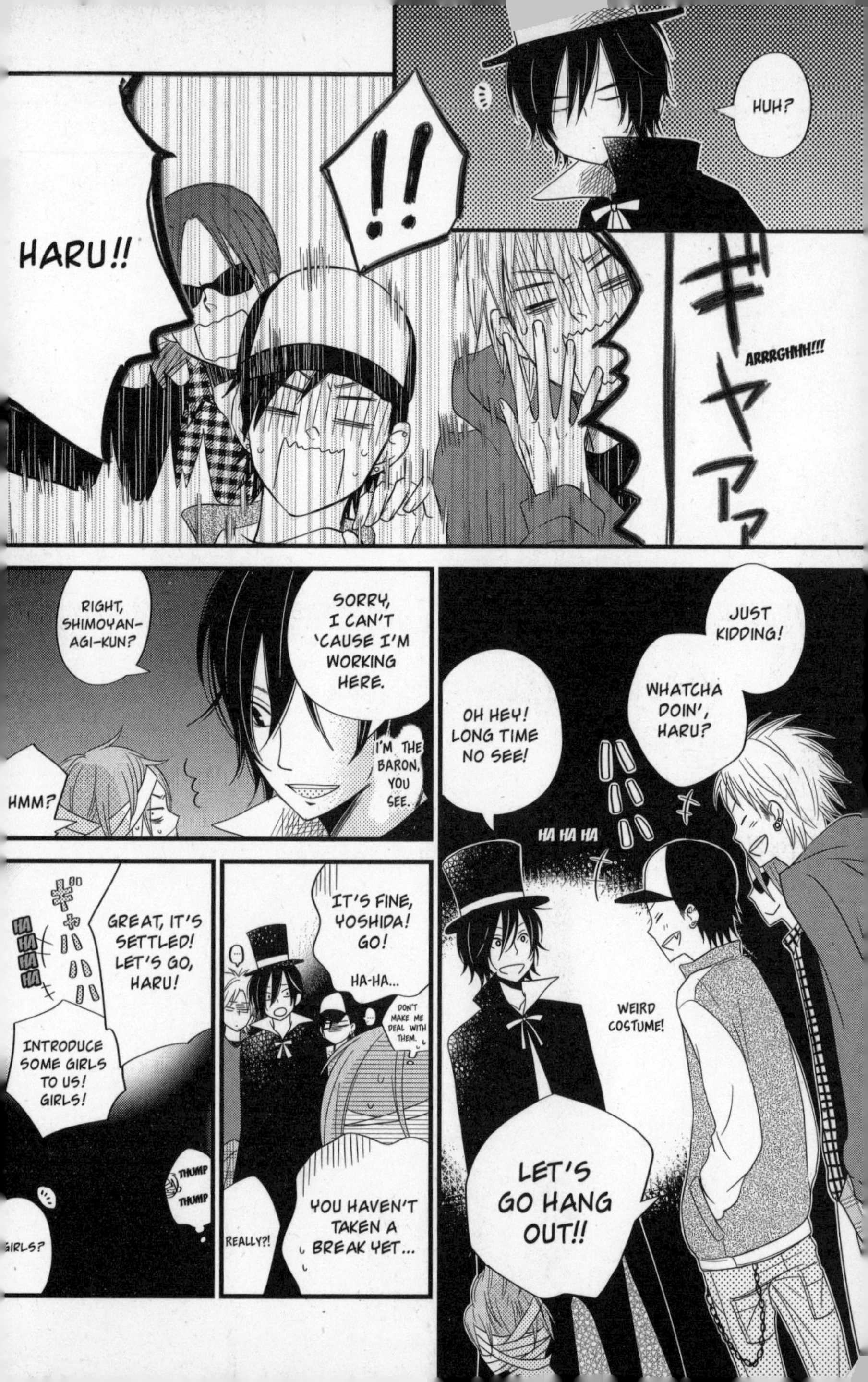
HUH?
...
ARRRGHHH!!!
!!
HARU!!
JUST KIDDING!
WHATCHA DOIN', HARU?
OH HEY! LONG TIME NO SEE!
HA HA HA
WEIRD COSTUME!
LET'S GO HANG OUT!!
SORRY, I CAN'T 'CAUSE I'M WORKING HERE.
I'M THE BARON, YOU SEE.
RIGHT, SHIMOYANAGI-KUN?
HMM?
IT'S FINE, YOSHIDA! GO!
HA-HA...
...
DON'T MAKE ME DEAL WITH THEM.
...
YOU HAVEN'T TAKEN A BREAK YET...
REALLY?!
GREAT, IT'S SETTLED! LET'S GO, HARU!
HA HA HA HA
INTRODUCE SOME GIRLS TO US! GIRLS!
THUMP
THUMP
GIRLS?

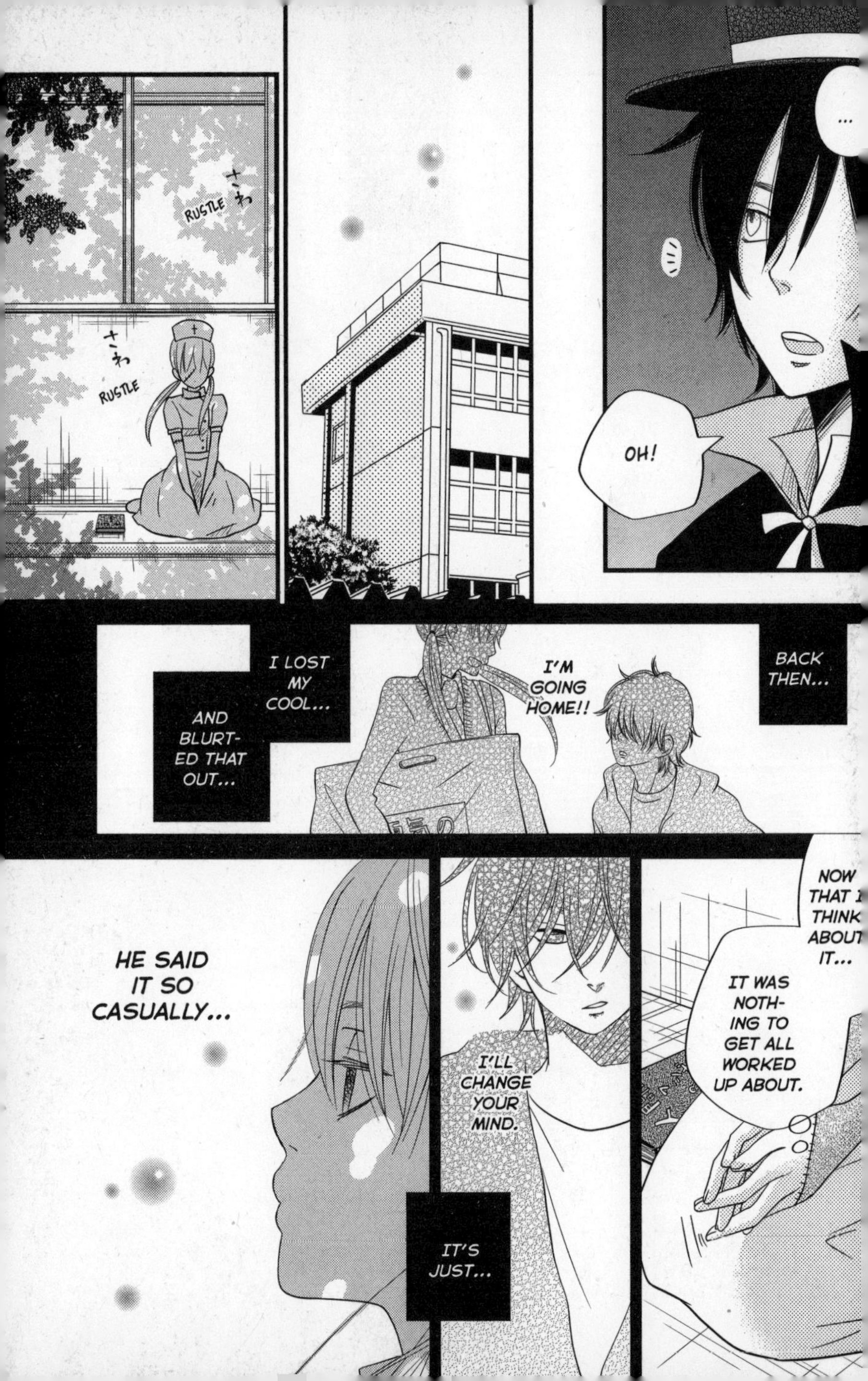
...
OH!
RUSTLE さわ
さわ RUSTLE
BACK THEN...
I'M GOING HOME!!
I LOST MY COOL...
AND BLURT-ED THAT OUT...
NOW THAT I THINK ABOUT IT...
IT WAS NOTH-ING TO GET ALL WORKED UP ABOUT.
I'LL CHANGE YOUR MIND.
IT'S JUST...
HE SAID IT SO CASUALLY...

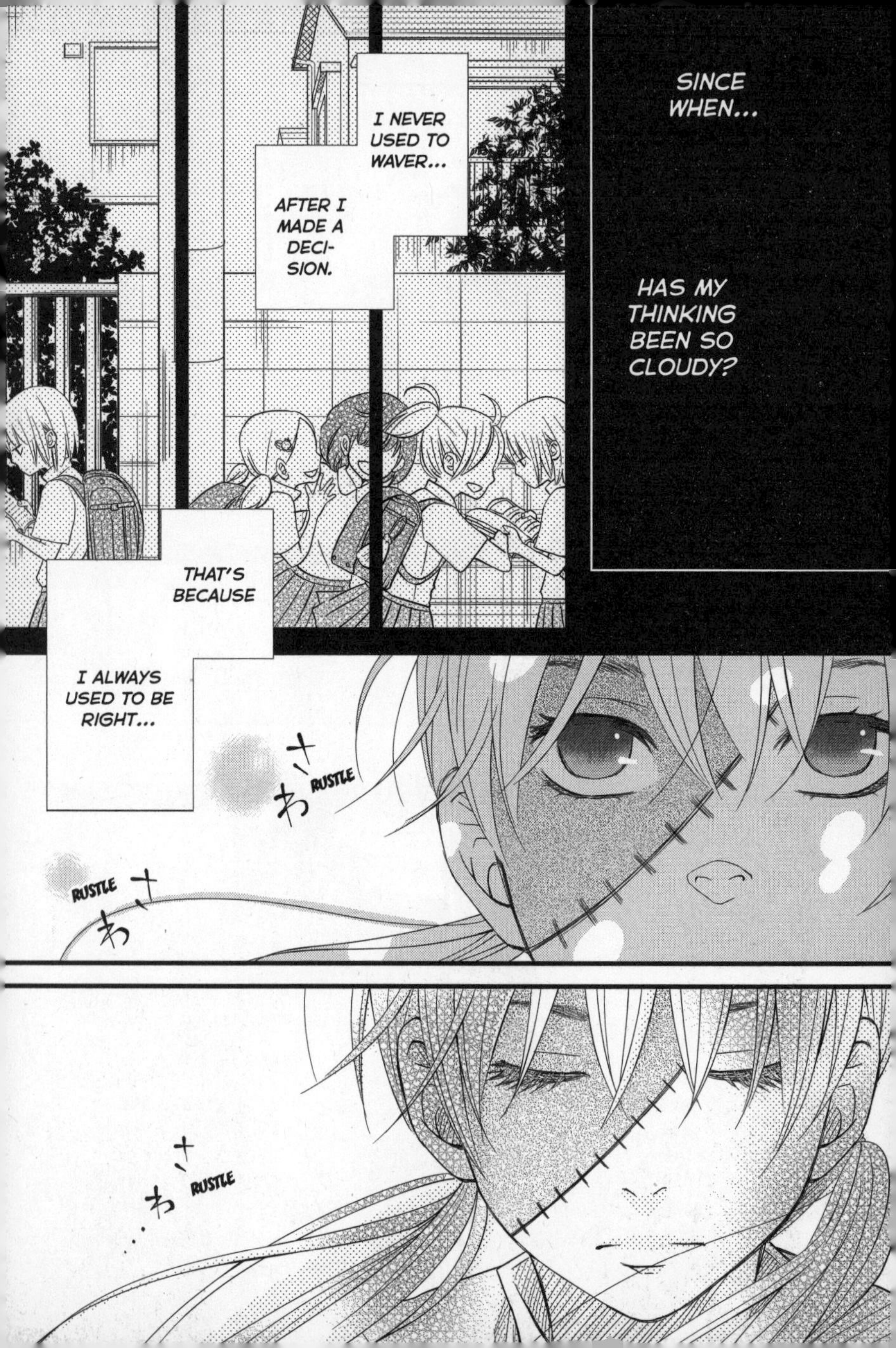
SINCE WHEN...
HAS MY THINKING BEEN SO CLOUDY?
I NEVER USED TO WAVER...
AFTER I MADE A DECI-SION.
THAT'S BECAUSE
I ALWAYS USED TO BE RIGHT...
さわ RUSTLE
さわ RUSTLE
さわ RUSTLE

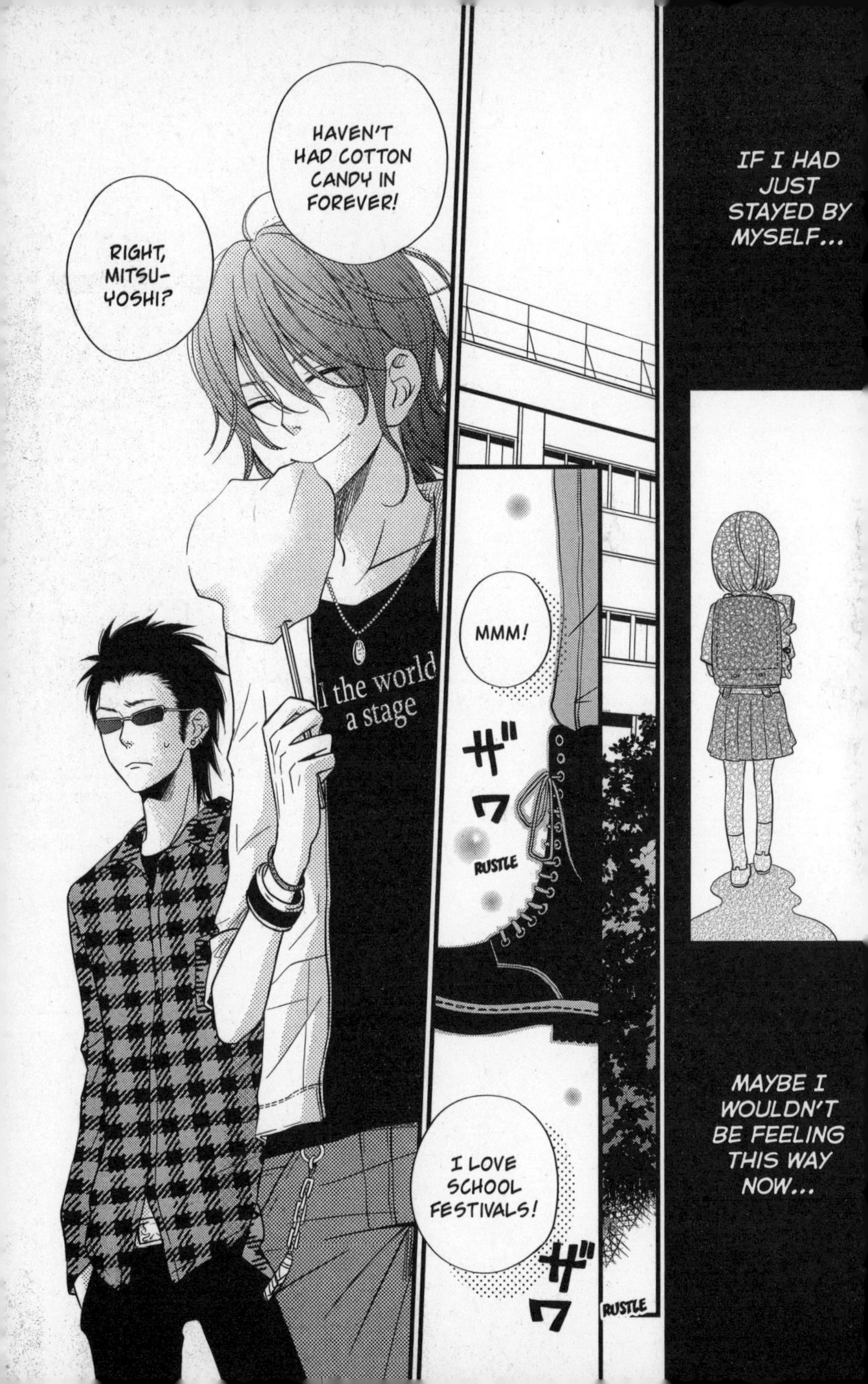
IF I HAD JUST STAYED BY MYSELF...
MAYBE I WOULDN'T BE FEELING THIS WAY NOW...
MMM!
ザワ
RUSTLE
I LOVE SCHOOL FESTIVALS!
ザワ
RUSTLE
HAVEN'T HAD COTTON CANDY IN FOREVER!
RIGHT, MITSU-YOSHI?
l the world a stage

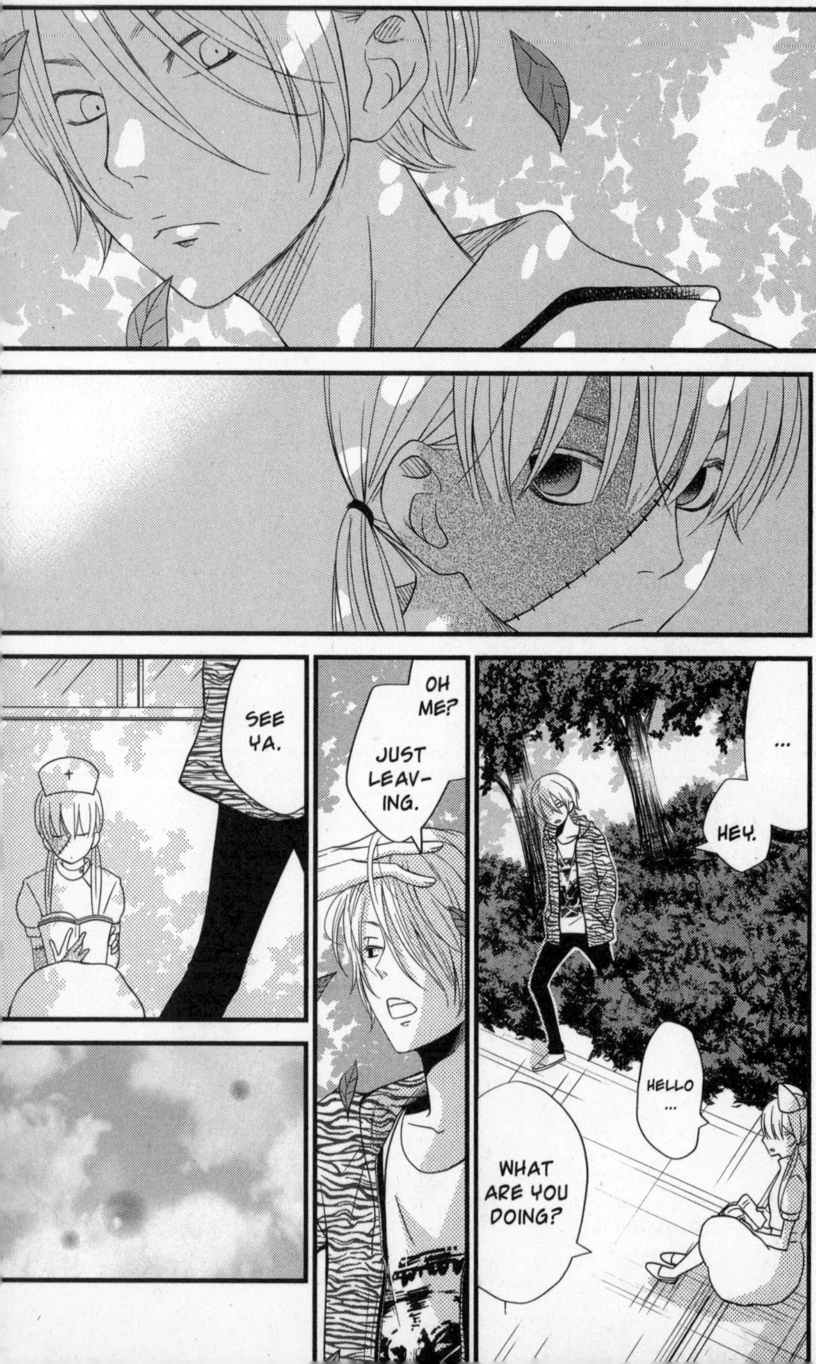
...
HEY.
HELLO ...
WHAT ARE YOU DOING?
OH ME?
JUST LEAV-ING.
SEE YA.

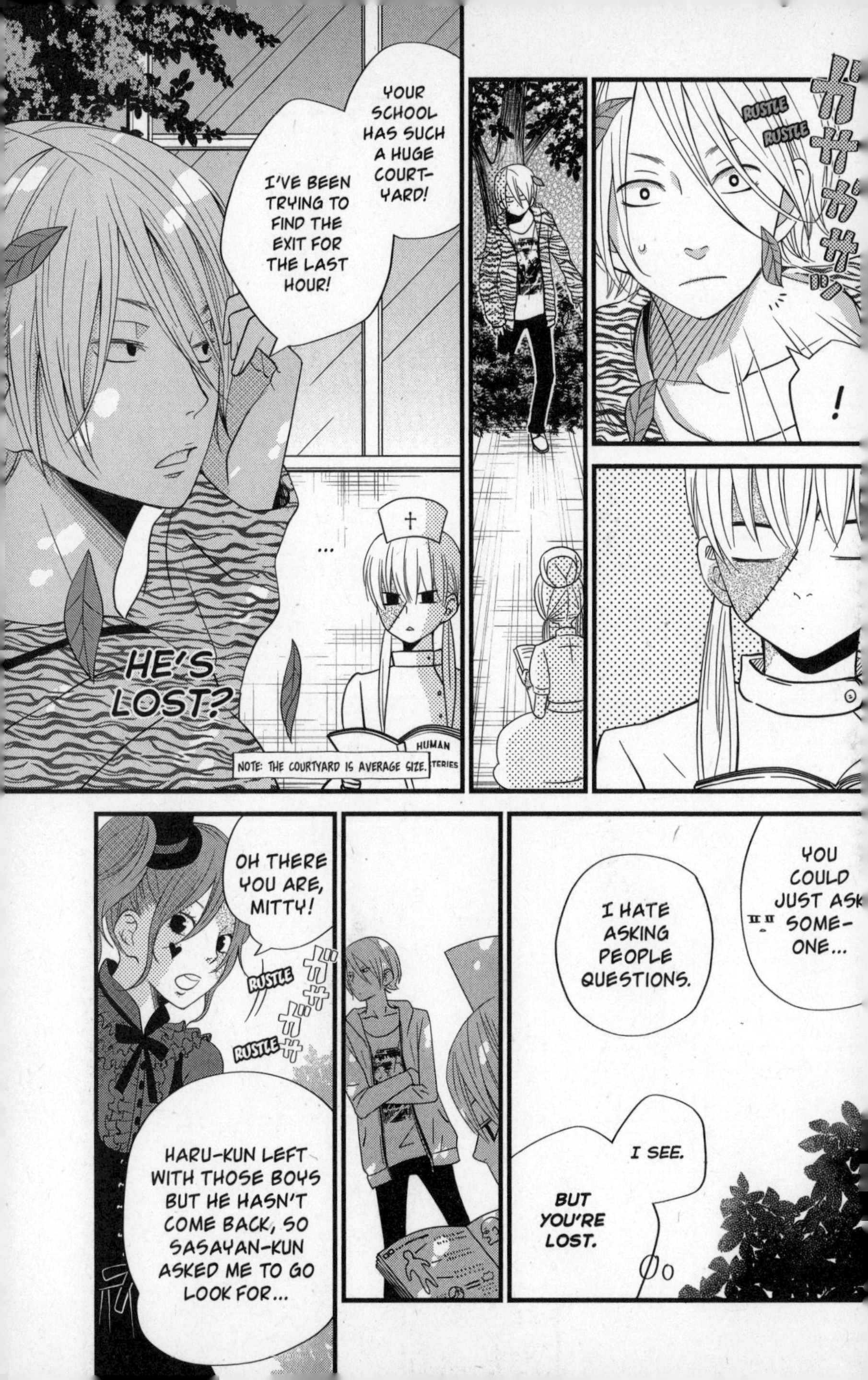
RUSTLE
RUSTLE
ガサガサッ
!
YOUR SCHOOL HAS SUCH A HUGE COURT-YARD!
I'VE BEEN TRYING TO FIND THE EXIT FOR THE LAST HOUR!
...
HE'S LOST?
HUMAN
NOTE: THE COURTYARD IS AVERAGE SIZE.
YOU COULD JUST ASK SOME-ONE...
I HATE ASKING PEOPLE QUESTIONS.
I SEE.
BUT YOU'RE LOST.
OH THERE YOU ARE, MITTY!
RUSTLE
ガサガサ
RUSTLE
HARU-KUN LEFT WITH THOSE BOYS BUT HE HASN'T COME BACK, SO SASAYAN-KUN ASKED ME TO GO LOOK FOR...

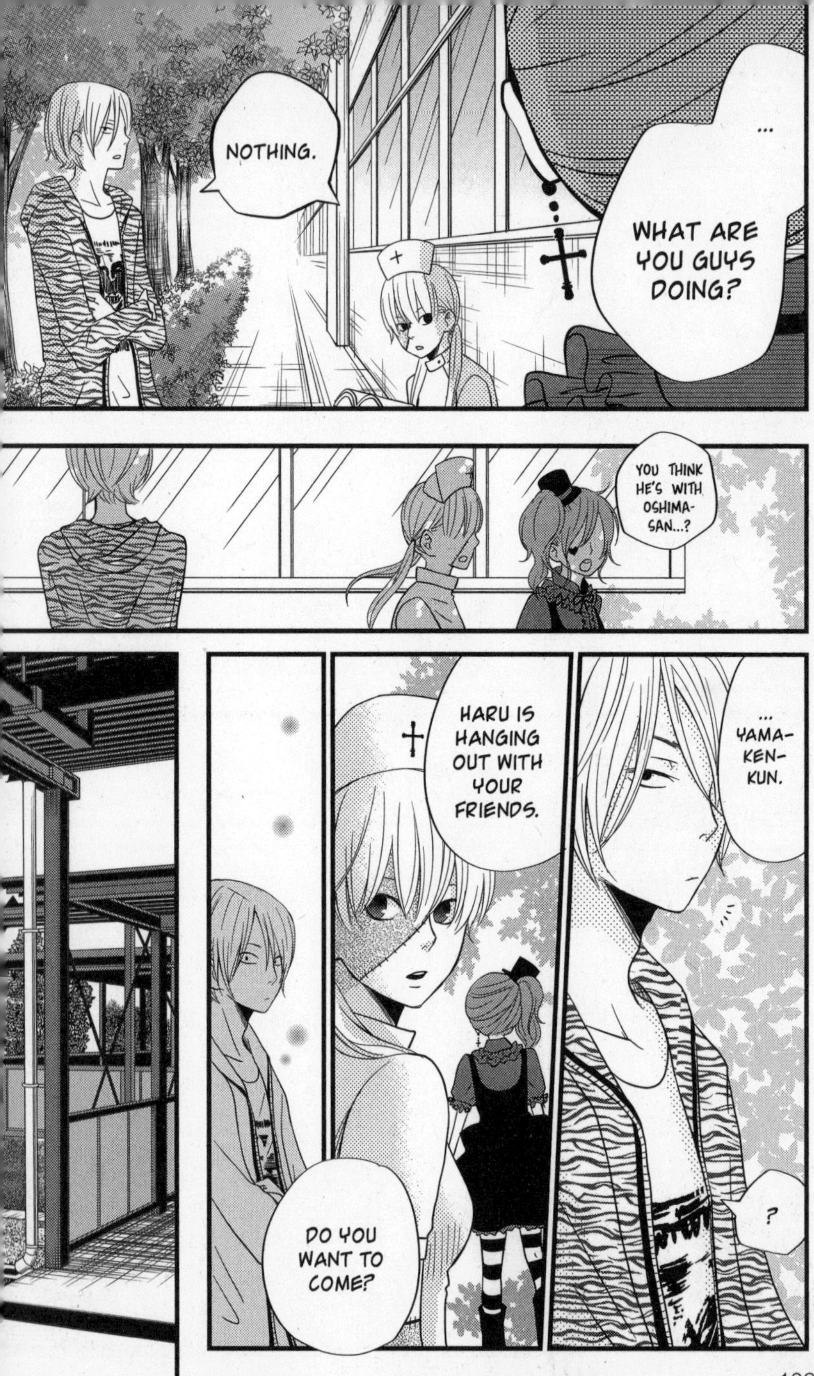
...
WHAT ARE YOU GUYS DOING?
NOTHING.
YOU THINK HE'S WITH OSHIMA-SAN...?
... YAMA-KEN-KUN.
?
HARU IS HANGING OUT WITH YOUR FRIENDS.
DO YOU WANT TO COME?

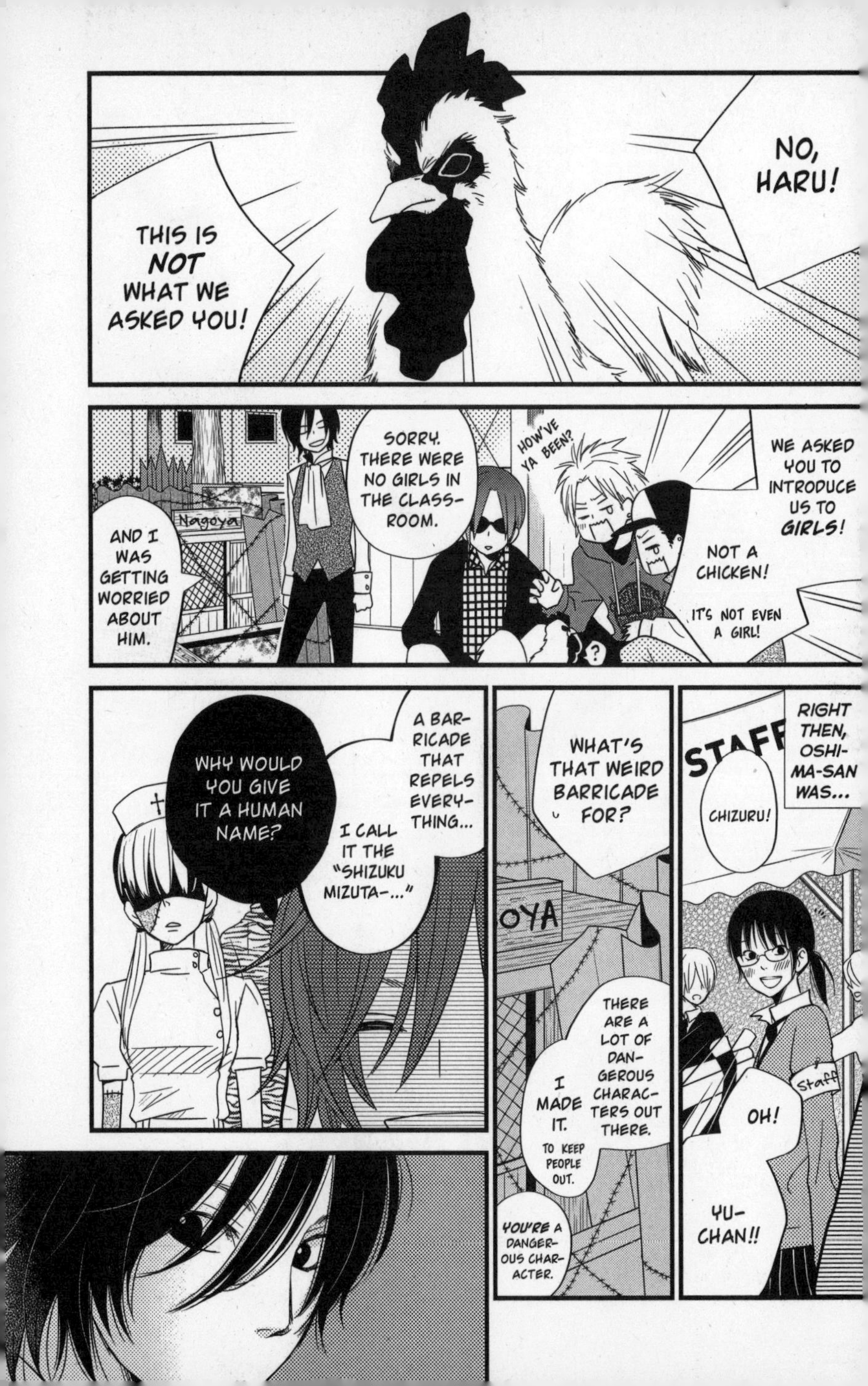
NO, HARU!
THIS IS NOT WHAT WE ASKED YOU!
WE ASKED YOU TO INTRODUCE US TO GIRLS!
NOT A CHICKEN!
IT'S NOT EVEN A GIRL!
HOW'VE YA BEEN?
SORRY. THERE WERE NO GIRLS IN THE CLASS-ROOM.
Nagoya
AND I WAS GETTING WORRIED ABOUT HIM.
RIGHT THEN, OSHIMA-SAN WAS...
STAFF
CHIZURU!
OH!
YU-CHAN!!
WHAT'S THAT WEIRD BARRICADE FOR?
THERE ARE A LOT OF DAN-GEROUS CHARAC-TERS OUT THERE.
I MADE IT.
TO KEEP PEOPLE OUT.
YOU'RE A DANGER-OUS CHAR-ACTER.
A BAR-RICADE THAT REPELS EVERY-THING...
I CALL IT THE "SHIZUKU MIZUTA-..."
WHY WOULD YOU GIVE IT A HUMAN NAME?

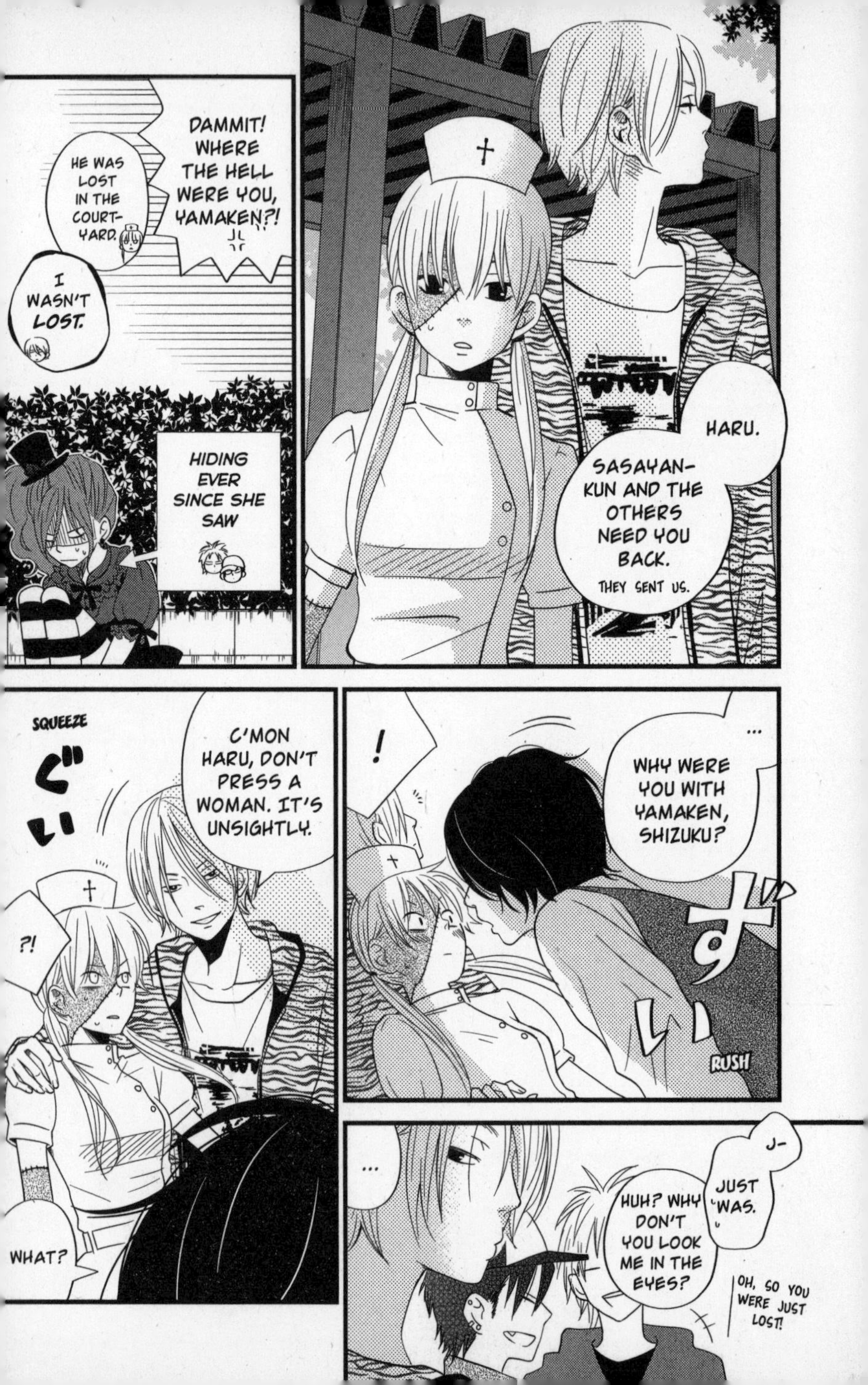
HARU.
SASAYAN-KUN AND THE OTHERS NEED YOU BACK.
THEY SENT US.
DAMMIT! WHERE THE HELL WERE YOU, YAMAKEN?!
HE WAS LOST IN THE COURT-YARD.
I WASN'T LOST.
HIDING EVER SINCE SHE SAW
...
WHY WERE YOU WITH YAMAKEN, SHIZUKU?
!
RUSH
J-
JUST WAS.
HUH? WHY DON'T YOU LOOK ME IN THE EYES?
OH, SO YOU WERE JUST LOST!
...
SQUEEZE
C'MON HARU, DON'T PRESS A WOMAN. IT'S UNSIGHTLY.
?!
WHAT?

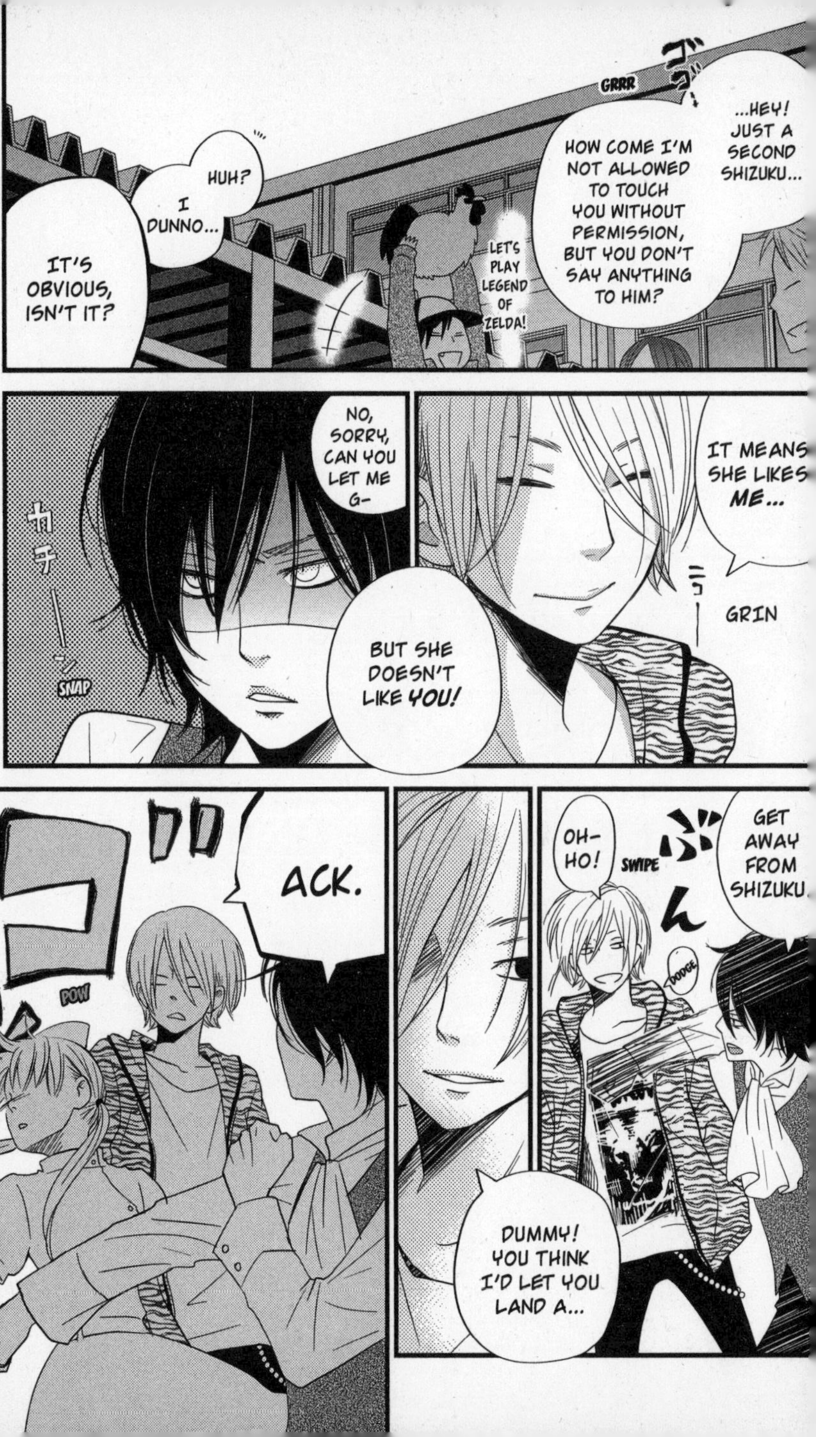
...HEY! JUST A SECOND SHIZUKU...
GRRR
HOW COME I'M NOT ALLOWED TO TOUCH YOU WITHOUT PERMISSION, BUT YOU DON'T SAY ANYTHING TO HIM?
LET'S PLAY LEGEND OF ZELDA!
HUH?
I DUNNO...
IT'S OBVIOUS, ISN'T IT?
IT MEANS SHE LIKES ME...
GRIN
NO, SORRY, CAN YOU LET ME G-
BUT SHE DOESN'T LIKE YOU!
SNAP
GET AWAY FROM SHIZUKU
ぶん
SWIPE
OH-HO!
DODGE
DUMMY! YOU THINK I'D LET YOU LAND A...
ACK.
POW

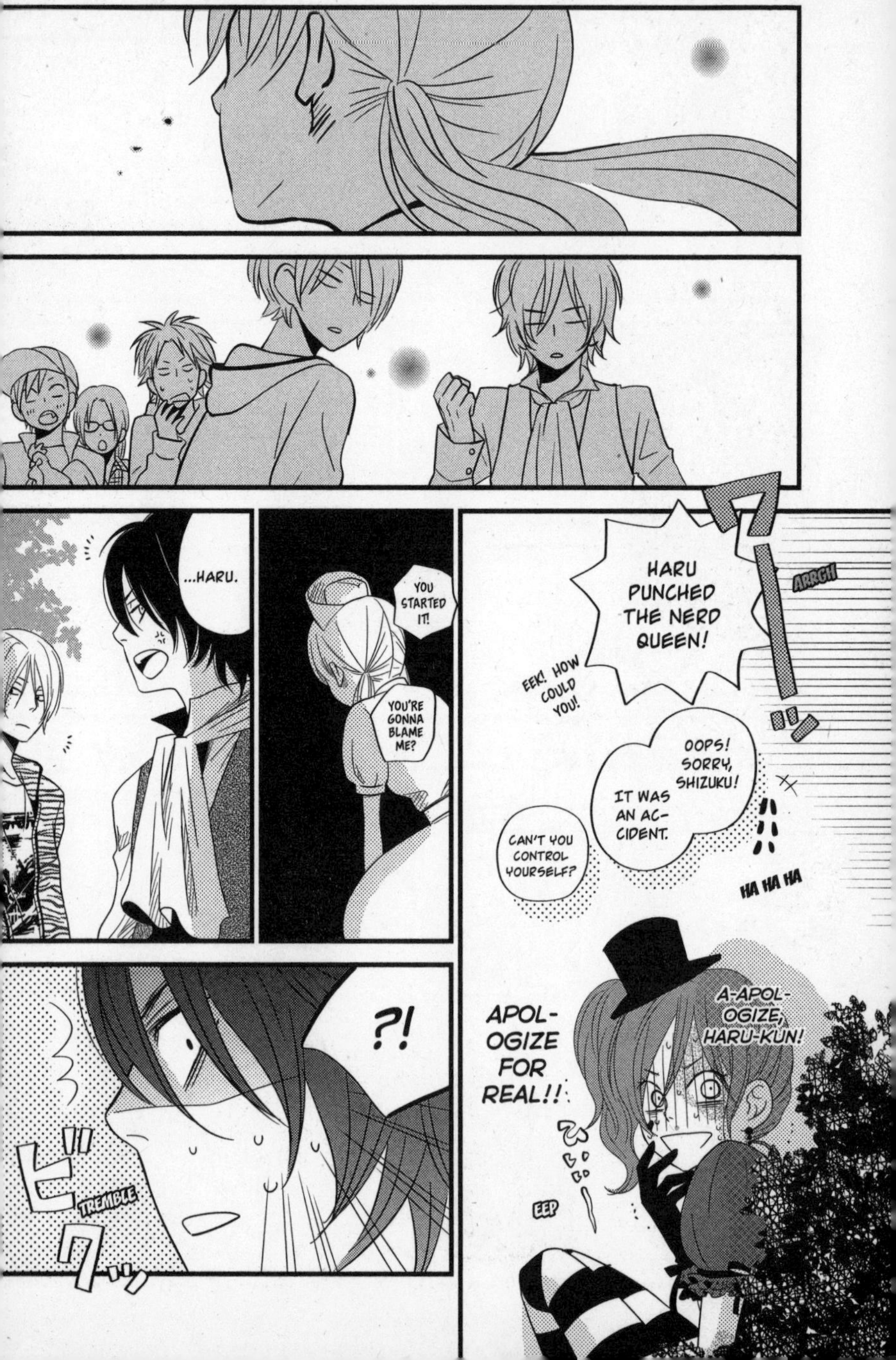
HARU PUNCHED THE NERD QUEEN!
ARRGH
EEK! HOW COULD YOU!
OOPS! SORRY, SHIZUKU!
IT WAS AN ACCIDENT.
CAN'T YOU CONTROL YOURSELF?
HA HA HA
A-APOL-OGIZE, HARU-KUN!
APOL-OGIZE FOR REAL!!
EEP
YOU STARTED IT!
YOU'RE GONNA BLAME ME?
...HARU.
?!
TREMBLE

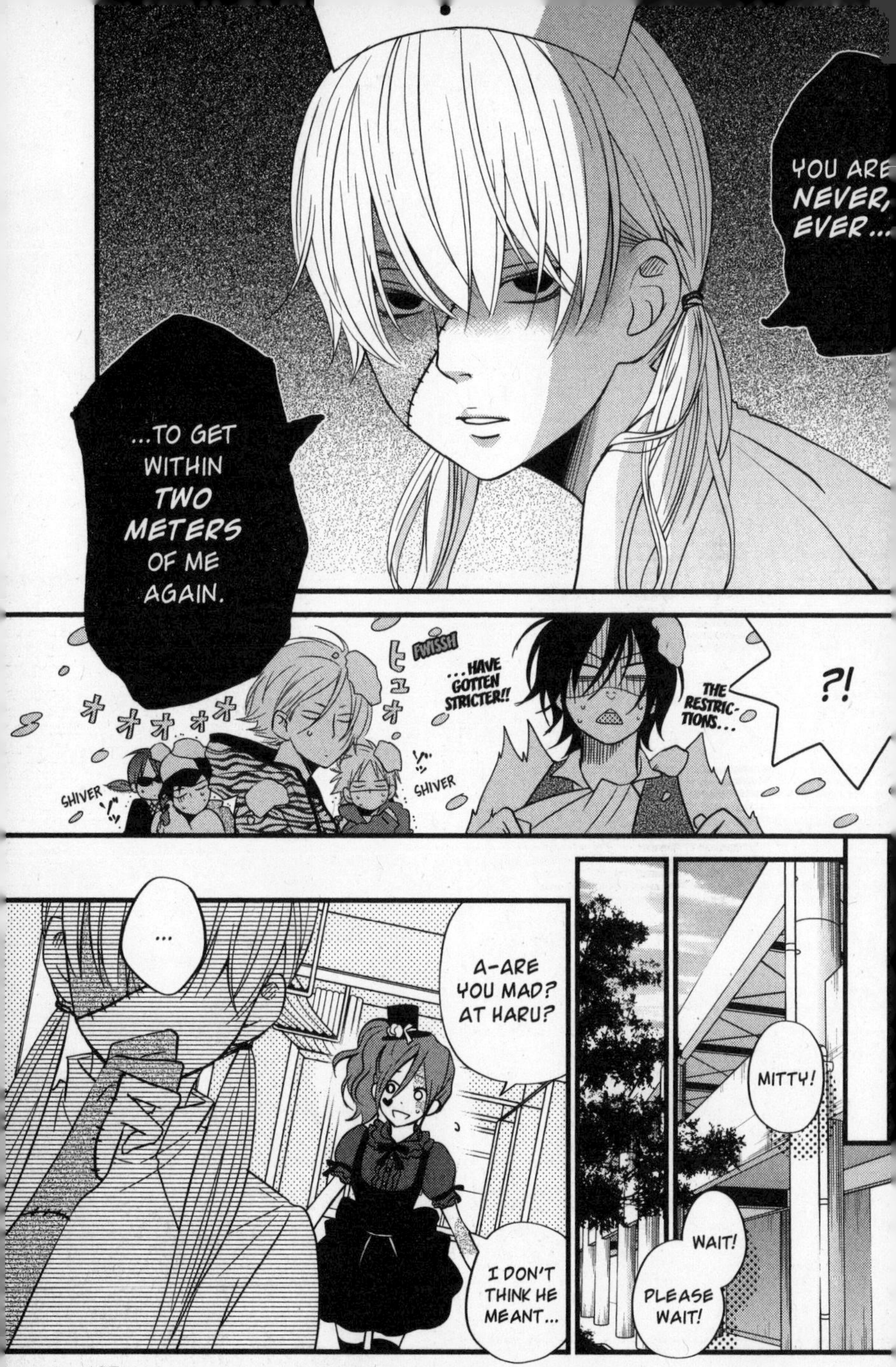
YOU ARE NEVER, EVER...
...TO GET WITHIN TWO METERS OF ME AGAIN.
?!
THE RESTRICTIONS...
...HAVE GOTTEN STRICTER!!
FWISSH
ヒュオ
オオオオオ
SHIVER
SHIVER
MITTY!
WAIT!
PLEASE WAIT!
A-ARE YOU MAD? AT HARU?
...
I DON'T THINK HE MEANT...

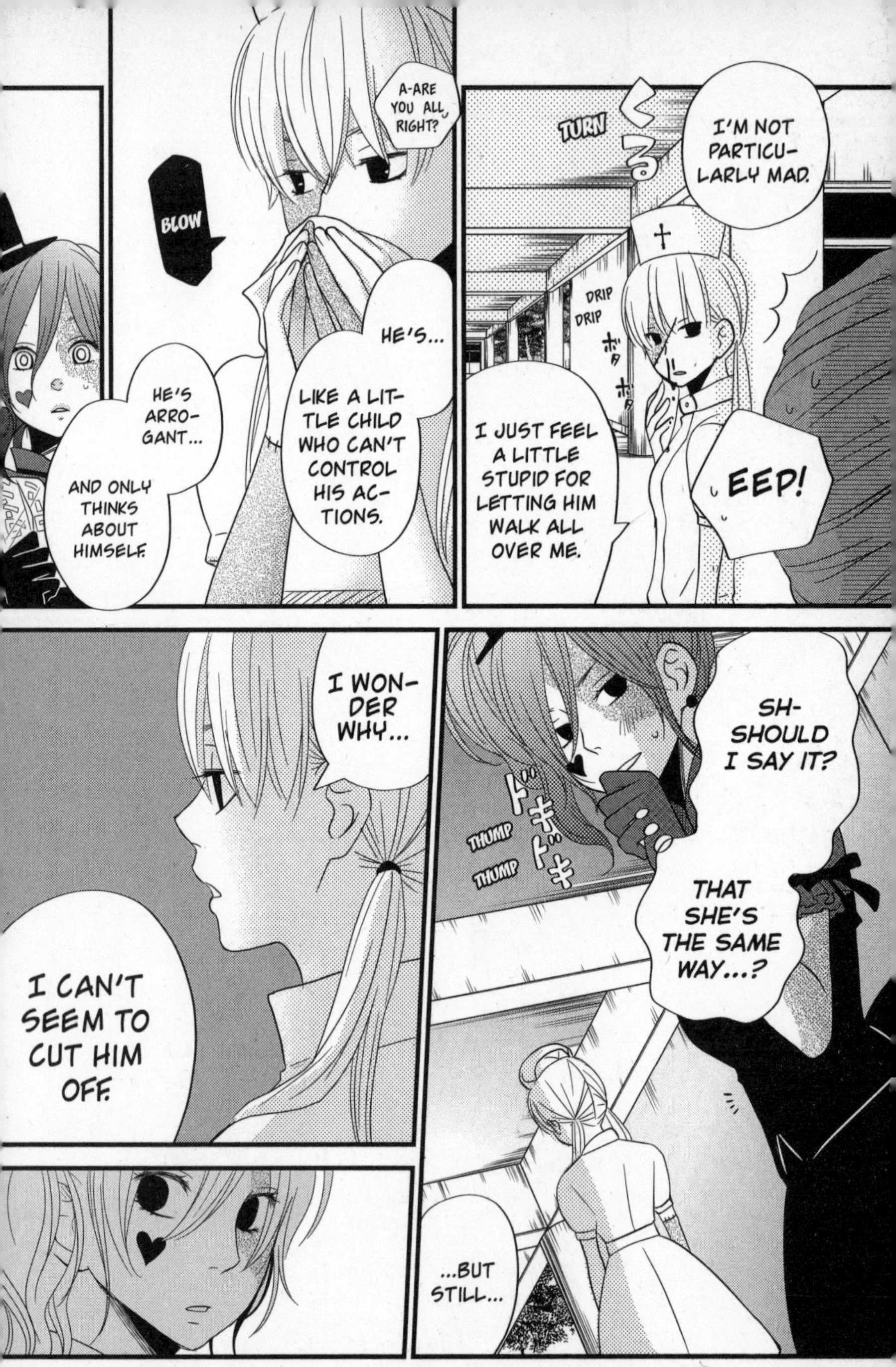
TURN
くる
I'M NOT PARTICU-LARLY MAD.
DRIP DRIP
ボタ ボタ
I JUST FEEL A LITTLE STUPID FOR LETTING HIM WALK ALL OVER ME.
EEP!
A-ARE YOU ALL RIGHT?
BLOW
HE'S...
LIKE A LIT-TLE CHILD WHO CAN'T CONTROL HIS AC-TIONS.
HE'S ARRO-GANT...
AND ONLY THINKS ABOUT HIMSELF.
THUMP THUMP
ドキドキ
SH-SHOULD I SAY IT?
THAT SHE'S THE SAME WAY...?
...BUT STILL...
I WON-DER WHY...
I CAN'T SEEM TO CUT HIM OFF.

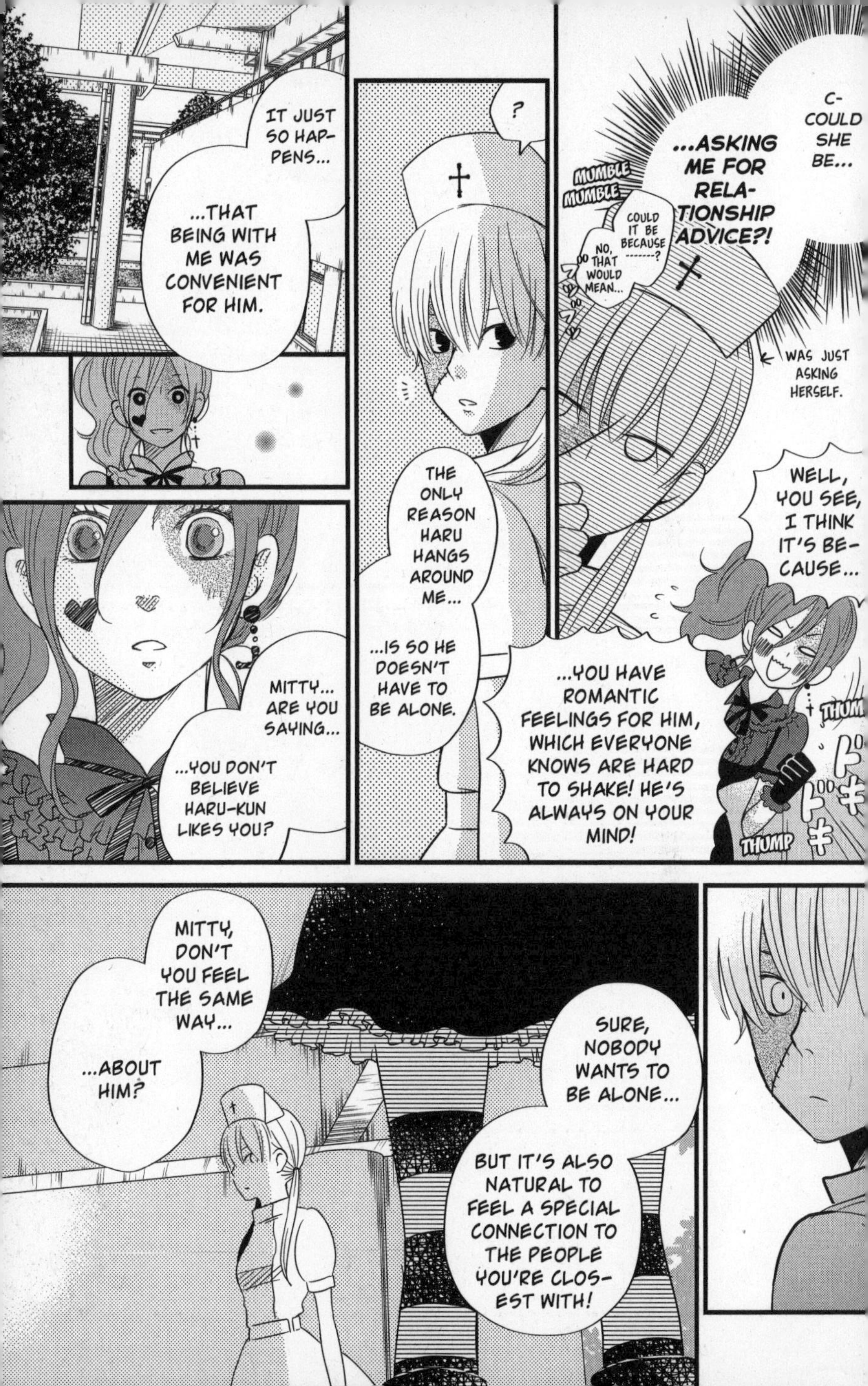
C-COULD SHE BE...
...ASKING ME FOR RELATIONSHIP ADVICE?!
COULD IT BE BECAUSE -------?
NO, THAT WOULD MEAN...
MUMBLE MUMBLE
WAS JUST ASKING HERSELF.
WELL, YOU SEE, I THINK IT'S BECAUSE...
...YOU HAVE ROMANTIC FEELINGS FOR HIM, WHICH EVERYONE KNOWS ARE HARD TO SHAKE! HE'S ALWAYS ON YOUR MIND!
THUMP
ドキドキ
THUMP
?
THE ONLY REASON HARU HANGS AROUND ME...
...IS SO HE DOESN'T HAVE TO BE ALONE.
IT JUST SO HAPPENS...
...THAT BEING WITH ME WAS CONVENIENT FOR HIM.
MITTY... ARE YOU SAYING...
...YOU DON'T BELIEVE HARU-KUN LIKES YOU?
SURE, NOBODY WANTS TO BE ALONE...
BUT IT'S ALSO NATURAL TO FEEL A SPECIAL CONNECTION TO THE PEOPLE YOU'RE CLOSEST WITH!
MITTY, DON'T YOU FEEL THE SAME WAY...
...ABOUT HIM?

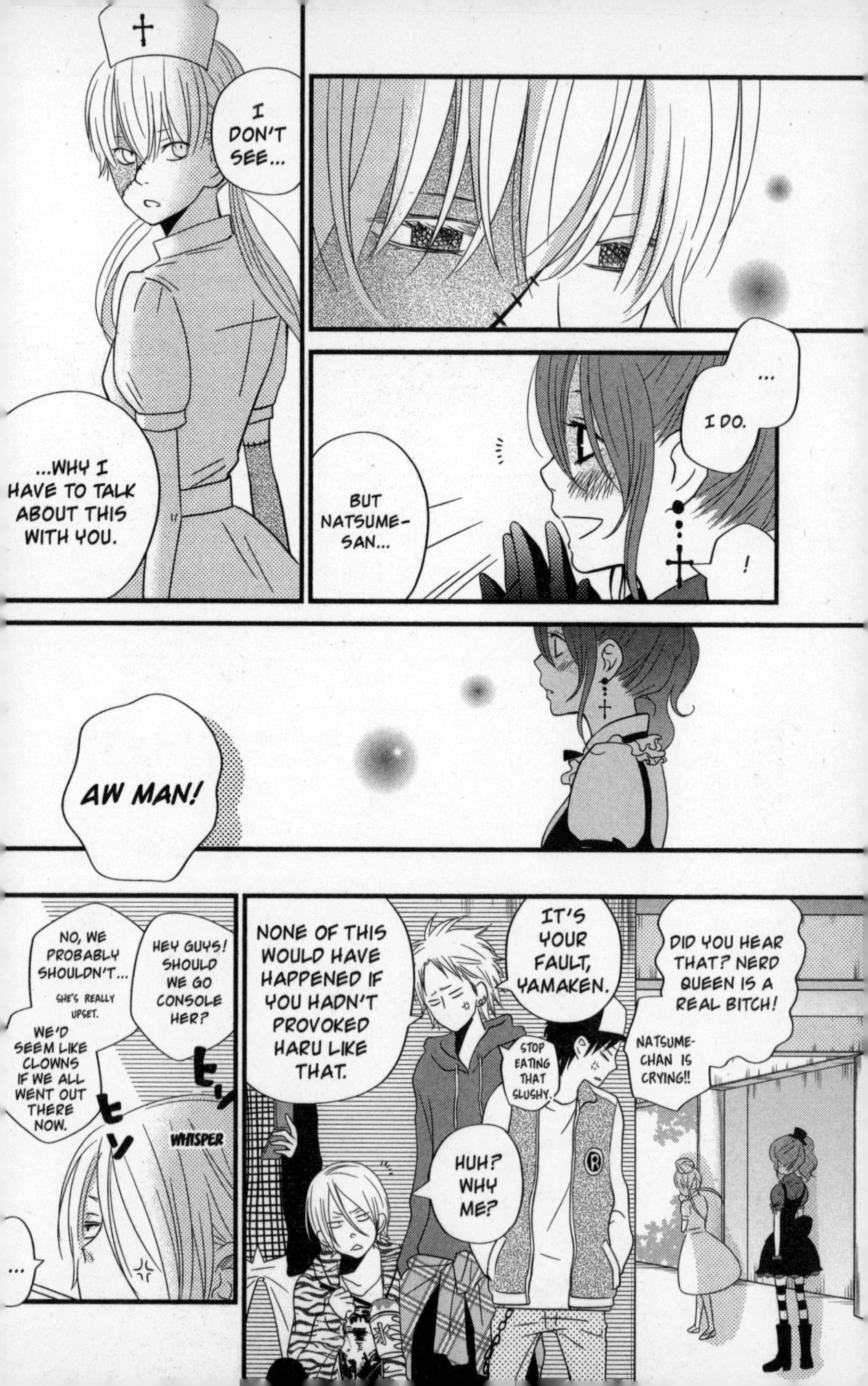
...
I DO.
BUT NATSUME-SAN...
!
I DON'T SEE...
...WHY I HAVE TO TALK ABOUT THIS WITH YOU.
AW MAN!
DID YOU HEAR THAT? NERD QUEEN IS A REAL BITCH!
NATSUME-CHAN IS CRYING!!
IT'S YOUR FAULT, YAMAKEN.
STOP EATING THAT SLUSHY.
NONE OF THIS WOULD HAVE HAPPENED IF YOU HADN'T PROVOKED HARU LIKE THAT.
HUH? WHY ME?
HEY GUYS! SHOULD WE GO CONSOLE HER?
NO, WE PROBABLY SHOULDN'T...
SHE'S REALLY UPSET.
WE'D SEEM LIKE CLOWNS IF WE ALL WENT OUT THERE NOW.
ヒソ ヒソ
WHISPER
...

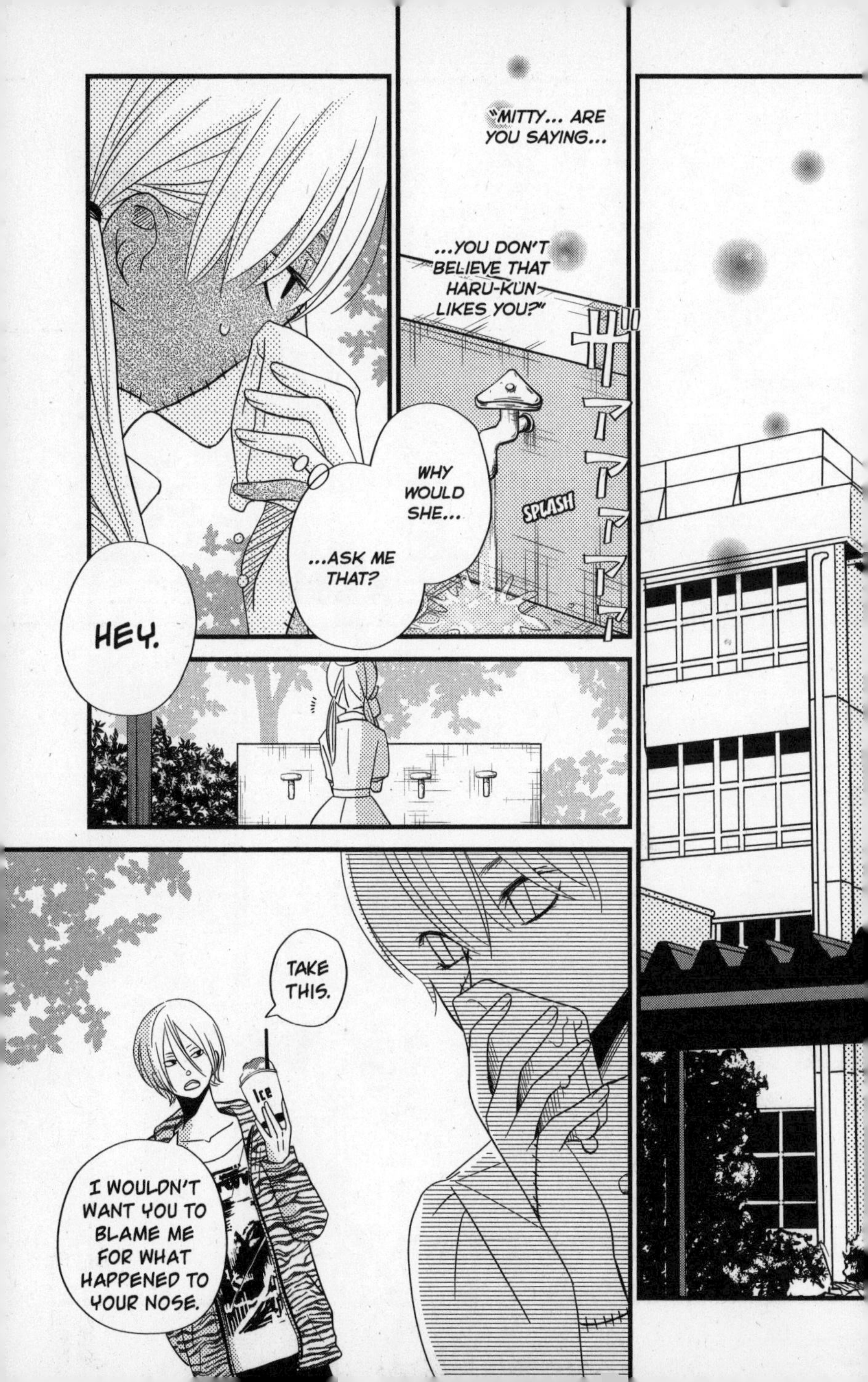
"MITTY... ARE YOU SAYING...
...YOU DON'T BELIEVE THAT HARU-KUN LIKES YOU?"
ザァァァァァ
SPLASH
WHY WOULD SHE...
...ASK ME THAT?
HEY.
TAKE THIS.
Ice
I WOULDN'T WANT YOU TO BLAME ME FOR WHAT HAPPENED TO YOUR NOSE.

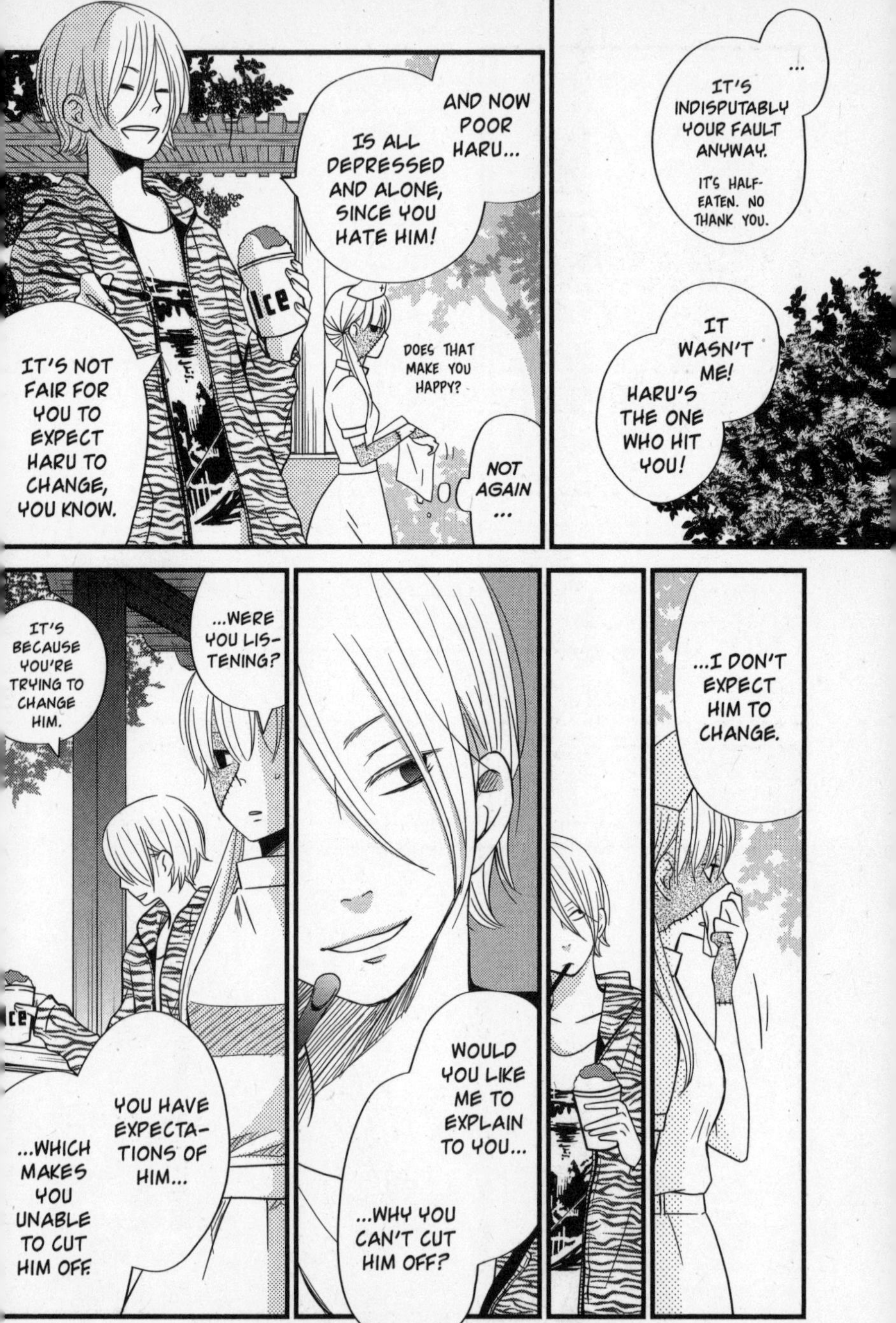
...
IT'S INDISPUTABLY YOUR FAULT ANYWAY.
IT'S HALF-EATEN. NO THANK YOU.
IT WASN'T ME!
HARU'S THE ONE WHO HIT YOU!
AND NOW POOR HARU...
IS ALL DEPRESSED AND ALONE, SINCE YOU HATE HIM!
DOES THAT MAKE YOU HAPPY?
NOT AGAIN ...
IT'S NOT FAIR FOR YOU TO EXPECT HARU TO CHANGE, YOU KNOW.
...I DON'T EXPECT HIM TO CHANGE.
WOULD YOU LIKE ME TO EXPLAIN TO YOU...
...WHY YOU CAN'T CUT HIM OFF?
...WERE YOU LISTENING?
IT'S BECAUSE YOU'RE TRYING TO CHANGE HIM.
YOU HAVE EXPECTATIONS OF HIM...
...WHICH MAKES YOU UNABLE TO CUT HIM OFF.

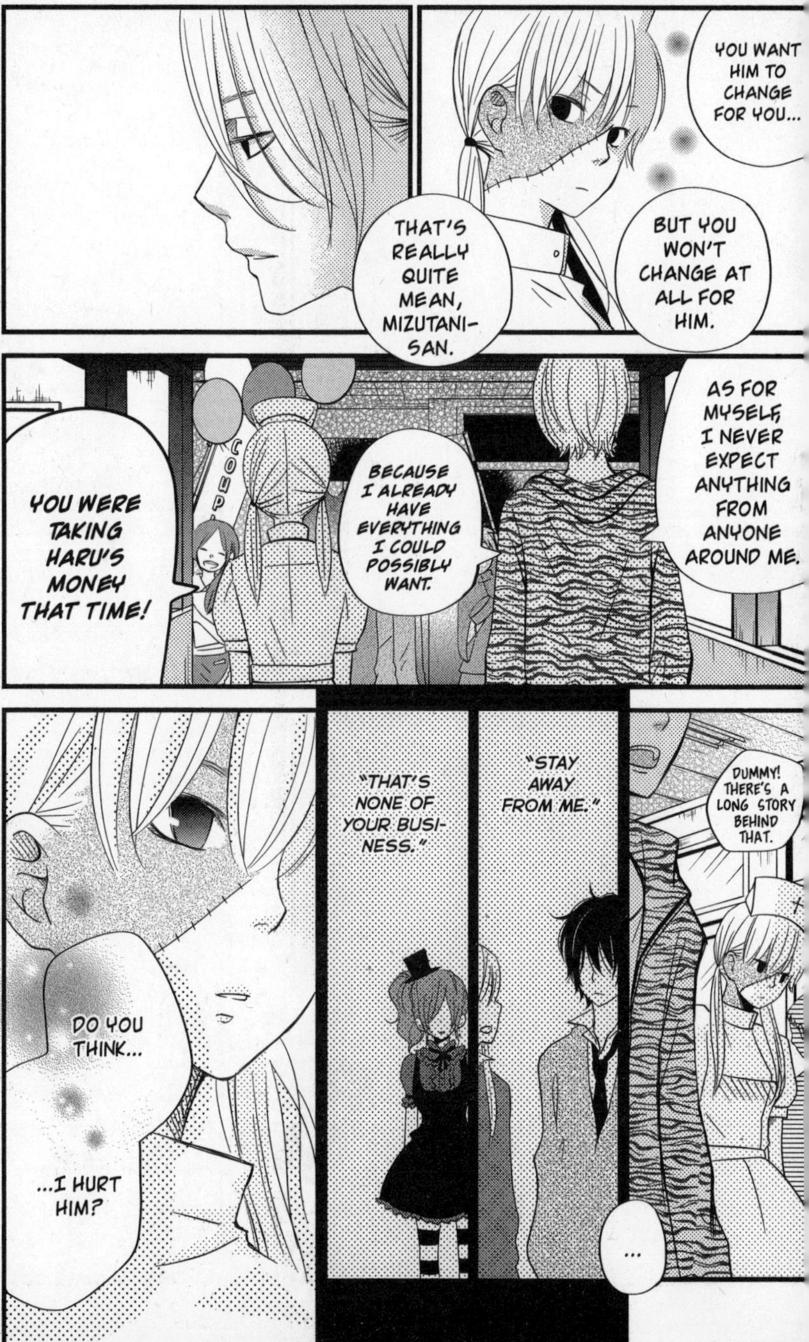
YOU WANT HIM TO CHANGE FOR YOU...
BUT YOU WON'T CHANGE AT ALL FOR HIM.
THAT'S REALLY QUITE MEAN, MIZUTANI-SAN.
AS FOR MYSELF, I NEVER EXPECT ANYTHING FROM ANYONE AROUND ME.
BECAUSE I ALREADY HAVE EVERYTHING I COULD POSSIBLY WANT.
YOU WERE TAKING HARU'S MONEY THAT TIME!
DUMMY! THERE'S A LONG STORY BEHIND THAT.
...
"STAY AWAY FROM ME."
"THAT'S NONE OF YOUR BUSI-NESS."
DO YOU THINK...
...I HURT HIM?

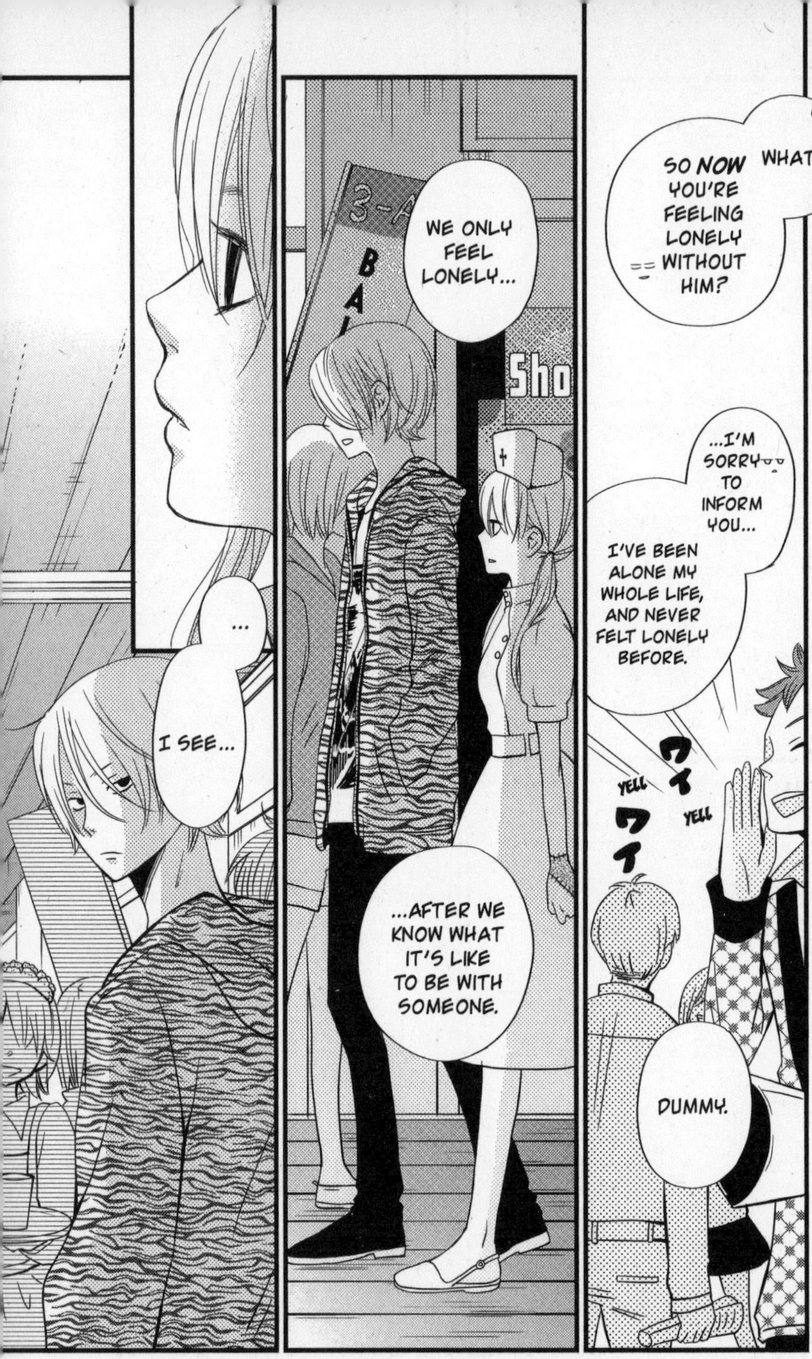
WHAT?
SO NOW YOU'RE FEELING LONELY WITHOUT HIM?
...I'M SORRY TO INFORM YOU...
I'VE BEEN ALONE MY WHOLE LIFE, AND NEVER FELT LONELY BEFORE.
ワイ YELL
ワイ YELL
DUMMY.
3-A
BA
Sho
WE ONLY FEEL LONELY...
...AFTER WE KNOW WHAT IT'S LIKE TO BE WITH SOMEONE.
...
I SEE...

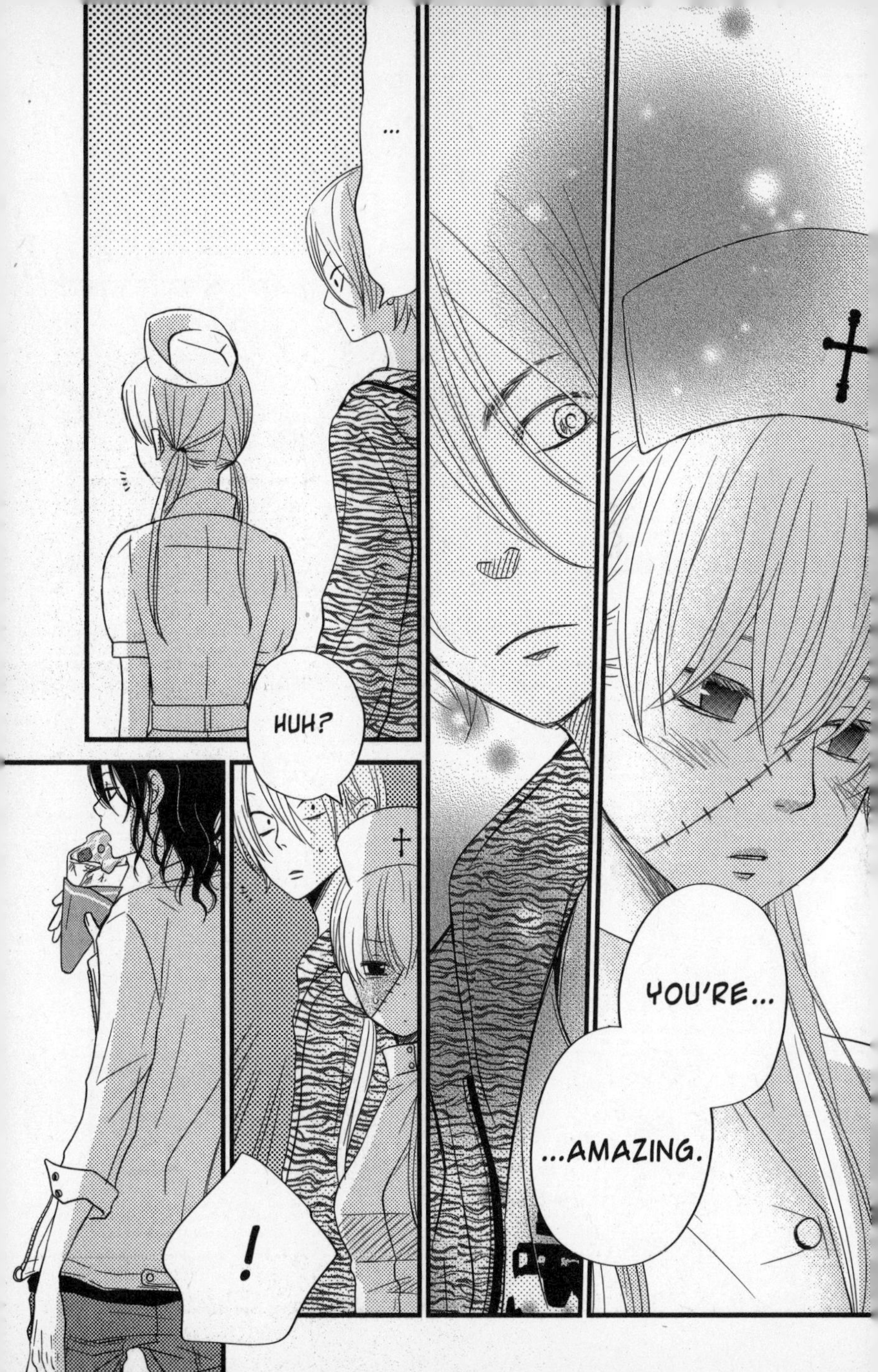
YOU'RE...
...AMAZING.
...
HUH?
!

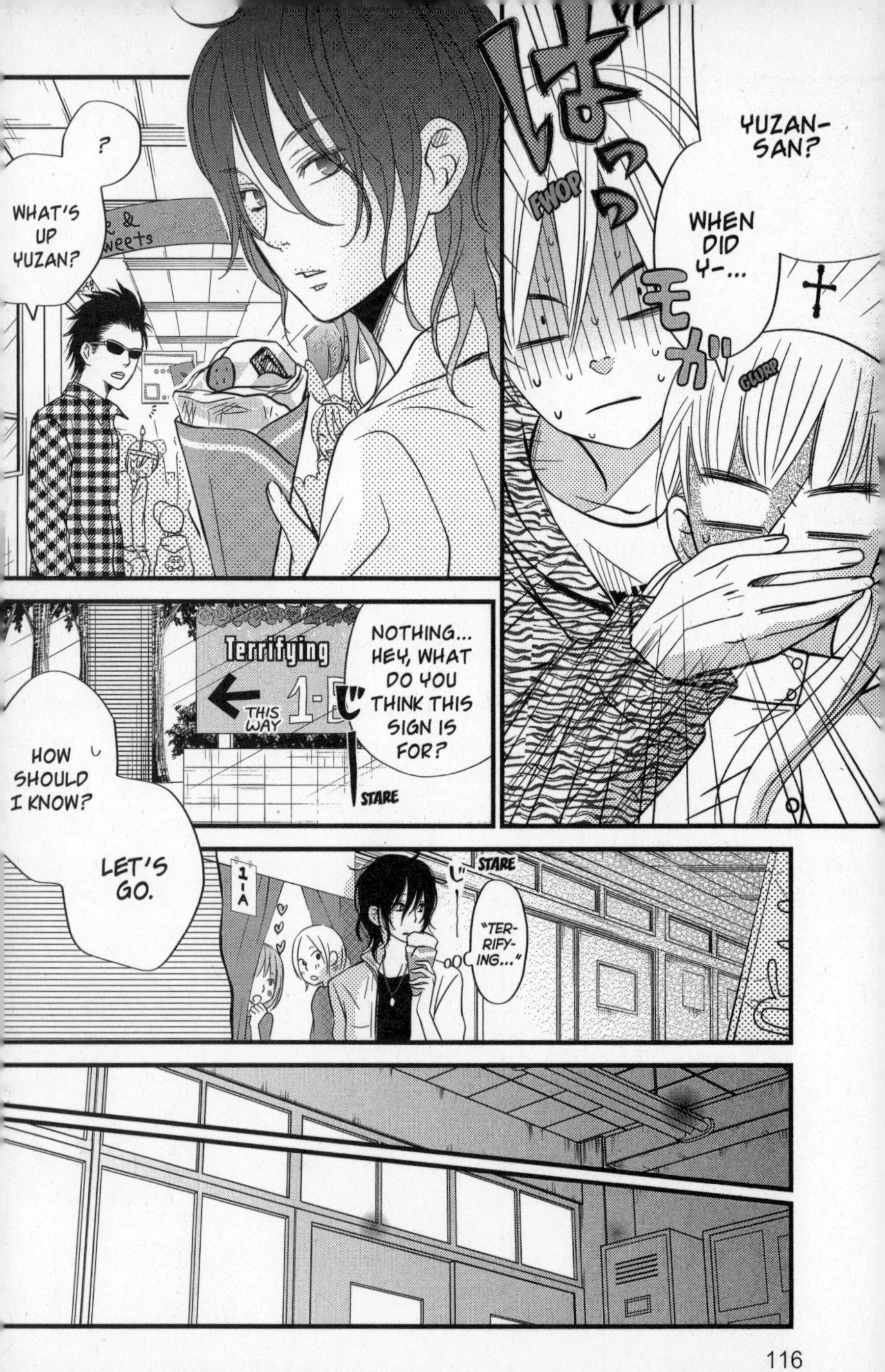
FWOP
YUZAN-SAN?
WHEN DID Y-...
GLURP
?
WHAT'S UP YUZAN?
Terrifying
THIS WAY
NOTHING... HEY, WHAT DO YOU THINK THIS SIGN IS FOR?
STARE
HOW SHOULD I KNOW?
LET'S GO.
STARE
"TER-RIFY-ING..."
1 A

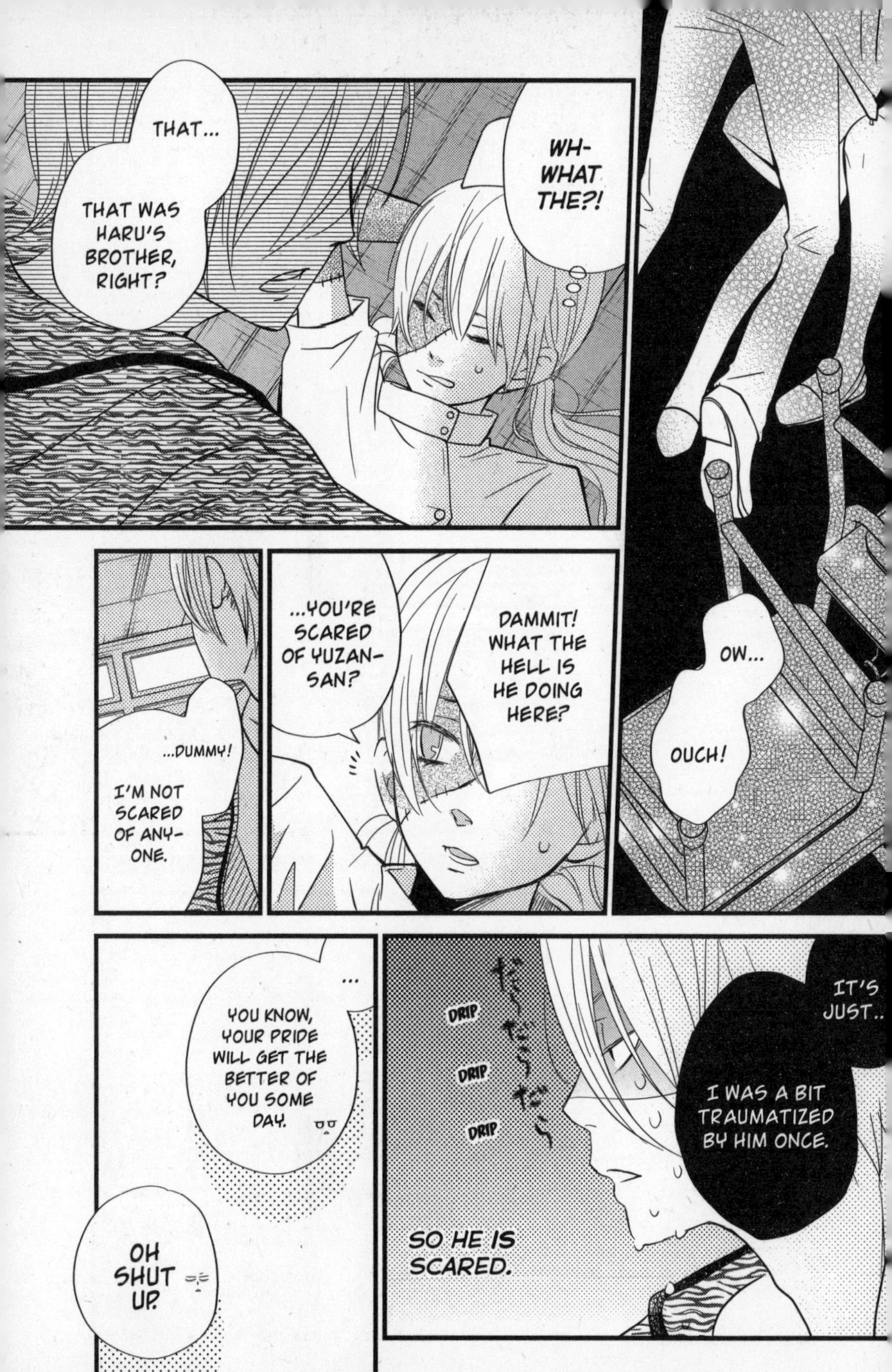
OW...
OUCH!
WH- WHAT THE?!
THAT...
THAT WAS HARU'S BROTHER, RIGHT?
DAMMIT! WHAT THE HELL IS HE DOING HERE?
...YOU'RE SCARED OF YUZAN-SAN?
...DUMMY!
I'M NOT SCARED OF ANY- ONE.
IT'S JUST...
I WAS A BIT TRAUMATIZED BY HIM ONCE.
DRIP
DRIP
DRIP
SO HE IS SCARED.
...
YOU KNOW, YOUR PRIDE WILL GET THE BETTER OF YOU SOME DAY.
OH SHUT UP.

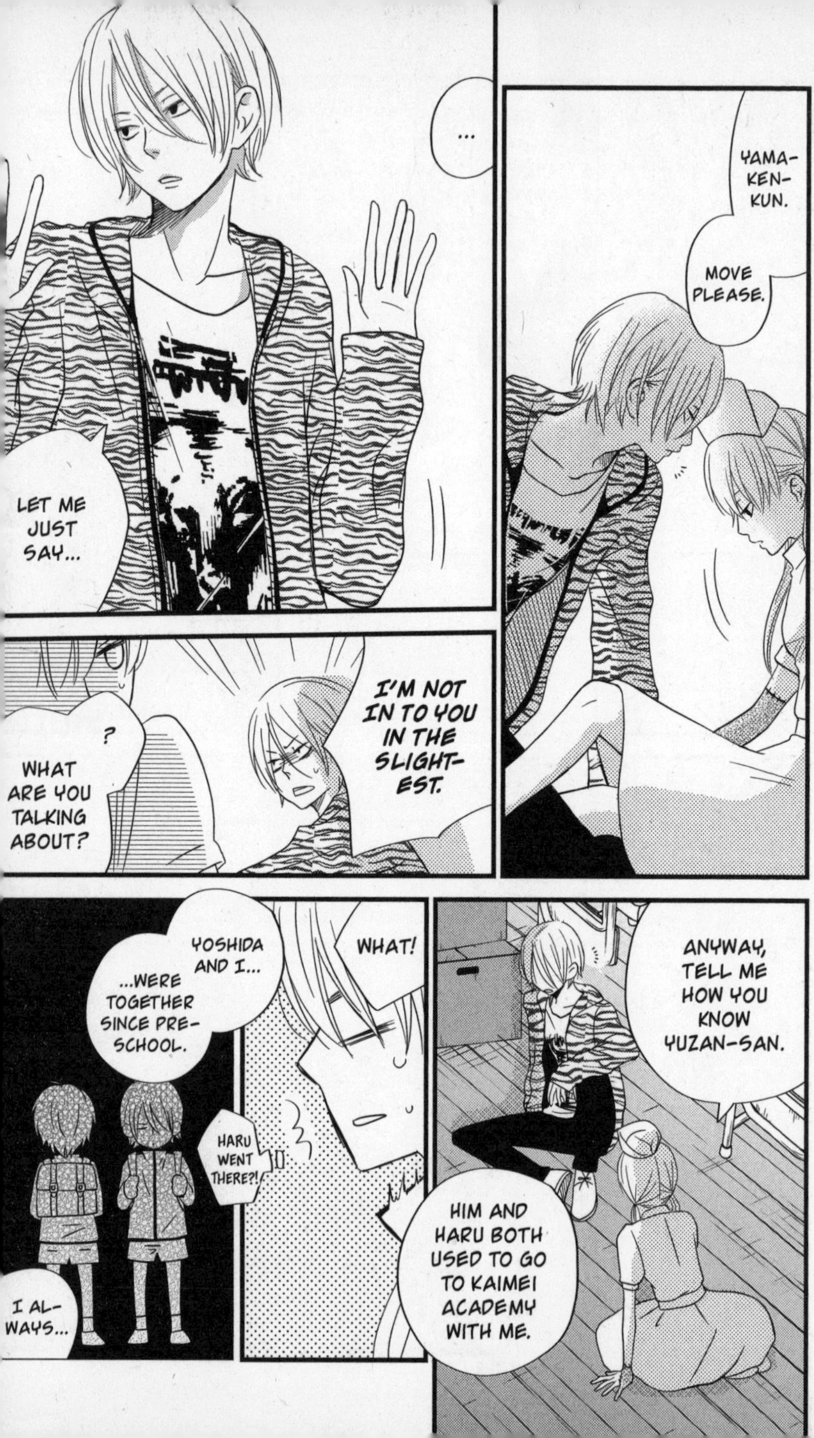
YAMA-KEN-KUN.
MOVE PLEASE.
...
LET ME JUST SAY...
I'M NOT IN TO YOU IN THE SLIGHT-EST.
?
WHAT ARE YOU TALKING ABOUT?
ANYWAY, TELL ME HOW YOU KNOW YUZAN-SAN.
HIM AND HARU BOTH USED TO GO TO KAIMEI ACADEMY WITH ME.
WHAT!
HARU WENT THERE?!
YOSHIDA AND I...
...WERE TOGETHER SINCE PRE-SCHOOL.
I AL-WAYS...

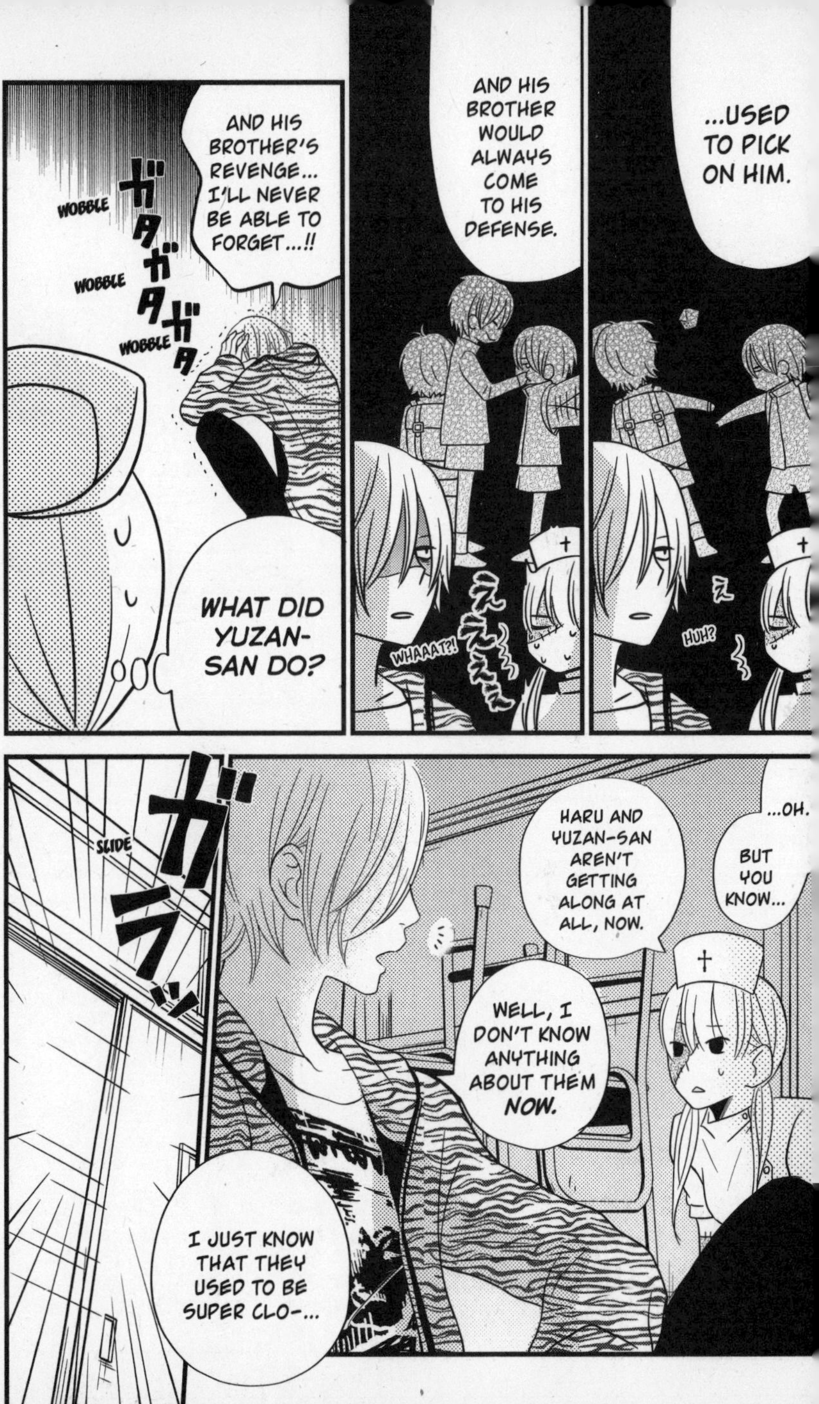
...USED TO PICK ON HIM.
HUH?
AND HIS BROTHER WOULD ALWAYS COME TO HIS DEFENSE.
WHAAAT?!
AND HIS BROTHER'S REVENGE... I'LL NEVER BE ABLE TO FORGET...!!
WOBBLE
WOBBLE
WOBBLE
WHAT DID YUZAN-SAN DO?
...OH.
BUT YOU KNOW...
HARU AND YUZAN-SAN AREN'T GETTING ALONG AT ALL, NOW.
WELL, I DON'T KNOW ANYTHING ABOUT THEM NOW.
I JUST KNOW THAT THEY USED TO BE SUPER CLO-...
SLIDE

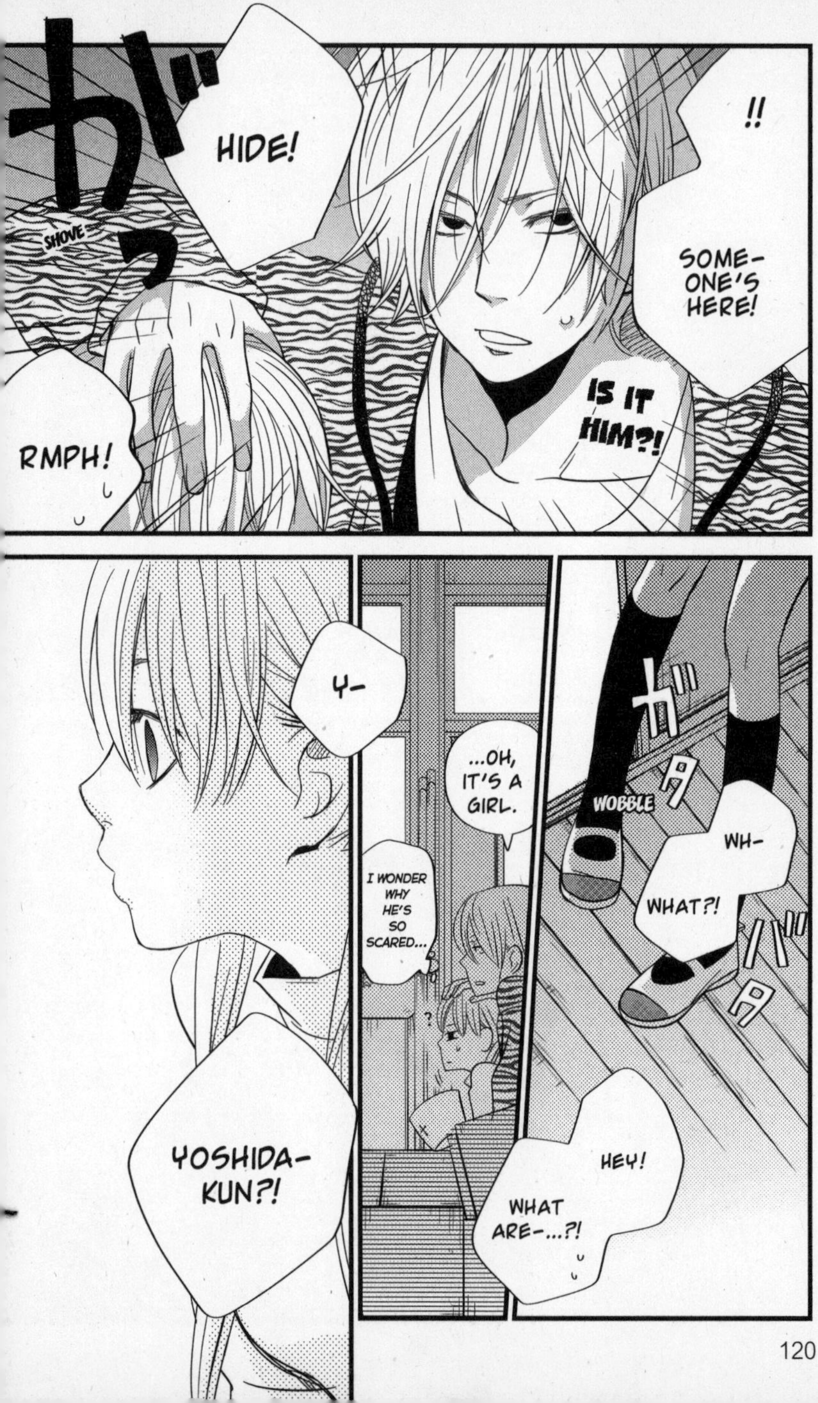
!!
HIDE!
SOME-ONE'S HERE!
IS IT HIM?!
SHOVE
RMPH!
WOBBLE
WH- WHAT?!
HEY! WHAT ARE-...?!
...OH, IT'S A GIRL.
I WONDER WHY HE'S SO SCARED...
Y-
YOSHIDA-KUN?!

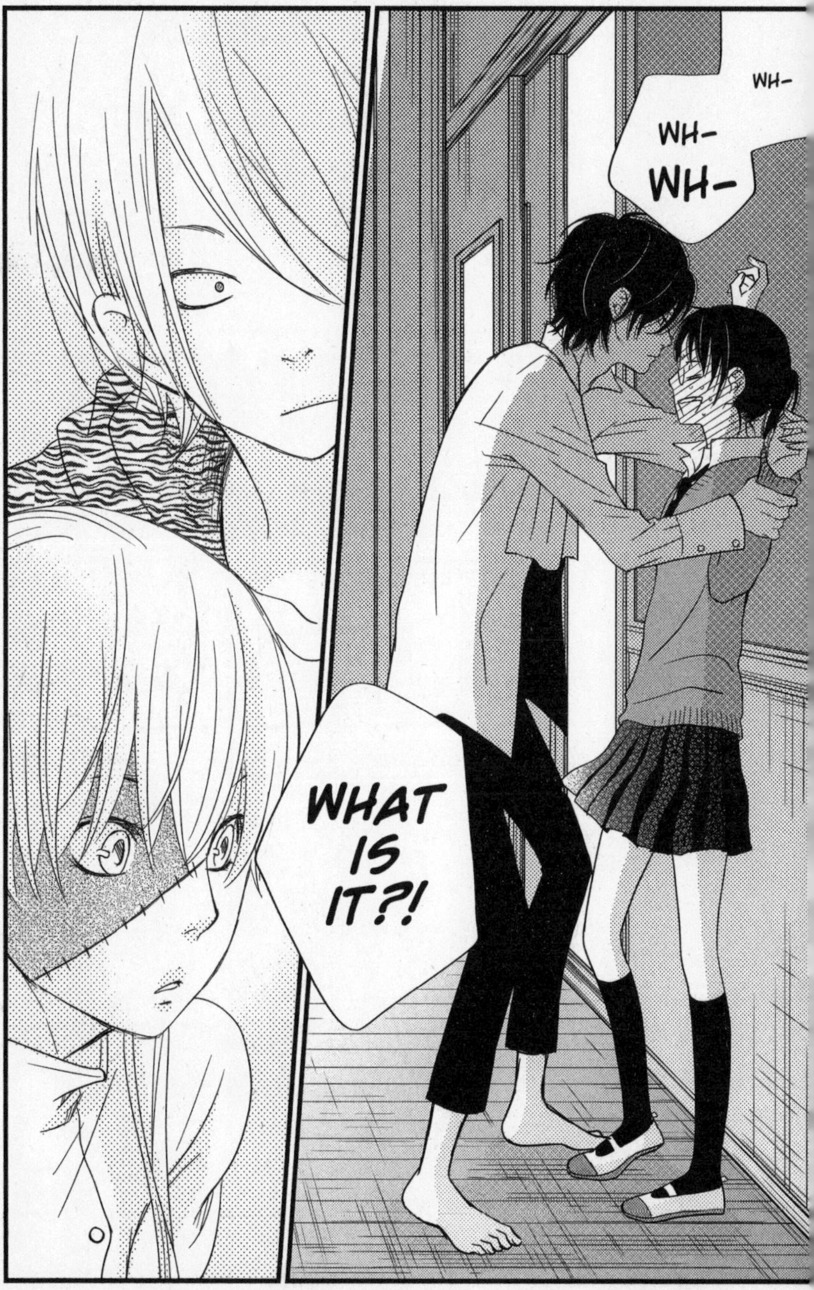
WH-
WH-
WH-
WHAT IS IT?!

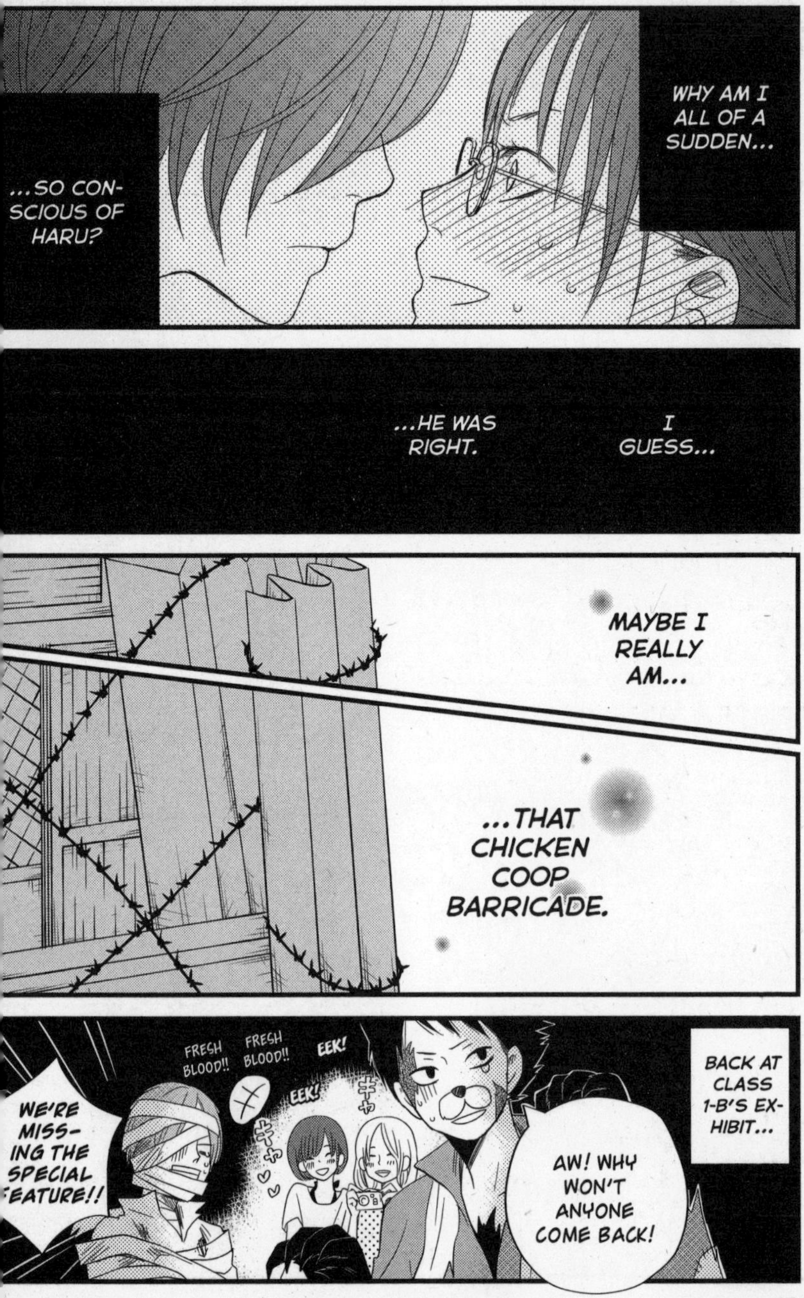

WHY AM I ALL OF A SUDDEN...
...SO CON- SCIOUS OF HARU?
I GUESS...
...HE WAS RIGHT.
MAYBE I REALLY AM...
...THAT CHICKEN COOP BARRICADE.
BACK AT CLASS 1-B'S EX- HIBIT...
AW! WHY WON'T ANYONE COME BACK!
EEK!
EEK!
FRESH BLOOD!!
FRESH BLOOD!!
WE'RE MISS- ING THE SPECIAL FEATURE!!

School Festival Prep 1

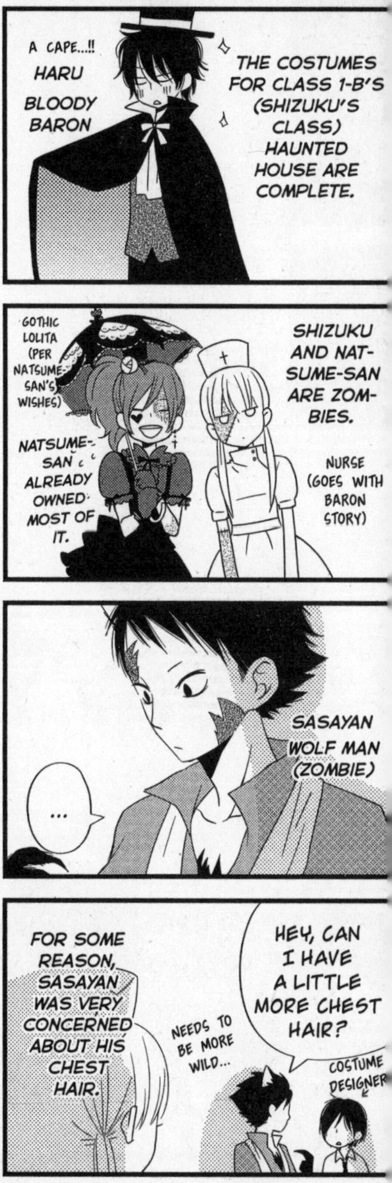
THE COSTUMES FOR CLASS 1-B'S (SHIZUKU'S CLASS) HAUNTED HOUSE ARE COMPLETE.
A CAPE...!!
HARU BLOODY BARON
SHIZUKU AND NATSUME-SAN ARE ZOMBIES.
NURSE (GOES WITH BARON STORY)
GOTHIC LOLITA (PER NATSUME-SAN'S WISHES)
NATSUME-SAN ALREADY OWNED MOST OF IT.
SASAYAN WOLF MAN (ZOMBIE)
...
HEY, CAN I HAVE A LITTLE MORE CHEST HAIR?
COSTUME DESIGNER
NEEDS TO BE MORE WILD...
FOR SOME REASON, SASAYAN WAS VERY CONCERNED ABOUT HIS CHEST HAIR.

School Festival Prep 2

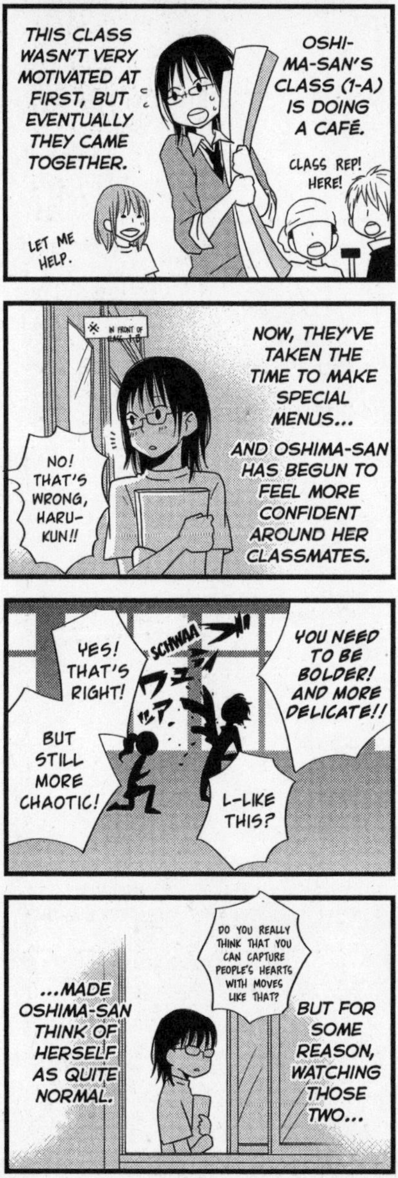
OSHIMA-SAN'S CLASS (1-A) IS DOING A CAFÉ.
CLASS REP! HERE!
THIS CLASS WASN'T VERY MOTIVATED AT FIRST, BUT EVENTUALLY THEY CAME TOGETHER.
LET ME HELP.
NOW, THEY'VE TAKEN THE TIME TO MAKE SPECIAL MENUS...
AND OSHIMA-SAN HAS BEGUN TO FEEL MORE CONFIDENT AROUND HER CLASSMATES.
※ IN FRONT OF CLASS 1-B
NO! THAT'S WRONG, HARU-KUN!!
YOU NEED TO BE BOLDER! AND MORE DELICATE!!
SCHWAA
L-LIKE THIS?
YES! THAT'S RIGHT!
BUT STILL MORE CHAOTIC!
BUT FOR SOME REASON, WATCHING THOSE TWO...
DO YOU REALLY THINK THAT YOU CAN CAPTURE PEOPLE'S HEARTS WITH MOVES LIKE THAT?
...MADE OSHIMA-SAN THINK OF HERSELF AS QUITE NORMAL.

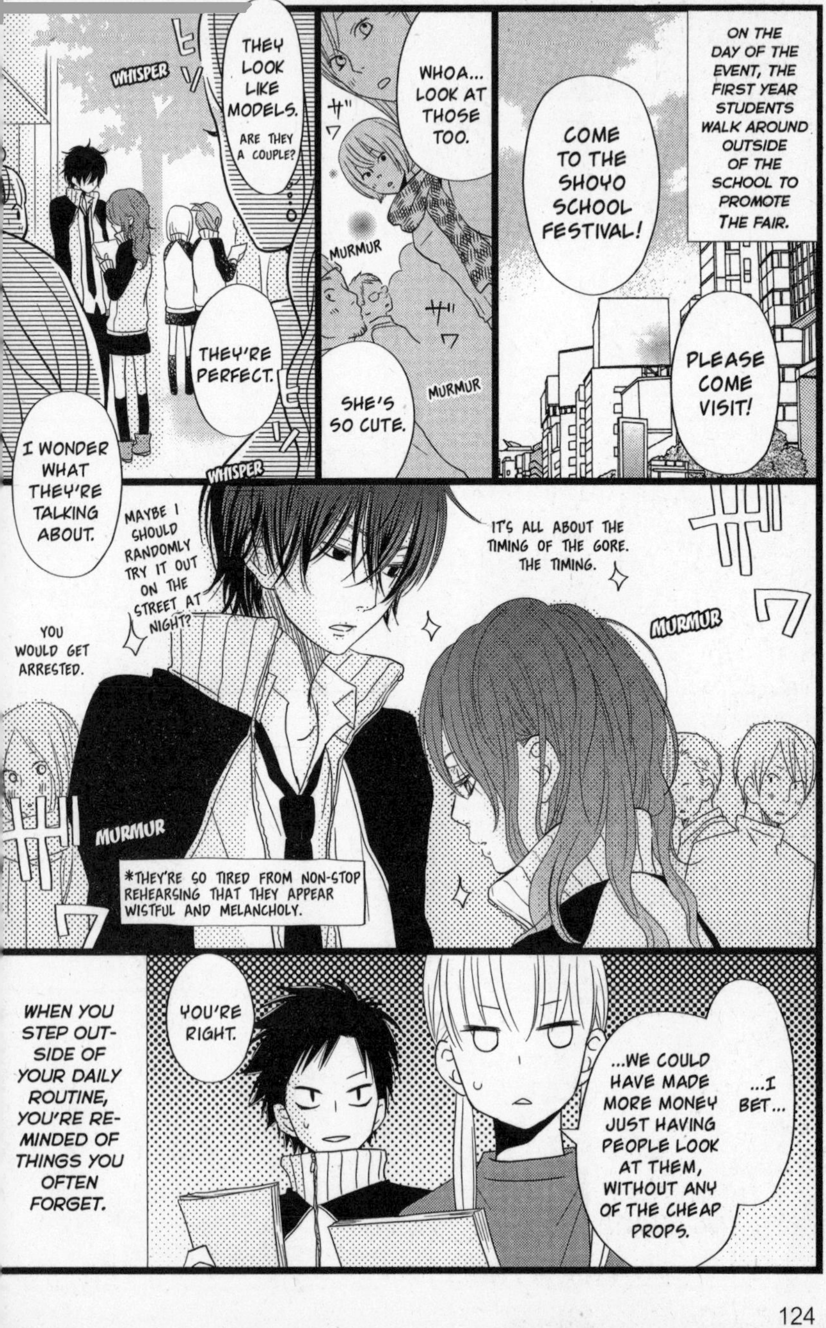
ON THE DAY OF THE EVENT, THE FIRST YEAR STUDENTS WALK AROUND OUTSIDE OF THE SCHOOL TO PROMOTE THE FAIR.
COME TO THE SHOYO SCHOOL FESTIVAL!
PLEASE COME VISIT!
WHOA... LOOK AT THOSE TOO.
ザワ
MURMUR
ザワ
MURMUR
SHE'S SO CUTE.
THEY LOOK LIKE MODELS.
ARE THEY A COUPLE?
ヒソ
WHISPER
THEY'RE PERFECT.
WHISPER
I WONDER WHAT THEY'RE TALKING ABOUT.
ザワ
MURMUR
IT'S ALL ABOUT THE TIMING OF THE GORE. THE TIMING.
MAYBE I SHOULD RANDOMLY TRY IT OUT ON THE STREET AT NIGHT?
YOU WOULD GET ARRESTED.
ザワ
MURMUR
*THEY'RE SO TIRED FROM NON-STOP REHEARSING THAT THEY APPEAR WISTFUL AND MELANCHOLY.
...I BET...
...WE COULD HAVE MADE MORE MONEY JUST HAVING PEOPLE LOOK AT THEM, WITHOUT ANY OF THE CHEAP PROPS.
YOU'RE RIGHT.
WHEN YOU STEP OUTSIDE OF YOUR DAILY ROUTINE, YOU'RE REMINDED OF THINGS YOU OFTEN FORGET.

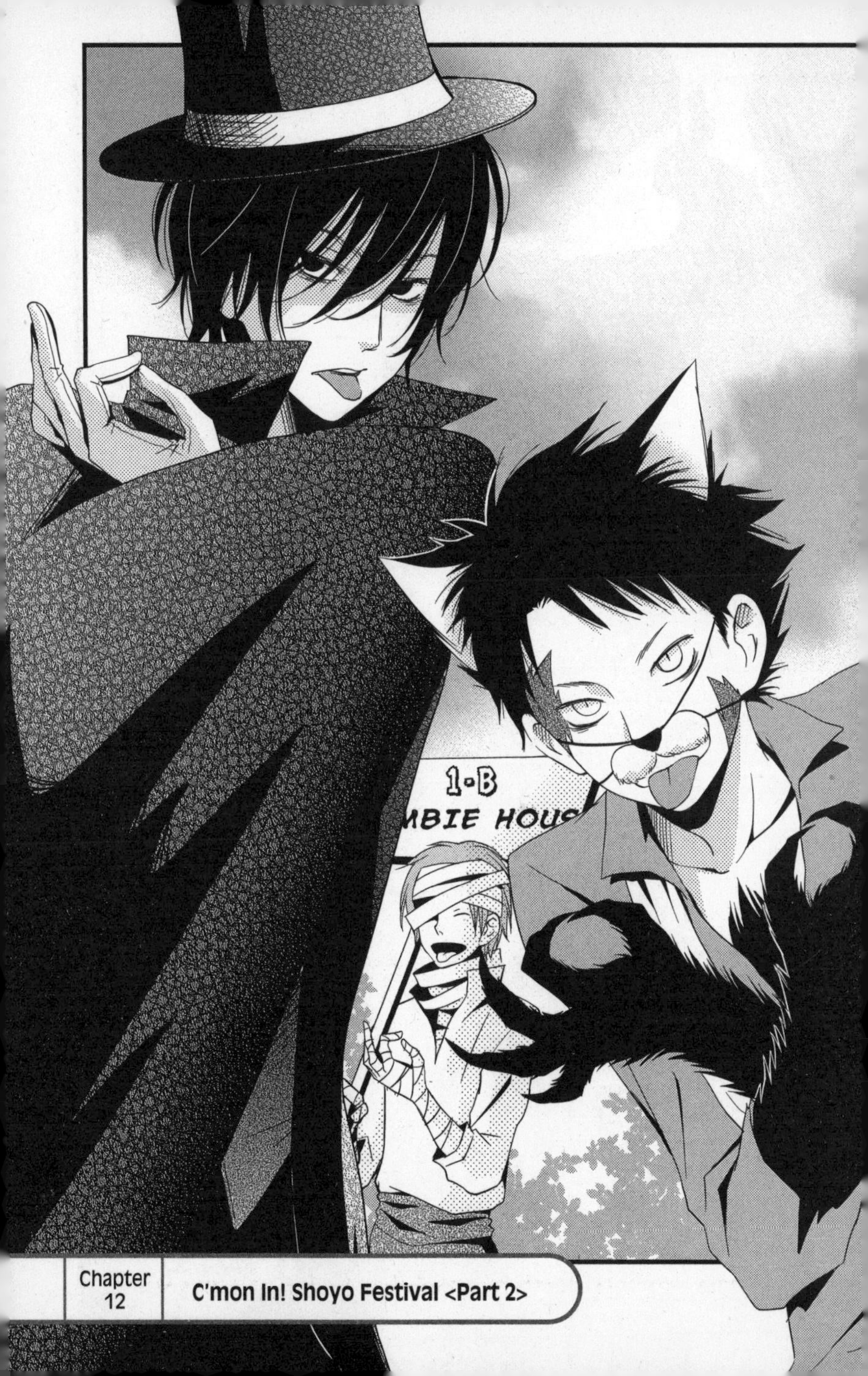
1-B
MBIE HOUS

Chapter 12 C'mon In! Shoyo Festival <Part 2>

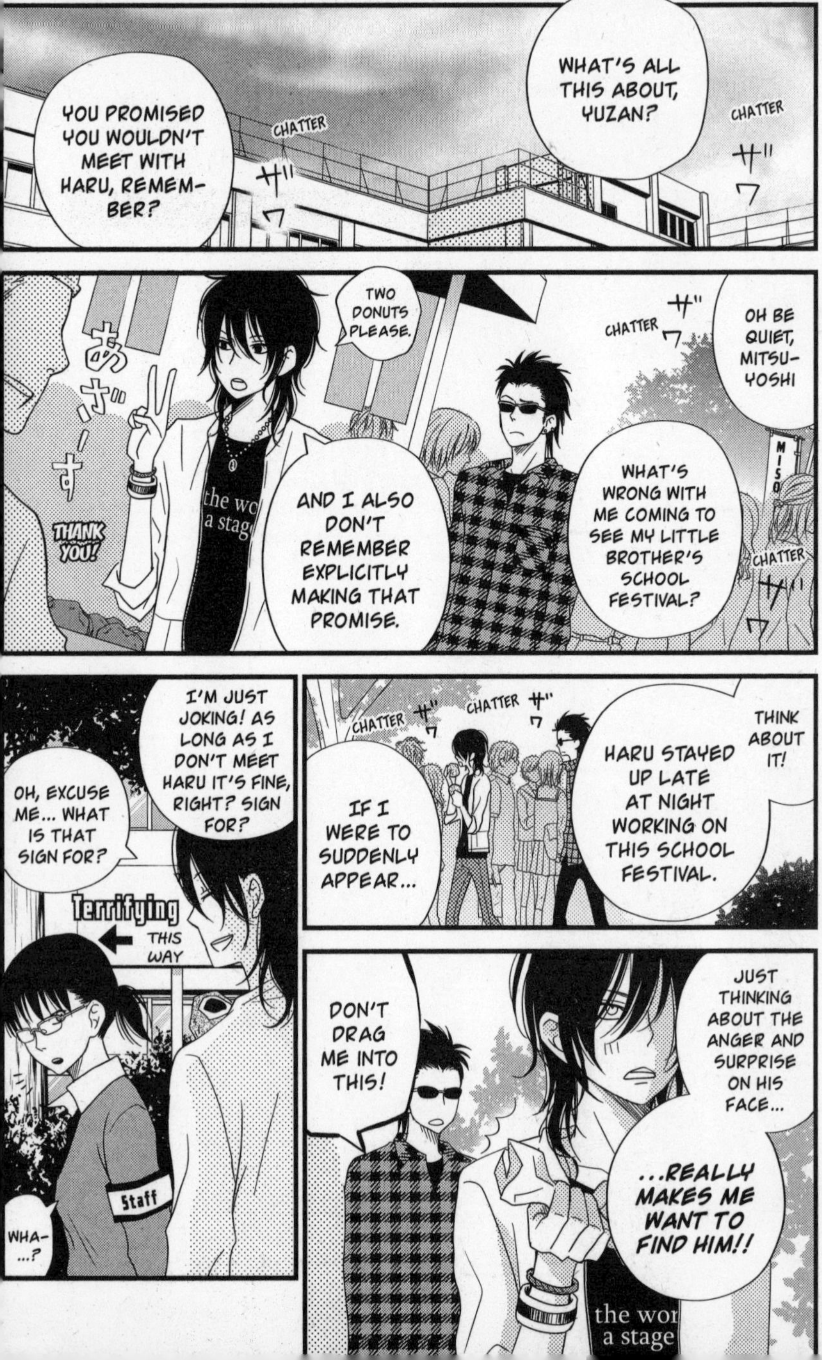
WHAT'S ALL THIS ABOUT, YUZAN?
CHATTER
ザワ
YOU PROMISED YOU WOULDN'T MEET WITH HARU, REMEMBER?
CHATTER
ザワ
OH BE QUIET, MITSUYOSHI
CHATTER
ザワ
WHAT'S WRONG WITH ME COMING TO SEE MY LITTLE BROTHER'S SCHOOL FESTIVAL?
CHATTER
ザワ
MISO
AND I ALSO DON'T REMEMBER EXPLICITLY MAKING THAT PROMISE.
TWO DONUTS PLEASE.
the wo
a stag
あざーす
THANK YOU!
THINK ABOUT IT!
HARU STAYED UP LATE AT NIGHT WORKING ON THIS SCHOOL FESTIVAL.
CHATTER
ザワ
CHATTER
ザワ
IF I WERE TO SUDDENLY APPEAR...
JUST THINKING ABOUT THE ANGER AND SURPRISE ON HIS FACE...
...REALLY MAKES ME WANT TO FIND HIM!!
DON'T DRAG ME INTO THIS!
the wor
a stage
I'M JUST JOKING! AS LONG AS I DON'T MEET HARU IT'S FINE, RIGHT? SIGN FOR?
OH, EXCUSE ME... WHAT IS THAT SIGN FOR?
Terrifying
THIS WAY
Staff
WHA-...?

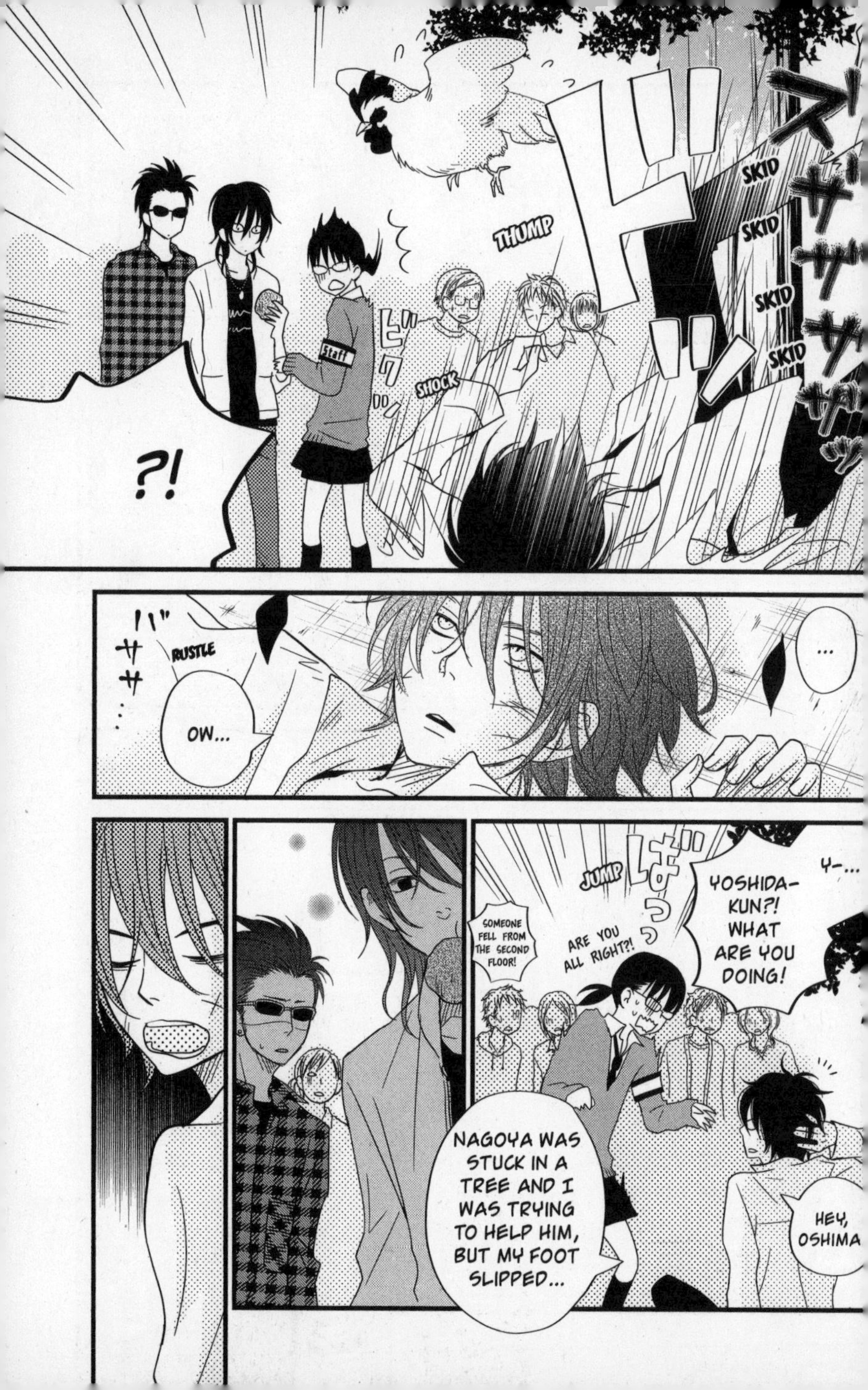
SKID
SKID
SKID
SKID
THUMP
SHOCK
?!
...
RUSTLE
OW...
Y-...
YOSHIDA-KUN?! WHAT ARE YOU DOING!
JUMP
ARE YOU ALL RIGHT?!
SOMEONE FELL FROM THE SECOND FLOOR!
HEY, OSHIMA
NAGOYA WAS STUCK IN A TREE AND I WAS TRYING TO HELP HIM, BUT MY FOOT SLIPPED...

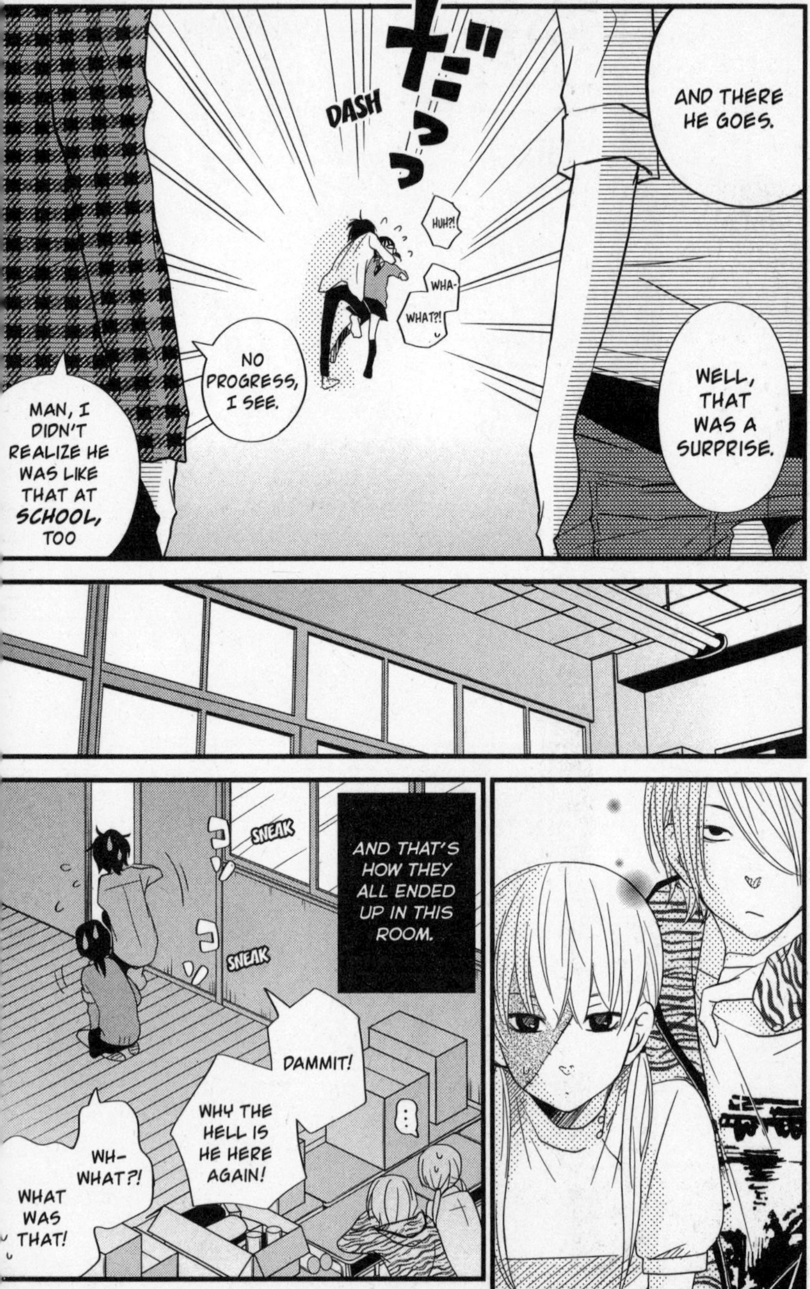
AND THERE HE GOES.
WELL, THAT WAS A SURPRISE.
DASH
HUH?!
WHA- WHAT?!
NO PROGRESS, I SEE.
MAN, I DIDN'T REALIZE HE WAS LIKE THAT AT SCHOOL, TOO
AND THAT'S HOW THEY ALL ENDED UP IN THIS ROOM.
SNEAK
SNEAK
DAMMIT!
...
WHY THE HELL IS HE HERE AGAIN!
WH-WHAT?!
WHAT WAS THAT!

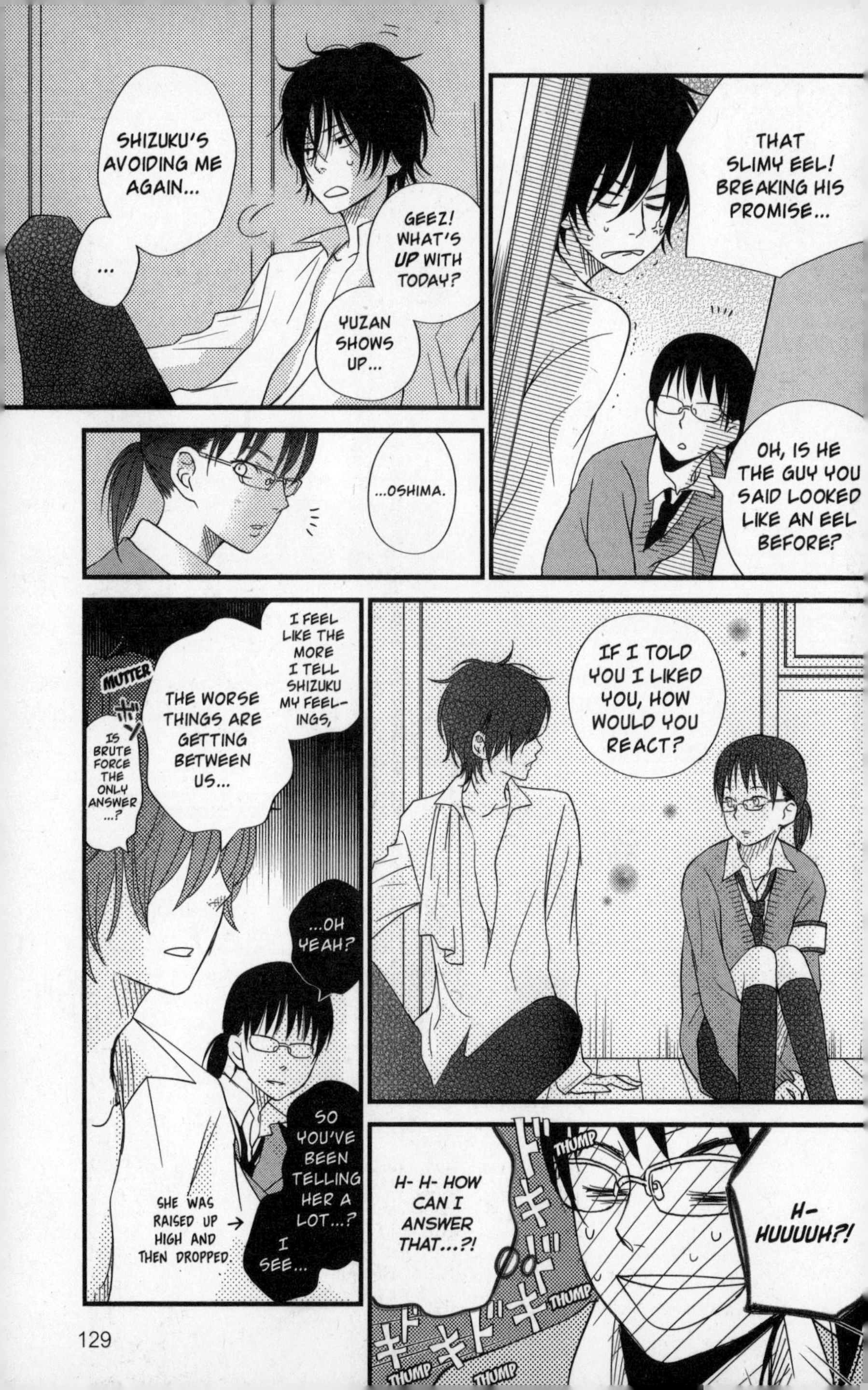
SHIZUKU'S AVOIDING ME AGAIN...
...
GEEZ! WHAT'S *UP* WITH TODAY?
YUZAN SHOWS UP...
THAT SLIMY EEL! BREAKING HIS PROMISE...
OH, IS HE THE GUY YOU SAID LOOKED LIKE AN EEL BEFORE?
...OSHIMA.
I FEEL LIKE THE MORE I TELL SHIZUKU MY FEEL-INGS,
THE WORSE THINGS ARE GETTING BETWEEN US...
MUTTER
IS BRUTE FORCE THE ONLY ANSWER ...?
...OH YEAH?
SO YOU'VE BEEN TELLING HER A LOT...?
I SEE...
SHE WAS RAISED UP HIGH AND THEN DROPPED.
IF I TOLD YOU I LIKED YOU, HOW WOULD YOU REACT?
THUMP
H- H- HOW CAN I ANSWER THAT...?!
H-HUUUUH?!
THUMP
THUMP
THUMP

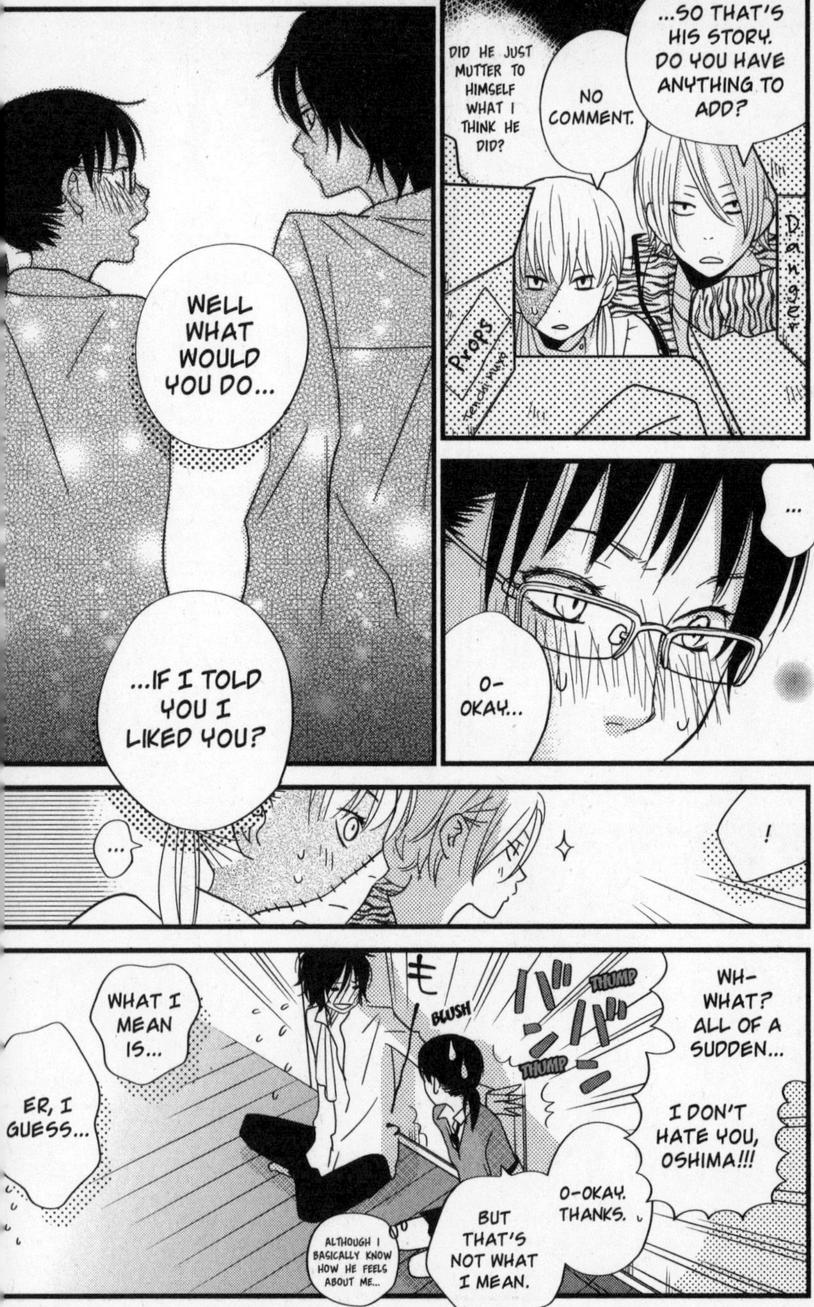
...SO THAT'S HIS STORY. DO YOU HAVE ANYTHING TO ADD?
NO COMMENT.
DID HE JUST MUTTER TO HIMSELF WHAT I THINK HE DID?
Danger
Props
...
O-OKAY...
WELL WHAT WOULD YOU DO...
...IF I TOLD YOU I LIKED YOU?
!
...
WH-WHAT? ALL OF A SUDDEN...
THUMP
BLUSH
THUMP
I DON'T HATE YOU, OSHIMA!!!
O-OKAY. THANKS.
BUT THAT'S NOT WHAT I MEAN.
ALTHOUGH I BASICALLY KNOW HOW HE FEELS ABOUT ME...
WHAT I MEAN IS...
ER, I GUESS...

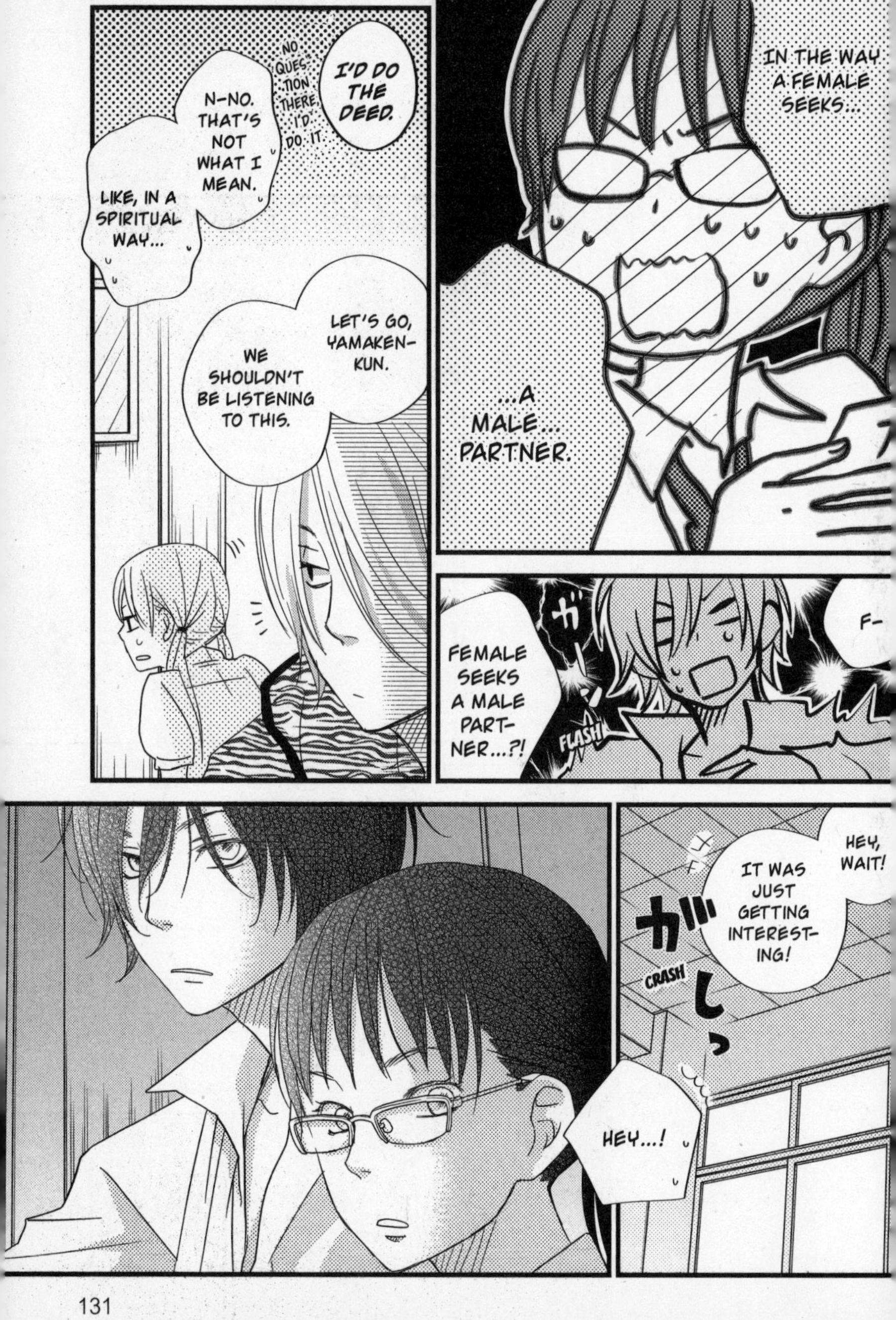
IN THE WAY A FEMALE SEEKS...
...A MALE... PARTNER.
F-
FEMALE SEEKS A MALE PARTNER...?!
FLASH
I'D DO THE DEED.
NO QUESTION THERE, I'D DO IT.
N-NO. THAT'S NOT WHAT I MEAN.
LIKE, IN A SPIRITUAL WAY...
LET'S GO, YAMAKEN-KUN.
WE SHOULDN'T BE LISTENING TO THIS.
HEY, WAIT!
IT WAS JUST GETTING INTERESTING!
CRASH
HEY...!

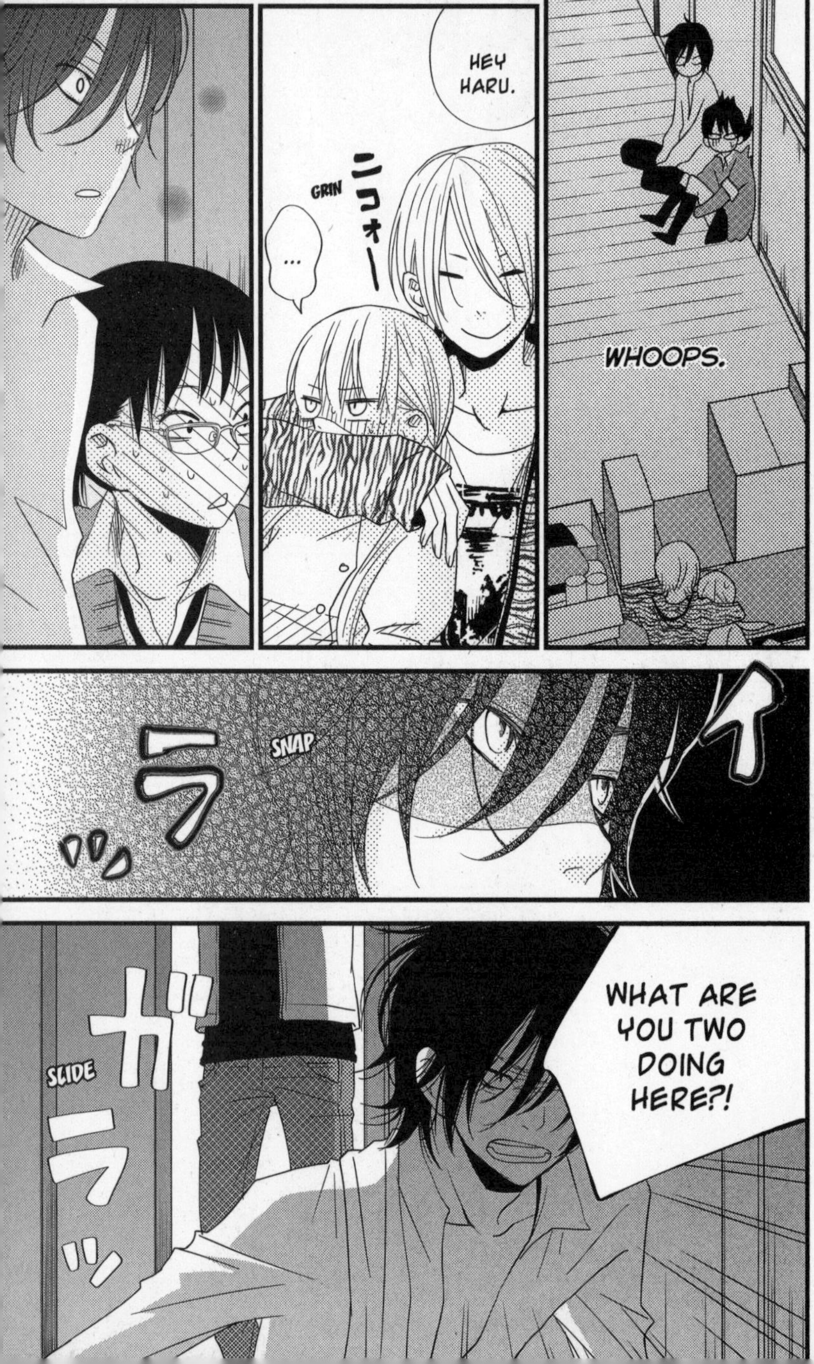
WHOOPS.
HEY HARU.
ニコォー
GRIN
...
イラッ
SNAP
WHAT ARE YOU TWO DOING HERE?!
ガラッ
SLIDE

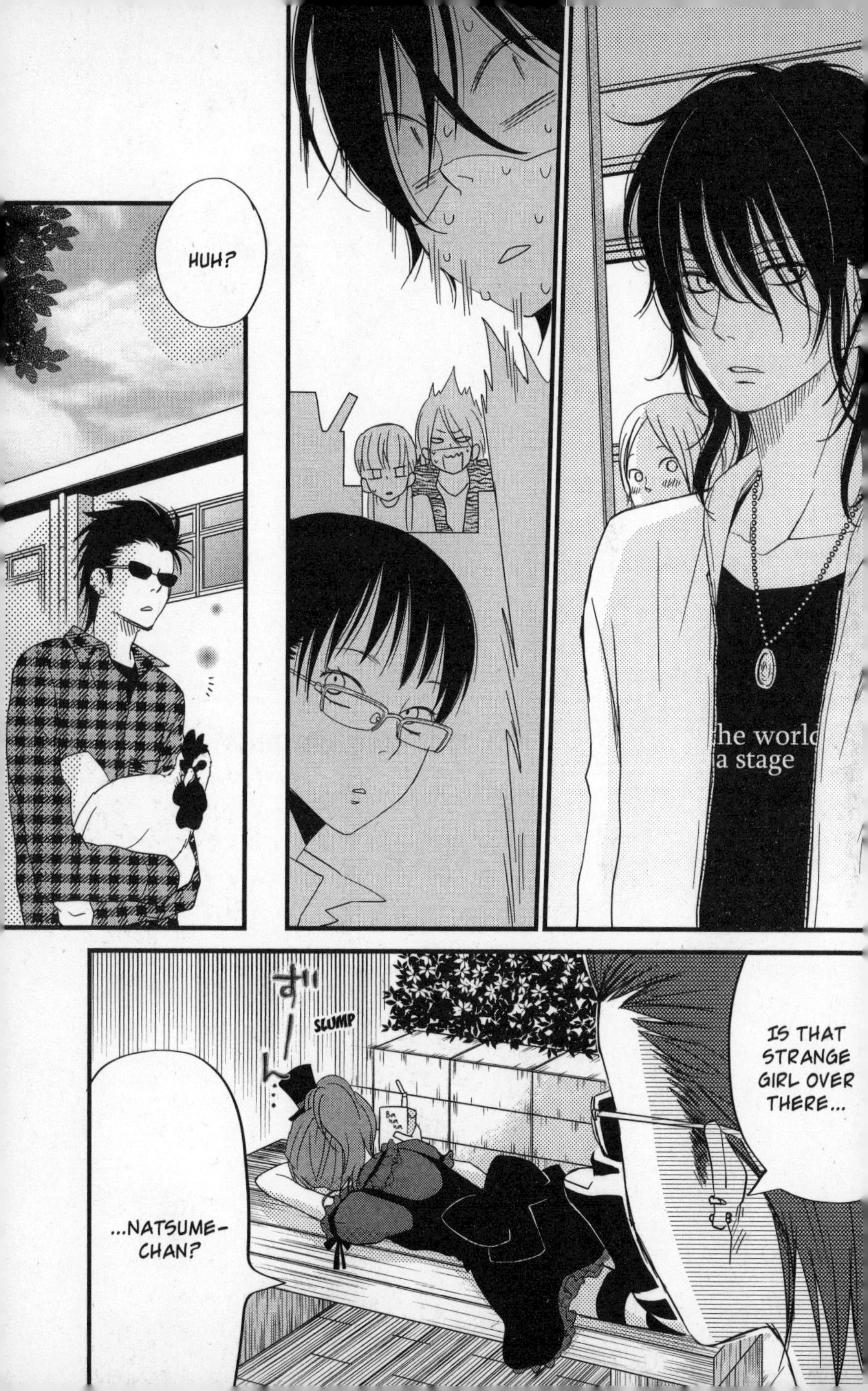
the world
a stage
HUH?
IS THAT STRANGE GIRL OVER THERE...
ずーん
SLUMP
...NATSUME-CHAN?

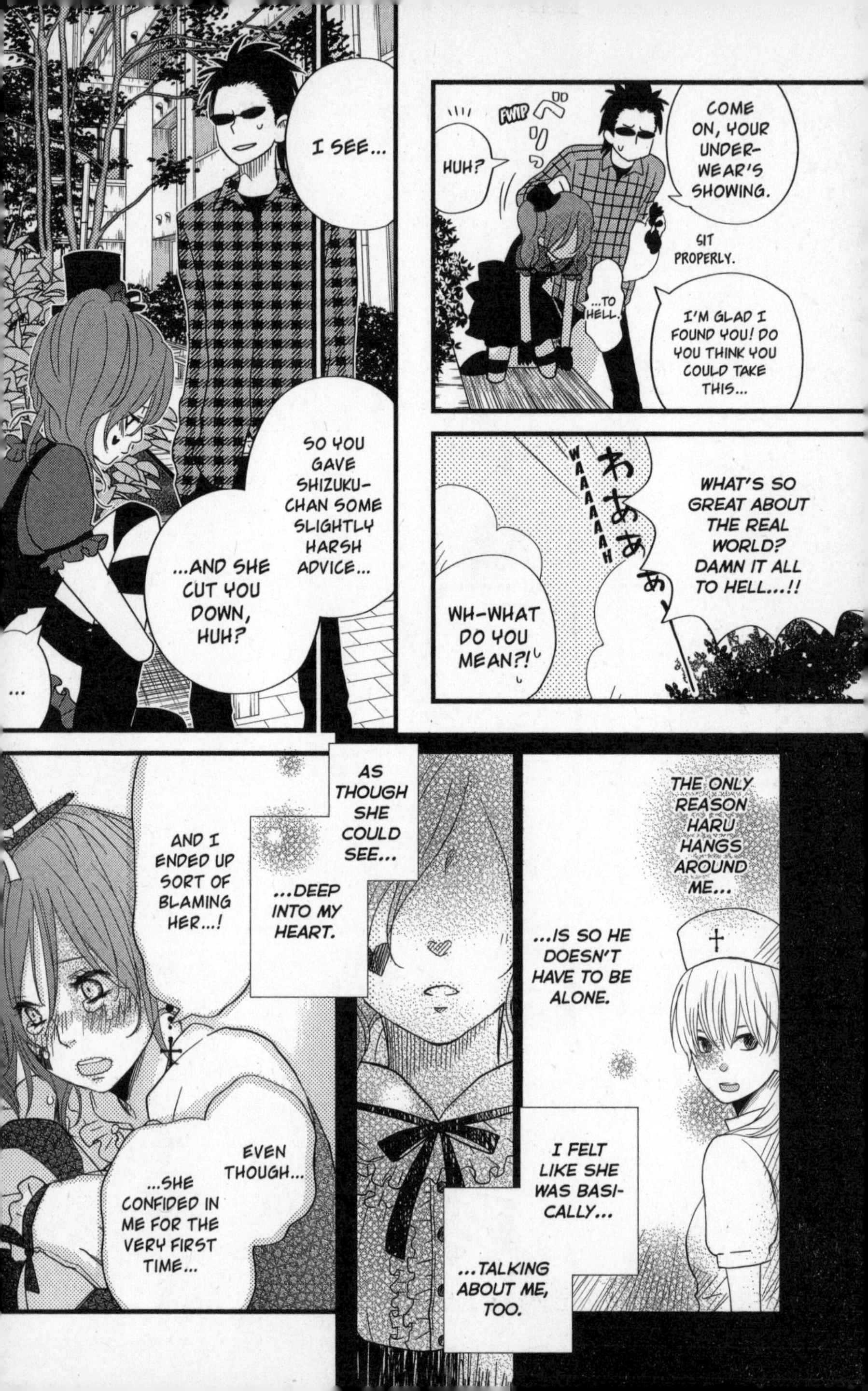
COME ON, YOUR UNDER-WEAR'S SHOWING.
FWIP べりっ
HUH?
SIT PROPERLY.
...TO HELL.
I'M GLAD I FOUND YOU! DO YOU THINK YOU COULD TAKE THIS...
WHAT'S SO GREAT ABOUT THE REAL WORLD? DAMN IT ALL TO HELL...!!
WAAAAAAAH わああああ
WH-WHAT DO YOU MEAN?!
I SEE...
SO YOU GAVE SHIZUKU-CHAN SOME SLIGHTLY HARSH ADVICE...
...AND SHE CUT YOU DOWN, HUH?
...
THE ONLY REASON HARU HANGS AROUND ME...
...IS SO HE DOESN'T HAVE TO BE ALONE.
I FELT LIKE SHE WAS BASI-CALLY...
...TALKING ABOUT ME, TOO.
AS THOUGH SHE COULD SEE...
...DEEP INTO MY HEART.
AND I ENDED UP SORT OF BLAMING HER...!
EVEN THOUGH...
...SHE CONFIDED IN ME FOR THE VERY FIRST TIME...

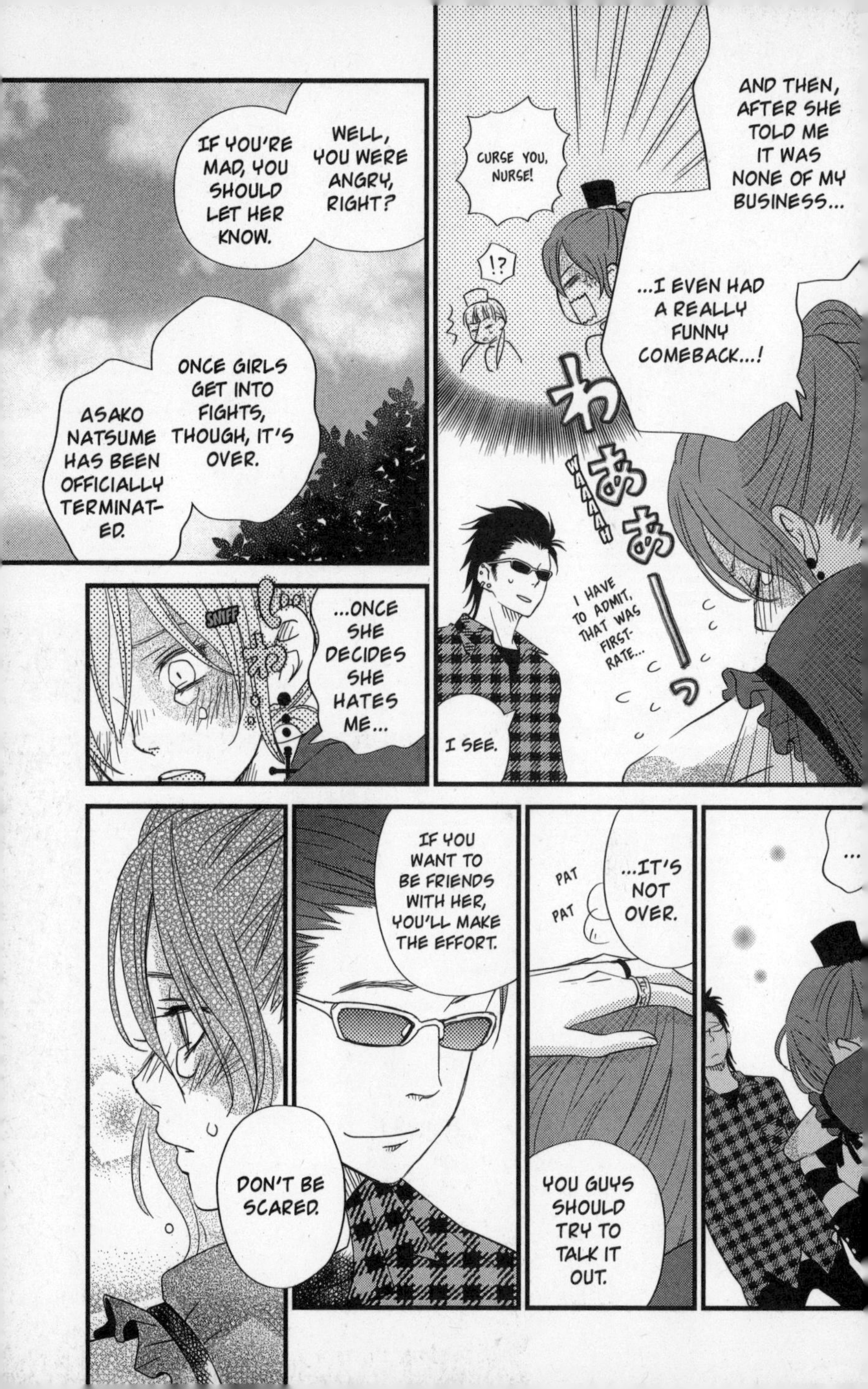

AND THEN, AFTER SHE TOLD ME IT WAS NONE OF MY BUSINESS...
CURSE YOU, NURSE!
!?
...I EVEN HAD A REALLY FUNNY COMEBACK...!
わああーっ
WAAAAAH
I HAVE TO ADMIT, THAT WAS FIRST-RATE...
I SEE.
WELL, YOU WERE ANGRY, RIGHT?
IF YOU'RE MAD, YOU SHOULD LET HER KNOW.
ONCE GIRLS GET INTO FIGHTS, THOUGH, IT'S OVER.
ASAKO NATSUME HAS BEEN OFFICIALLY TERMINATED.
SNIFF
...ONCE SHE DECIDES SHE HATES ME...
...
PAT PAT
...IT'S NOT OVER.
YOU GUYS SHOULD TRY TO TALK IT OUT.
IF YOU WANT TO BE FRIENDS WITH HER, YOU'LL MAKE THE EFFORT.
DON'T BE SCARED.

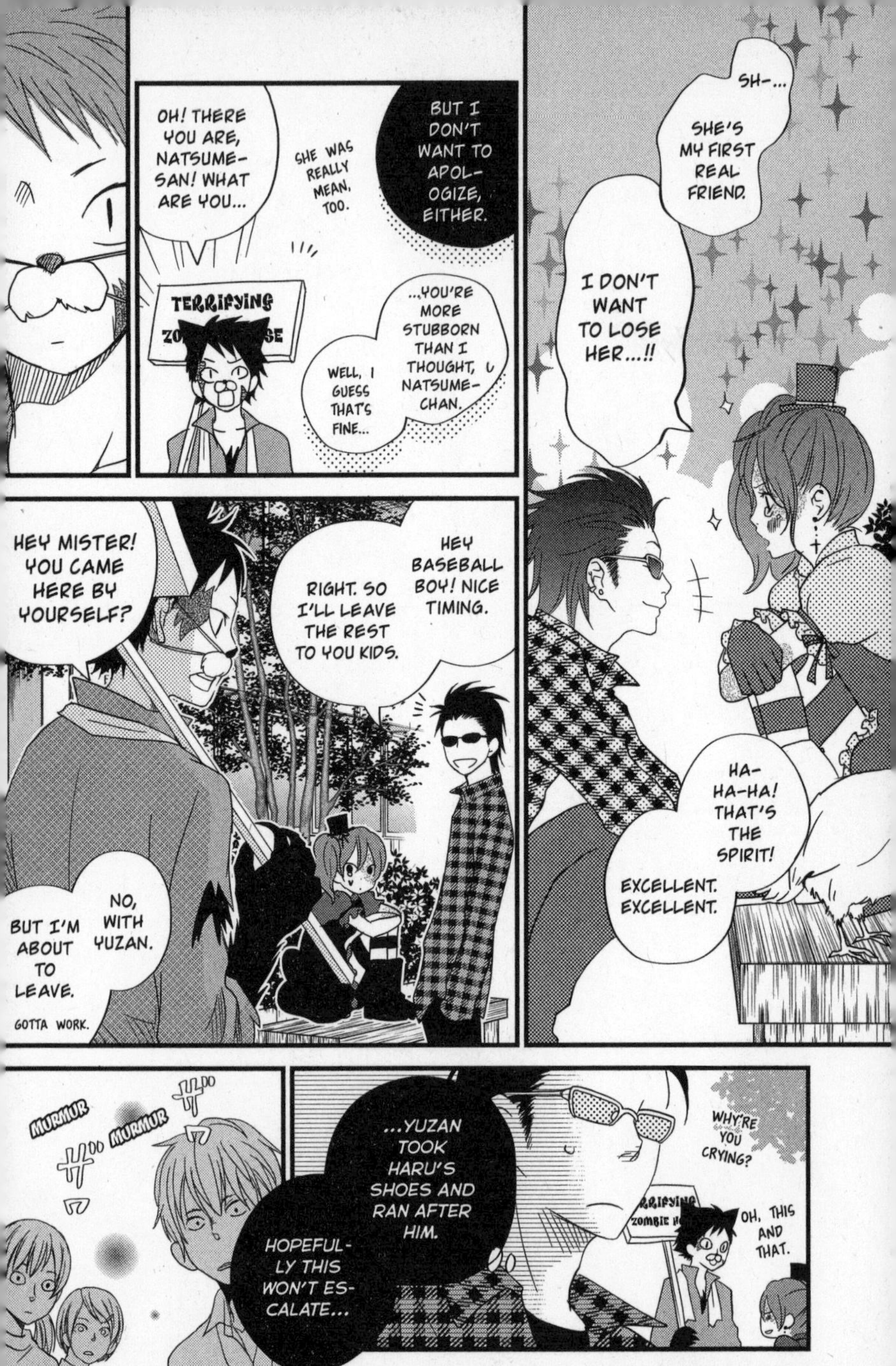
SH-...
SHE'S MY FIRST REAL FRIEND.
I DON'T WANT TO LOSE HER...!!
HA-HA-HA! THAT'S THE SPIRIT!
EXCELLENT. EXCELLENT.
BUT I DON'T WANT TO APOLOGIZE, EITHER.
SHE WAS REALLY MEAN, TOO.
OH! THERE YOU ARE, NATSUME-SAN! WHAT ARE YOU...
TERRIFYING
...YOU'RE MORE STUBBORN THAN I THOUGHT, NATSUME-CHAN.
WELL, I GUESS THAT'S FINE...
HEY BASEBALL BOY! NICE TIMING.
RIGHT. SO I'LL LEAVE THE REST TO YOU KIDS.
HEY MISTER! YOU CAME HERE BY YOURSELF?
NO, WITH YUZAN.
BUT I'M ABOUT TO LEAVE.
GOTTA WORK.
WHY'RE YOU CRYING?
OH, THIS AND THAT.
...YUZAN TOOK HARU'S SHOES AND RAN AFTER HIM.
HOPEFULLY THIS WON'T ESCALATE...
MURMUR
MURMUR

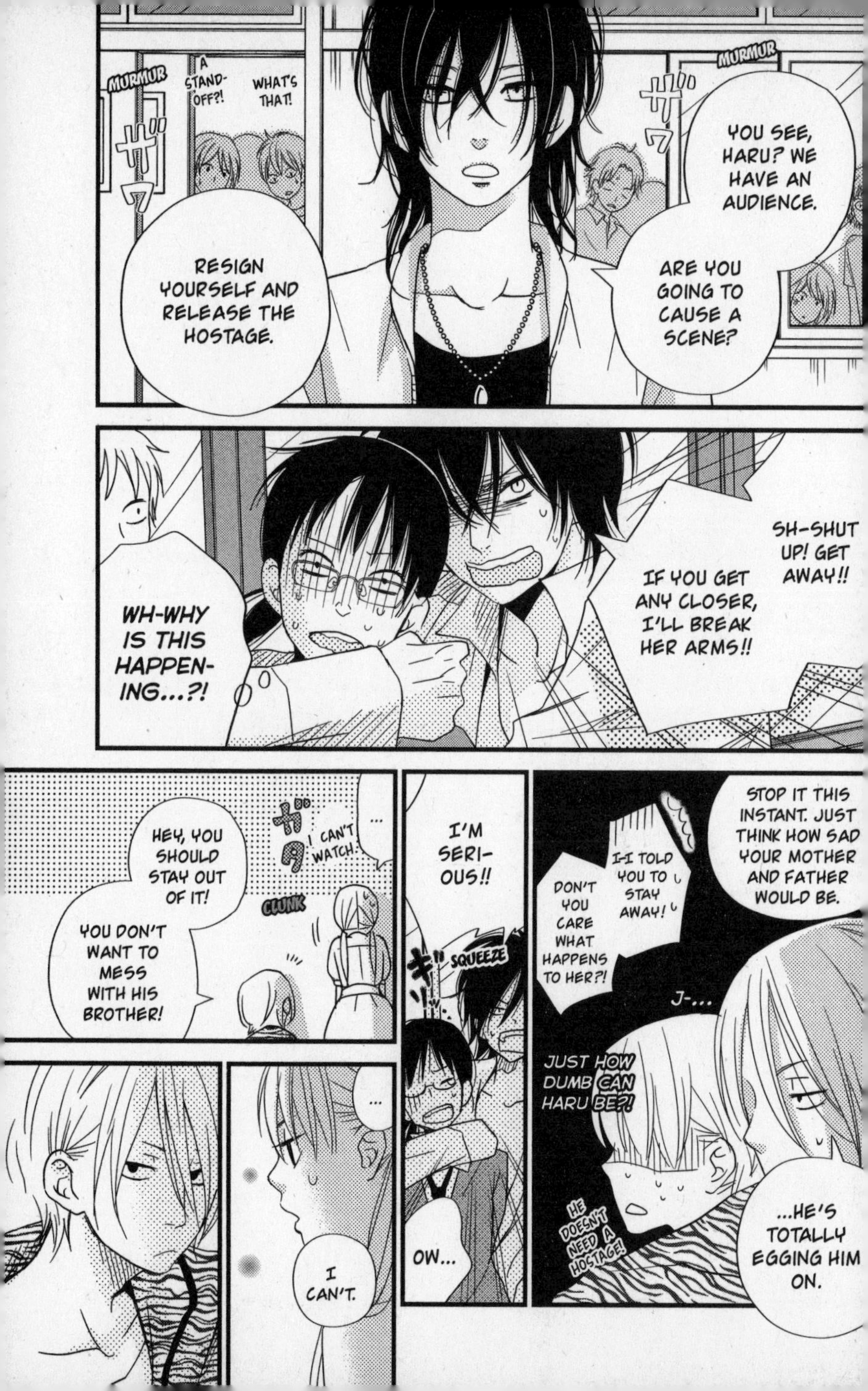
MURMUR
ザワ
YOU SEE, HARU? WE HAVE AN AUDIENCE.
ARE YOU GOING TO CAUSE A SCENE?
WHAT'S THAT!
A STAND-OFF?!
MURMUR
ザワ
RESIGN YOURSELF AND RELEASE THE HOSTAGE.
SH-SHUT UP! GET AWAY!!
IF YOU GET ANY CLOSER, I'LL BREAK HER ARMS!!
WH-WHY IS THIS HAPPENING...?!
STOP IT THIS INSTANT. JUST THINK HOW SAD YOUR MOTHER AND FATHER WOULD BE.
I-I TOLD YOU TO STAY AWAY!
DON'T YOU CARE WHAT HAPPENS TO HER?!
J-...
JUST HOW DUMB CAN HARU BE?!
...HE'S TOTALLY EGGING HIM ON.
HE DOESN'T NEED A HOSTAGE!
I'M SERI-OUS!!
SQUEEZE
OW...
...
I CAN'T WATCH.
ガタ
CLUNK
HEY, YOU SHOULD STAY OUT OF IT!
YOU DON'T WANT TO MESS WITH HIS BROTHER!
...
I CAN'T.

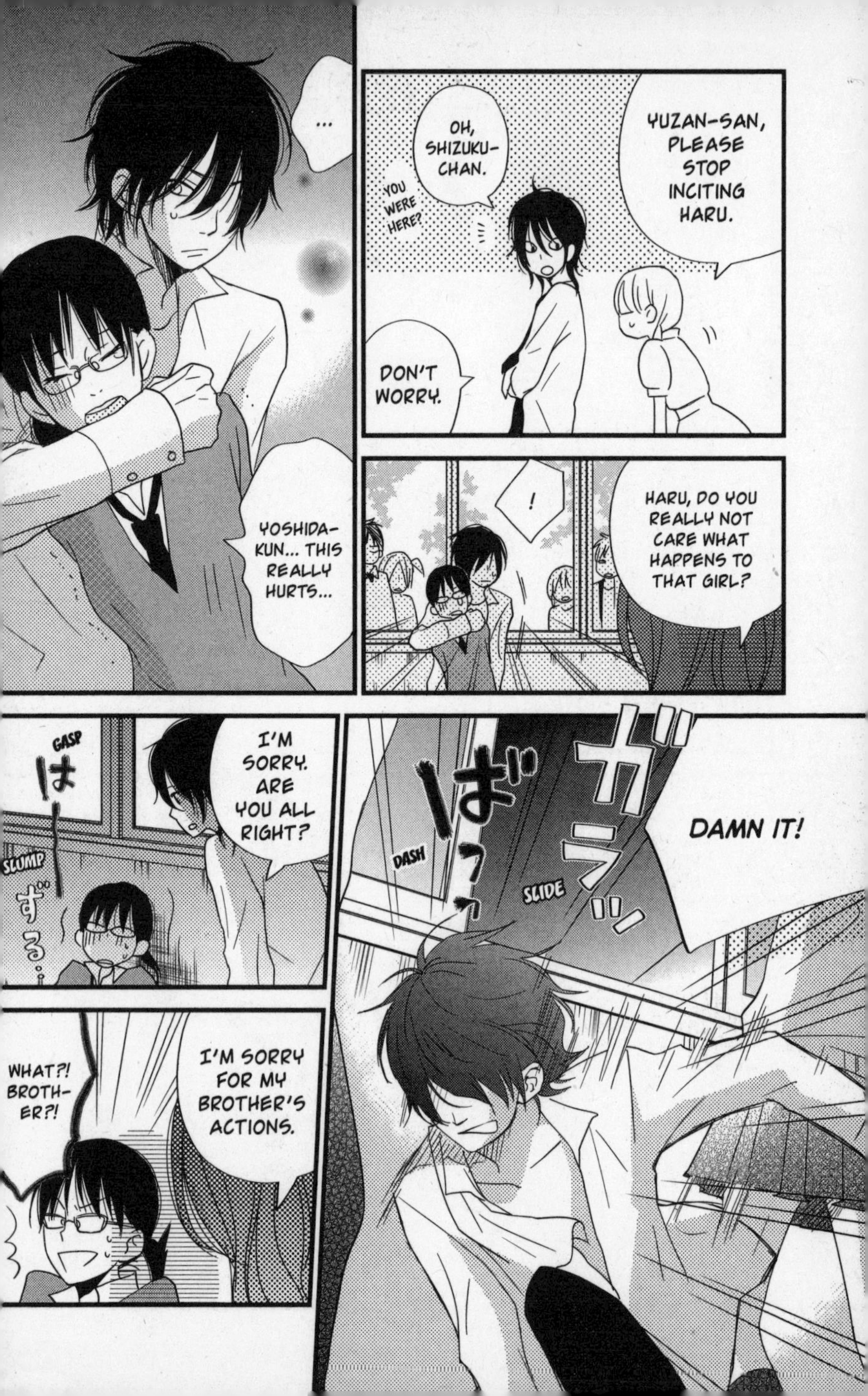
YUZAN-SAN, PLEASE STOP INCITING HARU.
OH, SHIZUKU-CHAN.
YOU WERE HERE?
DON'T WORRY.
HARU, DO YOU REALLY NOT CARE WHAT HAPPENS TO THAT GIRL?
!
...
YOSHIDA-KUN... THIS REALLY HURTS...
DAMN IT!
ガラッ
SLIDE
ばっ
DASH
I'M SORRY. ARE YOU ALL RIGHT?
はー
GASP
ずる
SLUMP
I'M SORRY FOR MY BROTHER'S ACTIONS.
WHAT?! BROTHER?!

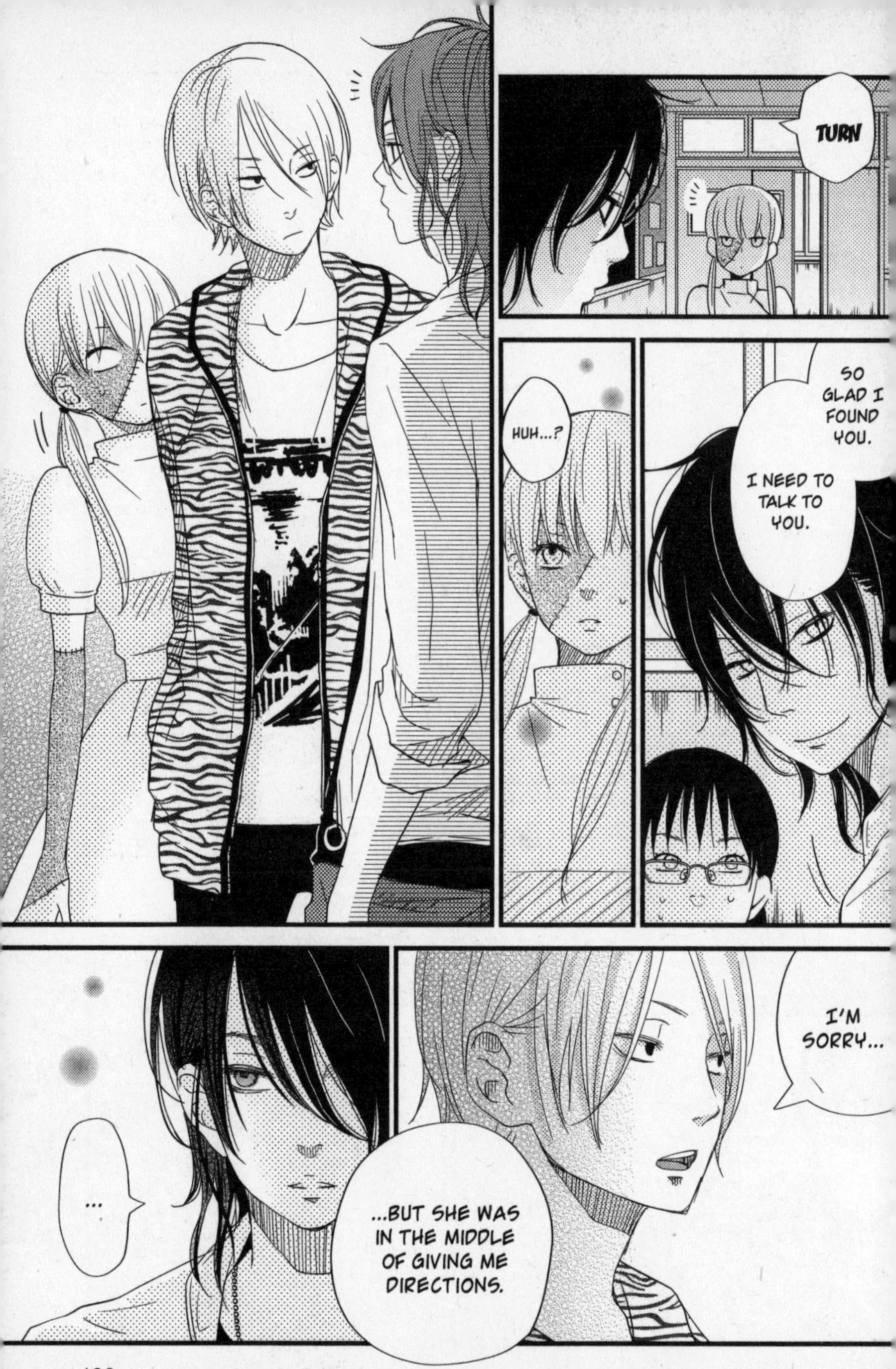
TURN
SO GLAD I FOUND YOU.
I NEED TO TALK TO YOU.
HUH...?
I'M SORRY...
...BUT SHE WAS IN THE MIDDLE OF GIVING ME DIRECTIONS.
...

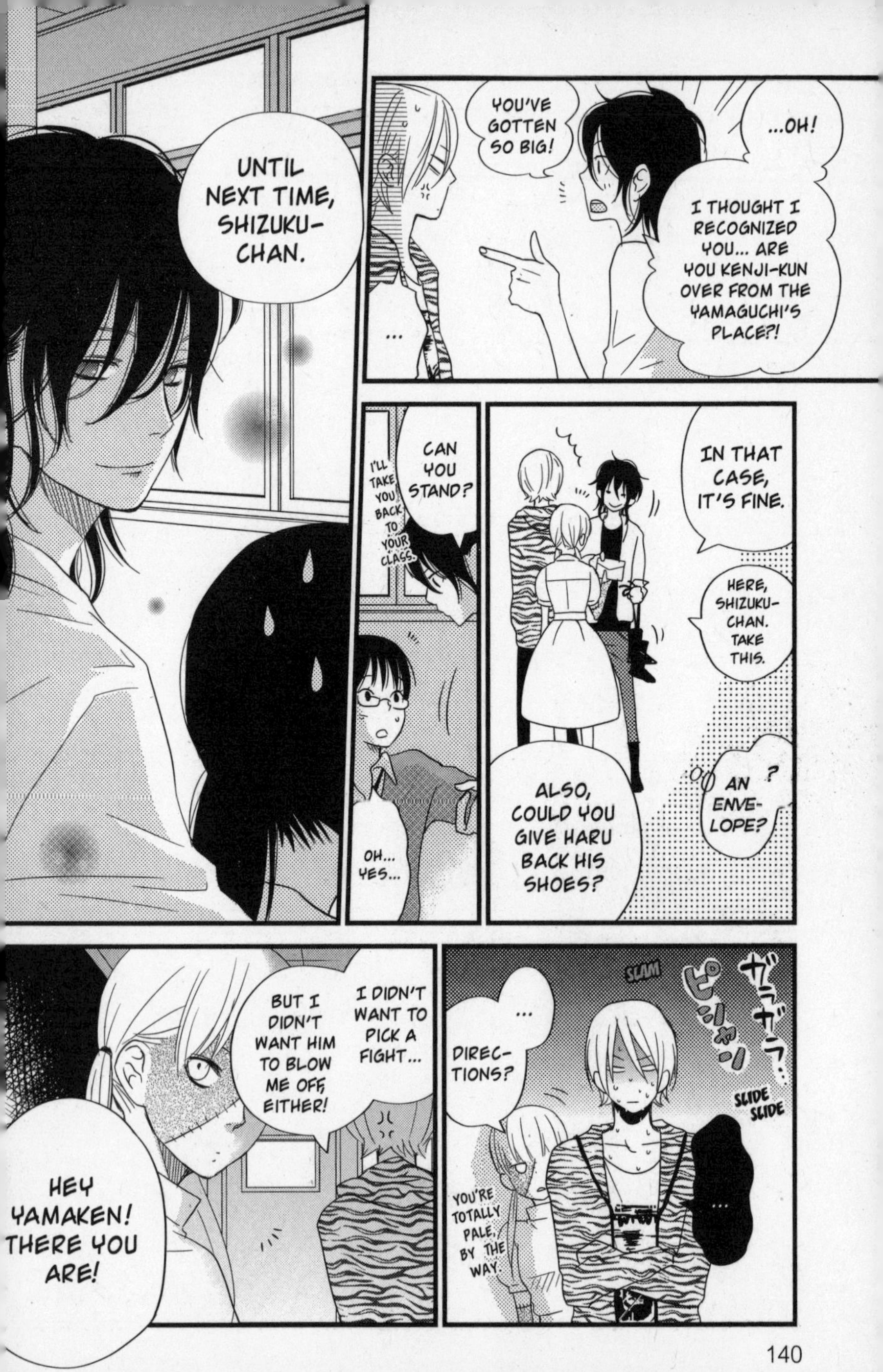
...OH!
I THOUGHT I RECOGNIZED YOU... ARE YOU KENJI-KUN OVER FROM THE YAMAGUCHI'S PLACE?!
YOU'VE GOTTEN SO BIG!
...
IN THAT CASE, IT'S FINE.
HERE, SHIZUKU-CHAN. TAKE THIS.
AN ENVELOPE?
ALSO, COULD YOU GIVE HARU BACK HIS SHOES?
CAN YOU STAND?
I'LL TAKE YOU BACK TO YOUR CLASS.
OH... YES...
UNTIL NEXT TIME, SHIZUKU-CHAN.
ガラガラ…
ピシャン!
SLAM
SLIDE SLIDE
...
...DIRECTIONS?
YOU'RE TOTALLY PALE, BY THE WAY.
I DIDN'T WANT TO PICK A FIGHT...
BUT I DIDN'T WANT HIM TO BLOW ME OFF, EITHER!
HEY YAMAKEN! THERE YOU ARE!

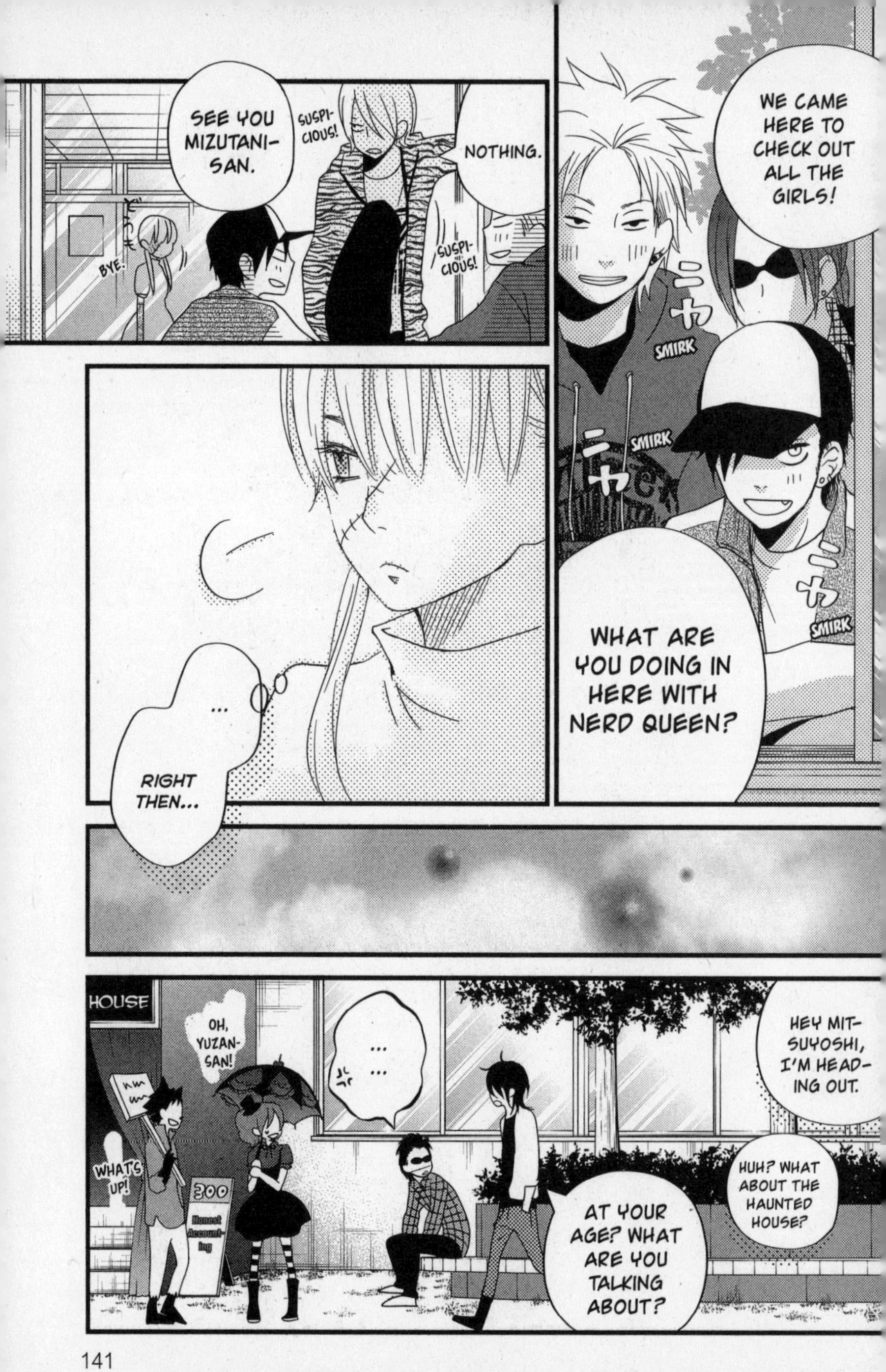
WE CAME HERE TO CHECK OUT ALL THE GIRLS!
SMIRK
SMIRK
SMIRK
WHAT ARE YOU DOING IN HERE WITH NERD QUEEN?
NOTHING.
SUSPI-CIOUS!
SEE YOU MIZUTANI-SAN.
SUSPI-CIOUS!
BYE.
...
RIGHT THEN...
HEY MIT-SUYOSHI, I'M HEAD-ING OUT.
HUH? WHAT ABOUT THE HAUNTED HOUSE?
AT YOUR AGE? WHAT ARE YOU TALKING ABOUT?
... ...
OH, YUZAN-SAN!
HOUSE
WHAT'S UP!
300
Honest Account-ing

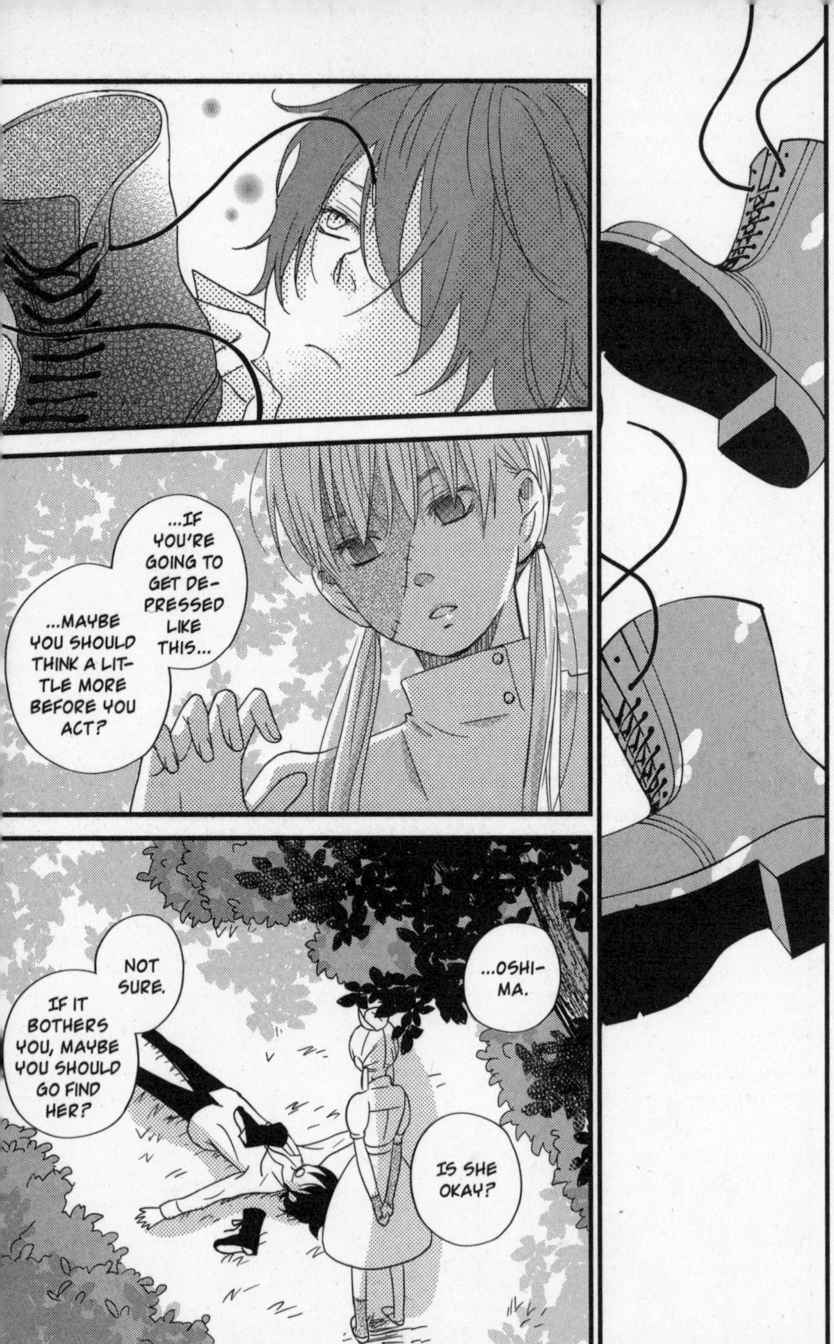
...IF YOU'RE GOING TO GET DE-PRESSED LIKE THIS...
...MAYBE YOU SHOULD THINK A LIT-TLE MORE BEFORE YOU ACT?
...OSHI-MA.
IS SHE OKAY?
NOT SURE.
IF IT BOTHERS YOU, MAYBE YOU SHOULD GO FIND HER?

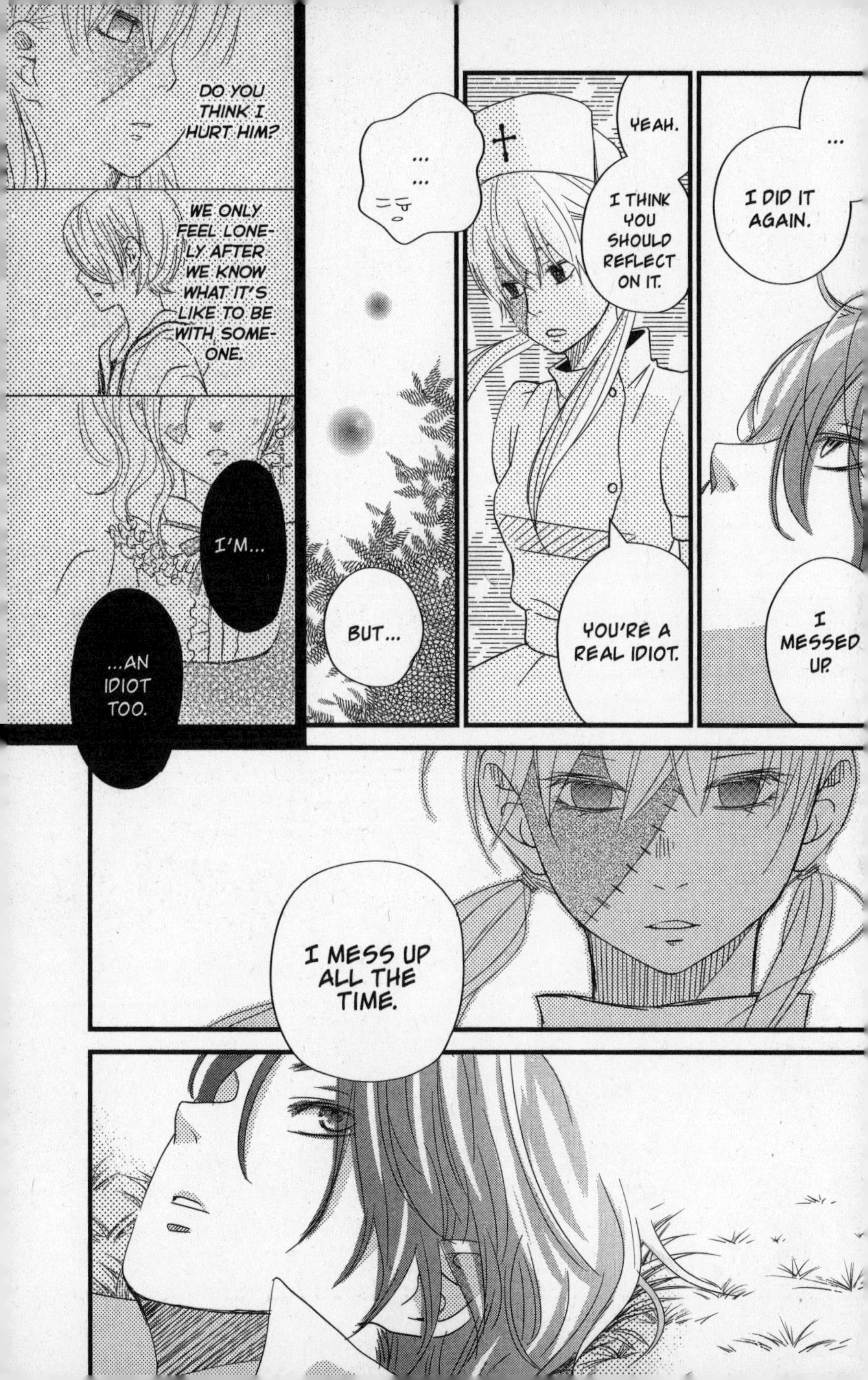
...
I DID IT AGAIN.
I MESSED UP.
YEAH.
I THINK YOU SHOULD REFLECT ON IT.
YOU'RE A REAL IDIOT.
... ...
BUT...
DO YOU THINK I HURT HIM?
WE ONLY FEEL LONE-LY AFTER WE KNOW WHAT IT'S LIKE TO BE WITH SOME-ONE.
I'M...
...AN IDIOT TOO.
I MESS UP ALL THE TIME.

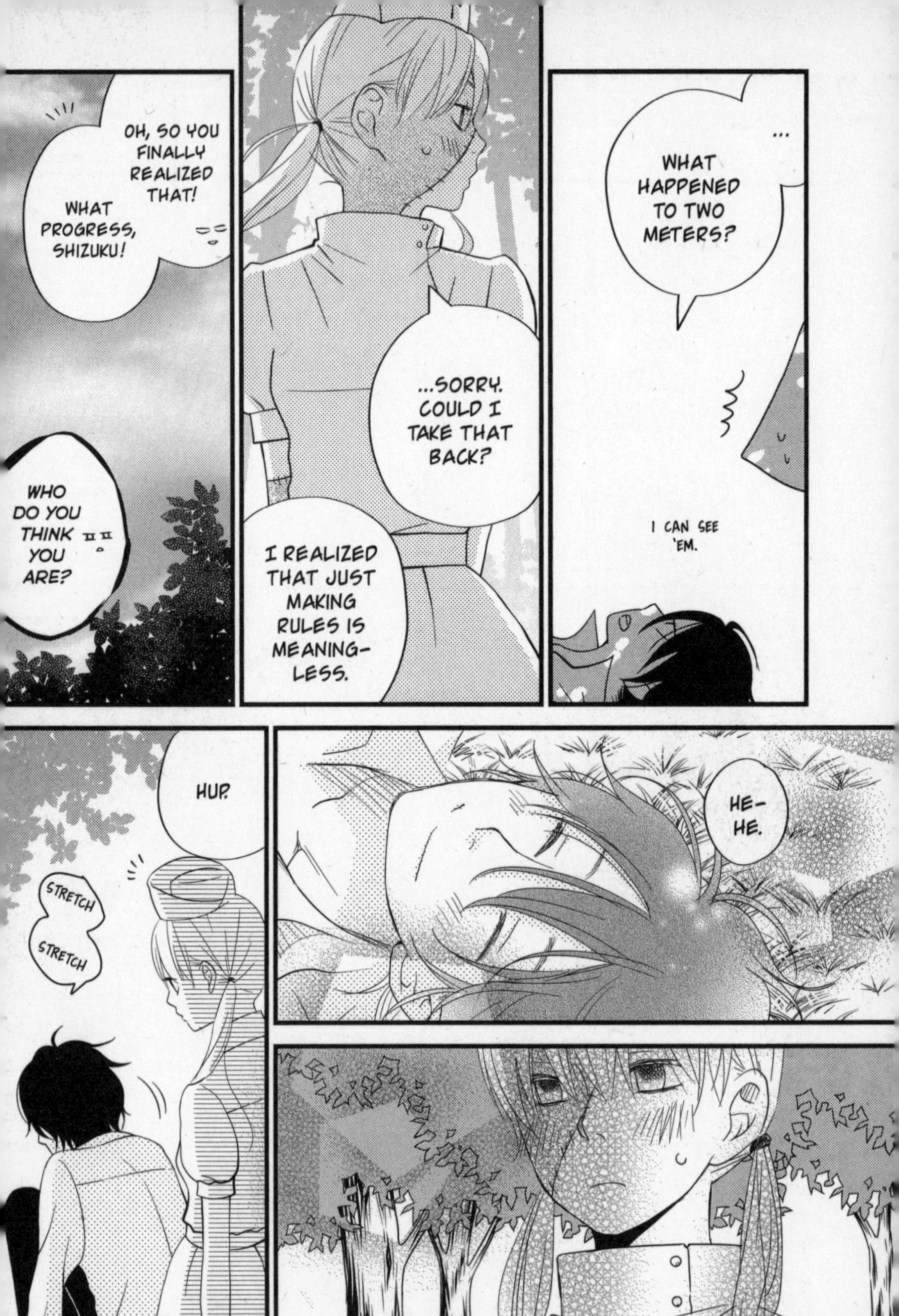
...
WHAT HAPPENED TO TWO METERS?
I CAN SEE 'EM.
...SORRY. COULD I TAKE THAT BACK?
I REALIZED THAT JUST MAKING RULES IS MEANING-LESS.
OH, SO YOU FINALLY REALIZED THAT!
WHAT PROGRESS, SHIZUKU!
WHO DO YOU THINK YOU ARE?
HE-HE.
HUP.
STRETCH
STRETCH

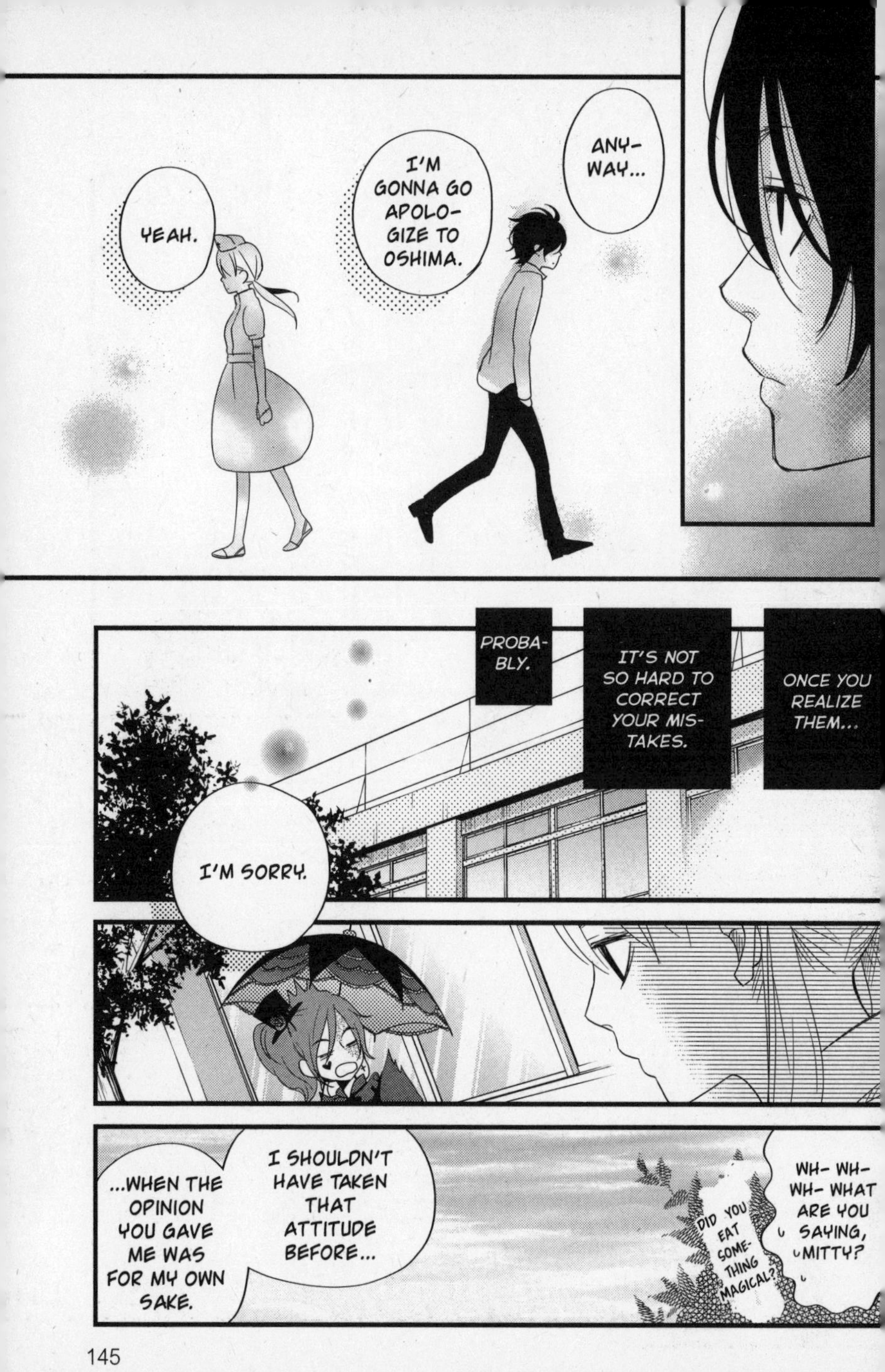
ANY-WAY...
I'M GONNA GO APOLOGIZE TO OSHIMA.
YEAH.
ONCE YOU REALIZE THEM...
IT'S NOT SO HARD TO CORRECT YOUR MISTAKES.
PROBABLY.
I'M SORRY.
WH- WH- WH- WHAT ARE YOU SAYING, MITTY?
DID YOU EAT SOMETHING MAGICAL?
I SHOULDN'T HAVE TAKEN THAT ATTITUDE BEFORE...
...WHEN THE OPINION YOU GAVE ME WAS FOR MY OWN SAKE.

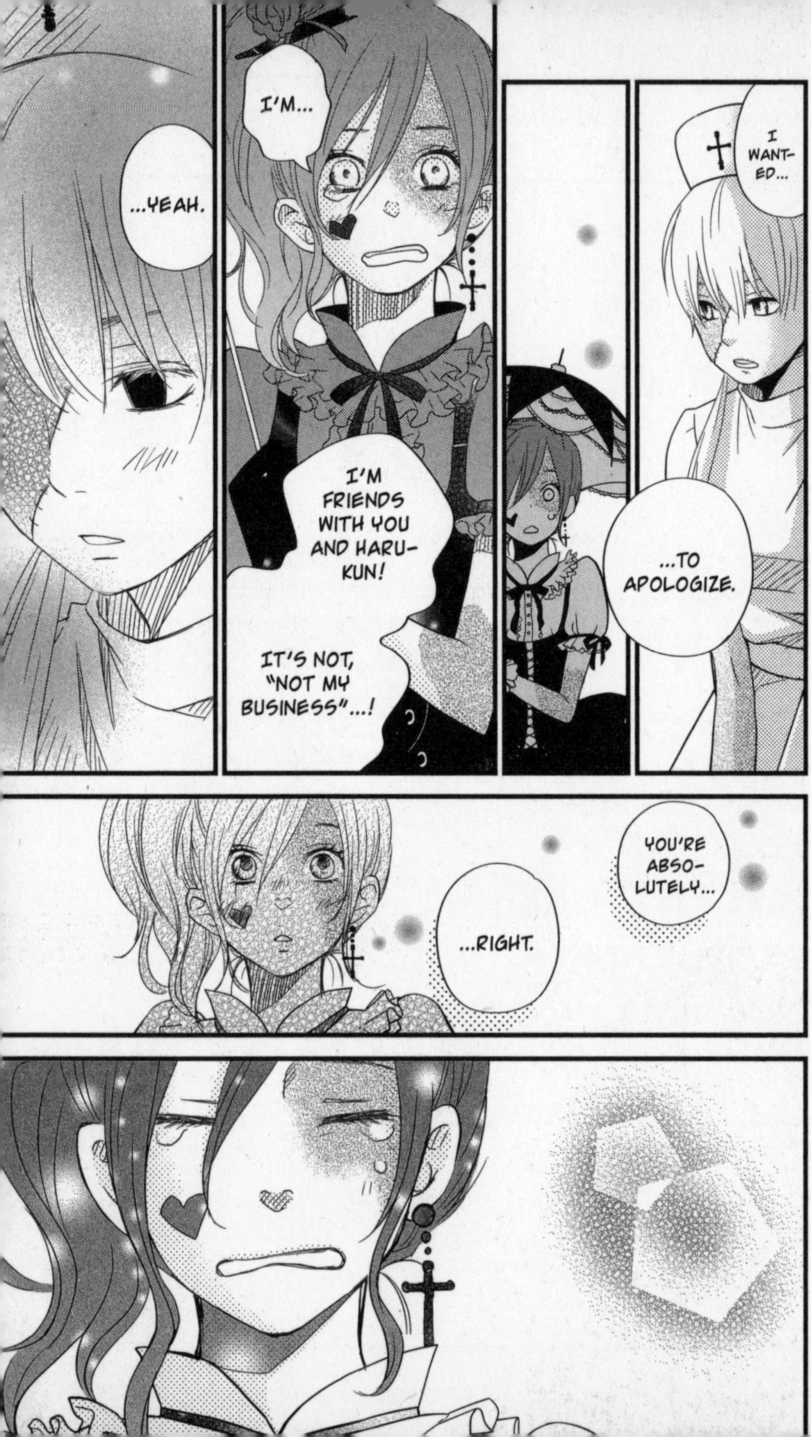
I WANT-ED...
...TO APOLOGIZE.
I'M...
I'M FRIENDS WITH YOU AND HARU-KUN!
IT'S NOT, "NOT MY BUSINESS"...!
...YEAH.
YOU'RE ABSO-LUTELY...
...RIGHT.

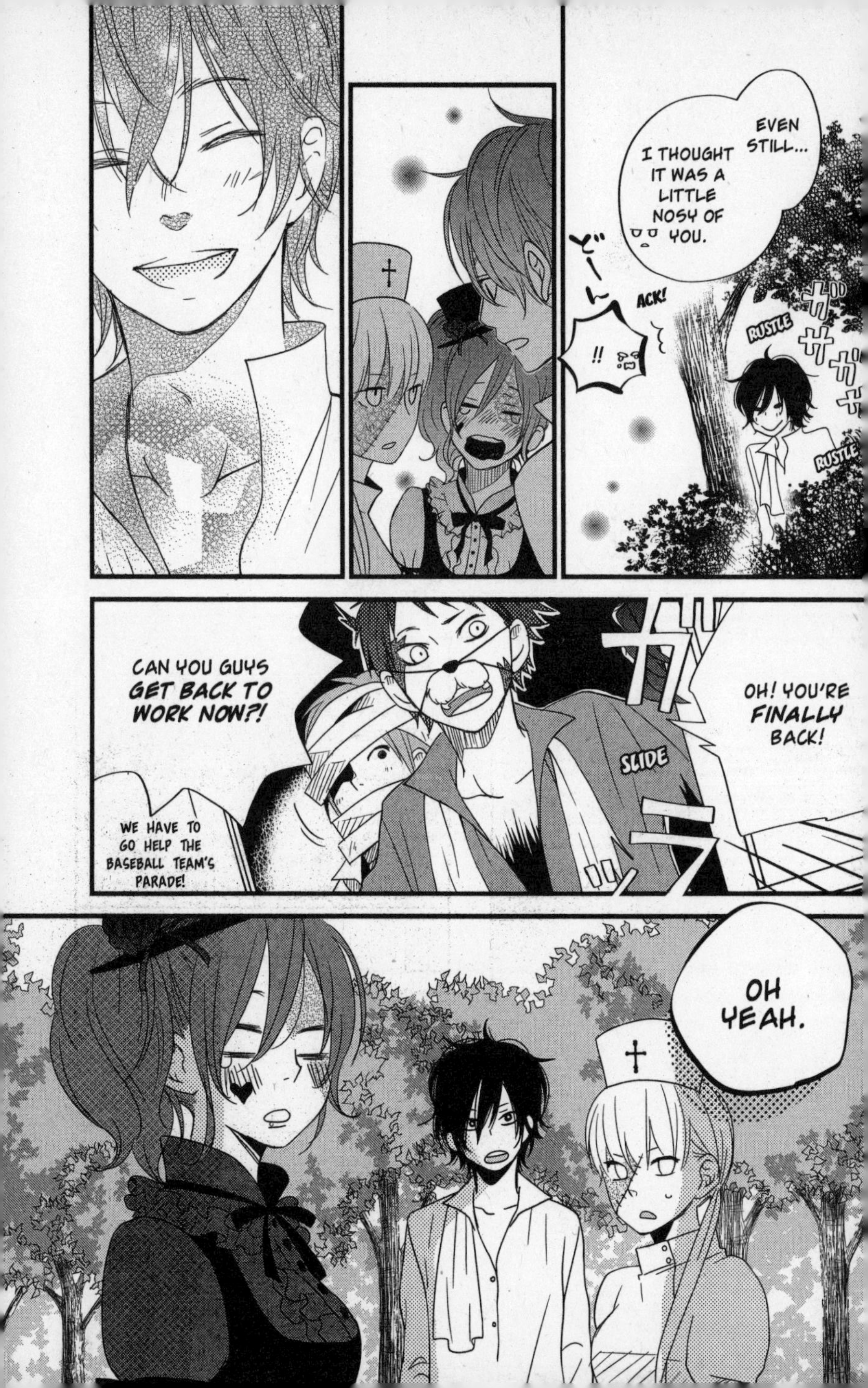
EVEN STILL... I THOUGHT IT WAS A LITTLE NOSY OF YOU.
どーん
ACK!
!!
RUSTLE
RUSTLE
OH! YOU'RE FINALLY BACK!
SLIDE
CAN YOU GUYS GET BACK TO WORK NOW?!
WE HAVE TO GO HELP THE BASEBALL TEAM'S PARADE!
OH YEAH.

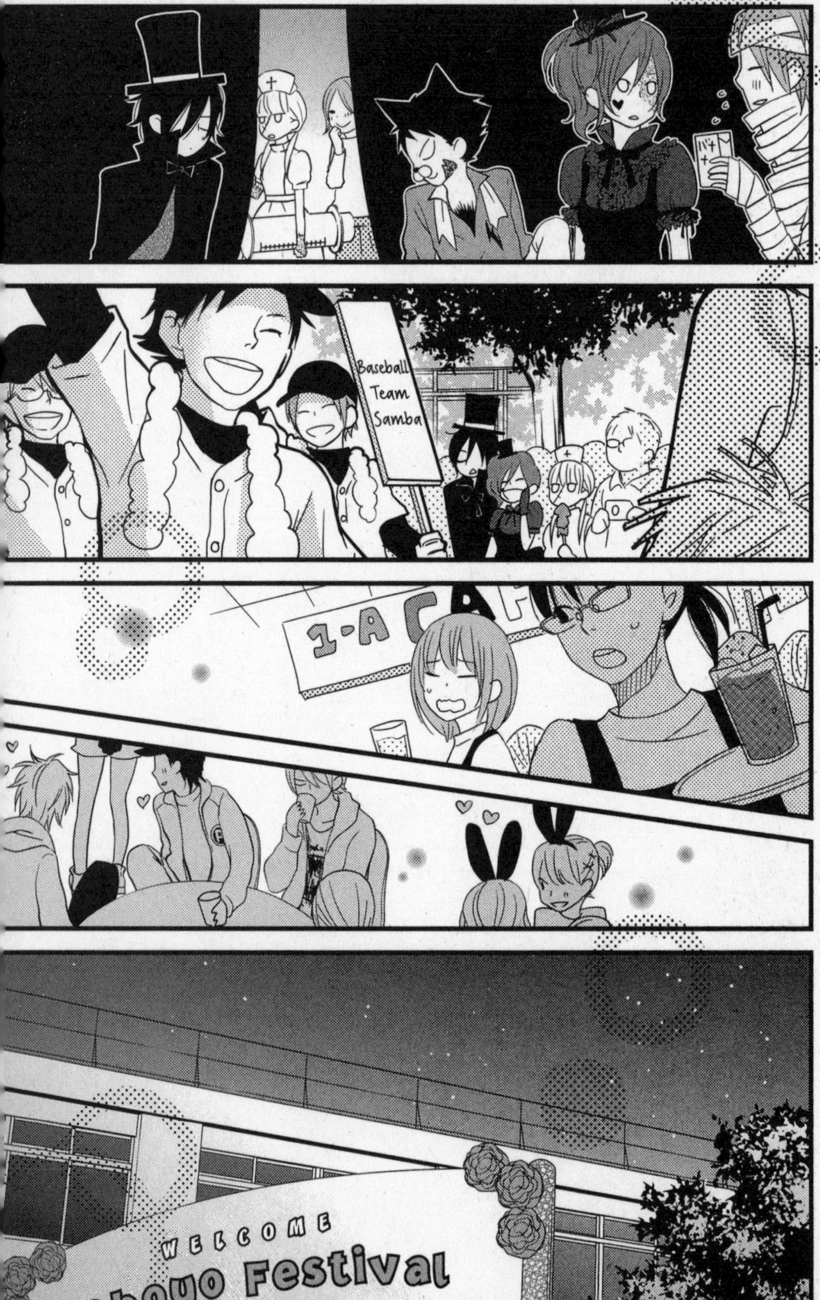
Baseball Team Samba
1-A
WELCOME
Shoyo Festival

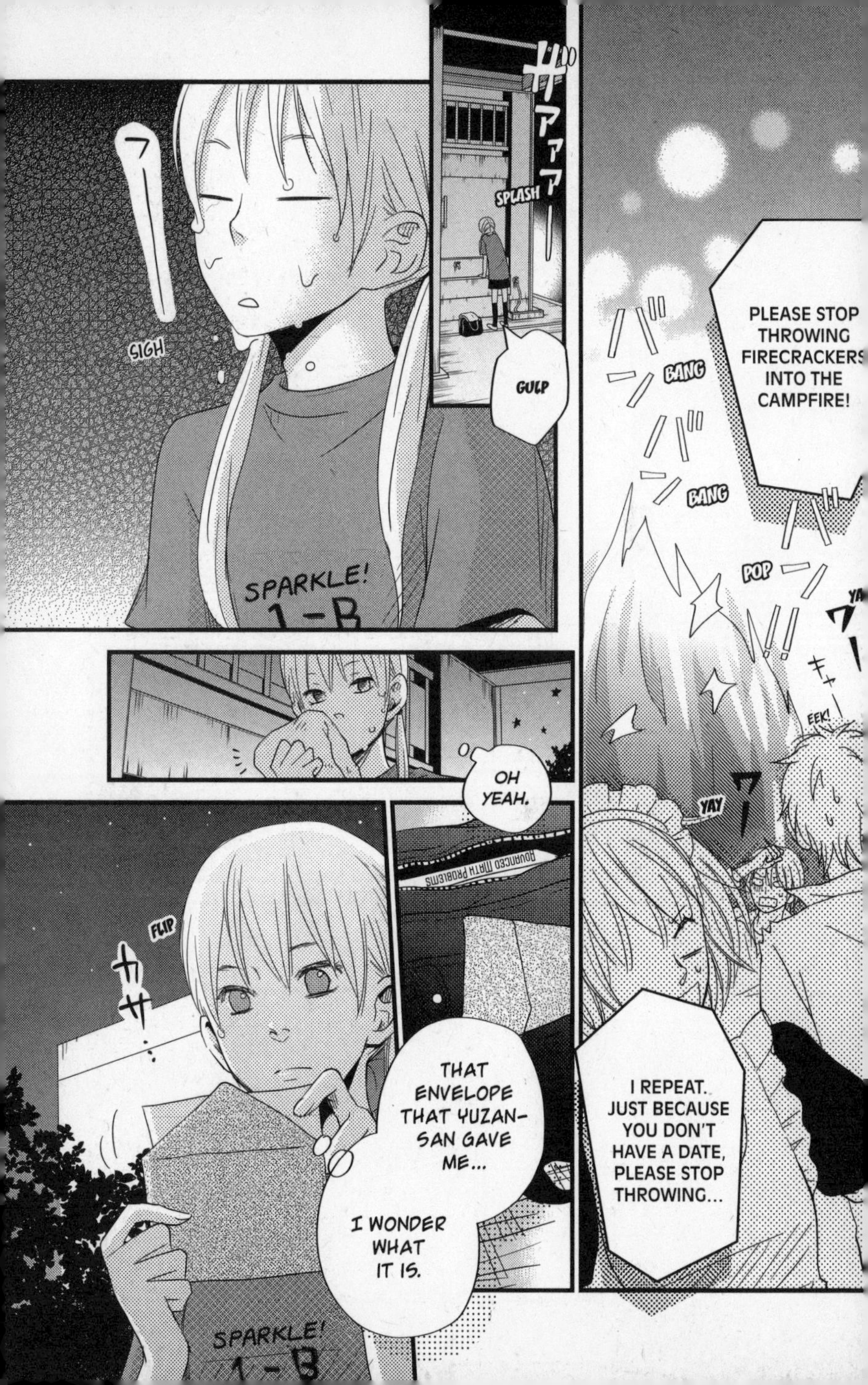
PLEASE STOP THROWING FIRECRACKERS INTO THE CAMPFIRE!
BANG
BANG
POP
EEK!
YAY
I REPEAT. JUST BECAUSE YOU DON'T HAVE A DATE, PLEASE STOP THROWING...
SPLASH
GULP
SIGH
SPARKLE! 1-B
OH YEAH.
ADVANCED MATH PROBLEMS
FLIP
THAT ENVELOPE THAT YUZAN-SAN GAVE ME...
I WONDER WHAT IT IS.
SPARKLE! 1-B

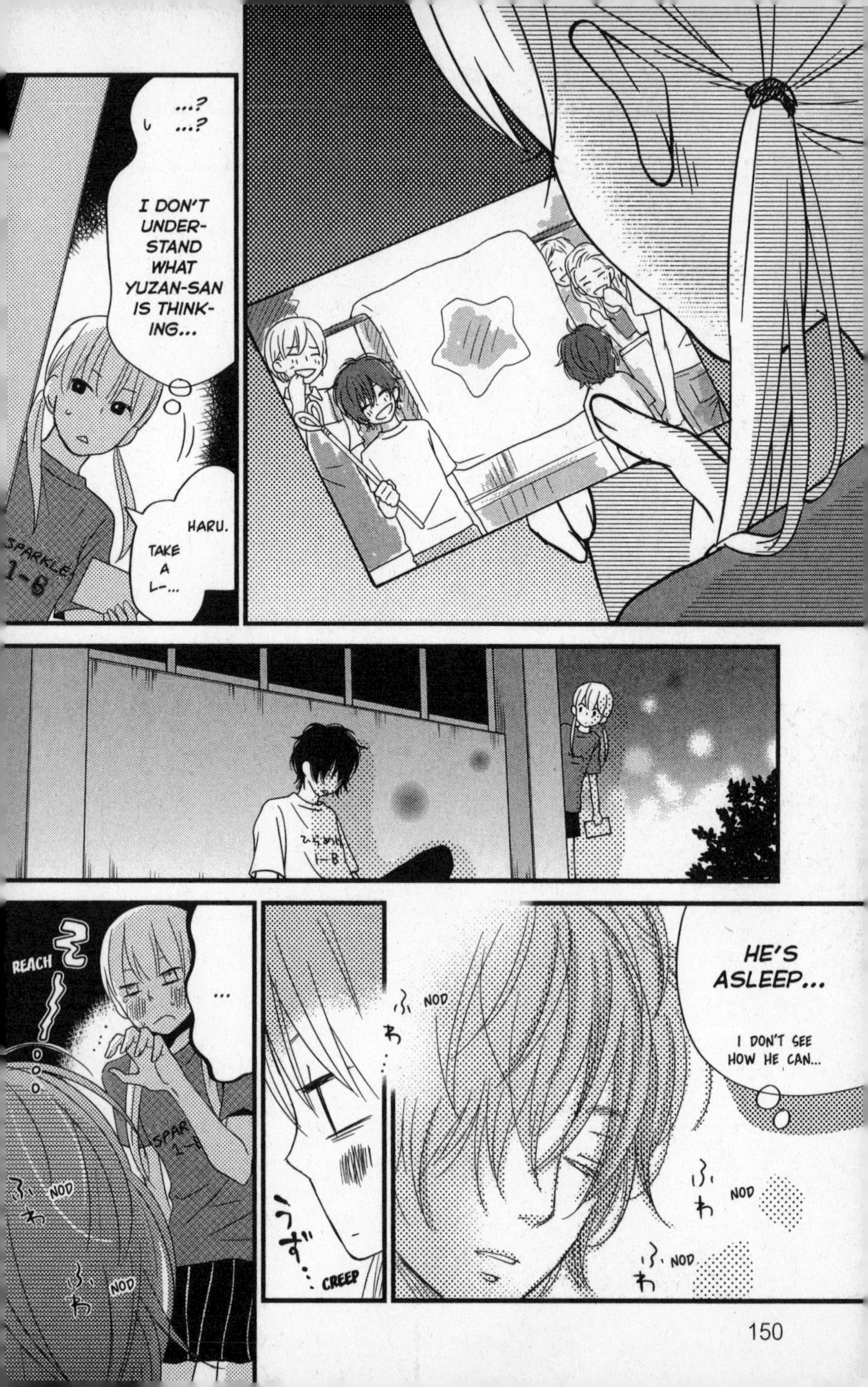
...?
...?
I DON'T UNDERSTAND WHAT YUZAN-SAN IS THINKING...
HARU.
TAKE A L-...
SPARKLE 1-B
HE'S ASLEEP...
I DON'T SEE HOW HE CAN...
ふわ NOD
ふわ NOD
ふわ NOD
ふわ NOD
うず... CREEP
...
REACH
ふわ NOD
ふわ NOD

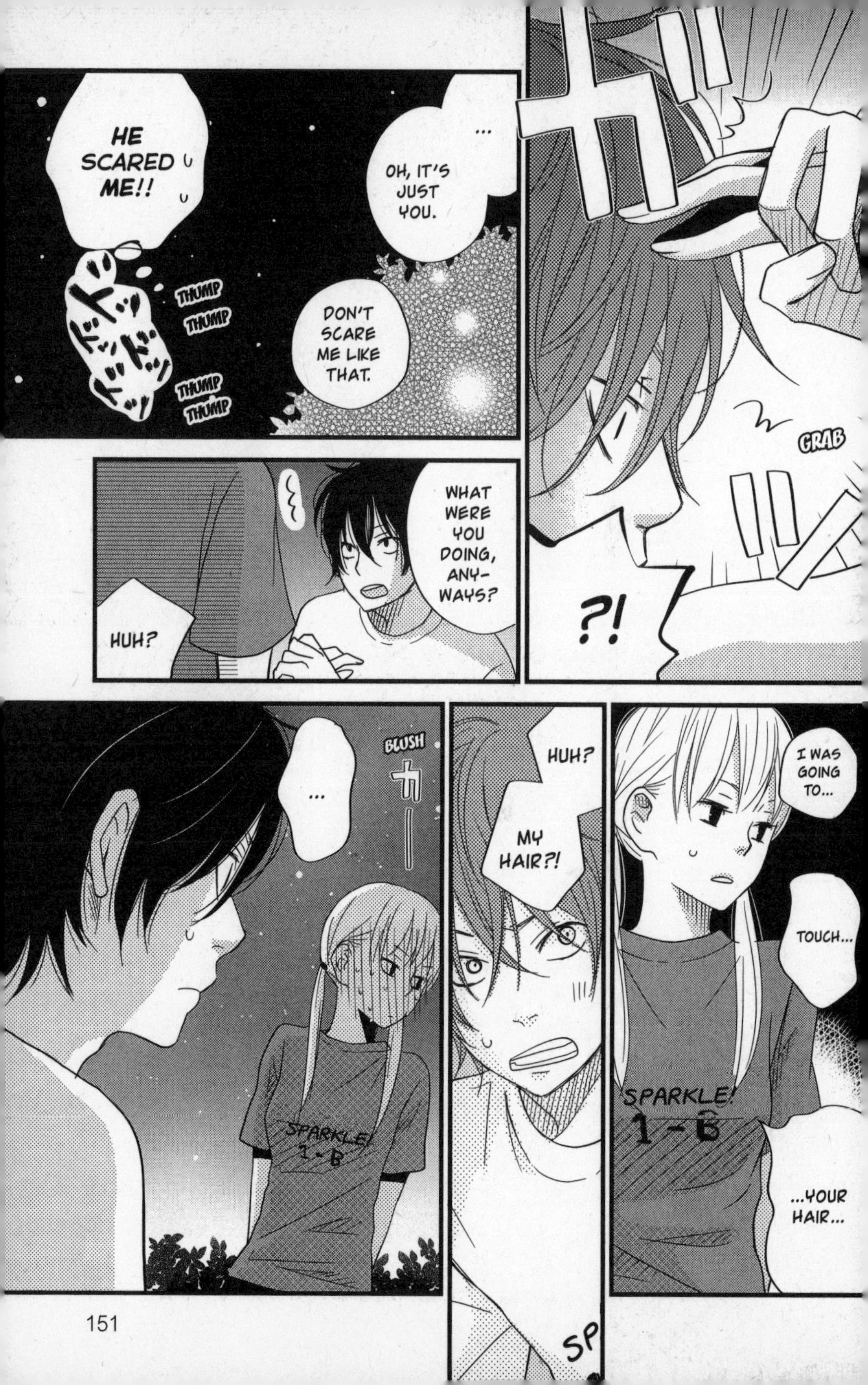
GRAB
?!
...
OH, IT'S JUST YOU.
DON'T SCARE ME LIKE THAT.
HE SCARED ME!!
THUMP THUMP
THUMP THUMP
WHAT WERE YOU DOING, ANY-WAYS?
HUH?
I WAS GOING TO...
TOUCH...
...YOUR HAIR...
SPARKLE! 1-B
HUH?
MY HAIR?!
SP
BLUSH
...
SPARKLE! 1-B

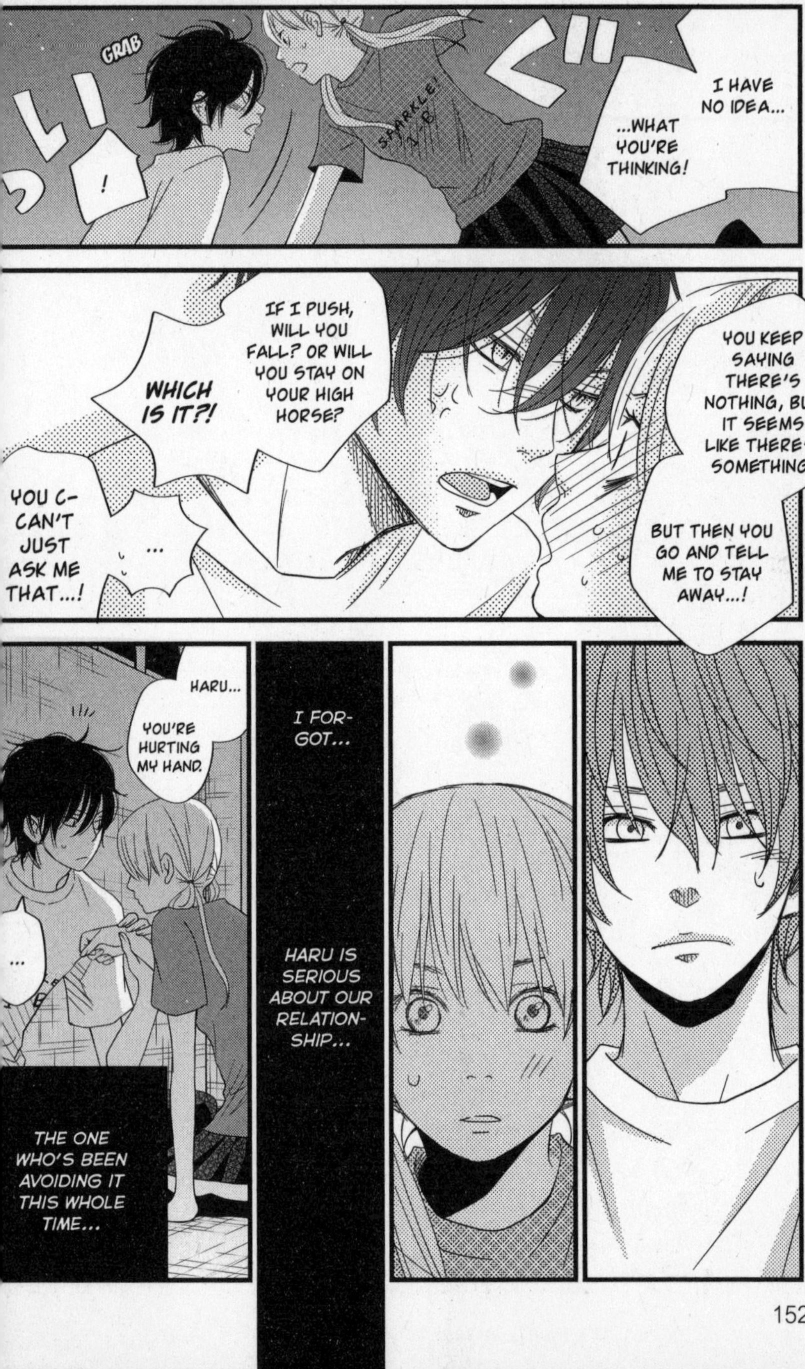
I HAVE NO IDEA...
...WHAT YOU'RE THINKING!
GRAB
SPARKLE! 1-8
!
YOU KEEP SAYING THERE'S NOTHING, BUT IT SEEMS LIKE THERE'S SOMETHING!
BUT THEN YOU GO AND TELL ME TO STAY AWAY...!
IF I PUSH, WILL YOU FALL? OR WILL YOU STAY ON YOUR HIGH HORSE?
WHICH IS IT?!
...
YOU C-CAN'T JUST ASK ME THAT...!
I FOR-GOT...
HARU IS SERIOUS ABOUT OUR RELATION-SHIP...
HARU...
YOU'RE HURTING MY HAND.
...
THE ONE WHO'S BEEN AVOIDING IT THIS WHOLE TIME...

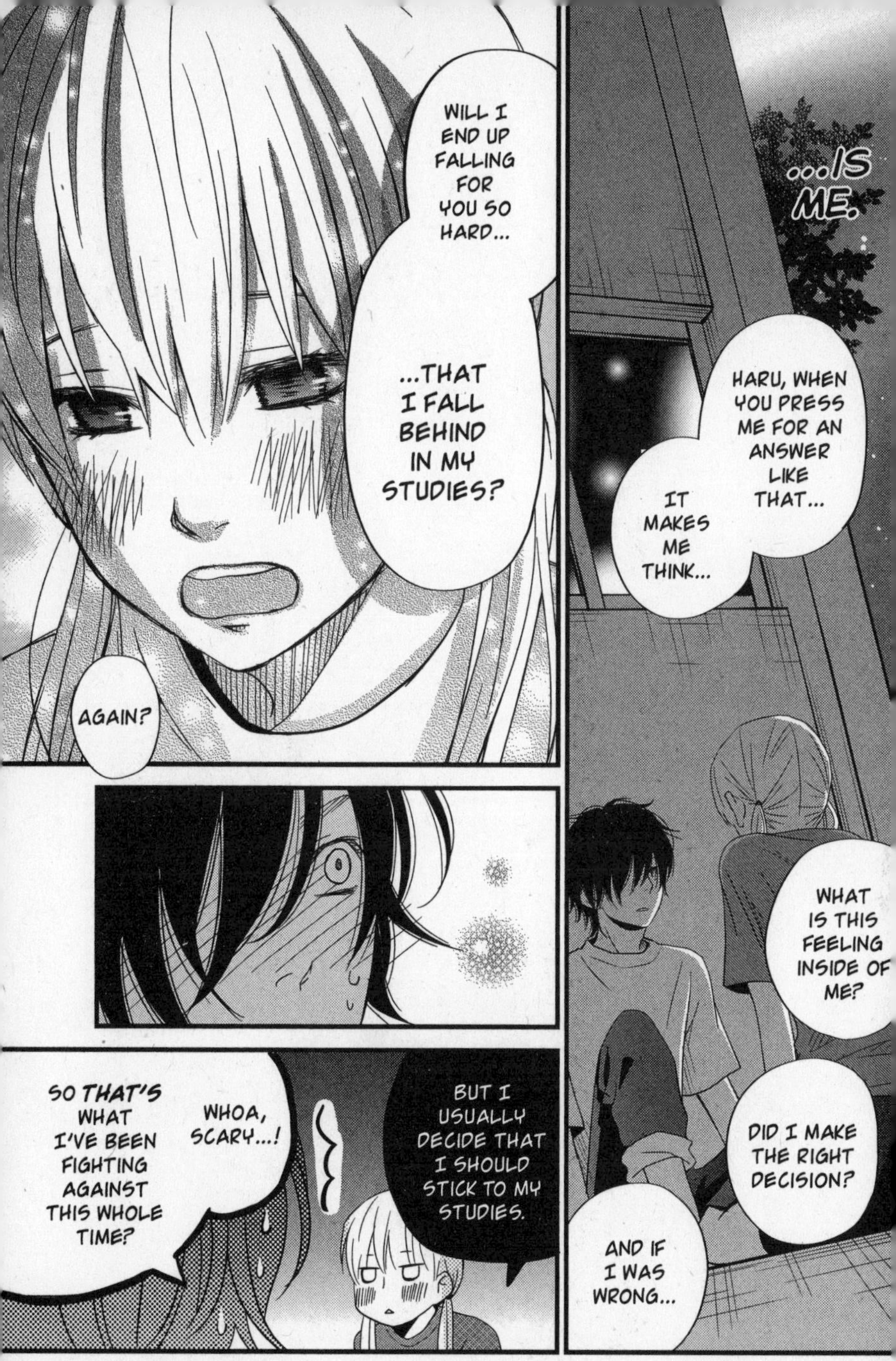
...IS ME.
HARU, WHEN YOU PRESS ME FOR AN ANSWER LIKE THAT...
IT MAKES ME THINK...
WHAT IS THIS FEELING INSIDE OF ME?
DID I MAKE THE RIGHT DECISION?
AND IF I WAS WRONG...
WILL I END UP FALLING FOR YOU SO HARD...
...THAT I FALL BEHIND IN MY STUDIES?
AGAIN?
BUT I USUALLY DECIDE THAT I SHOULD STICK TO MY STUDIES.
WHOA, SCARY...!
SO *THAT'S* WHAT I'VE BEEN FIGHTING AGAINST THIS WHOLE TIME?

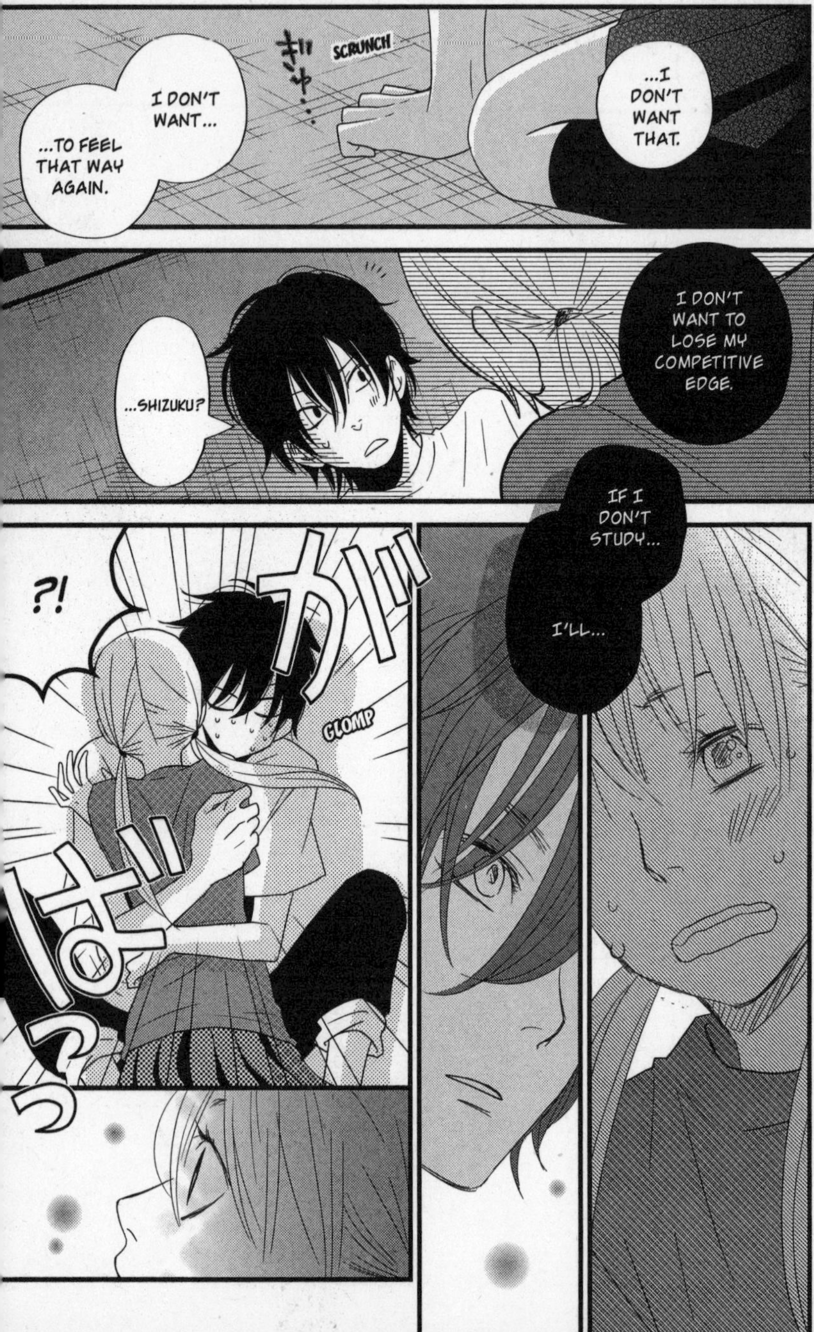
...I DON'T WANT THAT.
SCRUNCH
I DON'T WANT...
...TO FEEL THAT WAY AGAIN.
I DON'T WANT TO LOSE MY COMPETITIVE EDGE.
...SHIZUKU?
IF I DON'T STUDY...
I'LL...
?!
GLOMP

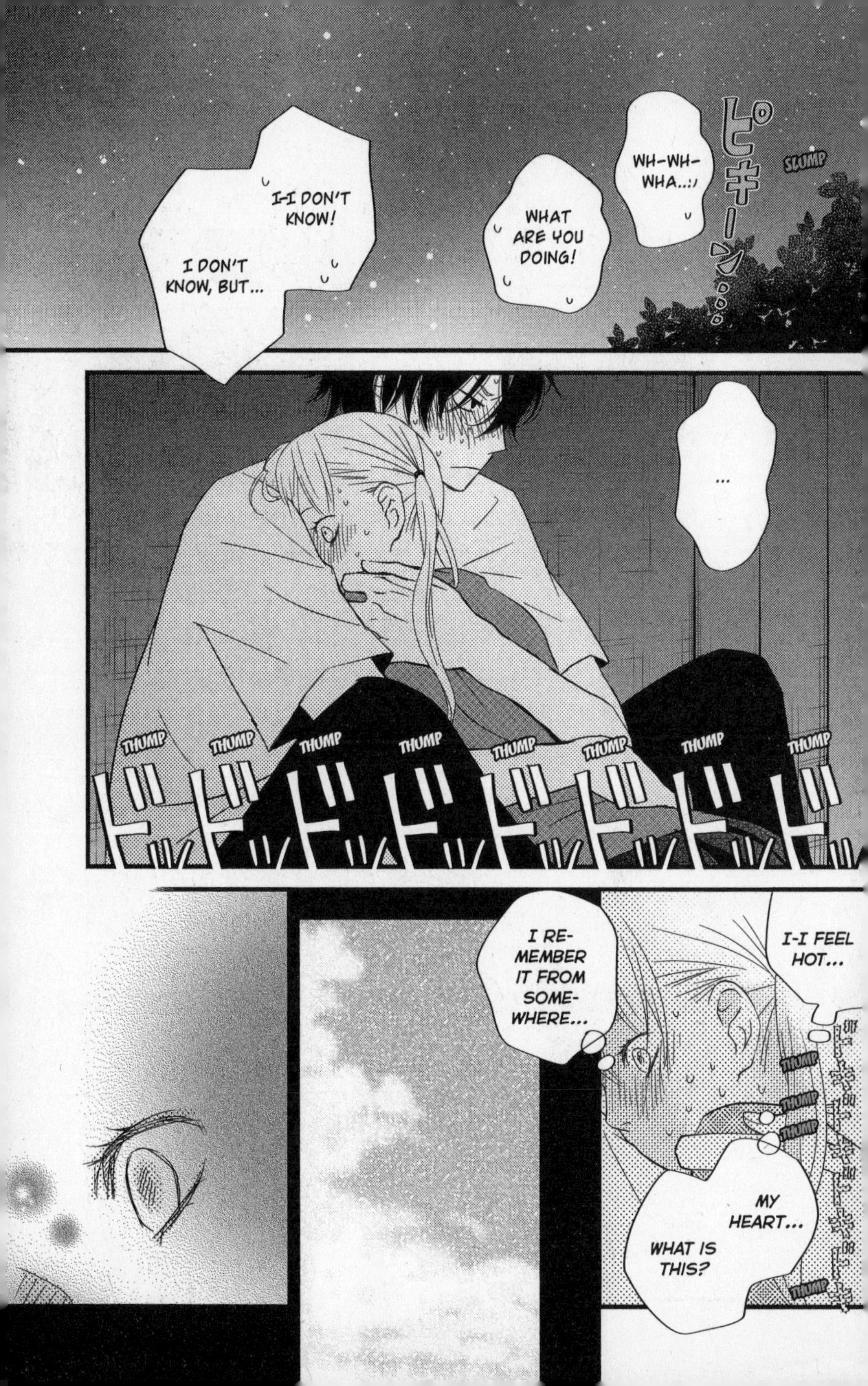
ピキーン。。。
SLUMP
WH-WH-WHA...!
WHAT ARE YOU DOING!
I-I DON'T KNOW!
I DON'T KNOW, BUT...
...
THUMP THUMP THUMP THUMP THUMP THUMP THUMP THUMP
ドッドッドッドッドッドッドッドッ
I-I FEEL HOT...
I RE-MEMBER IT FROM SOME-WHERE...
THUMP
THUMP
THUMP
MY HEART...
WHAT IS THIS?
THUMP

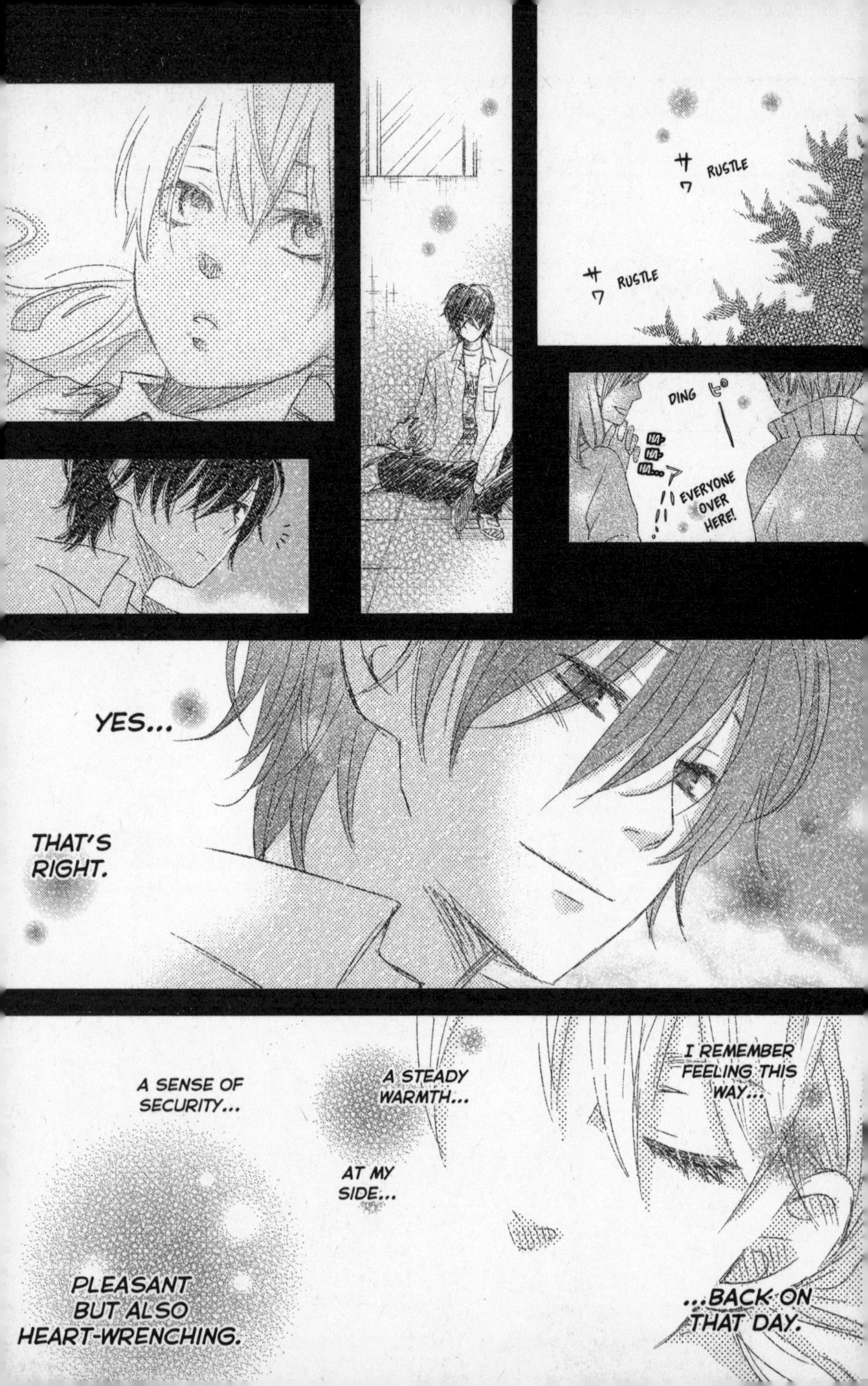

サワ
RUSTLE
サワ
RUSTLE
DING
EVERYONE OVER HERE!
YES...
THAT'S RIGHT.
I REMEMBER FEELING THIS WAY...
A STEADY WARMTH...
A SENSE OF SECURITY...
AT MY SIDE...
PLEASANT BUT ALSO HEART-WRENCHING.
...BACK ON THAT DAY.

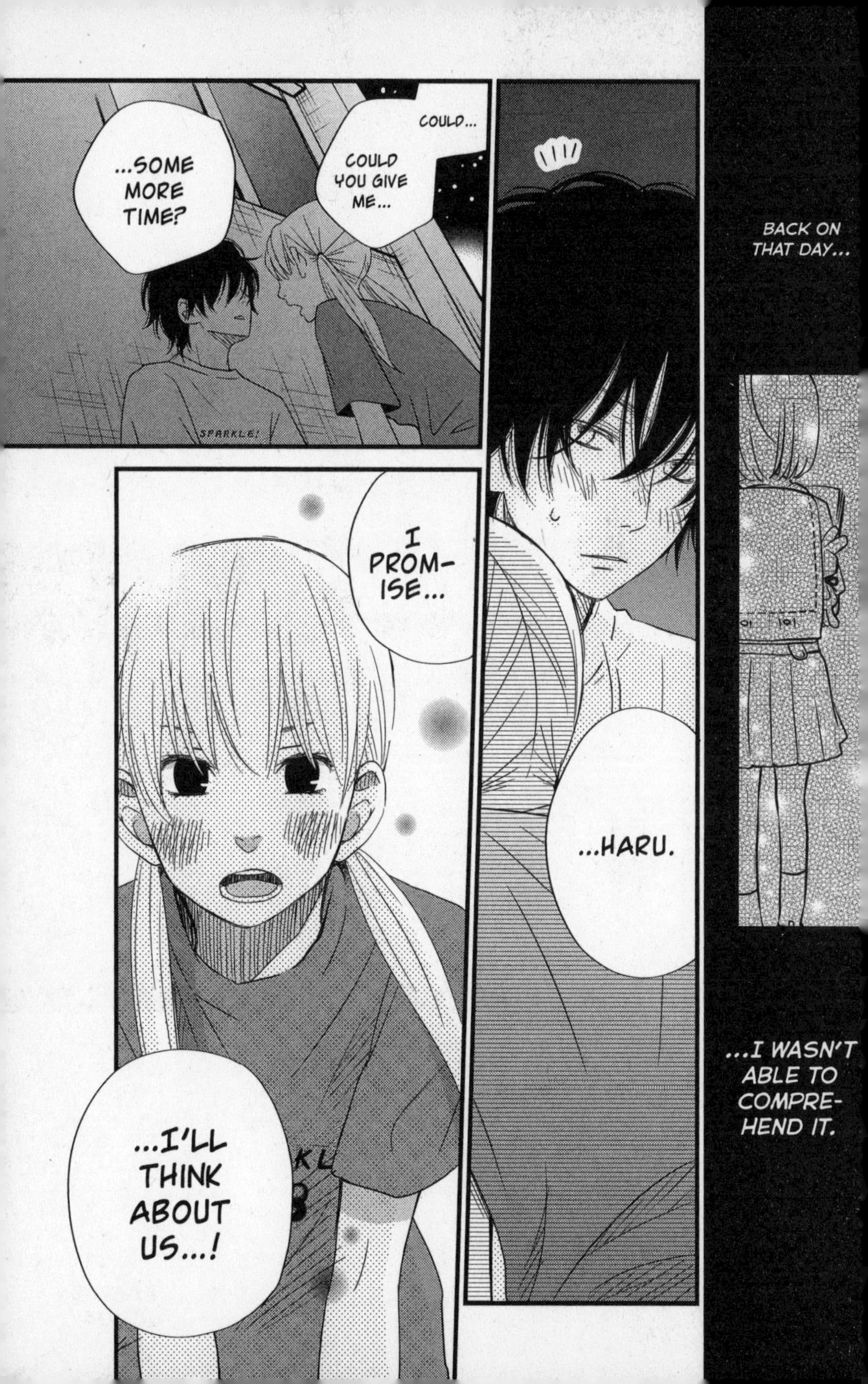
BACK ON THAT DAY...
...I WASN'T ABLE TO COMPREHEND IT.
...HARU.
COULD...
COULD YOU GIVE ME...
...SOME MORE TIME?
SPARKLE!
I PROMISE...
...I'LL THINK ABOUT US...!

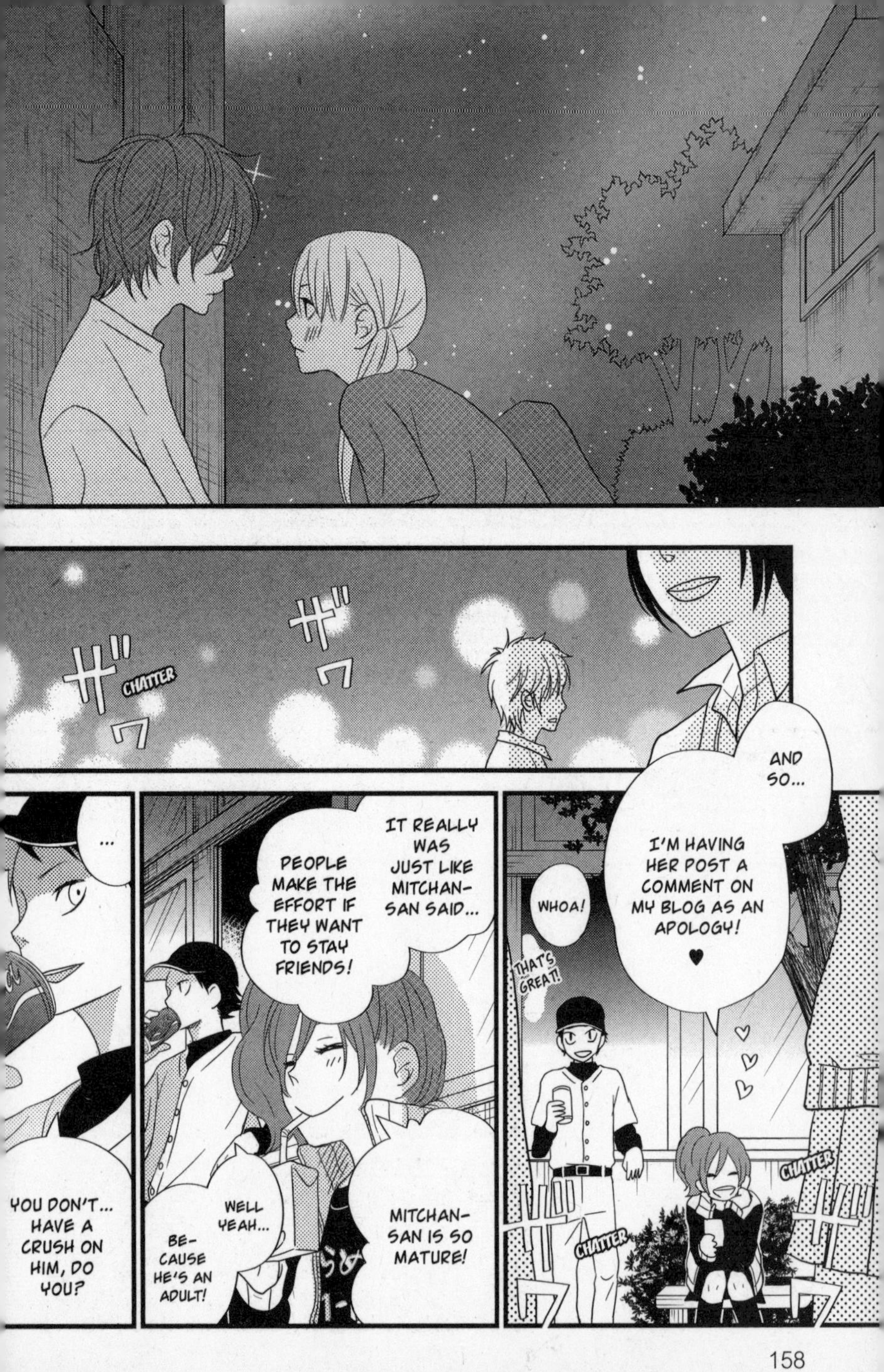
ザワ
ザワ
CHATTER
AND SO...
I'M HAVING HER POST A COMMENT ON MY BLOG AS AN APOLOGY! ♥
WHOA!
THAT'S GREAT!
CHATTER
CHATTER
IT REALLY WAS JUST LIKE MITCHAN-SAN SAID...
PEOPLE MAKE THE EFFORT IF THEY WANT TO STAY FRIENDS!
MITCHAN-SAN IS SO MATURE!
WELL YEAH...
BE-CAUSE HE'S AN ADULT!
...
YOU DON'T... HAVE A CRUSH ON HIM, DO YOU?

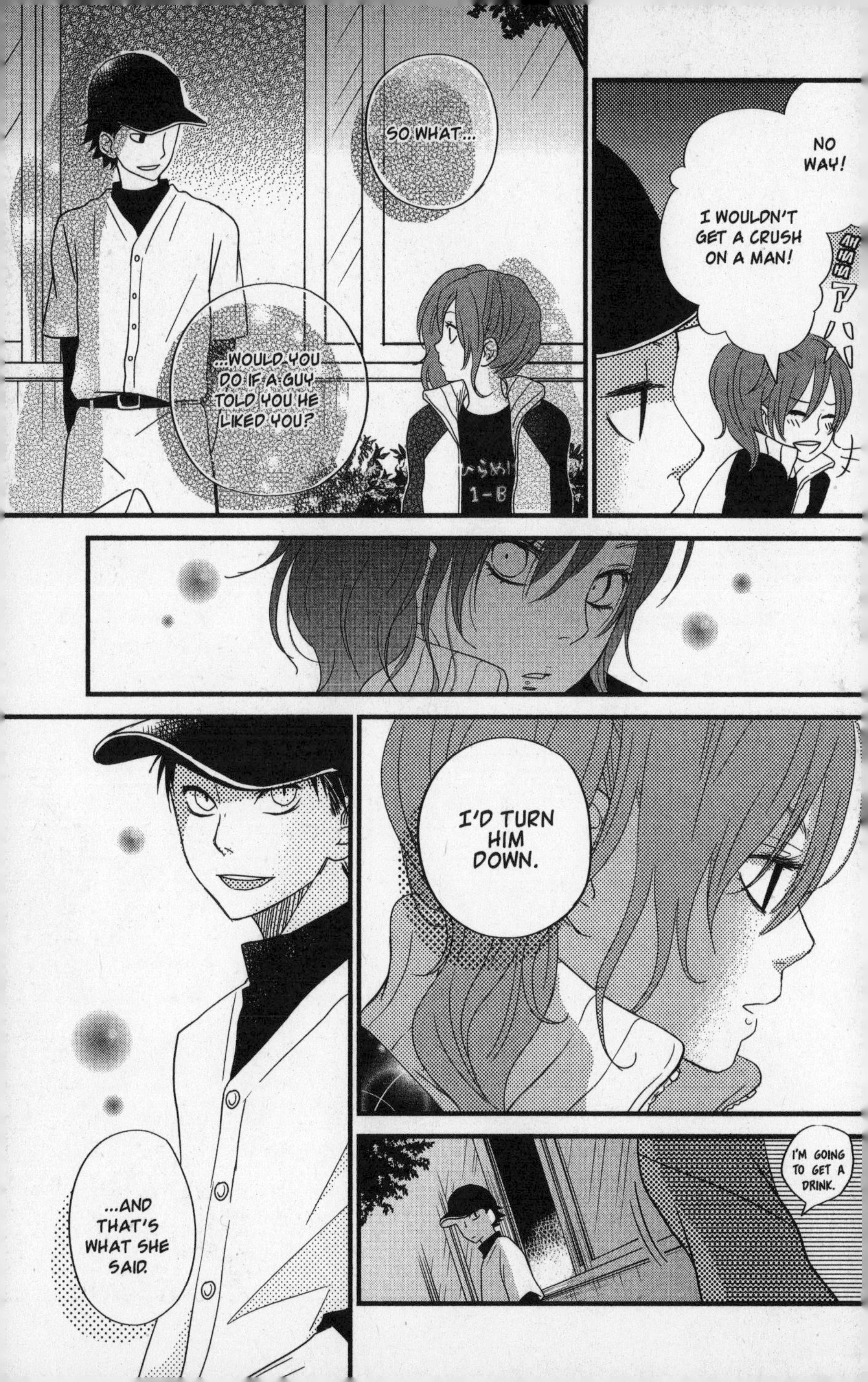
NO WAY!
I WOULDN'T GET A CRUSH ON A MAN!
AHAHA
アハハ
SO WHAT...
...WOULD YOU DO IF A GUY TOLD YOU HE LIKED YOU?
I'D TURN HIM DOWN.
I'M GOING TO GET A DRINK.
...AND THAT'S WHAT SHE SAID.

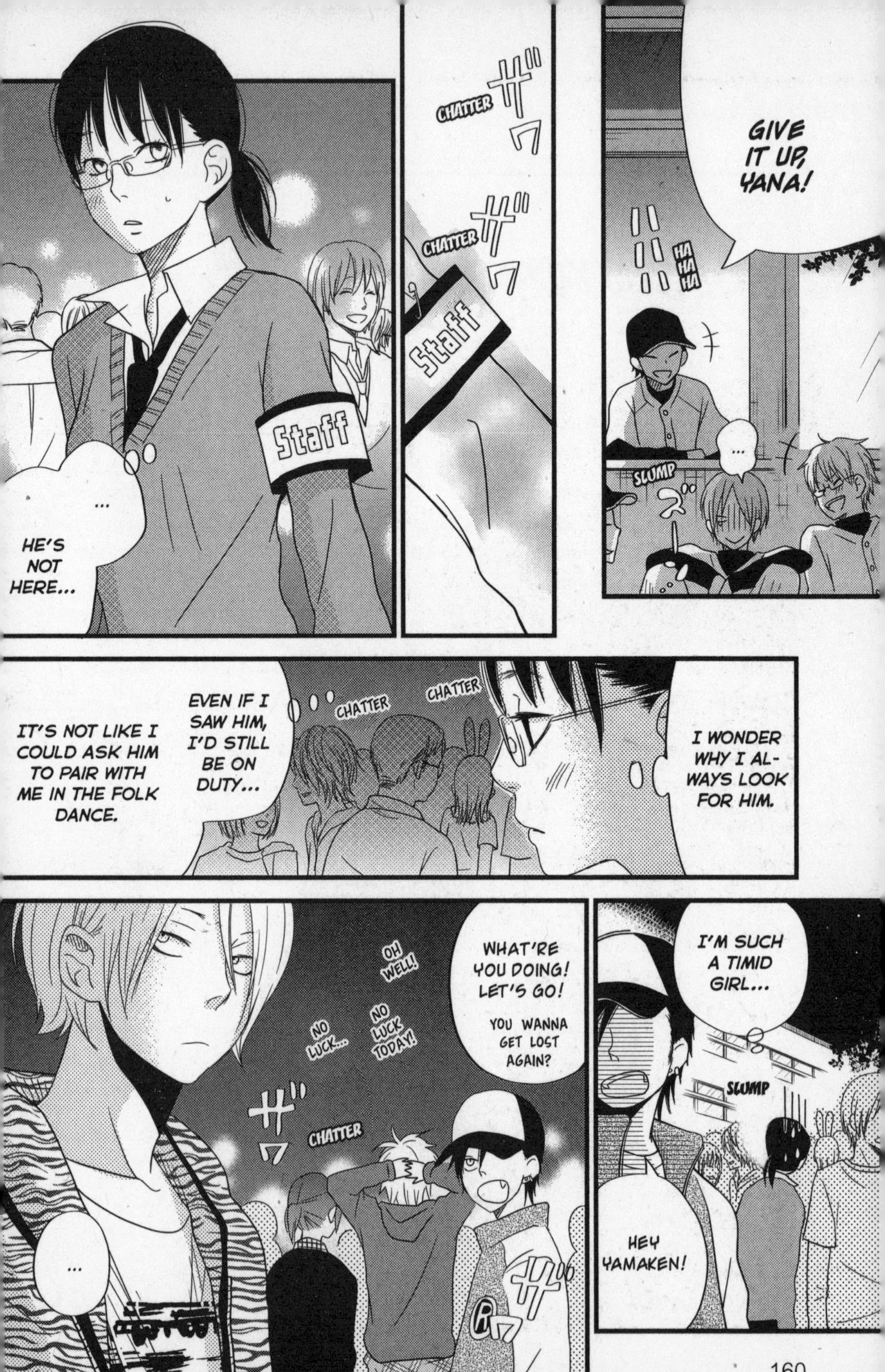
GIVE IT UP, YANA!
HA HA HA
...
SLUMP
CHATTER
CHATTER
Staff
Staff
...
HE'S NOT HERE...
I WONDER WHY I ALWAYS LOOK FOR HIM.
CHATTER
CHATTER
EVEN IF I SAW HIM, I'D STILL BE ON DUTY...
IT'S NOT LIKE I COULD ASK HIM TO PAIR WITH ME IN THE FOLK DANCE.
I'M SUCH A TIMID GIRL...
SLUMP
HEY YAMAKEN!
WHAT'RE YOU DOING! LET'S GO!
YOU WANNA GET LOST AGAIN?
OH WELL!
NO LUCK TODAY!
NO LUCK...
CHATTER
...

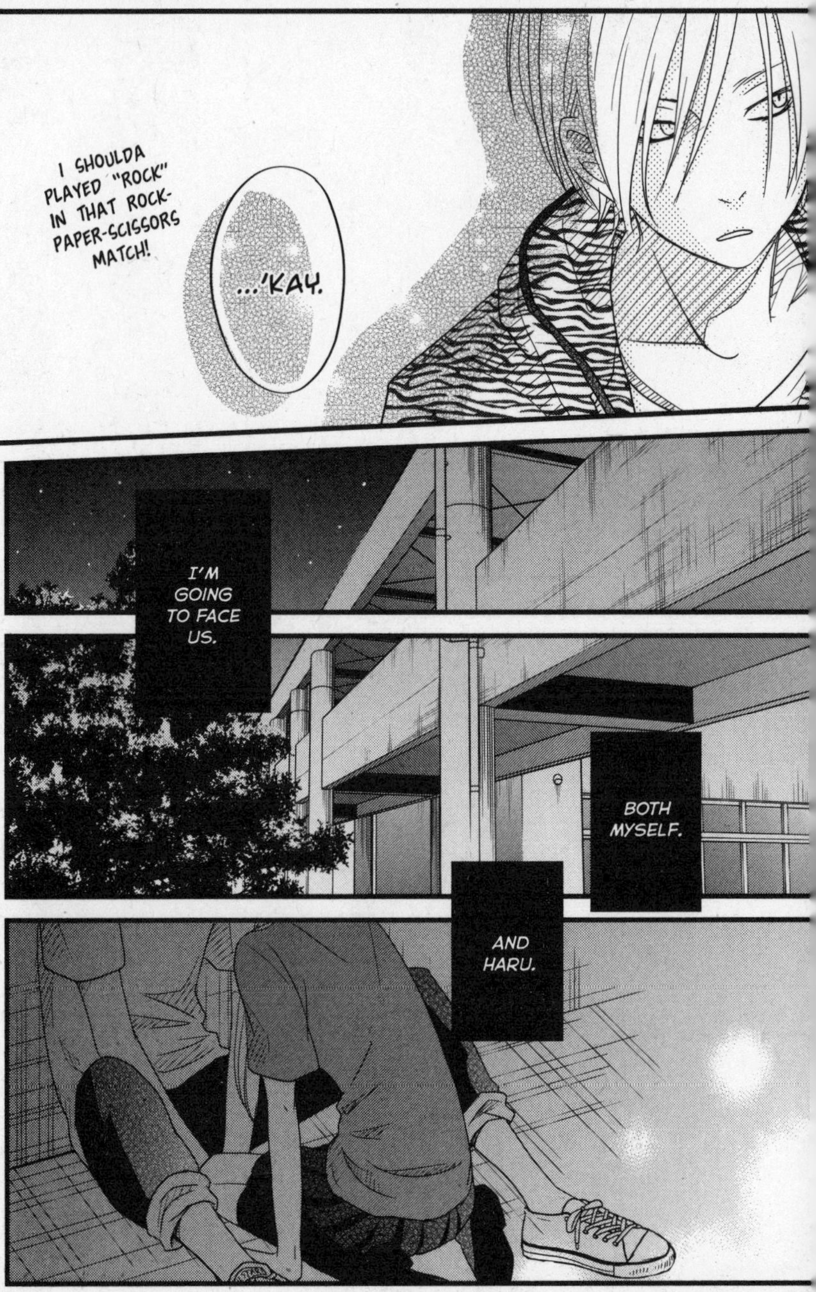
...'KAY.
I SHOULDA PLAYED "ROCK" IN THAT ROCK-PAPER-SCISSORS MATCH!
I'M GOING TO FACE US.
BOTH MYSELF.
AND HARU.

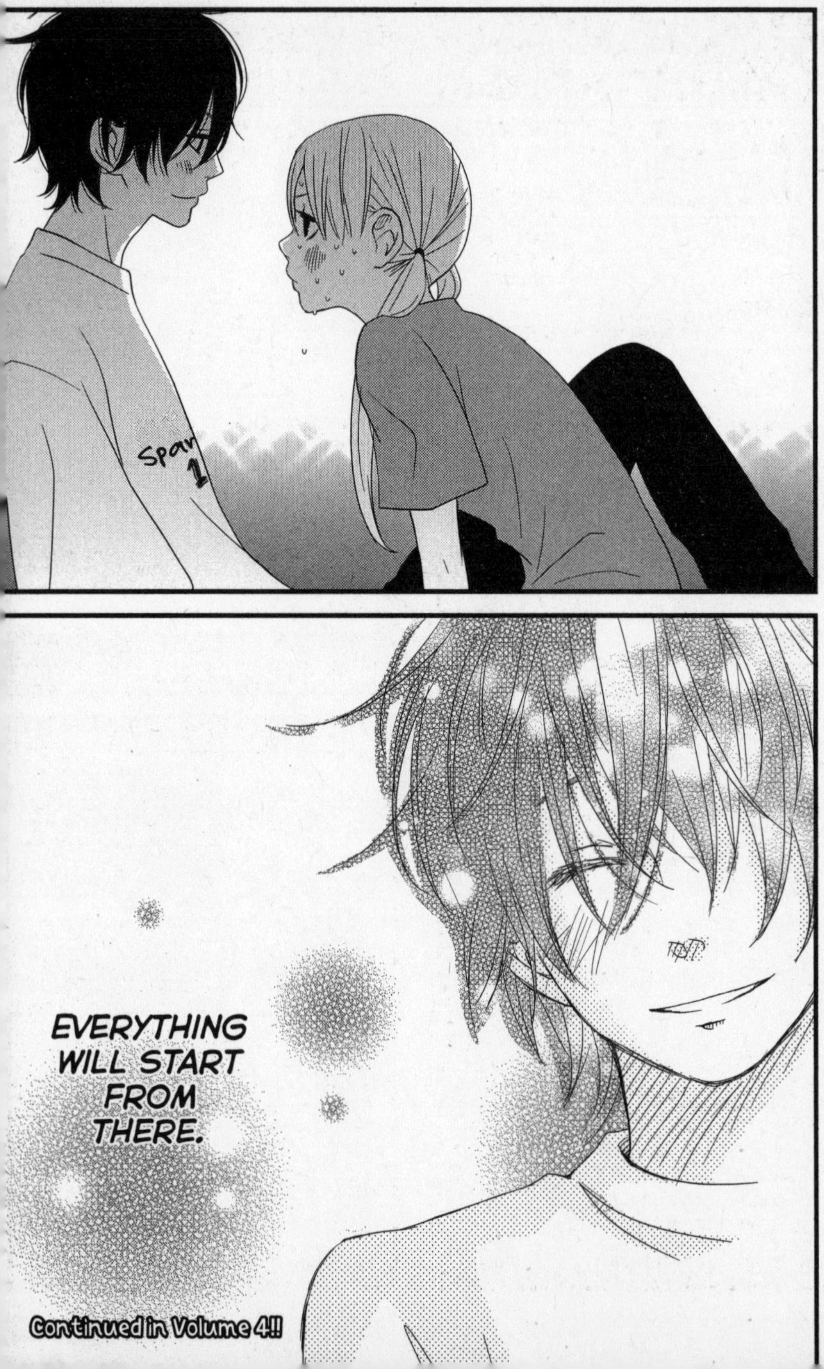
Spar
1
EVERYTHING WILL START FROM THERE.
Continued in Volume 4!!

It's Gotta Be That

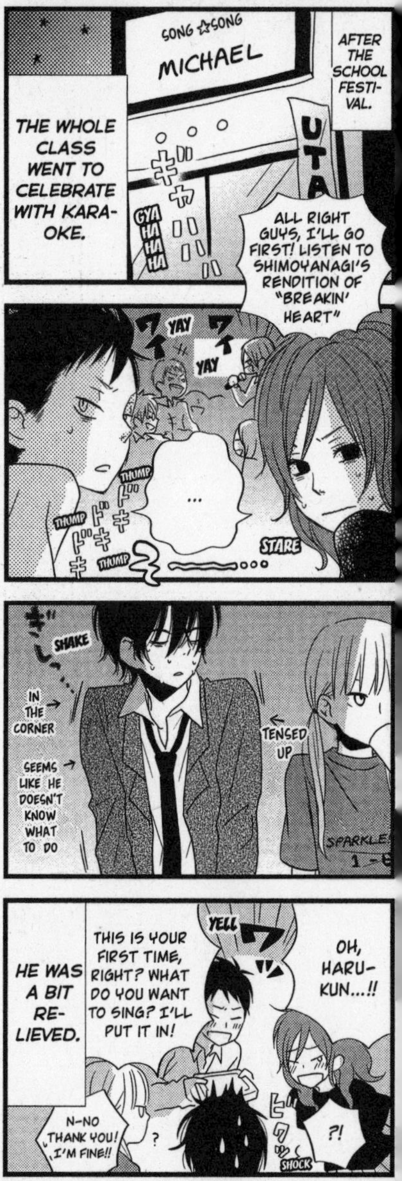
AFTER THE SCHOOL FESTI-VAL.
SONG☆SONG
MICHAEL
UTA
THE WHOLE CLASS WENT TO CELEBRATE WITH KARA-OKE.
GYA HA HA HA
ALL RIGHT GUYS, I'LL GO FIRST! LISTEN TO SHIMOYANAGI'S RENDITION OF "BREAKIN' HEART"
YAY
YAY
STARE
...
THUMP
THUMP
THUMP
TENSED UP
SPARKLE
SHAKE
IN THE CORNER
SEEMS LIKE HE DOESN'T KNOW WHAT TO DO
OH, HARU-KUN...!!
YELL
THIS IS YOUR FIRST TIME, RIGHT? WHAT DO YOU WANT TO SING? I'LL PUT IT IN!
HE WAS A BIT RE-LIEVED.
?!
SHOCK
?
N-NO THANK YOU! I'M FINE!!

Comment

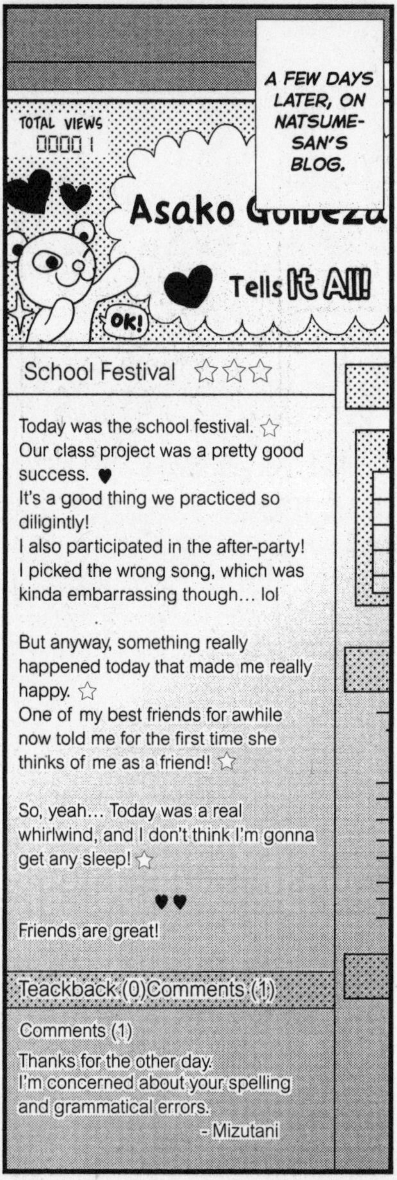
A FEW DAYS LATER, ON NATSUME-SAN'S BLOG.
TOTAL VIEWS 00001
Asako
Tells It All!
OK!
School Festival ☆☆☆
Today was the school festival. ☆
Our class project was a pretty good success. ♥
It's a good thing we practiced so diligintly!
I also participated in the after-party!
I picked the wrong song, which was kinda embarrassing though… lol
But anyway, something really happened today that made me really happy. ☆
One of my best friends for awhile now told me for the first time she thinks of me as a friend! ☆
So, yeah… Today was a real whirlwind, and I don't think I'm gonna get any sleep! ☆
♥♥
Friends are great!
Teackback (0)Comments (1)
Comments (1)
Thanks for the other day.
I'm concerned about your spelling and grammatical errors.
- Mizutani

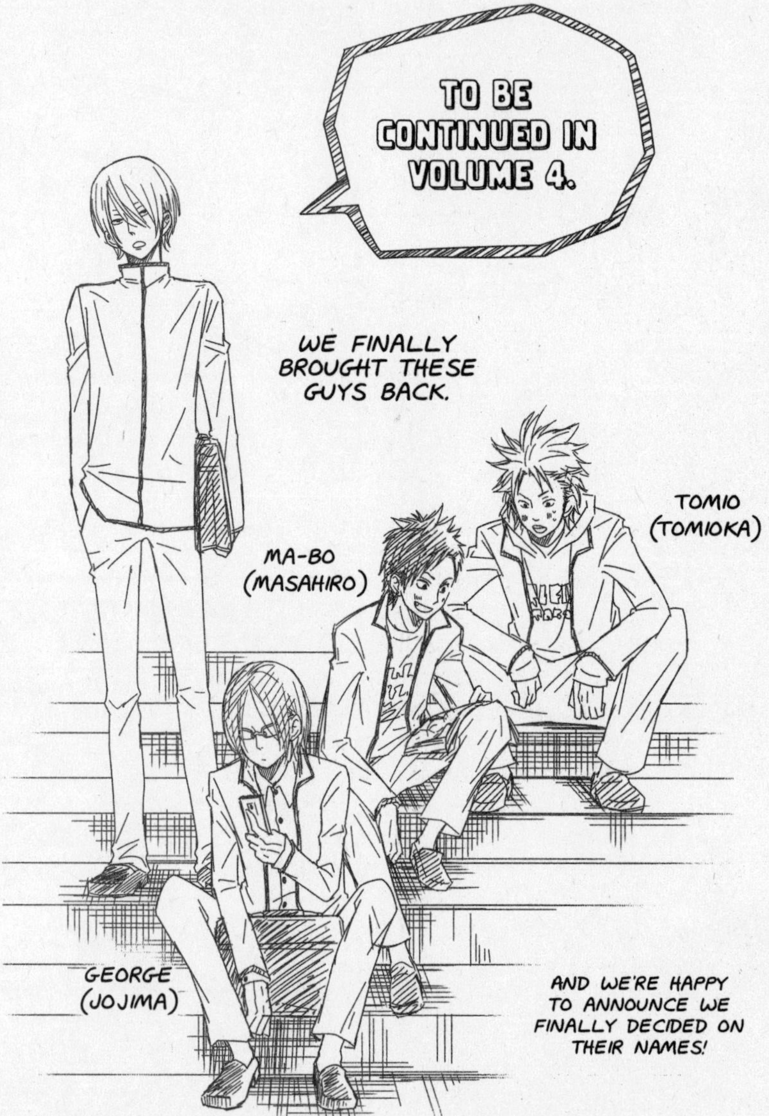
TO BE CONTINUED IN VOLUME 4.
WE FINALLY BROUGHT THESE GUYS BACK.
TOMIO (TOMIOKA)
MA-BO (MASAHIRO)
GEORGE (JOJIMA)
AND WE'RE HAPPY TO ANNOUNCE WE FINALLY DECIDED ON THEIR NAMES!

COMMENT

Robico

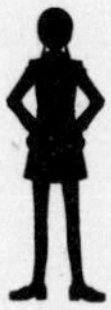

It's Volume 3.
When we started working on
this manga for publication,
my older sister kept
complaining how hard it was
to come over to visit me.
She's always had plenty of time
for video games, though!
She's an accomplished
Guild Master (Lv. 136) in a
certain online game.
...I'm a little worried about her.

Translation Notes

Japanese is a tricky language for most Westerners, and translation is often more art than science. For your edificaiton and reading pleasure, here are note on some of the places where we could have gone in a different direction with our translation of this book, or where a Japanese cultural reference is used.

Takoyaki, pages 44, 74

Takoyaki is a ball-shaped Japanese snack made of a wheat flour-based batter and cooked in a special takoyaki pan. It is typically filled with minced or diced octopus (tako), tempura scraps (tenkasu), pickled ginger, and green onion.

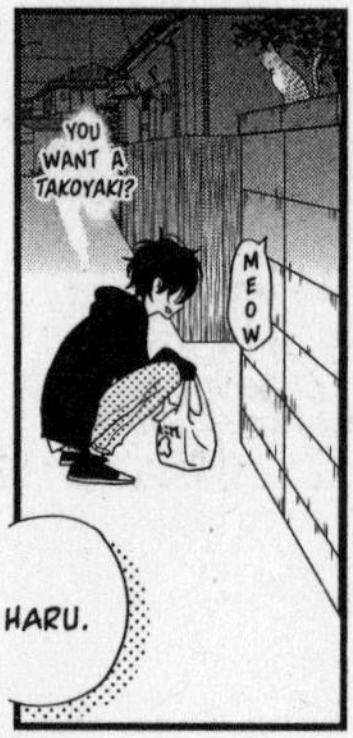
YOU WANT A TAKOYAKI?
MEOW
HARU.

Bon-odori, page 48

Bon-odori is a style of dancing performed during Obon, a Japanese holiday to honor the spirits of one's ancestors. The style of celebration varies in many aspects from region to region.

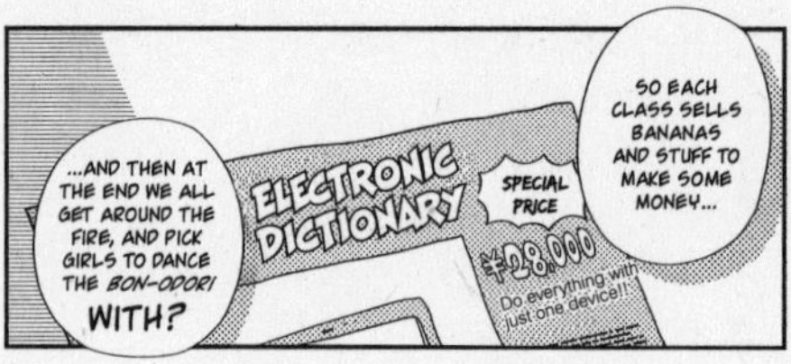
SO EACH CLASS SELLS BANANAS AND STUFF TO MAKE SOME MONEY...
SPECIAL PRICE
ELECTRONIC DICTIONARY
¥28,000
Do everything with just one device!!
...AND THEN AT THE END WE ALL GET AROUND THE FIRE, AND PICK GIRLS TO DANCE THE BON-ODORI WITH?

Cram School / Trial Test, pages 66

Cram schools are specialized schools that train their students to meet particular goals, most commonly to pass the entrance examinations of high schools or universities. Many students in Japan attend such schools, and in this volume, Shizuku is taking trial tests, likely based on the future college examination she will have to take in a few years.

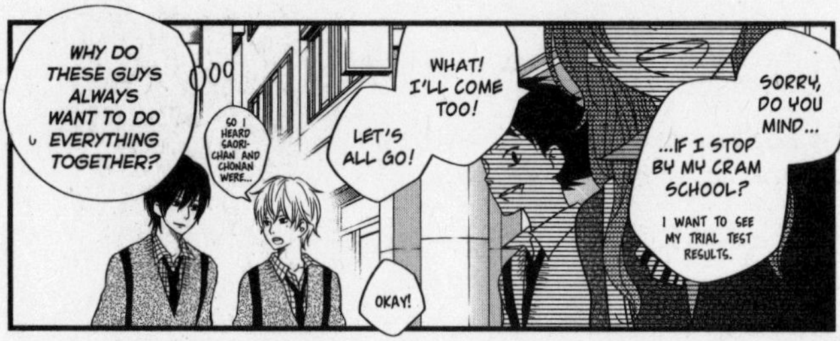
SORRY, DO YOU MIND...
...IF I STOP BY MY CRAM SCHOOL?
I WANT TO SEE MY TRIAL TEST RESULTS.
WHAT! I'LL COME TOO!
LET'S ALL GO!
OKAY!
SO I HEARD SAORI-CHAN AND CHONAN WERE...
WHY DO THESE GUYS ALWAYS WANT TO DO EVERYTHING TOGETHER?

My Little Monster volume 3 is a work of fiction. Names, characters, places, and incidents are the products of the author's imagination or are used fictitiously. Any resemblance to actual events, locales, or persons, living or dead, is entirely coincidental.

A Kodansha Comics Trade Paperback Original.

Published in the United States by Kodansha Comics, an imprint of Kodansha USA Publishing, LLC, New York.

Publication rights for this English edition arranged through Kodansha Ltd., Tokyo.

First published in Japan in 2009 by Kodansha Ltd., Tokyo as *Tonari no Kaibutsu-kun*, volume 3.

ISBN 978-1-61262-599-7

Printed in the United States of America.

www.kodanshacomics.com

9 8 7 6 5 4 3 2 1

Translator: Joshua Weeks
Lettering: Kiyoko Shiromasa